DATE DUE

JY 29 02		
AG 7 03		
MY 10 06		

Pakistan:

Islamic Nation in Crisis

First Edition
(1417 AH/1997 AC)

PAKISTAN:
Islamic Nation in Crisis

Ali Nawaz Memon

amana publications
Beltsville, Maryland

©1996 Ali Nawaz Memon
Published by **amana publications**
10170 Tucker Street, Suite B
Beltsville, Maryland 20705-2223 USA
Tel: (301) 595-5777   Fax: (301) 595-5888   e-mail: igfx@aol.com

Library of Congress Cataloging-in-Publication Data

Memon, Ali Nawaz, 1941(1360) -
    Pakistan: Islamic Nation in Crisis / Ali Nawaz Memon.
    p. (xiv, 362, 362) cm. 23
    Includes bibliographical references and index

ISBN 0-915957-66-3

    1-Pakistan -- Politics and Government -- 1988 -
    2- Pakistan -- Social Conditions.
    3- Pakistan -- Economic Conditions
I. Title

DS389.M46 1996   96-52865
954.9105 21

Printed in the United States by International Graphics
10170 Tucker Street, Suite B
Beltsville, Maryland 20705-2223 USA
Tel: (301) 595-5777 Fax: (301) 595-5888 e-mail: igfx@aol.com

DEDICATION

This book is dedicated with love and concern to the Islamic Nation as a whole which deserves to be an equal partner under the new world order; to the beloved people of Pakistan who are very discontented and should not rest until they have solved the basic problems facing them; to my late dear brother Ali Raza Memon whose persistent expression of discontent prompted me to write this book; and to all others who have been wanting to make a better Pakistan. May Allah show me the right path and give me courage to struggle harder for the good and against the evil! Ameen!

CONTENTS

PART TWO: KEY ISSUES AND SOLUTIONS

INTRODUCTION

As I try to understand what is going on in Pakistan, I am struck by the fact that Pakistanis started to become discontented soon after their independence. The discontent in East Pakistan led to the independence of Bangladesh in 1971. The level of discontent in the former West Pakistan which is currently known as Pakistan has been increasing and appears to have reached a new high in recent times. The purpose of writing this book is to understand the causes of basic discontent and explore possible solutions.

Feudalism as manifested by the concentration of both economic and political power has been a major cause. Both urban and rural dwellers have come to realize that the wealth and power of most of the prominent families of Pakistan is largely based on land grants from the British as a reward for defending them during the national mutiny of 1857 and thereafter. Since then, the system has been built upon personal loyalty first to the government of the day and then to the feudal lord himself. Those who have submitted and proven their loyalty have been rewarded and in time have become smaller lords in their own right. The rest of the rural population continued to suffer and have been deliberately denied opportunities for advancement, lest they mount an effective challenge to the feudal lord.

Conflict with India from the start, lack of sincere and honest leadership, corrupt politicians, slow growth of the democratic institutions, excessive power in the hands of civil and military authorities, widespread poverty and unemployment, breakdown of law and order, human rights violations, excessive influence and interference of the Western powers have all contributed to the current discontent.

In spite of all the discontent and the rather valid reasons for it, some astute observers feel that Pakistanis have seen nothing yet. The situation has a potential for getting a lot worse.

Those who visit Pakistan periodically are shocked by the visible growth in population in villages and towns. Data from UN agencies is beginning to confirm the growth. Based on a report from the UN population division, Pakistan's largest city, Karachi grew at a rate of 6.7% a year between 1970 and 1990. Its population is expected to grow from about eight million in 1990 to twenty-one million in year 2015. Karachi which was the 21st largest city in the world in 1990 is expected to become the 7th largest in 2015. Residents of Karachi are currently unhappy about lack of job opportunities and inadequate supplies of water, electricity, roads, and housing. Wait another twenty years. It is likely to get a lot worse.

The level and extent of ethnic and civil warfare taking place in Karachi and the rest of Sindh are condemnable. However, what took place in East Pakistan has not reached Pakistan's current borders yet. Rwanda, Somalia, and Liberia have experienced much worse. It is possible in Pakistan, but must be avoided at all cost.

On the economic front, the increase in the cost of living has been very upsetting to Pakistanis. However, the actual inflation of ten to 15 percent per year is very different from hyper inflation experienced by Latin American countries amounting to 100 percent per year. If people are worried about the high price of electricity, wait until it is doubled. The price must be increased soon to cover the cost of power purchased from privatized generation plants which will require imported oil and a return on private capital.

The devaluation of Pakistani rupee (rp) from about eight per dollar in the early 1970's to about 38 in 1996 has upset many people. They just do not know about the devaluation of the Turkish lira from about eight to 75,000 during the same period.

Violation of human rights in Pakistan is despicable. But it has been worse in Bosnia, Chile, Haiti, Liberia, Lebanon, and Somalia.

Relations with India have been bad. However, when BJP gains full power, as it is likely to do eventually, and carries out its policies toward Pakistan, Kashmir, and Muslims within their own borders, the situation has a potential for getting much worse.

The armed forces have ruled Pakistan for an excessive period and continue to claim a disproportionate share of the limited resources. However, to the sorrow of their fellow citizens, in many Muslim and non-Muslim developing countries, the forces have retained much greater control and squandered even a greater share of resources. The next martial law in Pakistan can be triggered by many plausible scenarios. The next Chief Martial Law Administrator (CMLA) may be a much worse person, and may choose to stay much longer.

Corruption and bribery have reached new levels in Pakistan. However, ask about it from someone who has lived in or visited Nigeria or even Egypt.

The economic gap between the developed world and underdeveloped countries of South Asia and Africa including Pakistan is very large. The television shows the difference every day. However, the gap is expected to widen and not narrow. In twenty years, per capita income of Pakistan may double to less than a thousand dollars a year. During the same period, it is expected to increase to almost fifty thousand dollars per person in the United States and to about seventy thousand in Switzerland.

People of Pakistan feel helpless and are giving up on the substantive improvement of the existing system. It is too tilted in favor of the ruling classes. They will never give up their privileged position. Even people in the highest levels of government have given up on the existing system and consider it beyond repair. People are increasingly thinking of revolution as the only way out. However, revolutions in other parts of the world have been very costly. There is massive destruction. Thousands die. Those who start revolutions rarely live to see it succeed. The new order built on destruction and blood is rarely better than the old one.

Pakistan needs dramatic changes. Drastic changes in policy and priorities are required. Above all, sincere leadership, peace, stability and dedicated labor are needed. However, there are a few long term options outside the democratic process. Unless the citizens take their democratic rights seriously and insist upon strict accountability, there is little hope.

Pakistanis should also remember that in spite of the secular nature of the government and limited political support for the religious parties, Pakistanis remain religious people. Islam is a powerful force in personal life and cannot be neglected. Successful solutions to the problems of Pakistan cannot be repugnant to the Islamic teachings; otherwise domestic consensus cannot be reached.

NOTE: The government of Prime Minister Benazir Bhutto was removed on November 5, 1996. However, Pakistan continues to face the issues of political leadership, poverty, unemployment, religious intolerance, law and order, ethnic strife, corruption, insecure borders, uncertain relations with the West, and national defense. Pakistanis continue to search for a clear vision and manifesto for change.

PART ONE:

BACKGROUND

CHAPTER 1

HISTORICAL SETTING

Cradles of Civilization

It is generally agreed that the first important civilizations of the world developed in four river valleys:

- the land between the Tigris and the Euphrates rivers in the Middle East (3100-1200 B.C.),
- the Nile River in Egypt (3100-1090 B.C.),
- along the Huang Ho (Yellow River) in China (1500-1027 B.C.), and
- along the region watered by the Indus River in what were the cities of Harappa and Mohenjo-daro in Pakistan (2500-1500 B.C.).[1]

Who the first inhabitants of the Indian Subcontinent were and where they came from, historians do not know. They have left no written records. From the rude and rough stones and the arrowheads dug up in the alluvial deposits of the great rivers of India, it is presumed that the first inhabitants, in general called aborigines, were gradually driven from their houses in the river valleys by other invading races. They fled to the mountains, where their descendants still live. These primeval people of the Indus river region are today categorized into three main groups: the Tibeto-Burma tribes, Oriya tribes and the Madras family. The resemblance of manners, complexion, religious beliefs and language suggest a common origin of Mongolia.[2]

Indus Valley Civilization (2500-1500 B.C.)

The ancient people who raised the edifices of the Indus Valley civilization some five thousand years ago are known to history as Dravidians. Their features and their Turanian affinities suggest that the Dravidians

---

[1] T. W. Wallbank, "World History," *The World Book Encyclopedia*, 21 (1994):352.

[2] A. Aziz, *Discovery of Pakistan* (Lahore: Sh. Ghulam Ali & Sons, 1957), pp. 2-3.

originated in the steppes of upper Asia from where they moved in successive
waves of immigration into the Indus Valley. They were eventually forced to
defend their country against the invading Aryans. When defeated they
became split into different groups, each having its own language and
institutions. The branches include the Madras (Tamil, Malayalam, Telugu,
Kanarese); the Gonds, and the Shudras (untouchable, low caste).[3]

The ruins of ancient villages and towns of the Indus Valley civilization
were discovered in the 1920's. Archaeologists found a civilization that
extended about 1,000 miles, from the foothills of the Himalayas to the Indian
Ocean, covering a much larger area than did the other three early
civilizations. The first Indus diggings were mainly at the two largest towns'
site—Mohenjo-daro (Sindh) on the Indus river and Harappa (Punjab) on the
Ravi River, a tributary of the Indus; other sites include Rana Chundai and
Zhob (Baloachistan).[4]

Archeology has revealed impressive ruins of a 4,500-year-old urban
civilization in Pakistan's Indus River valley. The reason for the total collapse
of this highly developed culture is unknown. A major theory is that it was
crushed by successive invasions (around 2,000 B.C. and 1,400 B.C.) of
Aryans, Indo-European warrior tribes from the Caucasus region in what is
now Russia. The Aryans were followed in 500 B.C. by Persians and, in 326
B.C., by Alexander the Great.[5]

Dravidians

Until 1920, there was but scant evidence of the existence of a highly
developed Dravidian civilization. Most of the information about them had
been derived from the unflattering expressions (Dasyus, Dasas, Asnosas,
Rakhshasas, etc.) used in referring to them in the songs and epics of the
victorious Aryans. These had been compiled in the famous work, the
Rigveda, the tales, legends, and traditions left behind by the Aryan
conquerors and interpreted by the Brahmans.

The ruins of the Indus Valley civilization show that the inhabitants had
developed well-planned towns, with buildings made from brick and streets
laid out in rectangular patterns. Houses had rooms built around courtyards;

[3] Ibid. pp. 2-3.

[4] *The World Book Encyclopedia*, 10 (1994):181.

[5] *U.S. State Department Profile* (U.S. Government Printing Office, 1995).

there were elaborate brick-lined drainage systems; and public bathing pools. Grains were stored in large warehouses and a system of weights and measures had been developed for commerce and other calculations. Craftsmen used copper, bronze, and silver to make various utensils and ornaments. Ivory and gold were used for jewelry and decorative furniture-making, an important craft in the society. Archeologists have found many stone seals engraved with animal and human forms; the more important seals are engraved with Indus writing that has yet to be translated. In fact, many scholars have attempted to decipher the writings of the Indus Valley people but without success.[6]

The excavations have also revealed that the Dravidians had established highly civilized and powerful empires. In the Rigveda we see or rather accidentally glimpse this conquest (Aryan conquest) from the Aryan point of view alone: they, the Aryans, are the heroes and scant tribute is paid to their contemptible Dravidian opponents, more skilled in the arts of peace than in those of warfare."[7] The memories of the battles and wars are alluded to in the Rigveda as a war of gods against demons: the invaders are described as the Aryan *"devatas, the deities of fire and light,"* the fair-complexioned and tall-statured heroes from the highlands of ancient Persia; while the enemies whom the Aryans crushed are scornfully portrayed as the "earth-born demons of ancient India . . . the black-skinned barbarians, noseless giants, man-eaters, dragons," etc. Says one poet, "Indra protected in battle the Aryan worshiper; he subdued the lawless. He conquered the black skin."[8]

By the discovery of the Harappa civilization, the "situation is, in fact, almost reversed, for the conquerors are seen to be less civilized that the conquered." The Aryans were "a people who had never known a city." When compared with the Dravidians, they were but a nation of savage barbarians who, exercising the profession of robbery under the honorable names of war and conquest, were determined to obliterate and did obliterate everything non-Aryan.[9]

The excavations reveal that while the Dravidians may have been valorous defenders of their land, they did not use iron implements of war. They possessed forts and knew the art of fortifying towns. However, no iron

---

[6] *The World Book Encyclopedia*, v. 10, pp. 182-3.

[7] Aziz, p. 10.

[8] Ibid., p. 12.

[9] Ibid., p. 10.

weapons have been found, only axes, spears, daggers, maces, slings, bows and arrows of copper, bronze and stone. Shields, helmets, and other defensive armor are noticeably absent. They also were fully familiar with wheeled vehicles, but do not seem to have used them in warfare.[10]

While the absence of advanced military weapons suggests a cause for the destruction of the Dravidians, so too does the absence of a spiritual discipline that so defined the feats narrated in the Aryan's Rigveda. Archeologists have failed to discover significant places of worship or temples of importance in their excavations. Instead there is evidence to suggest that the civilization had declined to the level of highly materialistic concerns and had engaged in a form of phallus-worship.

Aryans (1500-500 B.C.)

About 1850-1700 B.C., a central Asian people called Aryans began their assault on the civilized inhabitants of the Indus Valley. They came through the mountain passes to the Punjab region and began a series of wars of conquest which would eventually destroy the ancient civilization and replace it with a vastly different society, one which would dominate the area for many centuries.

As mentioned above, the term *Vedic* refers to Rigveda, an ancient collection of hymns the Aryan invaders composed to their various deities. The period during which the Aryan conquerors had barely advanced beyond the land of five rivers, the Punjab, and appeared as simple colonists, is called the Vedic Period and the Aryans of this time are in general labeled the Vedic people. The wants and aspirations of these Vedic people are expressed in the Rigveda. They ate beef, used fermented liquor, *Soma,* and they did not have any castes, i.e., *Brahmans, Kshatriyas* or *Vaishyas.*[11]

The Vedic hymns make it clear that the mobile, city-less invaders differed at every point from the long-static citizens whom they eventually conquered.[12] The first area which the Aryans of the Rigveda held consisted primarily of the Punjab and may have extended into the Doab of the Ganges and the Jumna. These Indo-Aryans regarded themselves as culturally different from and superior to the people whom they found in the land. They

[10] Ibid., p. 10.

[11] Ibid., pp. 16-17.

[12] *Crescent & Green: A Miscellany of Writings on Pakistan* (Freeport, N.Y.: Book for Libraries Press, 1970), p. 23.

disliked the ways of the non-Aryans, applied derogatory epithets to them, and condemned their religious practices, denominating them sorcerers and adherents of demons. When received in their society, whether as captives or otherwise, these non-Aryans were made to serve without privileges of citizenship and religion, an attitude generally considered one of the elements contributing to the formation of the caste system.[13]

Another important development was linguistic. The Aryans brought a language unrelated to any already existing in the subcontinent. It belonged to what is today called the Indo-European language family. The result was a linguistic clash, leading in varying measure, in different regions, to linguistic blending. As the Aryans have continued to live in the subcontinent and have fused with the non-Aryan, the conflict of languages, followed by blending, with the Aryan element being the dominant, has continued.[14]

The evidence of the Rigveda shows that during the centuries when the Aryans were occupying the Punjab and composing the hymns of the Rig-veda, the northwest part of the subcontinent was culturally separate from the rest of India. At this time, the closest cultural relations of the Indo-Aryans were with the peoples of what are today Iran and Afghanistan. The language and sacred texts of the later are preserved in the various works known as the Avesta, in inscriptions in Old Persian, and in some other scattered documents. After centuries, Aryan and non-Aryan civilization blended in the valley of the Ganges, especially about the sixth century B.C., to produce characteristically native Indian civilization, marked by distinctive features of social organization, legal institutions, religious practice philosophical speculation, and art forms. This was all encrypted in the Aryan language.[15]

Brahmanic Period

The age succeeding the Vedic Age is distinguished as the Brahmanic Age. In this period, the Aryan invaders advanced beyond the "land of the five rivers" and established powerful empires at Delhi, Oudh, Tirhut, and Bihar. In this period, the two poems of the Mahabharata and the Ramayana were composed and the spiritual conceptions and aspirations of the Aryans underwent a drastic change. The doctrine of transmigration was adopted, new

---

[13] Ibid., p.30.

[14] Ibid., p. 31.

[15] *Crescent*, p. 32.

deities arose, and the caste system developed. These have prevailed to modern times as basic Hindu doctrines.[16]

Except for the Rigveda, the remaining three Vedas and other religious books of the Hindus (such as Upanishads, Shastras, Aranyakas, Brahmanas, the two epics of the Ramayana and the Mahabharata, etc.) on which the Hindu social system rests were written in areas of the subcontinent which are outside the current boundaries of Pakistan.[17] It is generally agreed that the early Aryan invaders of the Indus Valley civilization shared a common religious origin with those who would later become Hindus.

However, it is apparent that the Aryans who stayed in areas which now constitute Pakistan did not evolve that particular form of Hinduism, with its caste system and other taboos, familiar to the modern world. It was only when they crossed the Sutlej and settled in the Gangetic Valley that this system developed. While settled in the Punjab, the Aryans had not yet become Hindu . . . The distinctive Brahmanical System appears to have been evolved after the Sutlej had been passed.[18] The castes were hardened by the time the Aryans occupied the middle land, i.e., the Gangetic Valley and distinguished themselves from their brethren in Sindh and the Punjab who were despised by them for not observing the rules of caste . . . and for their non-Brahmanical character.[19]

This could be explained by the very nature of the civilizations which they conquered in Pakistan and that which they found in the Ganges. The former had opposed them valiantly and in fact possessed greater culture and refinement. By the time the Ganges had been overrun, the Dravidians were far from the respected opponent of the Indus. Neither their valor nor their civilization could command respect. The development of the caste system from the same religious origins can be compared to the conquest of the Americas by Europeans who shared a common religion, Christianity, but who developed vastly different social and political systems in North and South America. So too, did the Aryans develop different societies in the Ganges Valley and the Indus Valley.

---

[16] Aziz, p. 20.

[17] Ahmed Abdulla, *The Historical Background of Pakistan and Its People* (Karachi: Tanseem Publishers, 1973), p. 17.

[18] Ibid., p. 16.

[19] Ibid., 17.

Persians (550-325 B.C.)

In the sixth century B.C., the historical records of the subcontinent become more abundant. During this time, the Persians (Achaemenian) crossed the mountains and reached the Indus plain. Persian kings such as Cyrus (558-529 B.C.), Darius I (521-486 B.C.) and Xerses (486-461 B.C.) extended the Persian empire until it eventually included the entire course of the Indus, from upper Punjab to the Arabian Sea.

The materials available to the scholar today show the northwestern part of the subcontinent was an economically advanced province in the last centuries of the first millennium B.C. to the early first millennium of our era. Herodotus describes the Indians inhabiting the part of the subcontinent under the Archaemenids as the most numerous of all peoples known to him, a people who "paid (to the Achaemenids) a tribute which was great in comparison to the others."[20]

The Persians extracted tribute from the conquered inhabitant but did not dramatically alter the social, political or religious customs of the region as had the Aryans. An important point to be noted is that even during the period that the area now constituting Pakistan was under Persian domination, it enjoyed complete autonomy. Its administration was under the control of several local rulers (rajas) who merely acknowledged the suzerainty of the Persians. The one generalization that can be made is that politically the northwest was again separate from central, northern, and eastern India. This fact clearly facilitated the invasion of the area by Alexander and contributed to the cultural divergence between the northwest and the rest of the subcontinent in the centuries that followed.[21]

Greeks (326 B.C. - 500 C.E.)

The legendary Macedonian king, Alexander (356-323 B.C.), began his conquest of Persia in 334 B.C. After historic battles that took his army through Egypt, Syria, and Persia, he entered Pakistan from the northern route at Swat. Through battles and diplomacy, he achieved dominion over a large area without much difficulty until he reached the territory east of Jhelum, where the famous Raja Porus inflicted considerable losses on the invaders. In spite of defeat, Porus was confirmed as ruler in his principality in

---

[20] Ibid.,p. 19.

[21] *Crescent*, pp. 32-33.

recognition of his prowess and patriotism. In fact, it is generally acknowledged that the Greeks had considerable respect for the people of the Indus Valley: "It is clear from classical accounts of Alexander's campaign that the Greeks were not unimpressed by what they saw in Indian (Pakistani) troops, in the austerity of the ascetics whom they met at Taxila, and in the purity and simplicity of the tribes of the Punjab and Sindh."[22] Alexander went as far as the river Beas, somewhere near Gurdaspur, where his army mutinied and forced him to begin the return home. He came down through the entire length of Pakistan, crossed the Hub River near Karachi and departed for home, dying along the way.[23]

The northern Indian troops recruited into the armies of Alexander and his successor came under the influence of Greek civilization (Hellenized) much earlier than other sections of the population. Indigenous troops were armed with Macedonian weapons and trained by Macedonian methods. Hellenization worked on the offspring of intermarriages between Macedonian soldiers and Asiatic women, as well as on the populations of numerous cities founded or rebuilt by the Graeco-Macedonian invaders. These cities were populated with foreign soldiers unable to provide further service and with local dwellers. Alexander himself married a Persian princess.[24]

Alexander's invasion of the Punjab (327-325 B.C.) is usually considered to mark the beginning of Greek influence upon the subcontinent. This resulted from the Greek conquest of the Persians more than from the actual conquest of the Indus Valley. By defeating the ruling Persians, the Greeks, in essence, inherited much of the subcontinent and began their Hellenistic influence on the area. During the centuries that followed, political rule was generally decentralized with much control being exercised by both Persian and Central Asian rulers. However, the Greek language was used considerably in administration and commerce while art and architecture acquired a distinct Greek character, though the subject matter was mostly Buddhist.

Many elements of Hellenism were assimilated by the native Indian culture, particularly in mathematics, medicine, and astrology and to some extent in literature and philosophy. Politically, during the time when Hellenism in India was decaying and in the centuries afterward, the northwest remained separate from northern and central India. The Gupta and Harsha

---

[22] Abdulla, pp. 20-21.

[23] Ibid.

[24] Ibid., pp. 24-25.

empires of the fourth and seventh century C.E. barely reached the Punjab and did not include Sindh.[25]

Alexander's defeat of the Persians left a vacuum in the northwest area of the subcontinent which was filled by the intrusion of India into Pakistan. For the first time in history, the flow came from the Ganges to the Indus. Chandragupta Maurya was able to establish a strong government in the Gangetic Valley which extended over most of northern India. Soon after Alexander's death, his successor Seleucus ceded the northwestern area (Pakistan) to Chandragupta peacefully. The area thus became a part of the Mauryan Empire in 300 B.C. without war. Hindu authority came with this new government.[26]

Buddhism

Siddhartha Gautama (563-483), the founder of Buddhism was born near the town of Kapilavastu, in the foothills of the Himalayas, in what is today called Nepal. By the time the Persians had been ousted by the Greeks, Buddhist missionary activities had begun to be prevalent throughout the subcontinent. Their influence continued to grow as Greek dominance decreased.

Of note is the fact that the third Mauryan emperor, Asoka, became Buddhist and the northwest area of the subcontinent (Pakistan) did not experience Hindu rule for very long. Under Asoka's rule, Buddhism was propagated effectively and the northwest subcontinent area (Pakistan) remained largely Buddhist until the arrival of Muslims in the eighth century.[27]

The Mauryan rule lasted for about one hundred years and was replaced by Greek-Bactrian rule. This period saw the increase of Greek and Buddhist influence, particularly under its most famous king, Menander (160-140 B.C.).[28]

The Graeco-Bactrian rule, like that of the Mauryan, lasted little more than one hundred years. Beginning around the first century B.C., waves of Turko-Mongoloid people such as the Sakas, Kushans, Huns, and Gujjars began to settle in Pakistan. In time, they constituted the overwhelmingly

[25] *Crescent,* p. 35.

[26] Abdulla, p. 22.

[27] Ibid.

[28] Ibid., p. 23.

predominant element of the population. This composition continues to this day. These waves were so dominant that everything was submerged or absorbed by it. All previous elements, Aryans, Iranians, and Greeks, simply lost their identity in this deluge and ceased to be recognizable.

In fact, the waves of Sakas were so enormous and their settlements so pervasive that Pakistan came to be known to Greek geographers as Scythia and in India literature as Saka-dipa. A unique feature of the Pakistan of this period is that it enjoyed a strategic spot in the corridor of trade and culture traveling between East and West. Bordering the two great empires of the time, Rome and China, Pakistan enjoyed easy access to art, architecture, science, and learning. For the most part, the area continued to be dominated by Buddhist beliefs and customs and only slight Hindu influences were present.

The greatest migration into Pakistan by Central Asian tribes extended over the 5th and 6th centuries of the modern era. This was the invasion by the Huns. The particular branch of the Huns who encamped in the Oxus Valley and eventually overran most of Pakistan was known as the Epthalite or White Huns. They were accompanied by other tribes, including the Gurjaras.[29]

This invasion by the Huns constitutes a major milestone in the history of Pakistan and northern India, socially and politically. Socially because the origin of almost all the tribes of Pakistan and those of Rajputana is traceable to them. No authentic family or class traditions go back beyond the Hun invasions. All genuine tradition of the earlier dynasties has been absolutely lost. The history of the Mauryas, Kushans and Guptas, as far as it is known has been recovered by scholars without help from living tradition. A large number of Afghan-Pathan tribes and most of the Rajput and Jat clans of the Punjab are, according to modern scholars, descended from the Epthalites, i.e., White Huns.[30]

Arabs (711 C.E.)

Pakistan's Islamic history began with the arrival of Muslim traders in the 8th century C.E. They established markets in the coastal Plain of Malabar. Soon after the death of the Prophet (PBUH), several expeditions were sent there, the first coming from Oman to the coast of India in 636-37 C.E. during

---

[29] Ibid., p. 30.

[30] Ibid.

the rule of Umar. Another expedition was sent in 643-44 during the rule of Uthman. His general, Abdullah bin Amar bin Rabi captured Kirman and besieged Sistan. He then proceeded to Makran where he defeated the combined forces of the kings of Makran and Sindh. During the rule of Muawiyah, the first Umayyad Khalifah (caliph), eastern Afghanistan came under Muslim authority.[31]

During the reign of the Umayyad Khalifah Walid, Muslim armies achieved great successes in the West, South, and East. Walid's general Musa bin Nusayr subjugated the whole of North Africa while his lieutenant Tariq conquered Spain. In the east, Qutaiba carried the banner of Islam far into Central Asia. Persia had already been overrun as far as the river Oxus. Under Hajjaj, the governor of Iraq, the spirit of conquest found its fullest scope.[32]

Muhammad bin Qasim. The invasion of Sindh is said to have been provoked by an act of piracy. The king of Ceylon had sent eight vessels containing valuable gifts to Walid and Hajjaj. These were plundered and the king of Sindh was held responsible. When diplomacy failed, Hajjaj received permission from the Khalifah to set out against Sindh.[33]

In fact, there were several reasons for the Arab desire to conquer Makran and Sindh. First, Sindhi forces helped the Persians in several earlier battles against Arabs. Second, when after the conquest of Persia by the Arabs some of their rebel chiefs sought refuge in Sindh, its Raja refused to surrender them to the Khalifah in spite of repeated requests. Third, Arab traders were being constantly harassed by pirates from the Makran and Sindh coasts; therefore a foothold in these areas was considered essential to safeguard Arab maritime interests.[34]

The first two expeditions were failures. The third expedition was placed under the leadership of Muhammad bin Qasim, the seventeen-year-old nephew and son-in-law of Hajjaj.[35]

The story of Muhammad bin Qasim has become one of Muslim history's great romances. His blooming youth, his dash and heroism, his noble

---

[31] Mohammad Arshad, *An Advanced History of Muslim Rule in Indo-Pakistan* (Dacca: Ideal Publications, 1967), p. 24.

[32] Ibid., p. 24.

[33] Ibid.

[34] Abdulla, p. 101.

[35] Arshad, p. 24.

deportment throughout the expedition and his tragic fall have invested his career with the halo of martyrdom. He marched toward India with a well-equipped army of 6,000 Syrian and Iraqi soldiers and 3,000 Bactrians. When he reached Makran, he was joined by the local Muslims and by many Buddhist Jats and Meds who had been oppressed by the Hindu kings of India. Muhammad reached Debal in 712 C.E. After a difficult battle, the Hindus were defeated and the town taken. He then conquered Nirun, crossed the Indus, and defeated the much larger Hindu army of Dahir. Additional victories at Brahmanabad and Multan propelled him to the borders of the kingdom of Kashmir.[36]

It is said that the death of Muhammad bin Qasim came when the daughters of the conquered Rajas were sent as captives to the Khalifah. They falsely accused Muhammad bin Qasim of having dishonored them. Upon hearing this, the Khalifah was so furious that he ordered that the young general's body be sent to his court sewn in cowhide. The order was complied with and the body was sent to the Khalifah. Upon seeing that the enemy of their father had been killed, the daughters confessed that they had fabricated the story. At this, the Khalifah ordered that they be dragged by horses until dead.[37]

Whether this legend is totally accurate is debated. Nevertheless, all historians agree that Muhammad bin Qasim's rule in Sindh was most liberal and his treatment of non-Muslims extremely just and fair. He was indeed harsh to opponents but never indulged in unnecessary cruelty or oppression. Religious tolerance was granted to Hindus who were allowed to rebuild temples damaged or destroyed during the fighting and compensation was paid to those whose property had been destroyed.[38]

The conquered territories were divided into districts ruled by Arab military officers. These Arab settlements developed and gradually grew into centers of commerce and culture. Revenue officers collected land revenue, zakat, jizya (the tax on non-Muslims in lieu of zakat) and other taxes. Local administration was left in the hand of the natives and the Brahmins were entrusted with high offices and were protected against opposition and violence.[39]

---

[36] Ibid.

[37] Ibid.

[38] Ibid., p. 29.

[39] Ibid., p. 30.

The principles of the Holy Qur'an took precedence over all laws and was applied to Muslims and non-Muslims. A Muslim Qazi decided cases but where Hindu subjects were involved, Hindu lawyers were engaged in helping him. All disputes relating to marriage, inheritance, adultery, etc., in which the parties were Hindus, were decided by the Hindus in their Panchayats.[40]

Sindh remained a province of the Khalifah only for a century and a half. The chief causes of the failure of Arab power were the sudden death of Muhammad bin Qasim and the stubborn resistance of the Rajput princes. Also, Sindh did not provide much material attraction to the Khalifah and Baghdad soon withdrew support of the Arabs in Sindh, leaving the rulers in a precarious situation. When, in 871 C.E., the Khalifah abandoned support, Sindh became a prey to disorder. The Arab settlers established small dynasties which lasted for about three centuries, until they were conquered by Muhammad Ghori.[41]

Being the easternmost province of the Umayyad and after that of the Abassid Khulafa'i (Caliphs) Sindh was loosely controlled. There were many internecine conflicts between petty Muslim rulers and between rival Muslim sects, particularly Sunnis and Ismailis. Since every development in the Muslim empire had its effect on the subcontinent, the Fatimid-Abbasid political rivalry with its religious manifestation in the Ismaili-Sunni controversy, found full echo here, particularly in the tenth century C.E.[42]

The result of the Arab conquest of Sindh was described by Stanley Lane Poole as a simple episode in the history of India and of Islam, a triumph without results. This is true in the sense that politically it had no permanent effect and in that the Arabs left no legacy of language, architecture, art, tradition, customs or manners. The Arabs however had brought with them a new religion and a new civilization which they introduced to the conquered peoples. In addition, Sindh became the link through which the fruits of Indian learning were transmitted to the Arabs, and by them made available to the world. Sindh facilitated the dissemination of Indian culture in Arab lands. The court of Baghdad extended its patronage to Indian scholars. Indo-Arab intellectual collaboration was considerable, particularly under the rule of the Khalifah al-Mansur (753-774) and Harun al-Rashid (780-808). Many Arab scholars were sent to the subcontinent to study medicine and pharma-

---

[40] Ibid.

[41] Ibid.

[42] Abdulla, pp. 106-7.

cology while many Hindu scholars were brought to Baghdad to teach and practice their medicine. In mathematics, the most important contribution of the Indo-Pakistan subcontinent was the introduction of what are known in the West as Arabic numerals and what Arabs themselves call the Indian numeral (*al-ruqum al-hindiyyah*).[43]

Indian philosophy also influenced the mysticism of Sufism. The close association of Sindh with Sufism is maintained to this day, and one of the most marked features of Sindh is the dominant place which Sufism occupies in the literature and religious life.[44]

Ghaznavid Rule

As the power of the Abbasid Khulafa'i (Caliphs) declined, numerous independent dynasties emerged in the eastern parts of the empire. Among them was a Persian one established in Bukhara, the Samanids. Here, many Turks were employed as royal attendants and in military service. The Turks were by this time a prominent group in the area. They had embraced Islam with great zeal and were noted for their bravery and fidelity. One of these Turks, Alptigin, had been in high office under the Samanids, but having lost his position, set out in 962 C.E. and establish an independent principality with its capital at Ghazni. This was the beginning of the next major period of Pakistani history, the Ghaznavid rule, which lasted almost two hundred years, until the end of the 12th century.[45]

In 976, Alptigin was succeeded by his one-time slave and later son-in-law, Subuktigin. Subuktigin extended this kingdom to Qandaher and soon came into conflict with the Hindu Raja, Jaipal, ruler of the Punjab at this time. The Muslim ruler eventually was able to defeat the Hindu Raja and extended his domain to Peshawar. Khurasan was later added.[46]

In 997, Subuktigin's son began to rule. His name was Mahmud and he was the first Muslim ruler to assume the title *sultan*. He added the southern areas to his kingdom by defeating the Ismaili and Carmathian rulers in Multan and Sindh, thus consolidating most of the northwest portions of the subcontinent. He also defeated his former ally, the Samanids. During his

---

[43] Arshad, p. 30.

[44] Ibid.

[45] Ibid., p. 33.

[46] Ibid.

more than thirty years of rule, Sultan Mahmud invaded India seventeen times, reaching Muthra, Kanauj, Baran, and Guwaliar, almost the whole of northern India felt his arms. He died in 1031 C.E.[47]

The results of Mahmud's victories were not permanent. He did not consolidate his conquests and the only lasting result of his expeditions was the permanent annexation of the Punjab. After his death, only a portion of Sindh and the Punjab acknowledged the suzerain of the Ghazni dynasty. In India, the political results of the invasion soon disappeared completely, leaving only a controversial legacy of conquest and economic disorder. So far, neither the Arabs nor the Ghaznavid Turks had succeeded in adding India to the growing empire of Islam.[48]

Culturally, however, Sultan Mahmud's invasion brought the civilization of the Hindus and the Muslims into close contact and led to mutual exchange of ideas and thoughts. Along with the Muslim soldiers and warriors came Muslim saints and scholars who permeated the rank of Indian society, promulgated Islam in India, and won many converts.[49]

The Ghaznavid rule in Pakistan lasted until 1187 C.E. During this period Lahore assumed considerable importance as the easternmost bastion of Muslim power and as an outpost for further advance in the east. It was a city of ghazis, saints and intellectuals. Apart from being the second capital and later the only capital of the Ghaznavid kingdom, it had great military and strategic importance. Whoever controlled this city was in a position to sweep the whole of East Punjab up to Panipat and Delhi.[50]

Delhi Sultanate

At the end of the twelfth century, the principality of Ghur was a mountainous province located between Ghazni and Herat. It was inhabited by hardy Afghans and ruled by militant Turkish kings who had once been subject to Ghazni rule. The Ghuri chief, Alauddin, fighting to avenge the death of his brothers defeated the Sultan of Ghazni and burned the city. When he and his son died soon thereafter, the Ghuri chieftains placed a nephew of Alauddin on the throne. His name was Ghiyas-uddin and when he

---

[47] Ibid., p. 32.

[48] Ibid., p. 39.

[49] Ibid., p. 39.

[50] Abdulla, p. 33.

conquered Ghazni completely, he turned it over to his brother, Shihabuddin, also known as Muiz-uddin Muhammad, popularly called Muhammad of Ghur. The two brothers shared power amicably: while the elder attended to local matters, Muhammad occupied himself primarily with expansion.[51]

Northern India at this time was divided into a number of independent petty Hindu kingdoms. Two hundred years earlier, Sultan Mahmud's expeditions had reached into India but had little permanent effect. The Rajput kingdoms survived his raids. In the absence of paramount authority, most of these Hindu kingdoms were independent and rarely cooperated.[52]

In 1175, Muhammad of Ghur began his Indian expeditions by attacking Multan; in 1179 he added Peshawar and in 1182 compelled the ruler of lower Sindh to acknowledge his suzerainty. In 1186, he captured Lahore and annexed the Punjab to his dominion. After a severe defeat at the hands of Hindus under the leadership of Prithvi Raj, Muhammad of Ghur defeated the Rajput Hindu princes in 1192 and captured their capital, Ajmer. After this victory, he and his generals conquered Delhi, Bihar, and Bengal.[53]

Muhammad of Ghur was a remarkable figure in medieval Asiatic history. Rising from the position of a small chieftain of Ghur, he laid the foundation of Muslim rule in Indo-Pakistan. He was both a great military leader and a prudent statesman. By the year 1203, Muhammad Ghuri was at the height of his power. His brother had died leaving him sole ruler of the extensive empire that extended from Afghanistan to Bengal.[54] His successors established the first dynasty of the Delhi Sultanate, the Mamluk (slave) Dynasty in 1211.

The territory under the Muslim ruler in Delhi expanded rapidly. By 1250, Bengal and much of central India were completely under the Delhi Sultanate. Several Turko-Afghan dynasties ruled from Delhi: the Mamluk (1211-90); the Khalji (1290-1320); the Tughlaq (1320-1413); the Sayyid (1414-51) and the Lodhi (1451-1526). As Muslims extended their rule into southern India, only the Hindu kingdom of Vijayanagar remained independent, until 1565 when it too fell. During this period, almost all the area in present-day Pakistan remained under the rule of Delhi.

---

[51] Arshad, p. 47.

[52] Ibid., p. 48.

[53] Ibid., p. 51.

[54] Abdulla, p. 33.

The sultans of Delhi enjoyed cordial relations with Muslim rulers in the Near East, but remained independent of their dominion. The laws of the land were based on the Qur'an and the Sharia; non-Muslim subjects were permitted to practice their religion but were required the payment of the *jizya* tax. Military camps and trading posts were established throughout the dominion and many of these eventually developed into small towns and cities. Perhaps the greatest contribution of the sultanate was its temporary success in insulating the subcontinent from Mongol invasions in the thirteenth century. The sultanate provided a common ground for Islam and Hinduism to meet and interact; this resulted in the "Indo-Muslim" fusion which left lasting monuments in architecture, music, literature, and religion.[55]

The sultanate suffered the sacking of Delhi in 1398 by Timur (Tamerlane) but revived briefly under the Lodhis before being conquered by the Mughals.

Mughal Period (1528-1858)

The Indo-Pakistan subcontinent in the sixteenth century consisted of a number of petty kingdoms, Hindu and Muslim, lacking common laws or institutions. The Delhi Sultanate, under the Lohdi ruler Ibrahim, was hard pressed to maintain authority over the various local rulers who constantly sought to rid themselves of the Sultan's yoke. Conspiracies, short-lived alliances and revolts were common. In this condition, the subcontinent was ripe for conquest.

The man who accomplished this was Zahiruddin Babur who established the Mughal dynasty which flourished until the middle of the nineteenth century. During the 16th and 17th centuries, the Mughals dominated most of South Asia with an empire marked both by administrative effectiveness and cultural refinement.

Babur was born in 1483 in Ferghana (present-day Uzbekistan). He claimed to be a descendant of both Chingiss (Genghis) Khan and Timur (Tamerlane). In his memoirs he calls himself a Turk, but his dynasty came to be known as Mughal. "Mughal had, in fact, become a generic term for warlike adventurers from Persia or Central Asia, and although Timur and all his line loathed the name, as that of their bitterest foes, it has been their fate

---

[55] Peter R. Blood, ed., *Pakistan, A Country Study* (Washington, D.C.: Library of Congress, 1995), p. 10.

to be branded by it."[56] His permanent place in history rests upon his Indian conquests, which open the way for an imperial line known as the Mughal dynasty.

Humayun, Sher Shah, Shah Jahan (builder of the Taj Mahal), Akbar (who attempted to establish his own religion), Aurangzeb (who greatly expanded the empire and championed Sunni Islam) are among the well-known Mughal kings who inherited and consolidated Babur's empire. Some excelled in military exploits, others were patrons of the arts, a few were devout Muslims.

During this time, when the empire grew rapidly, the differences between the subject populations (Muslims and non-Muslims) became great. Hindus, Buddhists, and Sikhs were always ready to challenge the Muslim Ulama in matters of worship and taxation. At times the *Jizya* was imposed and temples and non-Muslim institutions were closed while at other times the ruler gave non-Muslims considerable leeway in matters of worship.

The Mughal emperors sat on their thrones for more than three hundred years until 1858 when they were deposed by the English. Their rule represents the zenith of Muslim power and Islamic culture in the sub-continent, though their influence spread throughout the subcontinent unevenly. In some places, particularly south India, the Muslim element remained minor, occasionally negligible. In some others, such as the present Uttar Pradesh, the division of the population was equal between Muslims and non-Muslims. In still others places, there was a heavy preponderance in favor of Muslims, notably the northwest (Pakistan) where Islam was not only the religion of the rulers but where almost the entire population too had embraced the religion. Once again, the northwest area of the subcontinent had remained culturally distinct from the rest.[57]

From 1227 to 1739, a span of more than 500 years, Pakistan had remained a part of India primarily because of Muslim rulers. In 1739, Nadir Shah defeated the Mughal emperor and claimed Punjab (from Lahore westward), the Northwest Frontier Province (N.W.F.P.), Balaochistan, and Sindh as part of his kingdom. One of Nader Shah's generals, Ahmed Shah Abdali, succeeded him and established the kingdom of Afghanistan in 1747. He made the Pakistan territory part of his new state and claimed Kashmir, Peshawar, Daman, Multan, Sindh, and the Punjab up to the Sutlej. Thus, after centuries of attachment to India, Pakistan's westward attachments

---

[56] Arshad, p. 3.

[57] *Crescent*, p. 36.

were again revived. This became particularly important during the British period.

Sikhs: The close contact between Muslims and Hindus during the Mughal period produced several religious figures who taught unity of the two religions. Nanak was one of them. Nanak was a contemporary of Babur and outlived him by eight years. As almost all the Sikhs were originally Hindus, the Brahmin priests were hostile to the new religion. The first two successors of Nanak maintained cordial relations with Muslims. Akbar held the fourth Guru, Ramdas, in great esteem and granted him a plot of land with a pool at Amritsar. This pool was enlarged and upon it was built the famous Golden Temple. Henceforth, Amritsar became the headquarters of the Sikhs, as the followers of Nanak became known.[58]

Soon, however, the Sikhs and the Mughal authorities came into conflict during the rule of Jahangir and the fifth Guru, Arjun. According to the Sikh accounts, a Hindu revenue official of Jahangir became angry with Arjun because he refused to accept his daughter for his son. Jahangir fined the Guru but he refused to pay the fine. For this he was tortured and put to death. The death of Arjun is said to be the turning point in the history of the Sikhs. The period of peaceful evolution ended and the period of militancy began.[59] Sikh power would gradually grow and by the 19th century, an independent kingdom had been established in the Punjab headed by Ranjit Singh which extended to the Sutlej.[60] Sikh rule lasted for almost half a century until the British conquest in 1843.

The Mughal emperors were also the first to welcome Europeans into the sub-continent. Vasco da Gama led the first European expedition to India, sailing to the southwest coast in 1498. In 1510, the Portuguese captured Goa, which became the seat of their activities and from where they successfully challenged Arab power in the Indian Ocean and dominated sea routes. Under their protection, Jesuits established the first Christian missions on the subcontinent.[61]

It has been pointed out that except for the Maurya, Turko-Mughal and British periods—one Buddhist, one Islamic and one Christian— Pakistan remained independent or a part of empires located on her west. In fact, there

---

[58] Arshad, p. 99.

[59] Ibid.

[60] Abdulla, p. 35.

[61] Blood, p. 14.

have been more occasions when northern India was ruled by Pakistan-based kingdoms than Pakistan being ruled by northern Indian kingdoms. The Graeco-Bactrians with their capital at Taxila, the Kushans ruling from Peshawar, and the Sakas and Huns ruling from various cities in present-day Pakistan brought major portions of northern India under their control.[62]

British (1740-1947 C.E.)

Company Rule. The English came to India as traders. Their early history in India consists primarily of daring voyages, personal adventures and fights with the Portuguese or quarrels with the Mughal governor of Surat. Surat was the first lodgment of the British. They and the Dutch had been granted the right to establish factories there and very profitable trade was enjoyed by both European countries. Soon additional settlements had been established in Madras, Calcutta, and Bombay.

By the end of the 1600's, the Mughals were so dependent on trade with other countries that whoever controlled the seas had considerable influence over the rulers of the subcontinent. "The subjects of the Moghul cannot bear a war with the English for twelve months . . . without starving and dying by thousands . . . because by our war we obstruct their trade with all the Eastern nations, which is ten times as much as ours, and all Europeans nations put together."[63] By the beginning of the 1800's, British trading posts in India had been transformed from fortified trading posts (factories) to sovereign states where English law and order prevailed.

Mughal rulers permitted the merchants who carried their goods all over the world considerable latitude in established factories. The Dutch East India Company, the British East India Company, and later the French East India Company all vied for supremacy. The factories grew in area and population and armed company servants were used as militias. It was natural that they eventually became involved in politics. Plots and counter-plots, intrigues and subversion marked this period which was climaxed by the British East India Company, led by Robert Clives, defeating the forces of a local ruler in Bengal in 1757. By 1764, the British were in control of Bengal, Bihar, and Orissa; the Mughals maintained only titular control.

---

[62] Abdulla, pp. 35-36.

[63] J. T. Wheeler, ed., *Early Records of British in India* (Delhi: Ankit Book Centre, 1991), p. 89.

The British East India company expanded the area it controlled by two methods: agreements with local rulers under which foreign affairs, defense, and communications were controlled by the company while the rulers were allowed authority over most other affairs; and outright military conquest. The first method resulted in the so-called Native States, or Princely India, in which maharaja and nawab ruled; the second resulted in what was called British India.[64]

At the start of the nineteenth century, most of present-day Pakistan was under independent rulers. Sindh was ruled by the Muslim Talpur *mirs* (chiefs) in three small states annexed by the British in 1843. In Punjab, the decline of the Mughal empire had allowed the rise of the Sikhs, first as a military force and later as a political administration in Lahore. The kingdom of Lahore was the most powerful and expansive during the rule of Maharaja Ranjit Singh, when Sikh control was extended beyond Pesha-war. He added Kashmir to his dominion in 1839. After Ranjit Singh died in 1939, the British defeated the Sikhs and annexed the Punjab, including the present-day North-West Frontier Province. In 1850, the Treaty of Amritsar transferred Kashmir to the Dogra Dynasty who ruled the area under British oversight.[65]

The British gradually controlled most of the subcontinent through trade under the East India Company. Following an unsuccessful mutiny by the natives in 1857, the British government formally deposed the Mughals and assumed direct control. British traders arrived in South Asia in 1601, but the British Empire did not consolidate control of the region until the latter half of the 18th century. After 1850, the British, or those influenced by them, governed virtually the entire subcontinent.[66]

During British East India Company rule, revolts and mutinies by native troops under British control was not a rare occurrence. There also developed Islamic movements which regularly opposed English rule on Islamic grounds. In addition, Hindu traditions were also threatened: *sati* was condemned and the remarriage of widows encouraged.[67]

English education was spreading and Christian missionary activities convinced many that the British sought to convert the entire subcontinent to Christianity. The statements of English Christians often left a distinct

---

[64] Blood, p. 16.

[65] Ibid., p. 17.

[66] Ibid.

[67] Arshad, p. 145.

impression that the main interest of the British was to "confer on the countless millions of India, a higher and nobler gift of Christianity ... [Until the subcontinent] from Cape Comorin to the Himalayas embraces the religion of Christ and until it condemns the Hindu and the Muslim religions, our efforts must continue persistently."[68] Many Muslims and Hindus saw fighting the British as holy war.

The first major rebellion (1857) against the British is called the Sepoy Rebellion by English historians and the First War of Independence by Indian nationalists. The immediate cause for the mutiny by the sepoys, Indian soldiers employed by the company, was the introduction of a new rifle which had cartridges allegedly greased with cow or pig fat. The tips of these cartridges had to be bitten off by the soldiers before loading into the rifle. This outraged both Muslim and Indian soldiers who refused to use the cartridges. Fighting soon erupted and British soldiers were killed.[69]

The uprising failed primarily because the rebels lacked unity; Hindus and Muslims remained divided while princely rulers were unwilling to cooperate against their common enemy. In addition, the rebellion was limited to northern and central India and the fighting carried on primarily by sepoys of the Bengal army and some princely states. The British in fact called upon loyal native troops in other parts of the subcontinent to fight the insurgents; troops from the Punjab, particularly Sikhs, were especially valuable to the British.

The uprisings continued for a year but ultimately all the rebels were defeated. The uprising not only marked the end of the Mughal dynasty but it also heralded a period of persecution and exploitation of Muslims.[70] Though the rebellion had both Hindu and Muslim leaders, it was seen by the British primarily as a Muslim rebellion.[71] The property and possessions of the leaders were auctioned, travel was restricted and more important, Muslim leaders were discredited in the eyes of the British; in general, Muslims became isolated and powerless while Hindus prospered.[72]

---

[68] Aziz, p. 225.

[69] Blood, p. 18.

[70] Aziz, p. 256.

[71] Blood, p. 21.

[72] Arshad, pp. 146-47.

The British Raj. The revolt of 1857-58 marked the formal end of the Mughal Empire and also of company rule. The crisis created strong feelings in England against the East India Company and Parliament passed legislation which dramatically changed British rule in the subcontinent. It

- transferred authority from the East India Company to the British Crown, with Queen Victoria eventually being proclaimed empress of India in 1877; assured local princes of their rights and honor and promised the Indian people religious toleration and eligibility for public offices, despite caste or creed,
- adopted the policies of decentralization and "Indianisation," restoring legislative powers to the provinces,[73]and
- reorganized the army to include a greater proportion of English soldiers and sought to identify and segregate "martial races." Loyal Sikhs, Punjabis, Dogras, Gurkas and Pakhtuns (Pathans) were recruited while "disloyal" Bengalis and high-caste Hindus were discouraged from enlisting.[74]

The new rule also brought major social and economic changes to the subcontinent. For military, administrative and commercial purposes, the British improved transportation and communications. Irrigation canals were laid out in the Jamna, Ganges and Indus valley, with the latter becoming the largest irrigated area in the world. The expansion of irrigation in the Punjab led to the development of canal colonies, towns along the waterway settled mainly by Sikhs and Muslims. Punjab became the granary of India.[75]

Under the direct rule of the Crown, British expansion, termed the *forward policy,* continued into the north and northwest of the subcontinent. By 1887, Afghanistan and Baloachistan had been acquired though conquest, diplomacy, and purchase. However, British hegemony in the north-west frontier regions did not lead to direct administration similar to that in other parts of India. Local customs and laws continued, as did traditional lines of authority. To a large extent, the frontier served only as a buffer against the Russian empire and a training ground for the British Indian Army.[76]

After the rebellion of 1857, many Islamic leaders and activists eluded the British by fleeing to the mountainous northwest areas where they reorganized

---

[73] Ibid., pp. 148-49.

[74] Blood, p. 20.

[75] Ibid., p. 19.

[76] Ibid., p. 21.

and continued their agitation for *jihad* and emancipation from the British. A British historian of the time described the *Mujahideen* in these words:

> Besides constantly keeping alive a fanatical spirit of unrest along the Frontier, it has three times organized great tribal confederacies, each of which has cost British India a war. One government after another has declared it to be a source of permanent danger to our Rule, yet all our efforts to extirpate it have failed. It still continues the centre towards which the hopes alike of our disloyal subjects and of our enemies beyond the Frontier turn."[77]

The seeds of Muslim nationalism and the establishment of Pakistan are the subject of the next chapter.

---

[77] Hunter, *"The India Musalmans,"* p. 34. Quoted in Aziz.

CHAPTER 2

MODERN SETTING

Muslim Nationalism

The 1857 rebellion marked the end of the Mughal empire. The rebels had marched to Delhi in an attempt to restore the poet-emperor Bahadur Shah II to power and reestablish Muslim authority. When the English forces, with the help of loyal Punjabi soldiers recaptured Delhi, they banished the last of the Mughal emperors and assumed direct control of Indian affairs.

It should be noted that Hindus had been under the dominion of Muslims for hundreds of years. They, therefore, had learned how to be loyal subjects to another culture. Muslims, on the other hand, had to be taught who the masters were. Though the Mughals had been without real power for many years, they retained a semblance of independence which the British could not tolerate.

After the rebellion, Muslim leaders, not Hindus, were seen as the instigators of the uprising and the primary threat to British authority. The punishment inflicted on the Muslims by the victorious English was vicious and at times savage. Atrocious acts of reprisal and intimidation were followed by economic measures aimed at confiscating all Muslim wealth and possessions to render them powerless.[78]

Discrimination against Muslims continued long after the rebellion. The landed Muslim upper classes in the north Indian heartlands soon became culturally and politically isolated. These "Indian" Muslims failed to reemerge economically and produced no large group comparable to the upwardly mobile British-educated Hindu middle class. The former Muslim rulers of India now saw themselves becoming a permanent noncompetitive class in the British Raj, at the very time that the forces of Indian nationalism were gathering strength.

However, Muslims in the Punjab were rewarded for helping the British and became the dominant group in the northwest portion of the subcontinent. It was from this group that many future leaders of Pakistan would emerge.[79]

---

[78] Aziz, pp. 253-55.

[79] Blood, pp. 21-22.

While the Muslims in Delhi were reduced to abject poverty and broken in spirit, the rebellion continued unabated among many Muslims in provincial areas. Incidents of insurrection and calls to revolt continued throughout the 1860's, particularly among Wahabi leaders. British military force was unable to contend with an enemy spread over vast terrain and often supported by the local populace. As often happens in Muslim movements, the pulpits and mosques became the centers of revolt against foreign domination.

> It is not the traitors themselves whom we have to fear, but the seditious masses in the heart of our Empire, and the superstitious tribes on our Frontier, both of whom the Fanatics have again and again combined in a Religious War against us.[80]

After several defeats on the battlefield and failure to extirpate the Mujahideen, the British found it more effective to counter the insurgents with diplomàcy and subterfuge, often using bribery and deceit to foment dissension among the rebels and tribal chiefs and encourage discord and jealousy among various elements of the population.[81] It became clear to the British that the root of their problem was the theological foundation of the rebellious Muslims. It was Islam that the insurgents used to justify their cause and so Islam too became the target of British strategies, both military and economic.

> Under the decent name of donations, men were bribed according to their power and rapaciousness; and the conscience of many a sacred orator was tempered with and engaged to sound the trumpet of dis-cord. Mujahideen were branded with the odious name of "Wahabis" and the word "Wahabi" was put in use as an opprobrious epithet ... The people were preached and urged to view the Mujahids as apostates. The hirelings who declared themselves to be the true champions of the faith hurled their spiritual thunders against the Mujahideen and condemned them as enemies of the true God ... The torrents of the incessant and artful propaganda, under the cover of religious preaching ... shook the prestige and hold of the Mujahideen, and a large section of people genuinely and

[80] Hunter, p. 264.

[81] Aziz, p. 262.

seriously began to consider "whether or not the Mujahideen were true Muslims." This was the first effective blow inflicted on the revolution.[82]

The British continued to foster the spirit of religious discord and controversy. In a country with so diverse a population it was easy to magnify and exacerbate differences. Without an authoritative voice, Indian Muslims became divided regarding basic doctrines of Islam such as *jihad* and servitude to non-Muslim authority. British policy encouraged new interpretations and rewarded compromise and moderation. Hindus were favored with British education and government positions. Many Muslims who sought similar favors from the ruling authority had to conform their views to accommodate servitude. Jihad had to be rejected and British supremacy acknowledged.

This view was best expressed by Sir Sayyid Ahmed Khan who pleaded for an honorable servitude and who sought to halt the *jihad* which he felt had caused much grief among Muslim subjects. A passive Islam would be tolerated and would allow Muslims to survive, even prosper. By the middle of the 1870s, the spirit of rebellion had cooled and the Mujahideen were eventually silenced.[83]

Sir Sayyid Ahmed's Aligarth Movement grew in influence and prestige. Sir Sayyid considered access to British education as the best means to social mobility for the sons of Muslim gentry under colonial rule. He promoted Urdu as a national language and disdained politics, fearing domination by the Hindu majority. The Muhammadan Anglo-Oriental College (now Aligarth Muslim University) was founded in 1875. Most of its graduates sought administrative positions within the British system.[84]

One religious movement which was acceptable to the British was called the Deoband Movement and was led by Muslim scholars who were expanding traditional Islamic education and Islamic law to include new concepts applicable to contemporary Muslim society. They promoted publications in Urdu as opposed to traditional Arabic or even Persian texts.[85] They undertook efforts to organize Muslims throughout India; an element of

---

[82] Ibid., p. 269.

[83] Ibid., pp. 271-72.

[84] Blood, p. 22.

[85] Aziz, pp. 270-71.

the Deobandis would later favor the creation of a separate Muslim state and emerge as the Jamiat-ul-Ulama-I-Islam party.[86]

As English influence increased and Islamic unity decreased, a number of all-India associations were formed by English-speaking Indians who sought to assert their interests in manners more acceptable to the British. These associations were not formed along religious lines and frequently had Muslims and Hindus working together for a common cause.

In 1885, the Indian National Congress was founded, with British approval, to formulate proposals and demands to present to the British. The Congress served as a political debating society where the major issues of Indian society were discussed. Members came from all parts of Indian and represented a large variety of interests and religious groups; the majority, however, was Hindu.

Muslim leaders were divided over the issue of cooperating with the Congress. Some Muslims argued for cooperation, but many could not envision fair treatment under a Hindu majority. In 1906, the All-India Muslim League was founded in Dhaka to promote loyalty to the British and to "protect and advance the political rights of the Muslims of India and respectfully represent their needs and aspirations to the [British] Government."[87]

Partition and Independence

In 1913, the Muslim League formally adopted the same objective as the Congress—self-government for India within the British Empire. The First World War interrupted the movement but also gave new strength to the forces moving for independence. The Congress Party, led by Mohandas Gandhi, took the lead. Gandhi, a high-caste Hindu trained as a lawyer in England, urged his followers to adapt non-cooperation or civil disobedience rather than violence. "This meant rejecting offers of government positions, disregarding British laws, refusing to pay taxes, shunning army service, and boycotting British made goods."[88]

Hindus and Muslims struggled for independence together but the Congress and the League could still not agree on a formula that would ensure the protection of Muslim religious, economic, and political rights. Muslims'

---

[86] Blood, p. 22.

[87] Ibid., p. 23.

[88] Irving L. Gordon, *Reviewing World History* (New York: Amsco School Publications, New York, 1964), p. 383.

fear of domination by the larger Hindu population which out-numbered them three to one, finally brought an end to the alliance. The Congress was split in the 1930's when Mohammed Ali Jinnah withdrew his support to join the Muslim League which championed the cause of an independent Muslim Pakistan.

The idea of a Muslim state gained support in the 1930s as prominent Muslims such as Muhammad Iqbal and Jinnah envisioned separation. On March 23, 1940, Jinnah, now leader of the Muslim League, formally endorsed the "Lahore Resolution," calling for the creation of an independent state in regions where Muslims constituted a majority.

Figure 1:
Mohammad Ali Jinnah

At the end of World War II, the United Kingdom moved with increasing urgency to grant India independence. However, the Congress Party and the Muslim League still could not agree on the terms for a constitution or establishing an interim government. In June 1947, the British Government declared that it would bestow full dominion status upon two successor states —India and Pakistan.

Under the proposed arrangement, the various princely states could freely join either India or Pakistan. At the time of partition, British India consisted of eleven provinces including Bombay, Madras, Bengal, Punjab, and Sindh. In addition, there were 562 states ruled by princes.

Of all the princely states, Kashmir was the largest with an area of about 85,000 square miles. It is famous for its lovely valleys, beautiful lakes, snow -capped mountains, and artistic handicrafts. The majority of the people were Muslims but the ruler was a Hindu. There was much dissatisfaction within Kashmir including a serious uprising in 1932 resulting in a British commission of inquiry and exposure of corruption, neglect of education, and forced labor.

Hyderabad was regarded as the most important of all the princely states. Its ruler, Nizam, was considered as the richest man in the world. Nizam was a Muslim while the majority of the population was Hindu. As the demands for independence grew, the British decided, in principle, to divide the sub-continent between Hindus and Muslims. The Muslim majority areas were to become Pakistan and the rest would be left as India. The fate of the princely states was settled too with some important exceptions in Hyderabad and Kashmir. These two exceptions, particularly that of Kashmir, has since continued to haunt the subcontinent.

Consequently, a bifurcated Muslim nation separated by more than 1600 kilometers (1000 mi.) of Indian territory emerged when Pakistan became a self-governing dominion within the Commonwealth on August 14, 1947. West Pakistan comprised the contiguous Muslim-majority provinces of present-day Pakistan; East Pakistan consisted of a single province, which is now Bangladesh.[89]

After Independence

With the death in 1948 of its first head of state, Muhammad Ali Jinnah, and the assassination in 1951 of its first prime minister, Liaqat Ali Khan, political instability and economic difficulty became prominent features of post-independent Pakistan. After Pakistan's loss in the 1965 war against India, military leader Ayub Khan's power declined. Subsequent political and economic grievances inspired agitation movements which compelled his resignation in March 1969.

During the brief tenure of General Yahya Khan as martial law administrator, elections were held in 1970 in which the Awami League Party won an absolute majority in the parliament, capturing 167 out of 169 seats from East Pakistan. Frictions between West and East Pakistan precluded the

---

[89] U.S. Department of State Department Notes.

convening of the parliament and culminated in the 1971 army crackdown in East Pakistan, including the banning of the Awami League and the arrest of its leader, Sheikh Mujibur Rahman. Many of his aides and several million Bengali refugees fled to India, where they established a provisional government. Tensions escalated, and hostilities broke out between India and Pakistan in November 1971. The combined Indian-Bengali forces quickly overwhelmed Pakistan's army in the East. By the time Pakistan's forces surrendered on December 16, 1971, India had acquired control of a large area of East Pakistan.

Zulfiqar Ali Bhutto, whose Pakistan People's Party (PPP) had won a majority of the seats in West Pakistan in the 1970 elections, replaced Yahya Khan. East Pakistan became the independent state of Bangladesh.

Bhutto moved decisively to restore national confidence and pursued an active foreign policy, taking a leading role in Islamic and Third World forums. Although Pakistan did not formally join the Non-Aligned Movement until 1979, the position of the Bhutto Government coincided largely with that of the non-aligned nations.

Domestically, Bhutto pursued a populist agenda and nationalized major industries and the banking system. In 1973, he promulgated a new constitution accepted by most political elements and relinquished the presidency to become prime minister.

Although Bhutto continued his populist and socialist rhetoric, he increasingly relied on Pakistan's rural landlords. Over time the economy stagnated, largely as a result of the dislocation and uncertainty produced by Bhutto's frequently changing economic policies.

When Bhutto proclaimed his own victory in the March 1977 national elections, the opposition Pakistan National Alliance (PNA) denounced the results as fraudulent and demanded new elections. Bhutto resisted and, after endemic political violence in Pakistan, arrested the PNA leadership.

1977-1985 Martial Law

Anti-government unrest made the army restless. On July 5, 1977, the military arrested Bhutto and removed him from power. Martial law was declared and portions of the 1973 constitution were suspended. Chief of Army Staff Gen. Muhammad Zia ul-Haq became chief martial law administrator and promised new elections.

Zia released Bhutto and asserted that he could contest the elections scheduled for October, 1977. However, it became clear that Bhutto's popularity had survived his government and Zia postponed the elections. Subsequently, Bhutto was convicted and sentenced to death for alleged conspiracy to murder a political opponent. Despite international appeals on his behalf, Bhutto was hanged on April 6, 1979.

The Return of Democracy

On December 30, 1985, President Zia removed martial law and restored constitutional rights safeguarded under the constitution. The first months of 1986 witnessed a rebirth of political activity throughout Pakistan. All parties —including those continuing to deny the legitimacy of the Zia/Junejo Government—were permitted to organize and hold rallies. In April 1986, PPP leader Benazir Bhutto, daughter of Zulfiqar Ali Bhutto, returned to Pakistan from exile in Europe.

Following the lifting of martial law, Prime Minister Junejo attempted to make his Pakistan Muslim League (PML) a political party capable of competing with the PPP and its MRD allies on a national level. His increasing political independence and differences with Zia over Afghan policy resulted in tensions between them. Zia was a firm advocate of the Afghan Resistance, which had been fighting Soviet forces since they invaded Afghanistan in 1979; Junejo repeatedly expressed his concern over the effect the conflict and the presence of some three million Afghan refugees had on Pakistan's internal security.

On May 29, 1988, President Zia dismissed the Junejo government and called for November elections. In June, Zia proclaimed the supremacy in Pakistan of Shari'ah (Islamic law), by which all civil law had to conform to traditional Muslim edicts.

On August 17, a plane carrying President Zia, American Ambassador Arnold Raphael, U.S. Brig. Gen. Herbert Wassom, and 28 Pakistani military officers crashed on a return flight from a military equipment trial near Bahawalpur, killing all of its occupants. In accordance with the constitution, Chairman of the Senate Ghulam Ishaq Khan became acting president.[90]

---

[90] U.S. Department of State Notes.

Table 1.
Pakistan: Human Development Indicators[91]

	Pakistan 1970's	Pakistan 1990's	Low-Income Economies
Life Expectancy at Birth (Yrs.)	48 (1970)	59 (1992)	62 (1992)
Total Fertility Rate (Births per married woman)	7.0 (1970)	5.6 (1992)	3.4 (1992)
Infant Mortality Rate (Per thousand live births)	NA (1970)	91 (1991)	73 (1992)
Adult Literacy Rate (% of population age 15+)	24 (1977)	35 (1990)	60 (1990)
Primary Education Gross Enrollment Ratio (%)	47 (1974)	56 (1990)	101 (1991)
Secondary Education Gross Enrollment Ratio (%)	13 (1970)	21 (1990)	41 (1991)
Female	5	13	35

[91] Source: World Bank, *Pakistan Poverty Assessment*, (Washington, D.C.: The World Bank, 1995), Table 1.5, p. 53.

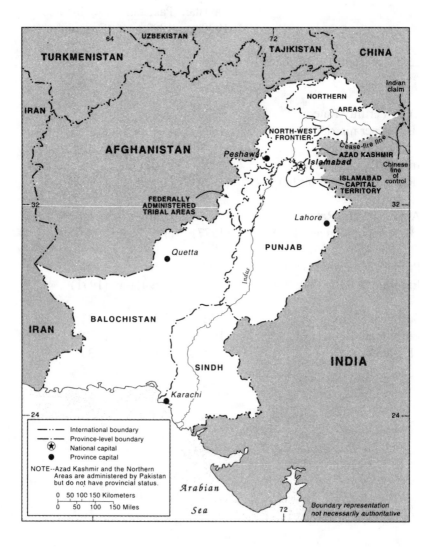

Administrative Divisions of Pakistan

CHAPTER 3

CURRENT CONDITIONS

> "The problem in this country is that the basic necessities have not been fulfilled — food, clothing, shelter, health and education. In fifty years of rule, they have only been thieving and enriching themselves." *A citizen.*

Overview

1. *Pakistan.*[92] Pakistan is located in Southern Asia along the Arabian Sea. It lies between latitude 24 degrees and 37 North and longitude 62 and 75 East. It is strategically located with Iran on the west, Afghanistan on the north and northwest, and the People's Republic of China on the northwest to northeast. It has more than 2900 kilometers of border with India; 2400 kilometers with Afghanistan; 900 kilometers with Iran; and 500 kilometers with China. It has more than 1000 kilometers of coastline.

Pakistan's land of 796 thousand square kilometers is almost twice the size of California. It presents a beautiful variety of landscape. The north to northwestern mountainous belt is largely barren, known for its rugged grandeur. It features many of the world's tallest peaks including the second tallest, K-2. The land beneath the Himalayas is fertile and tree clad. It grows a variety of fruit, tobacco, cotton, sugarcane, rice, and wheat.

Farther south lies the vast plain of the Indus River with an extensive irrigation network. The Indus basin is thickly populated and extensively farmed producing food and other cash crops. It contains most of the urban centers as well as the industries. Thar desert lies in the southeast, and marshy Rann of Katch in the east. Pakistan's large coast is on the Arabian sea.

The country is comprised of four provinces: Punjab, the North West Frontier (NWFP), Sindh, and Baloachistan; and the federally administered tribal areas. Based on the 1981 census, Pakistan's population was 84.3 million. Based on World Bank estimates, it was about 126 million in mid-1994.

---

[92] *Islamic Republic of Pakistan: A Profile* (Islamabad: Directorate of Films and Publications, Ministry of Information and Broadcasting, Government of Pakistan, undated).

Pakistan is accordingly, the eighth most populous country behind China (1191 million); India (912 million); the United States (261 million); Indonesia (190 million); Brazil (159 million); the Russian Federation (148 million); and Japan (125 million). Its current growth rate, about 2.9% per year, is one of the highest.[93] Punjab is the most populous province, followed by Sindh, NWFP, and Baloachistan.

The national capital is located in Islamabad. The largest city, commercial center, and capital of Sindh is Karachi. Lahore, the fastest growing commercial center is the capital of Punjab. Peshawar is the capital of the NWFP, and Quetta is the capital of Baloachistan.

More than 97 percent of Pakistan's population is Muslim. The rest represent nearly all the other religions of the world. The people speak Urdu, Punjabi, Sindhi, Pushto, Baloachi, Brahvi, Siraiki, and Hindko. Urdu is the official national language. A large number speak English. Most of the government business, particularly at higher levels is conducted in English.

2.   *Strategic International Setting.* For reasons of its geographical borders, cultural links, religious ties, and political relationships, Pakistan is a part of several formal and informal groupings and wears many international hats. Pakistan is:

- a member of the South Asian Regional Council along with India, Bangladesh, Nepal, Bhutan, Sri Lanka, and the Maldives;
- a close friend and ally of most Middle Eastern countries;
- a founding member of the Economic Cooperation Organization consisting of ten non-Arab Muslim countries, namely Iran, Pakistan, Turkey, Azerbaijan, Kazakhistan, Kyrgyztan, Turkmenistan, Tajikistan, Uzbekistan, and Afghanistan (accordingly, it is a friend and a partner of the Central Asian countries);
- a close friend of China helpful in opening doors to China for the West,
- a close friend of the United States, helpful in mobilizing all Muslims against the Soviet invasion of Afghanistan, which in turn contributed to the eventual collapse of the Soviet Union itself; and
- an active member of the Organization of the Islamic Conference (OIC), having played an important role in its formation and development.

Pakistan may not yet have found its "true calling," however it can be a powerful source of goodwill in the world.

---

[93] *World Development Report 1996* (Oxford: Oxford University Press, 1996), Tables 1 and 4.

General Discontent

3. *Promise of Pakistan Not Achieved.* The formation of Pakistan was meant to be a means of preserving and advancing Muslims in British India. Many Pakistanis feel that the original objectives of Pakistan have not been achieved. The partition of India and creation of a separate country for Muslims was expected to bring about immense benefits to all Muslims in terms of (a) prosperity and economic advancement; (b) spiritual freedom and development; (c) cultural and linguistic renaissance; and (d) establishment of a government dedicated to the welfare of the people, law and order, and freedom from exploitation and corruption. Most Pakistanis believe that these expectations have not been met.

Some argue that Britain's "divide and rule" policies and the actions of Pakistan's early leaders have sown the seeds of conflict and discontentment which continue to this date. They cite the many examples including:

- The "divide and rule" policy of Britain in the subcontinent was the prime motive for support of the Muslim League, not the welfare of Muslims. The rulers of Pakistan chose to continue this policy after independence.
- Britain's decision to leave India before resolving the status of Kashmir contained seeds of conflict for the subcontinent. The cost of this policy of inaction has been immeasurable.
- While Pakistan was carved out of India for the sake of Islam, most recognized religious leaders of the day opposed its creation. In fact, most of the leaders of the new nation did not even bother to follow the most elementary rituals of the religion.
- Promises of autonomy for the constituent provinces which were made in the Pakistan Resolution of 1940, and which had attracted the provinces to the new state, were broken. This lead to provincial rivalry, separatist movements and general disenchantment.
- British trained civil servants had ruled the alien masses through their control over a few landlords who in turn received government patronage. This practice has continued without regard for the true interests of the rest of the citizens of Pakistan.
- The majority population of newly independent Pakistan was alienated early through imposition of a national language which a majority did not understand or value.
- Leaders who had won elections in pre-partition days (e.g., in Bengal and in the Frontier) were quickly discarded by the new government of Pakistan and replaced by "yes men."

Initial Handicaps

The newly independent Pakistan started with many handicaps in 1947. It made its national life more complicated by adopting a number of ill-conceived policies.

4.   *Constitutional Instability.* Even though Pakistan had a constitutional assembly from the start, it took almost a decade to agree on the first constitution. Some have argued that quick agreement on the constitution would have meant a quick general election, which did not suit some prominent leaders, specially the first Prime Minister, Liaqat Ali Khan, who was a new immigrant and did not have a safe constituency. Hence the delay. Nevertheless, Pakistan is currently functioning under a modified third constitution.

Table 2: Pakistan--Changes in Constitutions

1947-56	Government of India Act of 1935
1956-58	The First Constitution
1958-62	Martial Law
1962-69	The Second Constitution
1969-73	Martial law
1973-77	The Third Constitution
1977-78	Martial law
1978-96	Modified Third Constitution

5.   *Too Many Political Parties.* Pakistan has a multi-party political system. Anybody can and does form a political party. The Muslim League, which led the independence movement, has changed hands several times. In the old days, everyone who came into power somehow claimed the Muslim League as his own. Currently, the Muslim League is claimed by three different factions—Nawaz Shariff, Junejo, and Chatta. There are a number of Islamic parties; Jamat Islami, founded by the late Maulana Maududi is the oldest. Zulfiqar Ali Bhutto formed his own Pakistan People's Party (PPP) in 1967. PPP is the largest party in the country with a political base in all of the provinces. The Mohajir Qomi Movement (MQM), Tehrik-e-Istqilal and the recently-formed Tehrik-e-Insaff, organized by famed cricketer Imran Khan are just a few more.

6.   *Frequent Changes in Government.* There have been frequent changes of government in Pakistan. The founder of the nation, Muhammad Ali Jinnah,

passed away in 1948, just over a year after independence. The first Prime Minister, Liaqat Ali Khan, was assassinated in 1951. The two events triggered much political instability and maneuvering by relatively unknown leaders. At the imposition of the first martial law on October 8, 1958, Pakistan had had four heads of states and seven heads of government during its first ten years.

Table 3: Pakistan--Changes in Government
Governor Generals (GG)/Presidents/Chief Martial Law Administrators (CMLA)

Mohammad Ali Jinnah (GG) 1947-48	Died in office
Khuwaja Nazimuddin (GG) 1948-51	Became Prime Minister
Ghulam Mohammed (GG) 1951-55	Incapacitated in office
General Iskandar Mirza 1955-58	Overthrown
General Ayub Khan (CMLA) 1958	Became President
General Ayub Khan 1958-69	Resigned
General Yahya Khan 1969-71	Resigned
Zulfiqar Ali Bhutto 1971-73	Became Prime Minister
Chaudhri Fazal Illahi 1973-78	Retired
General Zia-ul-Haq (CMLA) 1977-78	Became President
General Zia-ul-Haq 1978-88	Died in office
Ghulam Ishaq Khan 1988-93	Resigned
Wassim Sajad (Acting) 1993	Caretaker President
Farooq Laghari 1993-	Current President

Prime Ministers

Liaquat Ali Khan 1947-1951	Murdered
Khuwaja Nazimuddin 1951-53	Dismissed
Mohammad Ali Bogra 1953-55	Resigned
Chaudhri Mohammed Ali 1955-56	Resigned
H.S. Suhrawardy 1956-57	Resigned
I.I. Chundrigar 1957	Resigned
Firoz Khan Noon 1957-58	Overthrown
General Ayub Khan 1958	Office abolished; became President
Zulfiqar Ali Bhutto 1973-77	Overthrown; office abolished again
Muhammad Khan Junejo 1985-88	Dismissed
Benazir Bhutto 1988-90	Dismissed

Ghulam Mustafa Jatoi 1990	Caretaker President
Mian Nawaz Sharif 1990-93	Dismissed
Balakh Sher Mazari 1993	Caretaker President
Mian Nawaz Sharif 1993	Resigned
Moeen Qureshi 1993	Caretaker President
Benazir Bhutto 1993-1996	Dismissed

7.   *Long Periods of Martial Law*. General Ayub Khan led the first direct military rule in Pakistan. He remained in office for eleven years (1958-69). In 1969, when he was forced to resign under great political pressure, he decided to hand over authority to another military officer—General Yahya Khan—who assumed power in 1969. Khan was forced to resign in 1971. However, the two years saw a bloody civil war in the eastern wing of the country, a war with India, and the breakup of the country leading to Bangladesh's independence.

Khan handed power to an elected government led by Zulfiqar Ali Bhutto. However, Mr. Bhutto chose to keep the title of chief martial law administrator for almost two years. Mr. Bhutto's government was again replaced by military rule under General Zia-ul-Haq, who took over in 1977 and remained in office until 1988, when he was killed in a mysterious plane crash.

Since independence in 1947, Pakistan has been ruled directly by the army for about half of the time. During the other half, particularly since 1988, the army has played a prominent role in choosing the rulers—and in replacing them.

8.   *Involvement in too many conflicts*. Pakistan has had four wars with India. The first was over Kashmir in 1948. There was a brief battle over Ran of Katch in early 1965. It was followed by a major war over Kashmir in September 1965. Pakistan's civil war in East Pakistan led to a major war with India in 1971.

Pakistan has been an active player in the Afghanistan conflict since its start in 1978 and continues as such to this day. Pakistan is at least emotionally involved in the ongoing liberation movement in Kashmir—India claims that the involvement is much deeper.

9.   *Many Blessings*. Although Pakistan started out with several handicaps, it also started with many positive elements. Several of these have been built upon since then. Pakistan is blessed with a majority Muslim population sharing many uniting features. Pakistan has a large population and a diversity of people and land, a large area of land, huge financial resources, a sizeable

industrial base, highly trained manpower, media experience, strong community feelings and a belief in one Muslim nation, principles of good governance as enunciated by religion and faith, geopolitical strengths including natural resources and ownership of strategic areas, a well-trained armed forces, a strong civil service, and established institutions.

Since independence Pakistan has not matched the performance of several East Asian countries. Nevertheless, there has been much economic development in all sectors—agriculture, industry, transportation, education, and science. Many physical structures have been built throughout the country which did not exist at the time of partition. However, prosperity has not touched the majority.

A small part of the population has benefitted in economic terms, but for a vast majority, the promise of Pakistan has not materialized. This is confirmed by human development indicators shown below. The armed forces, civil service, judiciary, and premier institutions, such as Pakistan's railways and WAPDA, have lost some of their original glamor and promise. The dreams have been shattered and the majority has experienced little if any improvement in quality of life. Some of this can be attributed to the large increase in population. However, much of it may be due to poor government policies and greed of those in power.

Religious freedom has turned into sectarian violence. Ethnic strife caused by cultural and linguistic differences is widespread and growing. The governments have generally lacked essential Islamic qualities. Personal security, law and order are endangered; corruption has become open and the norm of the times. Exploitation by Hindus in pre-partition days has been replaced with exploitation by fellow Muslims.

Domestic Discontent

Some discontent is common in every country. In Pakistan, it has taken enormous proportions. It manifests itself as agitation against the government, magnified differences among the citizens, and conflicts and hostilities among the citizens and/or between the citizens and the government. The civil war in East Pakistan (Bangladesh) resulted in brutal action by the Pakistan army, military intervention by India, the capture of more than 90,000 Pakistani soldiers, and the breakup of the recently formed Islamic Republic of Pakistan. This war was the direct result of the discontent in the East Pakistan province. Some describe it as a struggle for control of the region's resources. Others attribute the civil war to the "feeling of superiority among the martial ethnic group" of West Pakistan. The leadership in Bangladesh has publicly accused their Muslim brethren in the Pakistani armed forces of having committed genocide, ethnic cleansing, and rapes.

Domestic discontent and ethnic strife in the remaining area of Pakistan has continued since then. Limited economic opportunities, an unfair distribution of the economic pie, and differences in language, culture and "degree of education" have been given as causes for the continuing strife and accompanying loss of life and property.

> "The Army blamed the politicians, the politicians the Army; the businessmen blamed the civil servants, the civil servants, the politicians; everybody blamed the landlords and the foreigners, and the left and the religious fundamentalists blamed everybody except the masses."[94]

Successive governments have chosen to use the army in Sindh and Baloachistan provinces, with a large expense of money and the loss of good will with local people, rather than solve the genuine local grievances.

10. *Typical Complaints*. Any observer visiting Pakistan would soon hear typical conversations among neighbors or family members voicing discontent regarding local and national conditions. Often-heard complaints include:
- The police stand around without enforcing many laws.
- Large numbers of people are unemployed and wander around in every part of the country.
- Ethnic problems are a reality which needs recognition and active search for solution.
- There exist mutual contempt and distrust among Punjabis, Sindhis, Mohajirs, and Pathans. Everyone offers reasons for disliking the others, and all expect more ethnic trouble in the future.
- People accuse the army of creating and/or sustaining MQM, Jiai Sindh and other ethnic organizations in the interests of the regimes in power.
- There is widespread corruption. The few honest government officials are shunted off to subordinate jobs. Individual custom appraisers earning the equivalent of $200 per month are individually millionaires.
- Lucrative posts are regularly auctioned.

[94] Emma Duncan, *Breaking the Curfew: A Political Journey Through Pakistan* (Arrow Books, 1989), p. 6.

- There are large numbers of weapons and military actions by public and private groups.
- The economic situation of the country is very weak.
- People are concerned and spend time gossiping about the future of the country.
- The American embassy is assumed to be actively involved in domestic Pakistani politics.
- There are internal divisions among all political parties but the leaders lack the courage to follow their conscience.
- The status quo is unlikely to continue for long.
- All groups are aiming at improving their position for the coming struggle.
- People have lost faith in the bureaucracy, the army, and the current political parties.
- A strong dictatorship is actually hoped for and expected—where it would come from is not clear.
- A conspiracy is suspected behind every action taken by government, political parties, and private groups.
- Financial capital is fleeing the country: people of power possess several passports, travel on different ones, and deposit assets abroad.
- Most people do not pay taxes, specially landlords and the self-employed.

Key Demands of People

11. *International.* As in other countries, people have international, national, provincial, and local levels of concerns. At the international level, people want a resolution of the Kashmir problem, peace on the borders, and good relations with all countries of the world, particularly the Muslim countries and the West.

12. *National.* At the national level, Pakistanis seek (a) humane and more civilized behavior from each other and the government; (b) improved governance including law and order, removal of corruption, and transparency in government; and (c) increased economic well being, including employment opportunities, provision of basic services, and increased purchasing power.

13. *Provincial.* From a provincial perspective, there are specific points in each province. Unfortunately there is limited consensus on the provincial issues among Pakistanis as a whole, and hence there has been limited progress in resolving issues.

14. *Sindh*. Sindh, as a whole, seeks increased autonomy (which is opposed by Punjab and the army) and an increased share of national resources (which is not possible without increasing the national revenue or decreasing the share of the army and of Punjab). MQM, which claims to speak for Karachi, seeks the removal of the quota system (opposed by Sindhis); bringing Biharis from Bangladesh (opposed by Sindhis); and the creation of a separate province for Mohajirs (opposed by Sindhis). The rest of Sindh demands affirmative action to make up for the past neglect (not possible without increasing national revenue or decreasing the revenue of the army and of Punjab) and an increased role for Sindhi language and culture (opposed by Urdu speakers).

15. *Punjab*. Punjab demands improved defense against India, further strengthening of the army, and continuation of the current level and pattern of development. The smaller provinces, particularly Sindh and Baloachistan, prefer changes in policies in each of these areas.

16. *Baloachistan*. Baloachistan demands affirmative action to make up for past neglect (impossible without increasing national revenue or decreasing the size of the army and the share of Punjab), increased autonomy (opposed by Punjab and the army), the increased share of national resources.

17. *North West Frontier*. The North West Frontier demands increased provincial autonomy, the settlement of the Afghanistan issue, the return of Afghan refugees to Afghanistan, and an acceleration of the current level of development.

The demands of Sindh and Baloachistan are opposed by at least one interest as indicated above. Punjab and to some extent the NWFP, which have the largest number of army personnel and a relatively higher rate of economic growth, continue with their agenda. While Sindh and Baloachistan are probably the most discontented provinces, it must be conceded that even Punjab and the NWFP are part of a very poor country and have many genuine economic needs.

Demands and Excuses

18. *Demands Summaries*. The above demands can be summarized and packaged as follows:
- provide sincere leadership,
- treat citizens with respect,
- reduce poverty and unemployment,

- make Pakistan richer,
- bring back religious tolerance,
- restore power to people,
- restore law and order,
- reduce ethnic divisions and regional inequalities,
- stop corruption,
- provide peace at the borders,
- normalize relations with the West, and
- provide affordable national defense.

19. *Excuses.* The government leaders over the years have acknowledged all of the above demands. However, they have not been able to pay due attention to them for what they have claimed to be a higher goal, the survival of Pakistan. All have claimed at one time or another that the very existence of Pakistan was in danger. Hence, the attention of the government and its leadership, and the limited resources available had to be diverted to the "survival" activities.

That Islam is in danger is another common proclamation of many of the leaders. "Protection of Islam" has become another high profile slogan used by leaders to elicit support.

The people of Pakistan are demanding integrated development. They are seeking economic, political, moral, and military development. The basic objectives in each of the four areas are clear, although the priorities and the required sacrifices for them are less appreciated.

20. *Economic Development.* The basic economic objective is to meet the needs of all Pakistanis in terms of adequate food, shelter, education, and health care. This can best be achieved through provision of adequate employment opportunities at reasonable wages, through both private and public sectors. Pakistan is rated by the World Bank and other development agencies as a low income country. However, in terms of purchasing power, it is far richer. Through greater emphasis on economic development, reduction in wastage, and better distribution of resources, a significant portion of Pakistan's basic needs can be provided. However, it has not been possible to achieve equitable distribution in spite of considerable public proclamations. Unless there are basic changes in policy and actions, it is unrealistic to expect improvement.

21. *Political Development.* The key political objective is continued existence and strengthening of representative government, answerable to the people of

Pakistan and therefore dedicated to their welfare. Pakistan has undergone a checkered history. For about half of the time since independence, the military has directly ruled the country. For the rest of the time, particularly since 1988, the military has been the king/queen maker.

The dictators have argued that Islam neither requires nor prohibits government based on "one man one vote." However, Islam requires consultation, mutual consent, freedom of speech, justice, and support for good and avoidance of evil. Many Islamic scholars have convincingly argued that democracy is the only way of meeting the Islamic requirements for the government. They assert that rule by those who do not have the welfare of the Muslim citizens and the pleasure of Allah as the twin prime objective is not desirable. They assert that Islam stands for stable government and urge citizens to follow their rulers only so long as they do not stray from the right path.

Political governments have been disappointing to the people. The people appear more than willing to give continued opportunity to the politicians, but survey after survey has demonstrated general disappointment with the leadership of the main political parties.

Moral Development: The Middle Path

Spiritually, Muslims believe in one God (Allah) and His messenger Muhammad (PBUH)[95], the Qur'an as the authentic source of all knowledge, the temporary nature of our life in this world, and the day of judgement. All sects appear to believe in these basic points. However, they appear to have different interpretations as one gets into greater details.

The Pakistani nation, as a whole, does not appear to follow the strict theocratic path followed by any of the religious parties. At the same time, they do not wish to support the corrupt politics of personal power and enrichment exhibited by several secular regimes. They strive for the middle path.

The basic objective of Muslims in Pakistan appears to be tolerant enough to let everyone have their own opinions as long as they maintain the basic beliefs of Islam. Declaring each other "kafir" (a disbeliever) due to differences in details of the religion often widens disputes among Pakistanis.

Pakistanis at times fail to treat each other as a part of same nation. Often they refuse to settle disputes among each other peacefully. Though their belief system tells them to do so, they do not always defend each other

---

[95] Peace and blessings (of Allah) be upon him.

against oppression and evil. Part of the problem is the leadership; and it is commonly accepted that Pakistanis are seeking better educated and more tolerant spiritual leadership.

Military Development

Militarily, Pakistan's objective is to be strong enough to defend its own borders and to render help to other Muslims in defense of their vital interests. The continued state of war with neighboring India has made this difficult. Pakistan is barely able to match a fraction of India's military capability and provide a deterrent. At the same time, most Pakistanis feel that the military has consumed an excessive share of national resources without achieving success in its assigned tasks. The main challenge is to meet the basic military objectives without totally bankrupting the country in the process.

The success of any military campaign depends on (a) a just and moral cause, (b) wisdom, bravery, and sincerity of the leadership, (c) a sense of the proper timing of an action in terms of suitability of the political conditions and physical circumstances, (d) the required size, organization, and discipline of the troops, and (e) superior equipment. Pakistan is seeking a consensus on all these points to achieve its objectives at an affordable price.

CHAPTER 4

WHO CONTROLS PAKISTAN?

Oh Allah! Lord of power (and rule), Thou givest power to whom Thou pleasest; and Thou strippest off power from whom Thou pleasant; Thou endowest with honour whom Thou pleasest, and Thou bringest low whom Thou pleasest: In Thy hand is all good. Verily, over all things Thou has power. (Qur'an 3:26)

The Constitution

22. *Constitutional Ideal*. The preamble to the constitution of the Islamic Republic of Pakistan states:

> **Whereas sovereignty over the entire universe belongs to Almighty Allah alone, and the authority to be exercised by the people of Pakistan within the limits prescribed by Him is a sacred trust;**
>
> **And whereas it is the will of the people of Pakistan to establish an order:**
> **Wherein the state shall exercise its powers and authority through the chosen representatives of the people;**
> **Wherein the principles of democracy, freedom, equality, tolerance and social justice, as enunciated by Islam shall be fully observed . . .**

The principles are wonderfully enunciated. The sovereignty of Allah is acknowledged. The people are supposed to control the sacred trust of Pakistan. The powers of the state are supposed to be exercised by the chosen representatives. But who gets to speak for the people and who, in fact, controls the government?

Constitutionally, the Prime Minister is the head of government and controls it. Of course, control cannot be absolute in a democratic form of government. The Prime Minister is constrained by the constitution in the following manner:

- The people have elected him/her and will judge his/her performance again during the next election.

- In Parliament, he/she must enjoy a majority vote in order to survive or face a vote of no-confidence and lose the position of prime minister.
- The president, the judiciary and others have powers too and cannot be forced into action by the prime minister.

The people are not convinced that the constitution is the ultimate arbitrator in Pakistan. Many rulers of the past have treated the constitution of the day with little respect. The framer of the current constitution, President Zulfikar Ali Bhutto, used it as he saw fit. His successor President Zia initially used "the law of necessity" and subsequently amended it to remove sections which interfered with his rule. Strong leaders or dictators are rarely constrained by their constitutions, particularly in the developing countries. Pakistanis continue to speculate as to who controls their country; and to whom they should turn to make their lot better.

Controllers of the Key Elements

The prime minister, the president, and the chief of army staff are the three most powerful individuals in Pakistan. If the three individuals holding these positions are in agreement, there is little that they cannot do. However, if the three are in disagreement, other powerful forces get involved and the outcome is unpredictable.

Agriculturists-Land Owners

The small farmers who actually work the soil are frequently too occupied with day-to-day living concerns to be actively involved in politics. The landlords who own the land which the farmers till in effect control the agriculture. In Pakistan, large parcels of land are held by a few landlords who exert considerable influence. The consumers are not organized enough to have any significant control over agriculturists. The landowners have agreed on a working arrangement to control their public regulators. Everyone knows how to keep the revenue officers and land registrar's office happy. The extent of feudal power is discussed below.

Industrialists

The Pakistani consumers have not matured enough to dictate demands to the industrial sector. Labor and even the hired management is at the mercy of the owners. The owners may be controlled to some extent by their financiers, and their regulators (the government). However, the owners have found ways to penetrate the financing agencies and the regulators. They seem to have come to an informal understanding about profit-sharing among themselves.

Foreign Powers

The U.S. Government is considered by many to be the single most important power in Pakistan. Its power is exercised through key local players tied to and dependent on the United States. For example, the Pakistani armed forces are dependent on U.S. assistance for (a) advanced technology, (b) weapons acquisition, (c) protection from potential enemies who can be incited to become aggressive or advised to seek peaceful solutions, (d) intelligence through U.S. satellites or agencies, (e) training of senior personnel, and (f) direct or indirect funding through international agencies or friendly governments on bilateral terms. Even though Pakistan has worked closely with China and Europe seeking diversity and independence, leaders of the armed forces recognize that the United States is aware of everything that they are doing. Little can be hidden and the best way is to heed U.S. advice and cooperate in every possible way.

Many senior Pakistani bureaucrats have received advanced degrees and training in the United States. They have raised their children in the United States and have relatives and property there. Most genuinely admire the open society, economic opportunities, and freedoms enjoyed by Americans. They see their children's future and even their own future retirement in America and are eager to follow suggestions from any representative of the U.S. Government.

Politicians also have come to believe that the key to power lies with the United States. Whether in or out of power, they lavishly entertain the visiting American dignitaries and make regular pilgrimages to Washington. As with bureaucrats, politicians send their children and relatives to study, work, and even settle in the United States.

Some European powers, particularly Britain and to some extent France and Germany, have similar linkages and loyalties among the armed forces, the bureaucracy and the politicians and enjoy significant influence. Muslim countries such as Saudi Arabia enjoy a great deal of respect and influence for reasons of (a) historic ties, (b) religious affiliation and control over the holy lands, (c) their ability to provide jobs, and (d) significant help they provided in the past in times of need.

China has considerable influence in Pakistan, too. It has been a reliable ally ever since the 1965 war with India. They have continued to help Pakistan, particularly in the fields of defense and diplomacy, to the extent they can.

Foreign donors (bilateral and multilateral), including the World Bank, the International Monetary Fund, the Asian Development Bank, and the government of Japan have a significant voice and influence with regard to economic policy. They refuse to lend and provide grants if the economy is allowed to fall beyond agreed targets or if certain critical policies are not followed.

Politicians and Their Parties

Pakistan has a multi-party political system. Anybody can form a party and many do. Political parties have been often formed to advance causes of a few or even a single individual. Such parties have died when the objectives were achieved or abandoned or simply with the death of the individual. Most parties have been hindered by limited appeal due to their regional, ethnic or sectarian composition.

Muslim League. As described in Chapter Two, the All India Muslim League (ML) was formed in 1906 to protect the interests of Muslims in British India. It spearheaded Pakistan's nationalist movement. However, following independence and the death of its two most prominent leaders, Mohammad Ali Jinnah and Liaqat Ali Khan, it rapidly lost its appeal. It came under the control of landlords and bureaucrats and lost touch with common citizens. The East Pakistani leaders became disillusioned and established the *Awami League* and other parties to struggle for their causes. In West Pakistan, the *Republican Party* gained control of the West Pakistan Legislative Assembly. Following martial law, General Ayub Khan revived the party as the *Pakistan Muslim League* (PML). It declined with the fall of the General. It was revived again by Prime Minister Junejo as PML-J. Subsequently former prime minister Nawaz Sharif has taken it over as PML-N.

Jamaat Islami (JI) was founded by Maulana Abul Ala Maududi in 1941 for the purpose of promoting Islamic values and causes in British India. It did not support creation of Pakistan as a separate homeland for Muslims principally because Islam is a universal religion and not subject to national boundaries. Following independence, JI sought to establish an Islamic state in Pakistan. It is opposed to Westernization, secularism, capitalism, socialism, bank interest, and birth control. It seeks to purge the community of deviant behavior and to establish a political system in which decision making is undertaken by a few pious people well-versed in the meaning of Islam. It has led the movements to expel the Ahmadiyya sect from Islam, pursued a defining role for Islam in the constitution, and sought to introduce Shariat laws. In spite of widespread feeling for Islam, JI won only four seats in the national assembly in the 1990 elections and three seats out of 217 seats in 1993.

The Pakistan People's Party (PPP) was founded by Zulfiqar Ali Bhutto in 1967 for purpose of bringing down the government of General Ayub. PPP adopted "Islam as our faith, democracy our polity, socialism our economy." It emerged as the largest political party in West Pakistan in the 1970 elections, and came into power following the separation of East Pakistan. While in power, PPP control increasingly moved to the wealthy landed elites. It won 155 out of 200 seats in the National Assembly elections of 1977, but was accused of widespread fraud. Subsequent riots led to imposition of yet another term of martial law and the eventual hanging of Mr. Bhutto in 1979. His wife Nusrat and daughter Benazir assumed control of PPP leadership as co-chairpersons. Following the death of General Zia, the PPP emerged as the largest party in the country in the 1988 elections and Benazir Bhutto assumed power as the prime minister. PPP lost the 1990 elections, but was voted back into power in 1993.

Muhajir Qaumi Mahaz (MQM). The MQM had its origins in the All Pakistan Muhajir Students Organization at Karachi University. The party was formed in 1984 by Altaf Husain to represent the interests of the Urdu-speaking Muhajir community. The party replaced the political power of the Muslim League, Jamat Islami and to some extent the PPP in two major urban areas of Sindh—Karachi and Hyderabad. It won thirteen out of 207 national assembly seats in 1988 elections and became a coalition partner of the PPP led government of Benazir Bhutto. Subsequent conflicts partially led to political instability and dismissal of the government. MQM won fifteen seats in the 1990 elections and joined the PML-N led government of Nawaz Sharif. For some time it enjoyed an unprecedented level of power particularly in Sindh in collaboration with Chief Minister Jam Sadiq Ali. MQM first played an active role in the ethnic riots in Karachi in 1986-87. Since then it has been accused of terrorism.

The government of Nawaz Sharif brought the army to control ethnic violence, robberies, kidnapping and terror in Sindh. The policy has been continued by the Benazir government. Since then, MQM has been in conflict with the government. MQM boycotted the National Assembly elections of 1993, but decided to participate in the Provincial Assembly elections and won most of the seats in the cities of Karachi and Hyderabad.

Awami National Party (ANP). The ANP was formed in 1986 by the merger of several left-leaning parties. Khan Abdul Wali Khan's political career has been built on intense Pakhtun nationalism inherited from his father Khan Abdul Ghafar Khan. The younger Khan became the first president of ANP. Its political base lies among Pakhtuns of the North-West Frontier Province (NWFP) and northern Baloachistan. The party won six seats in the 1990 national assembly elections, but won only three in 1993.

Jamiat-ul-Ulama-I-Islam (JUI). JUI was formed in 1945 following a split within Jamiat-ul-Ulma-I-Hind. It has gone through several organizational changes since then. Like ANP, its support base is in the NWFP and Baloachistan. JUI won six seats in the 1990 elections and four in 1993. It is led by Maulana Fazlur Rahman who succeeded his father in that position.

Tehrik-I-Istiqlal (Solidarity Movement) was formed by retired Air Marshal Asghar Khan in 1969. The party started with strong support among professionals but has failed to translate it into any electoral strength. Asghar Khan had been prominent in political agitation against Bhutto and subsequently against Zia. However, the party failed to win even a single seat in the 1993 elections.

Islami Jamhoori Ittehad (IJI) was formed in September 1988 as a political alliance to oppose PPP in elections. The alliance was composed of nine parties—ML and JI were the two largest. IJI succeeded in forming a provincial government in Punjab under the leadership of Nawaz Sharif. In the 1990 elections, IJI won 105 seats in the National Assembly versus forty-five seats for the Pakistan Democratic Alliance of which PPP was the main component. However, the alliance broke down before the 1993 elections.

PPP, PML (which is currently divided into three components), MQM, JI, ANP and JUI are significant among the existing political parties.

The political aspects of Pakistani government are controlled by those who can get the most votes in the national decisionmaking body. That, in turn, depends on getting elected at the levels of individual constituencies. The composition of the national assembly and the senate over the years has shown that the agriculturists have the largest representation within the assemblies. A few industrialists are beginning to invest well and are finding success in politics. Having observed the benefits which accrue to industrialists who set up industries, many of the agriculturists are also obtaining licenses and establishing their own individual enterprises. Only MQM can claim to be free of the influence of the agriculturists due to the fact that there is little agriculture within the boundaries of Karachi and Hyderabad.

Religious Leaders

Religious leaders exert an enormous influence over the citizens as the interpreters of the Qur'an and the Hadith. Devout Pakistanis respect Allah's will and are sincerely concerned about the Day of Judgement. Mosques in every village and on most street corners in urban areas provide a powerful venue for influencing common citizens. The political influence of religious leaders and their political parties has already been mentioned. However, their moral influence is far greater than seats in the National Assembly suggest. They have the ability to call people into the streets. They played a very large part in the campaign to overthrow Zulfiqar Ali Bhutto and helped sustain the rule of General Zia for the first several years. General Zia's patronage and the Afghan civil war have helped enhance their influence.

People of Pakistan yearn for restoration of moral values. Religious leaders continue to claim exclusive rights to moral values. Many Pakistanis dispute their claim but many others do not.

The Military

Article 243 of the 1973 constitution states that the federal government controls the armed forces. It gives the president power to raise and maintain active and reserve forces, grant commissions, and appoint the chiefs of staff of the army, navy and air force. Under article 242, the President is the commander-in-chief of the armed forces. The original intent was that the president would act according to the guidance of the prime minister. However, "the eighth amend-ment to the nominally "revived" but fundamentally altered 1973 constitution, promulgated in 1985 by President Zia, specifies in Article 90 that "national executive power is vested in the president". [96]

The army has tripled in size from its relatively humble beginnings in 1947. In the meantime, the country it is expected to defend has been reduced to half of the original size.

"Article 39 enjoins the state to enable people from all parts of Pakistan to join the armed forces. It does not, however, require proportional represen-tation of the provinces, and only modest progress has been made in making the military more geographically representative."[97] The military has pre-dominant representation from Punjab, with Pakhtuns as junior partners.

---

[96] Blood, p. 285.

[97] Ibid, p. 286.

Within Punjab, the northern districts provide the bulk of the soldiers. There is an increasing share of recruitment from the urbanized districts. However, there are relatively few soldiers from southern Punjab. There are a fair number of Mohajir officers. However, Sindhis and Baloach are conspicuously few. Different historical reasons have been cited for their exclusion. These include their poor relations with and lack of loyalty to the British colonial government, subservience of the people to their local feudal lords, relatively good economic conditions at home, and unwillingness to travel away from home.

The hope of creating a truly national army in contrast to the colonial army of the past has not been fully achieved in view of the regional recruitment patterns. The objective of having an Islamic force has occurred to some extent. However, given dependence on the West, particularly the United States, the emphasis on religion has been restrained. While Islamic leanings were more than welcome at the time of Jihad against communists in Afghanistan, they are much less welcome now that the United States and the sitting governments in Pakistan have distanced themselves from fundamentalism and emphasized secularism.

The army is subject to the prevailing situation within the country itself —regional polarization, materialism, and corruption. The officers largely feel pro-west but have much appreciation for the contribution and timely help of the Chinese. There is a desire for Islamic solidarity and declining hope of ever achieving it. There is strong mistrust of Indian intentions.

The army personnel tends to view civilians as disorganized, chaotic, corrupt, and disorderly. In contrast, they view themselves as disciplined, efficient, and clean. There is contempt for party politics and politicians in general. The army has gradually enlarged its role of being the protector of territorial integrity to being guardian of the ideological frontier as well as of political and economic stability. It has assumed the role of an ultimate arbiter in national affairs. As of this writing, it seems content with its covert role of being the king maker. There is limited if any overt desire to declare martial law again.

It is hard to predict the future. However, as the largest, best equipped, most organized, disciplined, efficient, and well-financed organization in the country, the military will remain a key if not the most dominating power in the country.

The military aspects of Pakistani government are controlled by the sitting decisionmakers, most of whom are within the military itself. The military, symbolized by the army chief of staff, started playing the role of kingmaker as early as 1953, barely six years after independence. At that time, Army

Chief General Ayub Khan joined hands with then Governor-General Ghulam Mohammed, who represented the bureaucracy, to dismiss Prime Minister Khawaja Nazimuddin.

The army continued to play the role of indirect king maker until October 1958 when General Ayub imposed direct military rule. The military led by General Ayub and then General Yahya, remained in power until the defeat of Pakistan by India in the war over East Pakistan (Bangladesh) and the break up of the country in 1971.

Figure 2:
General Ayub Khan

Figure 3:
General Yahya

Martial law resumed on July 5,1977, when Chief of Army Staff, General Mohammed Zia-ul-Haq, assumed power. He maintained absolute control until his sudden death in August, 1988. There has been a return to civilian rule since then, but only with the concurrence and under the watchful eyes of the miliary. The army has maintained the role of the king maker and has managed to change several prime ministers.

The justification for miliary rule has always been "an inept and corrupt civil leadership posing a threat to the country's security." General Zia introduced the additional factor of religion. Throughout its rule, the army has exercised absolute and unaccountable political, physical, and budgetary power. They have always viewed themselves as "the sole repository of all wisdom and the very epitome of the nation."[98]

Figure 4:
General Zia-ul-Haq

The history of army action shows that it moves only when there is a consensus within its leadership. The consensus comes only when the leaders, including corps commanders and the general headquarters, are in agreement. They, in turn, are influenced by their perception of what is good for the country and the military itself. A number of attempted coups d'etat, have failed because their leaders did not achieve a consensus within the army.

As strong as the army is, they can be influenced to some extent by the widespread mood of the people. In the past, discontent in major urban areas, Punjab in particular, has been significant. Conditions in Karachi alone have failed to initiate drastic action in recent times. The military tends be even more responsive to (a) suppliers of their finances, (b) suppliers of their equip-

---

[98] "The Beat of A Different Drum," *The Newsline* (Karachi: October 1995), pp. 43-44.

ment and technology, and (c) foreign military powers who can challenge them, i.e., the Western powers or neighboring armies.

Most Pakistanis feel that the army is the most powerful institution in the country and ultimately controls Pakistan. Constitutionally, the president, the prime minister, and the defense minister are supposed to control the army. In reality, when matters of interest to the military are considered, the generals usually make the ultimate decisions themselves. Even Zulfiqar Ali Bhutto, who successfully asserted civilian control over the armed forces for a number of years, recognized that fact.

> [Bhutto] understood, of course, that the army had brought him in, and that the army assumed it could always throw him out if he misbehaved too much or started to take extreme liberties, as it had thrown out Liaqat Ali Khan and Khuwaja Nazimuddin and Suhrawardy and Mujib, all those once-popular politicians who had stepped over the line of acceptable leadership behavior, whether in negotiations with India over Kashmir, in their Bengali separatism, or in treacherous secessionism. The army was Pakistan's protective wolfhound, always on duty, powerful enough to keep any enemy at bay or to destroy its "master" if he forgot the proper password or feeding hour.[99]

The army listens only to those who have stronger power. Most Pakistanis know that real material power in the world in 1996 lies with the West, particularly the United States. The army knows it and is therefore subject to considerable influence by the United States.

The Intelligence Agencies

Numerous intelligence agencies exist in Pakistan including the Inter Services Intelligence (ISI), the Military Intelligence (MI), the Directorate of Intelligence Bureau (DIB), the provincial Special Branches, and the Airport Security Force (ASF).

DIB, the premiere civilian intelligence agency, was set up soon after independence with the function of counter-espionage and monitoring hostile foreign powers and their diplomatic missions. It has been generally headed

---

[99] Stanley Wolpert, *Zulfi Bhutto of Pakistan* (Oxford: Oxford University Press, 1993), p. 184.

by senior police officers. However, over the years, its role has been expanded to keeping tabs on opposition politicians, tapping telephones, recruiting informers among journalists, and manipulating domestic politics through blackmail, harassment, disinformation campaigns against opponents, and keeping watch over other intelligence agencies.

The ISI was set up in the 1950s to perform all intelligence activities at home and abroad. There has been some overlap with DIB activities. During the martial law days of General Zia, DIB became overshadowed by Inter-Services Intelligence (ISI), whose role was greatly expanded with the Russian invasion of Afghanistan. The Afghan war resulted in close collaboration between ISI and the U.S. Central Intelligence Agency (CIA). Its resources were augmented through funding from the United States as well as from the Saudi government. It achieved a high profile and became "the biggest brother." Among other responsibilities, reportedly, it keeps an eye on the generals themselves to ensure their reliability to the regime.

The intelligence agencies have been used by each regime to help perpetuate power. However, after the death of Zia, ISI has allegedly even tried to determine who the ruler should be. It worked actively to create opposition to Benazir Bhutto during her first tenure as the Prime Minister, and actively promoted IJI led by Nawaz Sharif.

The intelligence agencies are credited with creation of MQM. Initially the purpose was to reduce the influence of Jamat Islami in Karachi. It came in handy for reducing the influence of PPP too. Former ISI chief, General Hamid Gul, once admitted, "it was necessary to create a countervailing force to the PPP, otherwise democracy could not have been restored." The task of putting the IJI together was assigned to ISI. The Chief of Army Staff, General Mirza Aslam Beg, took the decision in principle but left the nuts and bolts to Hamid Gul, who completed the job within weeks of the election.

There have been numerous committees and commissions established to coordinate intelligence activities. They have had little effect. "If democracy is to have meaning, the unregulated power of the intelligence agencies has to be limited to its national security functions. Their role has to be governed by legislation or statutory authority, as is the practice in much of the world. Only then will they be able to perform their vital national security task adequately."[100]

---

[100] Maleeha Lodhi and Zahid Hussain, "Pakistan's Invisible Government", in *The Newsline* (October 1992), pp. 22-34.

The Bureaucrats

The government is run on a day-to-day basis by the bureaucracy. The civil servants are supposed to be selected on the basis of their merit to implement policies of the government. Leaders of the government come and go, but the civil servants largely remain in place. Their own individual assignments change as they grow in seniority and experience; or as they fail or succeed in pleasing their superiors.

While the bureaucracy has been generally noted to be qualified, it is handicapped in a number of ways:

- The members of the elite Civil Service of Pakistan (CSP) are chosen through competitive examination while they are in their mid-twenties. In most cases, they are liberal arts graduates. They are good but generally not the best students because traditionally those have gone into medical and engineering fields.
- The members are trained to be administrators but not experts in any particular field. Knowledge of administration was sufficient during the colonial period or the early years of independence. However, it is inadequate for the current times of advanced technology and information when decisions regarding management and implementation of fairly sophisticated projects are required.
- Relatively few sitting federal secretaries or provincial secretaries have postgraduate education relevant to the departments that they head. This results in low quality decision-making.
- The officers are continually rotated in different geographical locations and different ministries with little opportunity of learning the subject at hand in depth. Sometimes a secretary of a particular department may be changed several times in a year which results in a lack of continuity in management.

23. The bureaucracy has been able to carry out its agenda because the elected representatives, i.e., the ministers to whom they report are often not educated, trained or sufficiently experienced. On the other hand, the ministers have the power to rotate the bureaucrats into position of relative power or relative obscurity. Accordingly, many civil servants accommodate ministers in order to maintain positive relations. The result has been an arrangement under which the bureaucrats are dedicated to personal agendas of the ministers but are left totally free to follow their personal agenda as long as the ministers' personal interests are not involved. The interests of the public receive the lowest priority.

In spite of political rhetoric, the civil servants have generally opposed deregulation because it takes powers of decision from their hands. In the interest of greater efficiency and sound management, it is imperative and urgent to recruit professionals at a higher level of administration in the government.

The bureaucracy generally flourishes in times of non-representative governments. It was at the peak of its power in the early years of independence. Their representatives, namely Ghulam Mohammed, Chaudhri Mohammed Ali, and Iskander Mirza, directly ruled the country until General Ayub assumed power in 1958. They have been very willing partners of the military during the times of martial rule. In spite of several setbacks at the hands of Ayub Khan, Yahya Khan, and Zulfiqar Ali Bhutto, the bureaucracy continues to hold tremendous power, probably second only to that of the military. They continue to make and break politicians at the local levels.

Elected Representatives

The elected representatives of the people collectively decide on whom the president, prime minister, chief ministers, and the ministers will be. The prime minister is the chief executive under the current arrangement. However, the president retains a large number of powers. The lower elected officials are supposed to make day-to-day policy decisions relating to their departments.

Once the top leaders are selected, the cabinet appointments come next. In Pakistan, the selection must be made from among the elected members. In case of a coalition government, the coalition partners have to agree on jobs in terms of numbers and portfolios. Everyone wants ministries with extensive powers and budgets. When it comes down to selection of individuals, loyalty is the single most important ingredient. Leaders are looking for a degree of competence, but no one is looking for competition. Persons with high degrees of both loyalty and competence will be welcomed but will be difficult to find. People with high degrees of competence but low levels of loyalty will be suspect. People with high degrees of loyalty and low levels of competence will often be picked.

The next step relates to putting the "right civil servants in the right place" so that the ministerial instructions can be carried out. It amounts to choosing just the right person among hundreds of members of the civil service for the key ministries in Islamabad and the provinces. Wishes of the ministers, relevant members of the national and provincial assemblies, relevant politicians, senior military officials, and senior civil servants already selected have to be taken into account.

Following the change of provincial chief minister in Punjab in September 1995, several newspapers including the Urdu Weekly Pakistan Post gave a detailed listing of posting of key officials in the province, including the chief secretary, inspector general of police (IG), several secretaries, commissioners, deputy inspectors-general, deputy commissioners, superintendents of police, etc. It gave names and explained how each of the key officials picked was related to one or more of the important persons, and owed the job to the identified VIPs.[101] It was clear that not many posts were filled on the basis of merit or the special suitability of people for the jobs. Loyalty and willingness to carry out instruc-tions remain the main criteria.

With the help and support of the bureaucrats, the person in charge must be able to reward their friends and supporters and punish the enemies. There are many ways to reward and punish, (some are discussed in various parts of this book). As a minor example reported in the press, one Ali Sher Rahopoto, a favorite of Sindh Chief Minister Abdullha Shah received a Sindh Government Pajero car at auction for 380,000 rupees. He sold it for 1,280,000. He made a quick profit of 900,000 rupees or more than $25,000.

There are much higher levels of reward for the favorites. On the other hand, those out of favor can be punished through lodging of false complaints with the police, arrest, detention for an extended period without being brought before magistrates, long jail sentences, and worse.[102] People routinely die in well-staged encounters with the police.

At times, they go as far in running of the government as they wish to. They bring in their own "experts or technocrats" to advise them on specialized subjects such as finance, defense, commerce, etc. In practice, the ministers are subject to a great deal of "guidance" from the prime minister. Members of the assem-blies who do not hold cabinet posts are, nevertheless, very important within their respective constituencies. They play important roles in local administration, local development projects, and all forms of political patronage.

The National Media

In Pakistan, as in most developing countries, the media, particularly the national press, is controlled by elite families with economic empires extend-

---

[101] *The Weekly Pakistan Post* (Urdu), (15-21 Sept. 1995), pp. 1 and 7.

[102] "Rival Survival,"in *The Newsline,* Karachi, (September, 1995), pp. 52-53.

ing to newspapers and magazines. The families symbolize private wealth and public power. The line between politics and public information is thin. One foot in the press ensures a mouthpiece for any politician, and one foot in politics ensures the private interests of the press owners. Also typical of most developing world media, the Pakistani press supports right-wing, pro-business governments. They have been accused of playing leading roles in bringing down relatively liberal regimes. Media owners have made deals with governments to secure and enhance power and publishing rights. The government influences editorial policy and when it differs from the government's point of view, conflict is often minimized by low-key reporting. If the press decides to build up someone or some cause, they give prominent and positive coverage. If they do not, they just ignore and, if necessary, assault.

The means of government control are varied from outright censorship in times of dictatorial control to almost complete freedom of the press in times of liberal democratic regimes. The government uses legal mechanisms and eco-nomic enticements, such as allocation of subsidized newsprint paper and public advertisements, to keep the press under control.

The Pakistani press is to be congratulated for producing editors such as the late Razia Bhatti of *Newsline Magazine* who pioneered investigative reporting, which brought her into direct conflict with public and private powers. The press has often exposed excesses of public and private sectors and has supported independence of the national judiciary.

Nevertheless, the press has been accused of (a) allegiance to personal rather than public interests; (b) cooperating with dictators by keeping people unin-formed, spreading misinformation, and facilitating their continuation in power; and (c) fanning fires of communalism and sectarianism by exaggerating and sensationalizing stories. In recent times, the press has been accused of subservience to MQM interests in Karachi as a result of their ethnic affiliation, blackmail, threats to their personal safety, and fear of attacks on their property.

On the positive side, there are indications that some elements of the national press have decided to push for national reforms. They have united in protecting press freedom. Pakistan continues to look for a free and constructive role from the national press.

Ethnicity of the Mighty Ones

Overview. The most powerful individuals in Pakistan are well protected. Simple and relatively uneducated landlords of yesterday have educated their children at home and abroad. Members of their extended families have penetrated all centers of power: Some have remained in politics and have contacts within the government and opposition, some have gone into civil service, some have joined the armed forces, perhaps a daughter has been married into an industrial family. The result is that the key groups have become interrelated. Similarly, the industrialists have branched out in politics, media, civil service, and the armed forces. Over the years, they have become wealthier and more experienced. They all have contacts with foreign powers and have established solid credentials with them. These groups are powerful and exclusive. Entry at the higher levels is possible but extremely difficult.

The average man in the urban street or on the rural farm acknowledges the power and vast network of the mighty ones. However, the earlier universal feeling of respect for important and powerful individuals may be changing into a feeling of indifference or even enmity.

There are foreigners as well as Pakistanis with great power. The mighty foreigners are generally officials of governments or international organizations. They need not and, in fact, do not control every Pakistani. They identify, influence, and promote key individuals among the politicians, armed forces, bureaucrats, industrialists, agriculturists, etc. They maintain day-to-day contacts with Pakistani institutions at home and abroad. They take advantage of estab-lished networks and develop prestige and influence through contacts already in place. Some Pakistanis feel that the mighty foreigners enjoy very significant influence. Others feel that estimates of their influence are highly exaggerated. The truth probably lies somewhere in between.

Domestically, mighty ones are a class by themselves. Ethnic barriers do not stop them. They unite on issues of mutual interest to them. The feudal landlords unite against agricultural income taxes, regardless of their respective ethnicity. The industrialists fight for tax exemptions. The bureaucracy joins hands with any who can offer benefits and advantages. Of course, the army acts as a unit under its leadership.

Nevertheless, ethnicity is a fact of life in Pakistan. It plays a subtle but significant role in many aspects of Pakistani life. It is useful to understand where the leaders come from.

There are religious leaders in all parts of the country. However, looking at the prominent *ulama* of the day, they are largely from Punjabi, Pashtun, and Urdu speaking Mohajir communities, in that order. The powerful landlords belong to Punjabi, Sindhi, Pashtun, and Baloach communities. Mohajirs do not hold significant amounts of agricultural land. The industrialists are largely from Punjabi, Pashtun, and Mohajir communities. Only a few Sindhis have ventured into industrial ownership. The political leaders are largely from Sindh and Punjab. The military leaders are mostly from Punjabi, Pashtun, and Mohajir communities. Most of the leading bureaucrats belong to Punjabi, Pashtun, and Mohajir communities.

The following matrix indicating ranking of power among five major communities of the country may give an overview of the ethnicity of those who control Pakistan. The highest ranking is one and lowest is five. The ranking is based on results of an informal survey conducted by the author.

	Punjabi	Sindhi	Mohajir	Pashtun	Baloach
Spiritual leaders	1	4	3	2	5
Economic leaders	1	4	3	2	5
Agriculture	1	2	5	3	4
Industry/mining	1	5	3	2	4
Banking/finance	1	4	3	2	5
Political power	1	2	4	3	5
Votes	1	2	4	3	5
Political leaders	2	1	4	3	5
National Press	1	4	2	3	5
Military leaders	1	5	3	2	4
Bureaucracy	1	4	3	2	5

Based on ethnicity, people from Punjab have an overwhelming dominance over other communities in the country. Pashtuns have emerged as the second most powerful group in the country. Mohajirs are more powerful than their numbers would indicate. They are really more powerful than Sindhis or Baloachs. They are the third most powerful group. Although Sindhis have held very visible leadership positions in the political arena, in the opinion of the author, they emerge as fourth followed by Baloachs.

Rise and Fall of Zulfiqar Ali Bhutto

After the success of his party on the basis of "*roti, kapra, makan*" (i.e., food, clothing, and shelter), the late Mr. Bhutto tried to change the power structure and confronted all traditional centers of power. He saw the feudal landlords and industrialists, particularly those who were not with him, as the enemies. On a personal level, he treated them with little respect. He threatened them with radical land reforms in order to break their hold on the peasants. He tried to break up the industrial power of the "twenty-two most powerful families" and actually nationalized most of their holdings. On the other hand, he gave a lot of respect and protection to labor who started the *gherao* (encirclement) movement, which literally took over the industries until its demands were met.

Figure 5:
Zulfiqar Ali Bhutto

He went after the bureaucrats by summarily retiring hundreds of them and recruiting hundreds of outsiders. Soon he found that the newcomers, many of whom were party loyalists, began to behave like the rest of the bureaucrats. He retired generals and promoted others at will. However, eventually he came to realize that:

- He could not fulfill all the promises he made to the people. Their needs were too many and the resources were too limited. He could not count on their loyalty on the basis of delivery of goods to them. He had to resort to traditional way of getting their support.
- Support of the landlords and *pirs* was needed to control the rural areas and to win the rural constituencies.
- Industrial production was essential. Government officials would have to run the industries. Labor could not be left unchecked for the sake of industrial production.

- Military support was necessary for continuity of power. Their loyalty was essential and would be maintained through a large military budget, equipment, and manpower.

With the passage of time, the former revolutionary and populist became like other rulers. Over time, he gave an ever-increasing share of political power to the feudal lords; he kept labor at bay and relied heavily on the bureaucracy and the military to get his policies implemented. Eventually, the West became unhappy over his nuclear and even his Islamic solidarity policies; industrialists whose assets were nationalized refused to make new investments; people who had been promised so much became impatient; and finally, his handpicked generals turned against him and removed his government. The new government, under the leadership of General Zia, did much to restore the earlier power of feudal lords, industrialists, the bureaucracy and, of course, the military. Few gains accrued to the common citizen.

Power of Benazir Bhutto

Many Pakistanis believe that current Prime Minister Benazir Bhutto has recognized the importance of the West under the new world order and found that the road to power in Pakistan first passes through Washington. She has always maintained friends among Democrats in the United States Congress. Since Hillary Clinton's visit to Pakistan in March, 1995, Benazir has continued direct and very cordial links to the White House. She presents an acceptable international agenda and does not challenge the basic policies of the United States. She enjoys greater freedom of action and support than others in a comparable position.

As previously discussed, many feel that the late Prime Minister Bhutto lost power because of his stance against the United States, particularly on the nuclear issue. Working too hard on behalf of Islamic solidarity also did not endear him to Washington, although Islam was not perceived in the same manner at that time as it is today. His daughter has seen the writing on the wall and gone all out to court U.S. support. Has she gone too far? Some Pakistanis think so.

Passage of the Brown Amendment by the U.S. Congress has facilitated release of some previously paid for but blocked equipment. Negotiations have begun for the purchase of new aircraft from other sources. Military needs continue to receive the highest priority in budget allocations. Even if direct aid to Pakistan remains restricted, the United States can indirectly provide limited military aid by providing continued international economic assistance. It can also continue the flow of essential arms through other channels.

With the United States firmly in her corner, the army is unlikely to confront her. In fact, her relations with the army have improved recently; this has made her position even more secure. Catering to basic budgetary and equipment needs of the army would have the result of making the military a second source of power.

Figure 6:
Benazir Bhutto

A third key ingredient of Benazir's power base is the memory of her father. Millions of the poorest of Pakistanis continue to have a fondness and respect for him and his descendants. The only threat to her in that area is from her brother. As long as the family does not self-destruct, a large reserve of voters is theirs to tap.

With the United States, the army, and a large vote bank, Prime Minister Bhutto appears to be feeling secure. Charges of corruption, inefficiency, unemployment, violence, and the breakdown of law and order have all had limited impact on the present government of Pakistan. Burning issues of the day and discontent among a vast majority of the people remain dormant, perhaps until the next elections. Even then, the people will not have a free hand. They will only be able to choose among the candidates presented to them. The opposition parties do not appear well-organized and have been unable to offer anything better. In addition, local feudal lords and other powerful interests remain in positions of control. They continue to limit the options of the people.

Is There a Secret Group?

The president, prime minister, armed forces, intelligence agencies, bureaucracy, landed aristocracy, industrialists, and politicians all wield considerable power. On the international level, the Western superpowers, particularly the United States, know how to protect their interests. However, is there a formal secret group which is developing strategic policy and controlling the country?

Many people in position to know the truth deny the existence of a "secret super group" which controls Pakistan. As noted earlier, during normal times, if the three most powerful individuals—the prime minister, the president, and the army chief—are in agreement, there is no room for others. Powerbrokers become visible in times of disagreement among the three. As new elections approach, high officials and interest groups try to influence the timing and subsequently, the results of each election in their favor.

If the election gives a clear majority to someone, it is difficult for the "sitting ruler" to deny them the power without sacrificing the political process, as happened after the 1970 elections. At that time, denial of power to the Awami League of East Pakistan led to independence of Bangladesh. However, if the election results are not clear-cut, all the mighty ones—the president, chief of army staff and his corps commanders, the most influential civil servants, elder statesmen, and envoys from the United States, Europe, China, and Saudi Arabia—try to play the role of kingmakers. The president, the chief of army staff, and the U.S. envoy probably become the three most important players. However, once the new prime minister is selected and sworn in, he or she assumes power and decides to whom to delegate it. The kin makers then return to their traditional roles.

Changing the Power Structure

Given the considerable amount of discontent in Pakistan, people are looking for ways to change the power structure. It can happen through a number of ways.

24. *Commitment of People to Change.* Optimistic observers argue that the commitment of Pakistanis can make change happen. People, as a whole, are seen as the true masters, in the form of voters, consumers, taxpayers, and workers in all sectors. Unfortunately, their ability to protect their long-term interests is tied to their stomachs, which force them to take a short-term view of life and not jeopardize the short-term interests. At times, Pakistanis fail to display persis-tence or intellectual and emotional maturity which reflects their true priorities. They remain content with emotional and feel-good slogans. Rising education and economic standards are helping the general population to articulate their feelings. Hopefully, they will demonstrate their commitment to change.

Machiavelli best expressed the idea that politicians will behave better when they depend upon a virtuous population than when they depend upon one which is indifferent to moral considerations. A community in which crimes, if any, are made widely known, functions more effectively than one in which there is strict censorship. Education and awakening of the popula-tion as a whole is a prerequisite. Such awakening is taking place among the urbanites, but a vast majority of the country is still oblivious.

Pakistan's history has shown that if the people really want something badly enough, they can stand up to the establishment of the day. They mobilize and get support wherever they can. The examples include:

- determination of the people of East Pakistan to gain autonomy and eventually independence,
- success of the People's Party in the West Pakistan in the 1970 elections,
- success of the people in destabilizing Mr. Bhutto's government in 1977,
- success of the people in bringing Benazir Bhutto to power through the 1988 elections, and
- success of MQM in a series of elections in Karachi.

25. *Change in Land Ownership Patterns.* Land reform, particularly in terms of reducing the ability of the landed aristocracy financially to control blocks of votes of their tenant farmers, is essential. Previous efforts have been blocked by the landed aristocracy because of their large representation in the legislature and because land is, in part, also owned by the military and the bureaucracy. Politicians belonging to industrial families or of urban background are continuing to push for reform in this area.

26. *Reducing the Cost of Elections.* Lowering the cost of participating in elections will encourage the middle class and educated people who do not have vested interests to venture into the electoral process. The current cost

of election campaigns at provincial and national levels is so high that most of the qualified potential candidates from lower or middle classes are forced to look for fixed salary jobs rather than to run for elective offices.

On the other hand, leaders of the political parties are often forced to give party nominations to those who can win the elections. It means that party nominations often go to those who have wealth to spend and a captive bank. In rural constituencies, the big landlords are the obvious choices. Accordingly, most of Pakistan's elected members of the provincial and national assemblies are land–owners. In a parliamentary form of government, only the elected members can be ministers. Accordingly, most of the cabinet ministers are also landlords. In order to have a wider representation of the people, ways must be found to reduce the cost of elections. Public financing of elections and fun raising at the grass–roots level is often mentioned.

27. *Proportional Representation.* A change in the constitutional arrangements may be necessary which would change the method of electing representatives. Elections at the level of each constituency may be limited or eliminated while elections of slates of candidates at the national level, based on total votes received by the party, may be introduced. This would break the control of the local feudal lords on their constituencies and focus attention on each party's program and qualified personnel.

28. *Education of the Imams.* Religious leaders need improved skills in terms of teaching and understanding the Qur'an through interpretation (*tafseer*), traditions *(hadith),* comparative religions and relevant social sciences which will make them more effective and sensitive to real issues facing the people. Given the high position occupied by Islam in the daily life of Pakistanis, the religious leaders could begin to play a more meaningful role.

29. *Positive Influences from Abroad.* Support and positive influences from outside forces can help, too. If Western countries and the Islamic block of nations tried to influence the military, bureaucracy, and religious leaders to focus on agreed-upon priorities for the benefit of people, Pakistan would benefit greatly. Why would they do it? The West claims to want to strengthen democracy, improve human rights, and enrich the lot of the local citizens. They have helped with technical and financial assistance. This will be an opportunity for them to do something more fundamental without incurring financial cost. For the Islamic governments, it should be a policy naturally emanating from their religious affirmations.

PART TWO:

KEY ISSUES AND SOLUTIONS

CHAPTER 5

POLITICAL LEADERSHIP

There is the type of man whose speech about this world's life may dazzle thee, and he calls Allah to witness about what is in his heart; yet is he the most contentious of enemies (Qur'an 2:204).

And there is the type of man who gives his life to earn the pleasure of Allah; and Allah is full of kindness to His devotees (Qur'an 2: 207).

Past Achievements

30. *Leaders.* Pakistan has had leaders who have made some exceptional achievements. Even their opponents admire:

- QAID AZAM MUHAMMAD ALI JINNAH'S ability to get the idea of Pakistan accepted by the British government and the Hindu majority, to unite a majority of Muslims of the subcontinent, and to organize the new government of Pakistan from scratch.
- GENERAL AYUB'S ability to channel national energies to economic development in the early years of the first martial law starting 1958.
- ZULFIQAR ALI BHUTTO'S ability to sense and represent the feelings of common people over several years, build a new political party from scratch in spite of total opposition from the government of the day, suffer solitary confinement in jail under subhuman conditions, and accept execution rather than compromise with his military captors on matters of principle.
- GENERAL ZIA'S personal modesty and his efforts to introduce Islamic socio-economic system.
- JUENJO'S efforts to revive political and press freedoms.
- BENAZIR BHUTTO'S ability to launch a successful campaign against a martial law government at a tender age with few resources, and to bear and survive the hardships of separation from her family, and the miseries of jail.

- NAWAZ SHARIF'S emphasis on private sector initiative.
- MOEEN QURAISHI'S attempt to introduce accountability and to collect over due loans from powerful and influential individuals.

At the same time, not many people have admired the personal dictatorship of Jinnah after independence; the well-publicized corruption of Ayub's son; the arrogance of Bhutto; the misuse of religion and the state apparatus to continue Zia's regime; the new heights of corruption reached during the regimes of Benazir and Nawaz Sharif; the personal enrichment of martial law administrators at provincial, district and local levels; nor the almost continuous self-enrichment of most political leaders and civil servants.

Figure 7:
Nawaz Sharif

Distrust of Government

Oh ye who believe! Why say ye that which ye do not? Grievously hateful is it in the sight of Allah that ye say that which ye do not. (Qur'an 61:2-3).

31. *Lack of Sound Leadership.* While Pakistanis do not have enlightened religious leadership to help resolve day-to-day issues, they have lacked

political leadership, too. Successful leaders usually have many common attributes. Very few leaders of Pakistan's government possess the requisite qualities. Rarely, do they

- possess honesty and integrity and follow up on promised actions, or possess competence and the required skills;
- look forward, visualizing positive future events and making them happen;
- provide inspiration for people, mobilizing them for hard work and sacrifice for the publically stated goal;
- enjoin the good and forbid the evil; or
- recognize that they do not have all the answers, and therefore seek effective mutual consultation.

People are neither blind nor unappreciative. On rare occasions when their leaders have demonstrated one or more of the above qualities, people have responded and followed enthusiastically.

Approach of the Leaders

32. *Machiavellian Practices.* Many citizens feel that instead of following the teachings of Allah and His Prophet, the leaders of Pakistan have been following the advice of the fifteenth century philosopher Niccolo Machiavelli: The focus is on achieving and keeping power. In *The Prince,* among other things, Machiavelli suggested what most Pakistani officials practice:[103]

- Power is for those who have the skill to seize it in free competition.
- Popular government is preferred not because of rights, but because popular governments are less cruel, unscrupulous, and inconstant than tyrannies.
- A ruler will perish if he is always good; he must be as cunning as a fox and as fierce as a lion.
- The ruler must keep faith when it pays to do so, but not otherwise. On occasion, the ruler must be faithless.
- The ruler must be able to disguise his character well, and be a great feigner. It is not necessary for a ruler to have all great qualities and conventional virtues, but it is very necessary to seem to have them.
- The people are so simple and so ready to obey present necessities, that one who deceives will always find those who allow themselves to be deceived.

---

[103] Niccolo Machiavelli, *The Prince*, translated by George Bull (London: Penguin Books, 1981).

- The ruler should seem to be religious.
- There are three groups of people: the ruler, nobles, and the people. All should have a part in the constitution, then they will keep each other in check. Each group should have legal rights in proportion to their real power. For consideration of stability, it would be wise to give more power to people.
- It is futile to pursue a political purpose by methods that are bound to fail. If the end is good, the ruler must choose means adequate to its achievement.
- Success means achievement of purpose, whatever it may be.
- The question is ultimately one of power.
- Power often depends on opinion, and opinion upon propaganda. In the propaganda, it is desirable to look more virtuous than the adversary. Victory goes to the side which has the most of what the public considers to be virtue.
- Civilized men are almost certain to be unscrupulous egoists. The men of large cities are already corrupted.

On the other hand, Pakistani officials ignore Machiavelli's point that politicians will behave better when they depend upon a virtuous population than when they depend upon one which is indifferent to moral considerations.[104]

The Arrogance of Power

33. *Many Types of Arrogance.* The leadership often manifests haughty, disdainful behavior which reflects many different types of arrogance. There is arrogance of gras root support, of wealth, of righteousness, and of power. The Bhuttos have been accused of arrogance based on their support at the grassroots level. Leaders from feudal and business classes, including Nawaz Sharif, demonstrate faith in their wealth. The leaders from religious parties have sometimes exhibited the arrogance of righteousness. Past and present military leaders, as well as top civil servants, are generally arrogant on the basis of their power within the government. Regardless of their personal acts and behavior, the leaders view themselves as above the rest of the Pakistani citizens.

The middle class is restive and has not been able to assert itself in politics. On the other hand, relatively few leaders from that class have ven-

---

[104] Bertrand Russell, *A History of Western Philosophy* (New York: Simon and Schuster, 1945), pp. 504-11.

tured into politics. The needs of daily life have not left much opportunity for them to venture in politics. Some among them have made the attempt, and a few have achieved relative success. The middle class of Karachi has been the singular exception. Their MQM has had great political success. Unfortunately, as discussed elsewhere in this book, the opportunity appears to have been misused.

Structural Barriers to Representative Leadership

Despite the Islamic emphasis on mankind's noble purpose in life, there is little effective motivation coming from Pakistani leaders which encourages this noble purpose. In practice, the leadership demonstrates conspicuous emphasis on self-interest. Lack of truly representative leadership may be attributed to some of the existing structural barriers, including:

- the lack of public insistence on personal accountability and the requirement to set a good example by the leaders,
- the current electoral system requiring great personal wealth and vote banks and producing the election of the same types of representatives as in the past—wealthy, feudal, and industry/business representatives,
- excessive reliance on powerful individuals rather than institutions while the individuals continue to erode and weaken the institutions with impunity,
- lack of independent and honest watchdog institutions,
- a reluctance of the best youngsters to enter politics—brighter students continue to pursue medical and engineering carrer while the considerable brain drain of most educated people with initiative continues, and
- the conflict with India has created insecurities and phobias which often overshadow rational and economic considerations in the decision-making process.

34. *Reasons for Lack of Trust.* Unquestionably, theirs is a serious lack of trust in governments in Pakistan. While there may not be scientific surveys to prove it, Pakistanis have not had trust in their governments for a long time. There are many reasons for it:

- Lack of trust in the leader. Many of them are perceived by their citizens to lack honesty, competence, vision, and genuine commitment to the welfare of citizens as their primary objective.
- Lack of direct participation in government. Governments in Pakistan have been directly in the hands of the military for considerable periods of time. The people have had no say in their ascendence to power. Even

with "democratic" governments, citizens have openly questioned the results of the elections. In the few elections perceived as honest, the elected leaders changed their priorities soon after assuming power. Thereafter, they have become dedicated to preservation of power.

- Excessive protection and immunity provided to high government officials under the law. Occasionally, some politicians and bureaucrats have received exemplary punishments. In most cases, the high officials remain unpunished. Accountability at the next election is the only protection for the citizens. Even that is often meaningless because the democratic process is interrupted by coups d'etat and little choice in quality candidates.

- Questionable independence of the press. The Pakistani press is shackled due to the need to protect the political interests of the owners, generate revenue through government-sponsored advertisements, and protect "national security." While there are increasing examples of responsible and bold reporting, the press remains restricted.

- As a result of freer airwaves and satellite transmissions of international TV and other media, people can see continual economic progress in many countries, some of which were poorer than their own not long ago. They can also see improvements in the economic status of Pakistani leaders themselves. But they see little real change in the lives of a majority of the population.

The people are dissatisfied with the three practical leadership options available to the nation. At the time of this writing, the government headed by Prime Minister Benazir Bhutto was being periodically accused of unprecedented corruption. The Prime Minister's spouse was accused of being one of the main beneficiaries. The opposition under the former prime minister, Nawaz Sharif, had an equally bad performance, with his family's industrial empire being one of the main beneficiaries of corruption. They are equally disenchanted by the third option, return to military rule, because of the poor performance of the previous military regimes.

Role of Opposition Parties

While there are genuine complaints against the leaders in power, there is widespread dissatisfaction against the leaders in the opposition, too. It is felt that Pakistan's political leaders have performed poorly and that the same leaders have performed even worse in the role of opposition.

The first rule of democratic government is to accept the electoral verdict of the people, no matter how thin the margin of victory may have been. While the winners move into office, the losers assume the role of loyal opposition. They keep an eye on government policies and workings, they offer constructive criticism and alternate solutions, they improve their own internal organization, they make changes in their leadership, and they prepare for the next election.

In Pakistan, the tradition has been to refuse to accept the results of the election, to label the government fraudulent, and to focus on toppling it. Very little attention has been paid to playing the democratic role of opposition or protector of the interests of the common people. In recent years, each opposition has continually attacked the honesty and motives of leaders of the governing party. Oddly, however, they are never able to prove any misconduct in courts of law when they themselves are in power and have an opportunity to do so. They are continually talking of betrayals regarding policies in Kashmir and nuclear issues, emotional topics which they failed to solve while they were in power. However, little is said about unemployment, poverty, religious intolerance, corruption at all levels of the government, land reform, taxation policy or most other issues of concern to the average citizen.

Never has the leader of the losing side been replaced for the poor performance of his party at the elections. Never are internal party elections held to revitalize the party. The opposition simply waits for the ruling government to do something wrong and tries to catch it in the act. The focus is on toppling the government.

Lately, the attacks have become less civilized in language and have actually become physical in nature. There is much room for improving the role of opposition parties in the parliament and outside. People have come to question the motives of the opposition. The problem lies with both political groups—those who occupy the halls of power and those who sit in opposition.

Role of the Press

Despite periodic restrictions, particularly during military regimes, Pakistan's press has not been totally restricted. In the 1990s, it has enjoyed an unprecedented degree of freedom. Many daily newspapers including *Dawn, News, Jang,* and the *Frontier Post*, and periodicals including the *Herald* and *Newsline,* have used this freedom to report on what is wrong in the society and in the government. Nevertheless, not much follow-up action has been taken. Certainly not much corrective action has followed. The press has rarely insisted upon it. Several reasons have been suggested:

- The press is generally owned and controlled by politicians and other vested interests who may not be as unhappy with the *status quo* as they pretend to be. Press revenue is dependent on advertisements which are largely controlled by the government; in addition, the government subsidizes paper used for printing and regulates its distribution. Therefore, the owners do not go beyond a certain limit to demand or take action against anyone.
- People generally know the facts but are too weak to do anything about it; a widespread cynicism is prevalent in the country.
- Government officials know that the system is corrupt, and most of them are involved in some form of corruption; press disclosures are not going to have serious repercussions against them.
- Even those who have been caught and gone to jail realize that with connections and money, life can be often made tolerable inside. They will eventually come out and use the period in jail as a badge of honor; people will forgive them and even give them more chances to govern.

With such a state of affairs, there is little incentive and considerable risk to the owners and editors of the press to search persistently for reform. Hence, their actions are often for public consumption and are not to be taken seriously.

Lack of Accountability

Like all other citizens of the state, the political, civil, and military leaders have to be held accountable for their actions. In theory, under the current law there is financial and political accountability. In addition, Pakistanis generally believe in final accountability on the day of judgment. In practice however, the system does not work so well.

To start, excessive immunities provided under the law have to be reduced. The leaders have also become experts in avoiding financial accountability. In spite of regular and detailed audits, very few if any can be convicted in courts of law for financial mismanagement or personal benefits derived. In recent times, accusations of bribery against the governments of Benazir Bhutto and Nawaz Sharif have been innumerable. Nawaz Sharif's government tried its best to convict Asif Zardari and other PPP leaders but could prove nothing in two years. Similarly, Benazir's government has tried for two years to prove something against key members of the Nawaz Sharif government but has had limited success.

In general, political accountability has been limited. There have been frequent changes in governments in Pakistan, partly because of the dissatisfaction of people. But the leaders manage to convince the people that they were thrown out for some other cause. They claim to be martyrs, and the public believes them. In due course, the new regime is found to be no better than the old one and thrown out. The earlier one comes back in power.

Need for Improved Governance

35. *Increased Accountability*. Based on its experience in developing countries, the World Bank has suggested a number of ways to improve governance.[105] Increasing accountability is one of the elements. It includes:

- Increased decentralization of government with delegation of responsibility and authority to local governments which are physically closer to and tend to be more sensitive to the concern of the common citizens.
- Increased financial accountability through establishment of infrastructure for sound financial management. This includes (a) critically assessing the country's accounting and auditing standards, laws, and regulations; a degree of independence of auditors in public and private sectors is needed as is the capacity to undertake accounting and audit work and training arrangements; (b) introducing improved budgeting, accounting, and information systems; (c) building professional cadres of accountants and auditors; and (d) strengthening the legal framework of modern accounting practice.
- Strengthened anti-corruption strategies by (a) reducing opportunities for bribery (rent-taking) by simplifying rules and by replacing administrative mechanisms with market ones; (b) Tax reform, based on lower, uniform rates and simpler rules and the strengthening of tax administration and record-keeping; (c) Regulation reform, such as the abolition of price controls, the simplification of license requirements, and similar deregulation measures; and (d) Privatization, to reduce the size of the state enterprise sector under bureaucratic control.

36. *Strengthening Institutions*. Almost every past government has been accused of destroying public institutions. In view of massive unemployment, the policy makers face continual pressure to recruit more people. This has led to ever-increasing staffing levels which are way beyond the capacity of the

---

[105] World Bank, *Governance: The World Bank's Experience*, (Washington, D.C.: The World Bank, 1994), pp. 12-20.

institutions to support. The same policymakers have insatiable personal and party desires to use the institutions for private gains. There is an urgent need to improve controls and reduce incentives for corrupt behavior. The required measures include:

- civil service reforms to restore a professional, accountable, realistically paid, and well-motivated bureaucracy;
- strengthening public procurement systems through the reform of laws, more transparent procedures, adoption of improved bidding documentation, competitive bidding, and staff training;
- modernizing public sector accounting, upgrading internal audit capacity, and strengthening the supreme audit institution;
- reforming the judiciary to reduce long delays and inconsistent rulings, improved compensation for judges and relevant staff, automation of information systems and improved physical infrastructure, better training for law students and practitioners; and
- reforming the legislative branch to improve review and formulation of policy, automating information systems and communication links between executive and legislative branches of the government, and providing the required training.

37. *Judicial Reform.* "Creating wealth through the cumulative commitment of human, technological, and capital resources depends greatly on a set of rules securing property rights, governing civil and commercial behavior, and limiting the power of state . . . there must be mechanisms to resolve conflicts based on the binding decisions of the judiciary; and procedures should exist for amending the rules when it becomes necessary."[106] There is a need to address issues relating to inappropriate laws, uncertainty in their application, weak enforcement, arbitrary discretionary power, inefficient court administration, slow procedures, and the subservience of judges. The government should consider doing the following:

- remove inequalities through laws that discriminate by race, religion, ethnic affiliation, national origin, or gender;
- simplify trade and customs procedures, encourage new business, and generally improve the legal environment for the private sector;
- ensure that there is a mechanism for equal protection for the weak, including minorities, women, and the poor;
- ensure improved court administration; and
- learn from the legal experiences of other countries.

---

[106] Ibid. p. 23.

The judicial assertion of independence from the executive branch of government, under Chief Justice Sajjad Shah is commendable. However, a way must be found to ensure that the exercise of independence is based on principles of law and not personal interest or ego.

38. *Transparency and Disclosure of Information.* There are occasions when governments correctly withhold information from the public (e.g., on national security issues). However, generally non-transparent decision-making provides opportunities for private gain and arrangements which may not be in the best interest of the public. Transparency equates with more open government, deterrence to corruption, competitive public procurement, less room for bribery, and higher chances of exposure.

Transparency is needed in the private as well as in the public sector. For example, accurate and timely financial information, in a standard format, must be required of private enterprises in order to assess credit risk and facilitate new investment. In addition, as state enterprises are privatized and become public utilities, it is necessary for the protection of consumers to set up or strengthen regulatory agencies.

39. *Free Media.* The freedom of media is important in keeping the public informed and encouraging and sustaining public awareness and debate of current issues. It also encourages accountability and discourages corruption in public officials and politicians.

Transparency requires pressure from people, political commitment, supportive institutions, free media, and continual vigilance. Pakistan needs accountability and transparency. Both must be introduced to the maximum extent.

Leadership Needs

Today Pakistanis are seeking a different kind of leader. They would welcome leaders who recognize the weaknesses and strengths of the nation and question the status quo. Pakistani leaders must:
- recognize the general distrust of government, the reasons for such distrust, and they must attach a high priority to restoring trust;
- accept and effectively play whatever role voters assign to them through the electoral process, either in government or as opposition;
- carry out the mandate of the people through constitutional means;
- improve governance through accountability, institutional reform and strengthening, judicial reform, and transparency;

- diagnose all issues presented to them honestly and correctly based on the citizen's interest rather than their own;
- challenge the political process by searching for opportunities, learning from people closest to the problems, experimenting with alternative approaches, and taking appropriate risks;
- enlist the help of others to get tasks done—delegate and teach others;
- strengthen their supporters and make them feel ownership and involvement in the whole effort;
- use authority effectively and set good examples;
- plan and publicize victories of good over evil, even if they are small, providing the taste of success and thereby energizing frustrated citizens;
- select people for assignments on merit, recognize those with unique talents, reward extraordinary effort, appreciate the job well done;
- give priority to developing future leaders, devote effort to human resource development of the nation, seek out special talent in everyone, train them, and get them ready for the task; and
- seek support of Allah through prayer and seek citizen support through transparency of action.

While there is much that Pakistani leaders must do to improve their performance, the common citizens of Pakistan must recognize and insist on several basic points:
- Political change must take place in conjunction with social change.
- Leaders must have a good understanding of economic issues in order to cope with current needs and expectations.
- Leadership must be encouraged from the top down as well as from the bottom up.
- Steps must be taken to ensure that leaders feel obligated to the populace and that votes will be given and received voluntarily.
- Leadership must be decentralized to provincial and local government.
- Leaders most knowledgeable about the concerned issue must be given the authority to resolve it.

CHAPTER 6

CONDITION OF THE PEOPLE

"It is not righteous that ye turn your faces towards East or West; but it is righteousness to believe in Allah and the Last Day, and the Angels, and the Book, and the Messengers; to spend your substance out of love for Him, for your kin, for orphans, for the needy, for the wayfarer, for those who ask, and for the ransom of slaves; to be steadfast in prayer, and give Zakat, to fulfil the contracts which ye have made; and to be firm and patient, in pain (or suffering) and adversity, and throughout all periods of panic. Such are people of truth, the God fearing." (Qur'an 2:177)

Slogans

Throughout Pakistan's history, politicians and military rulers have tried to attract attention and in some cases motivate through different slogans. The founding father, Jinnah, focused on unity, discipline, and faith. After years of political anarchy, the first martial law under Ayub Khan focused on order in daily life. Zulfiqar Ali Bhutto talked of "*roti, kapra, makan* (food, clothing, and shelter)." Most leftist groups have focused on secularism and liberalism. The religious parties and Zia ul Haq talked about a return to orthodox Islam.

All have had good reason for focusing on these points. These points were and continue to be important. However, somewhere along the way, Pakistanis have forgotten the basic qualities of being human, *insaniyat*, in Islamic terms. It is generally agreed that it is most important to be a good human being. If this basic quality of *insaniyat* is cultivated, from the leaders down to the citizenry, much would be resolved.

Pakistanis must become accountable to themselves based on spiritual and social needs. Their religion has established the basic traits which are essential to success. These traits must be cultivated on a personal basis before they can be institutionalized nationally.

Wasted Potential

Pakistan is blessed with many assets. However, it is unable to use its strength collectively for the common good of Pakistanis or the Muslim *ummah* at large. The country is unable to put the powerful message of Islam, strong community feeling, principles of good governance, and geopolitical strengths to greater use. Pakistan's other strengths such as financial resources, an industrial base, and a skilled population could be of greater value if it were fully utilized. In comparison to some of Pakistan's neighbors and to the West, Pakistanis are a long way behind and often at their mercy.

There is much criticism of Pakistanis, largely by Pakistanis themselves. But there has also been much economic progress. Comparing the country to the Pakistan of 1947, every indicator of economic, political, and military develop-ment will show growth and maturity. But there have been many setbacks, too. Pakistan and its people could have been much further along than they are.

Success of Pakistanis Abroad

Pakistanis have experienced great success working for others overseas. Pakistani doctors provide the backbone of the medical profession and health care in Great Britain. They helped build much of the oil rich Middle East: universities, roads, bridges, buildings, water supplies, electric power plants, business management, medical professions, etc.—all bear the label of Pakistani labor. In spite of the failure of the Bank of Commerce and Credit (BCCI), Pakistani talent in banking is visible in most international banks— Citibank, Chase, Grindlays—all have Pakistani workers and managers at all levels of management.

The United Nations and its specialized agencies—from the Secretariat to the World Bank, UNESCO, the World Health Organization, the World Food Organization—all have workers and senior officials from Pakistan. Many African countries have numerous middle level Pakistani officials and advisors.

Pakistanis who have migrated to the United States have achieved success in education, the sciences, technology, and business. They are active in social and community development and while they have yet to achieve noticeable political success, they have established valuable ties with local elected officials, congressmen, senators, and even the White House. They are becoming effective advocates for Pakistani interests and for Islam.

On the whole, Pakistanis are able to organize themselves and others in order to produce valuable output in a timely manner. Yet at home they appear to be a completely disorganized people, lacking work ethics and producing relatively little.

Achievements at Home

Problems at home begin with the lack of adequate organization in government, social divisions exacerbated by colonialism, limited economic opportunities, and bureaucratic impediments. Despite these problems, Pakistanis have achieved much at home.

Economic development at the national level and by individuals since independence has been substantial. Pakistanis have demonstrated that they can make the best out of the worst circumstances. Their ability to adapt to new technology and to new markets has been remarkable. Given the chance, they can certainly compete economically.

Among the achievements which Pakistan has attained since 1947, the following are most notable:

- a relatively modern economy has been created with the share of manufacturing equaling that of agriculture at 25% of GDP;
- agriculture has been modernized, having moved from subsistence to exports of cotton, high quality rice, and fruits;
- poverty has been reduced;
- manufacturing has moved beyond processing agricultural products toward producing transport and electrical equipment and consumer electronics;
- a large degree of urbanization has taken place, with more than a third of the population living in urban areas, about a half of whom live in cities of one million or more and enjoy the relative comforts of urban life;
- a well-educated work force of several hundred thousand has emerged, with well-recognized skills in banking, hotel management, airline operations, shipping, and computer software development;
- a large pool of people working abroad, with many in highly skilled operations and several thousands of them having access to capital that they would be willing to invest in the country; and
- based on World Bank estimates, its purchasing power of per capita income is almost double that of India—$2130 in 1994, as compared to $1280 for India.

On the international economic front, Pakistan has survived despite the loss of the Indian markets at the time of partition. In recent times, as a result of the collapse of the Soviet Union, there have been some unforeseen trading opportunities with Central Asia and also improved trading options with fast developing economies in East Asia, including China. The growing Pakistani community in Europe and North America can be a source of investment capital and managerial talent. [107]

Similarly, there are many Pakistanis outside the government who are busy in constructive social and welfare activities. Abdus Sattar Edhi's work in establishing and operating the Edhi Foundation has resulted in help for millions of Pakistanis who in turn continue to contribute generously to expand his work. Akhtar Hamid Khan has significantly helped peasants in East Pakistan and is now busy helping people of Orangi in Karachi and elsewhere. The Agha Khan's Rural Support Program has provided considerable help to many. Asma Jahangir and her colleagues have focused on human rights with some success. Imran Khan's work in establishing a larger cancer hospital has been appreciated by all.

In the land of corrupt bureaucrats, there must be thousands of honest teachers, doctors, engineers, clerks, police officials, etc., who refrain from illicit gain. They inspire millions of other Pakistanis. In their hearts, even the corrupt officials wish that they could emulate the good ones. Certainly, the bad ones hope and pray that their children will turn out to be better than themselves.

Spiritual Weaknesses

A divided people, easy to manipulate and easy to purchase, Pakistanis face many spiritual problems: different interpretations of Islamic teachings, few and weak religious leaders, poorly educated religious teachers, difficulty of understanding Arabic, restricted roles of women, careless practice of Islam, and excessive craving for the Western way of life. Some may be guilty of making religion more difficult than it is. All will agree that individual and collective reform is needed.

Islamic Nation Model

"...And take a provision (with you) for the journey, but the best of provisions is right conduct . . . " (Qur'an 2:197)

On the whole, are Pakistanis good Muslims? Well-documented surveys are not available. Only Allah knows what is in the heart of one hundred

---

[107]Shahid Javed Burki, "Pakistan's Economy in the Year 2000," an article discussed during a 1996 meeting of the Washington Policy Analysis Group.

million plus Muslims in Pakistan. It is totally between Allah and each individual. Nevertheless, one can make an attempt to gauge the overall situation in order to determine where they are and where they should be aiming to go.

40. *Religious Practices.* Pakistanis maintain Islam as the national religion and as such the following appears to be the norm:
- Most consider their religion and, at least, minimal prayer essential; while a large number of urban and a smaller number of rural people may not be praying regularly, a large number are.
- The virtue of charity is taught at an early age. Although most probably do not pay a fair share, some *zakat* is deducted from all bank accounts.
- Pakistanis possess a strong belief in Allah and the prophethood of Muhammad (PBUH). With exceptions, most Pakistanis see future events to be the will of Allah and, at times, neglect to exert effort to attain future results.
- Pakistanis exhibit a strong faith in prayer to Allah. The faith is extended to intermediaries as well; many people visit the graves of saints to ask them to intercede on their behalf.
- Pakistanis are concerned about the weakness of Muslims in the world; while most do not know what to do about it, they continually search for ways to help.

41. *Declining Moral Values.* Many assert that Pakistani citizens are plagued by declining moral values. Flattery, lying, and cheating for the sake of personal advancement come rather easily. Bribe-giving and taking is accepted as a way of life. Those who need to get some work done from the state apparatus are happy to pay something to get their work done. People in authority are eager to maximize their personal fortunes and are happy to accept and even demand the bribe. People are running after money at all levels and are happy to go to any means to get it—sell drugs, adulterate food, deny others their rights, kidnap, even cause or commit murder. There is an urgent need for improvement of moral values at all levels of Pakistani society.

Many Pakistanis recognize the problems and are speaking up against the status quo. However, they do not know what to do about it. They want change, but do not know how to bring it about. They can be mobilized for change as long as their personal interests are not adversely affected.

42. *Other Weaknesses.* Pakistanis are aware of their national weakness in four critical areas: spiritual, economic, political, and military. While Pak-

istan's performance in East Pakistan and some other areas of the country leaves a lot to be desired, Pakistanis are always eager to help Muslims abroad. Pakistan has been an enthusiastic and effective supporter of Muslim organizations and causes around the world. Pakistanis in general wish that they had the power to do more. They feel relatively weak due to domestic and external constraints (among Muslims and non-Muslims) against supporting the Muslim agenda.

43. *Divisive Issues.* Unfortunately, Pakistanis are active in ethnic, sectarian, and other divisive causes. Nevertheless, they have a reasonably good understanding of, and relations with the West. They recognize the importance of issues on which there is a convergence of views with the West, and are willing to place greater focus on those matters.

44. *Medina Model.* Establishment of an ideal Islamic state as established by the Holy Prophet (PBUH) in Medina remains a dream that many Pakistanis have. In recent times, there have been attempts to set up Islamic governments in Iran, Saudi Arabia, Pakistan, and Sudan. But the emphasis appears to have been on compliance with rituals and duties toward Allah. Little has been done for social justice and meeting duties toward mankind. The ideal model has not been successfully replicated because the required characteristics of Islamic leadership are missing. A consensus has not been reached on how to deal with challenges of the new times.

Economic Issues

Despite the progress to date, Pakistanis face many economic issues: low per capita income, widespread poverty, poor distribution of resources, large illiterate and poorly trained manpower, large unemployment, corruption, misuse of resources, and excessive dependence on foreign aid. The relatively small size of Pakistan's economy and the general poverty of the citizens is one of the reasons the nation does not command the international respect it seeks.

45. *Abuse of Power.* While Pakistan's national leaders have been unable to handle power judiciously, average Pakistani citizens in any position of authority often do equally poorly. A truck or bus driver who has control over his vehicle may drive it without much regard for anyone else on the road. In fact, the current violence in Karachi reportedly started some years ago when a careless Pathan bus driver ran over a young Mohajir girl. The common

behavior of laborers and clerks in government offices often reflects the arrogance and selfishness of senior officials. Many shopkeepers cheat through adulteration of goods or fraudulent weights and measures if they have a chance. Many political workers have turned into criminals in Karachi and elsewhere, showing how far common decency has deteriorated over a period of time. Union leaders are sometimes as arrogant as management. The union boss of the United Bank Limited reportedly stripped a senior vice-president naked in the presence of the bank staff and clients. In another instance, he urinated on the bank president's desk to demonstrate his contempt for the management.[108]

Political and International Issues

Pakistanis clearly face many political and international issues. As in many Muslim countries, these include but are not limited to widespread lack of trust by Muslims in their own governments, being a party or parties to many conflicts around the world, division among Muslims, limited freedom of press, lack of an agreement on the definition of Islamic government, human rights violations on a massive scale at home, fear of Muslims in the West, and poor image of the Muslims around the world.

46. *Personality Complexes.* Many Pakistanis have an inferiority complex vis-a-vis Westerners. Perhaps the explanation lies in Pakistan's colonial back-ground. However, anyone with a European/American complexion who speaks English is seen to be a superior human being. Perhaps they have more money and will make some available, or they might hold some important position and provide employment. Whatever the reason, Pakistanis treat them much better than they treat fellow Pakistanis.

Pakistanis often lack constructive aggressiveness and positive competitiveness with each other and with the outside world in the world marketplace. This too may reflect the recent colonial past and the suppression of individuality and creativity which goes along with being subject to foreign authority.

47. *Is Islam Holding Pakistan Back?* Some Pakistanis strongly feel that Islam is holding the nation back in economic, political, cultural, and scientific fields. Most practicing Muslims would challenge such a view, asserting that, to the contrary, Islam fosters education and commercial enterprise. They

---

[108] *The Herald,* Karachi, (June, 1996), p. 93.

point to many affirmations in the Qur'an and in the Traditions *(Ahadith)* exhorting believers to seek knowledge, to reflect on creation, to actively to engage in trade, etc.

The problem appears to be based on the confused teachings by some of Pakistan's less-educated religious leaders. Their limited knowledge of Qur'an and the authentic *Hadith* often results in their followers being misled and misguided. It is true that the basic purpose of human creation is to worship Allah. Nevertheless, the Qur'an and Hadith go on to assert the human obligation to balance this world with the next and to struggle for the welfare of humanity. While Muslims need to be ready for death which may happen in the very next moment, they are also encouraged to excel in this world for as long as they are alive.

The importance of education and learning has been emphasized in the Qur'an and *Hadith* numerous times.

"...From among His servants, it is the learned who fear Allah. Allah is Mighty and Oft-Forgiving." (Qur'an 39:28)

Nevertheless, despite its commitment to Islamic practices, the government continues to tolerate illiteracy and a poorly trained citizenry. In scientific education and research, Pakistanis are even further behind. The result is that they are almost totally dependent on Western countries.

Education, Training and Research

48. *Large Illiterate and Poorly Trained Manpower.* Based on 1991 data, the adult illiteracy rate was 4% for high income countries; 35% for the world as a whole; and 40% for low income countries. At least seventeen Muslim majority countries had adult illiteracy rates of 50% to 82%. Only 18% to 50% of the people of these countries can read and write in their native language. In many countries of Muslim Africa more than 70% were illiterate. 65% were illiterate in Pakistan and Bangladesh; 52% in Egypt; 46% in Iran; and 43% in Algeria.

Some Muslim countries are making efforts to improve their situation by spending a reasonable part of their central government expenditure on education. Others are not. Data is not available for all countries, and some, like the United States, fund education through property taxes collected and spent at the local government level.

Some comparative data is illustrative. Singapore spent 19.9% of the central government's budget on education in spite of insignificant illiteracy in 1991. Israel spent 10%. Many African countries and Bangladesh spent about 10% too. Pakistan's central government spent 1.6%. The provincial governments of Pakistan found additional funding. However, the total was a fraction of the required amount.

Like most developing countries, the Muslim countries are far behind in science and technology. Tariq Husain of the World Bank has pointed out some interesting but alarming numbers. Japan has 3,500 scientists and engineers per million of population; the US has 2,700; Europe has 1,600; Asia (minus Japan) has 100, and Africa has fifty. While the data for Muslims as a group is not available, the number of scientists and engineers is probably somewhere between fifty and 100 per million. The same report indicates that 90% of world research potential is concentrated in about thirty-five countries with 25% of the world's population.[109]

The latest available data indicates that more than 70% of Pakistan's people are illiterate, (i.e., unable to read, write or count). Launching a massive literacy program is a must. An educated populace leads to political accountability and stability, economic progress, use of technology, enhanced household management, and improved stability. The quality of education of the literate population is also in question.

49. *Cheating at the Educational Institutions.* For the last fifteen to twenty years, Pakistan has been facing a serious problem of cheating at educational institutions. The grading is done on the basis of final examinations which are held annually. These are meant to be closed-book and strictly monitored. Nevertheless, students have gotten into the habit of copying. They copy from previously prepared notes, and textbooks. The lucky ones copy from tailor-made answers to the examination questions as prepared by experts and delivered inside the examination hall.

There is cheating at different stages of the educational process. Payments or influence is used for:
- gaining admission to educational institutions,
- finding out in advance what questions will be asked on the examination,
- copying during the examination or having someone else take the examination for you, and
- manipulating higher marks from the person who grades the examination.

---

[109] Ali Memon, *The Islamic Nation* (Beltsville: Writers' Inc. International, 1995), p. 70.

The result is that Pakistan is producing many illiterates from its educational institutions. The same people rely on influence and money to obtain jobs. Unless something is done to stop this vicious cycle, their children will be equally ignorant. Pakistan will be burdened with a generation of fake degree holders.

Pakistan can expect to fall further behind in scientific research and advanced technology unless there is (a) some major improvement in their education policy, (b) an increase in expenditure on education, and/or (c) an improvement in relation with theWest permitting increased access to advanced learning.

The Pakistan government and private organizations need to spend a large share of their resources on developing science and technology. A science-friendly atmosphere needs to be created. Students must learn applied science and technology on a massive scale and be able to carry out research of all kinds. Well justified, planned and executed expenditure on advanced technology projects need to continue in spite of competing demands.

Other Critical Areas

50. *Mixing of Politics and Violence.* During recent years, intimidation has been increasing as a tool for getting votes and then power. In the past, some landlords used strong-arm tactics to make sure that their tenants in rural areas vote for them. Of late, urban politicians have discovered the benefits of having lawless thugs in their camps.

The political scene at many universities is dominated by bold mercenaries who are feared on the campus and in their neighborhoods. Violence is now used on a large scale to intimidate an entire population in a geographical area. In the violence of Karachi, a political party is showing its strength through massive acts of violence. The ideological debates have given way to the politics of guns and rocket launchers. If a group with, say, 5000 guns manages to achieve its goals through violence, it will be very appealing for the opponents to negate it with 10,000 guns. This bodes poorly for the democratic process.

51. *Exclusion of Women from the Market Economy. Women in Pakistan, An Economic and Social Strategy* (World Bank 1990), describes the situation which is common in Pakistan and may be even worse in other Muslim countries. It indicates that a major obstacle to the country's transformation into a prosperous middle-income country is under-investment in people, particularly women. Women, who constitute half of the population, cannot

participate effectively either as contributors or as beneficiaries. In many social contexts, women are accorded esteem and importance; but on most counts, the status of women in Pakistan is among the lowest in the world.

Within the family, women are responsible for training children. However, they are performing below their potential. Women's education is essential to improve the health and education of all the family, to slow population growth to the level desired by the family itself, and to increase economic productivity. Women's labor and income are already very important for survival of poor families in both urban and rural areas. Improvement in their access to credit, new technology, required inputs, markets, and formal sector employment will allow women to raise their productivity, and hence contribute to family welfare, and overall economic development.

Without education, women can only play the traditional role of home caretakers. They remain ignorant and dependent. They produce more children than wanted by the family, lose more of them than necessary, and remain poor. There is a need to remove overt legal and regulatory dis-crimination against them. Political leadership, Islamic scholars, and the media can play a vital role. Increasing opportunities for women is essential to improving economic per-formance and promoting equity.

Health Services

Health standards are generally low in Pakistan which is partly reflected in low average life expectancy and a high infant mortality. All families are ultimately responsible for their own health. However, their ability to take correct decisions are a function of their education, particularly health educa-tion and financial position (i.e., ability to pay for the required health services as needed). The poor are generally lacking in both areas. Governments can help by

- implementing economic development policies which will benefit the poor;
- increasing the cost effectiveness of health expenditure programs;
- expanding investment in schooling and health education, particularly for girls;
- financing and ensuring delivery of basic clinical services, including immunization against all childhood diseases;
- minimizing the external threats to public health through controls over infectious diseases, environmental pollution, and the availability of illegal drugs and addiction;

- raising the educational and professional standards of medical personnel; removing theft and corruption in publicly owned medical facilities;
- improving management of government medical facilities through decentralization to the extent possible;
- requiring public and private suppliers to compete in providing drugs and clinical services;
- ensuring provision of basic services to all citizens;
- encouraging social or private insurance for clinical services outside the basic essential services; and
- facilitating continual increase in scientific knowledge in preventive, diagnostic, and curative areas.

Public Service

People have become cynical about the idea of public service. Even though they can see the selfless efforts of organizations such as the Edhi Foundation, they are skeptical about their true purpose. Public service through charitable organizations is suspected of having personal agendas or little meaning. People see "do gooders" come and go, and some are even misused. They do not take them seriously.

If an influential and powerful person is behind an organization, some support will be forthcoming, largely as a favor to the founder or other powerful patrons. Otherwise, there is little collective effort to help the needy. How can people be motivated to provide public service? This remains a difficult challenge for Pakistan in light of reduced religious motivation and increased secular trends. Good examples will obviously help. Punishment for those who cheat the public in the name of charity will also help restore confidence.

Rural Population and Feudal System

52. *History.* Feudalism may be defined as (a) a political system of local government and of military organization for protection; (b) an economic system of self-sufficient agricultural manors and of land holding in return for goods and services; and (c) a social system of rigid class distinction and an unchanging way of life.[110]

Historically, feudalism arose in Europe between the 5th and 9th centuries. Lawlessness and disorder were widespread. The central governments

---

[110] Gordon, pp. 71-77.

were unable to provide protection against invaders and roving bands of highway robbers. The small farmers turned to a local strongman, usually a noble. The farmer gave his land to the noble and in return, the noble promised him protection and allowed him to keep farming the land. By the 9th century, almost all the farmers in Europe had surrendered their property and freedom in exchange for protection. They became serfs.

In parallel, many kings rewarded their fighting men with conquered land. The fighting men became land-rich nobles. As the kings became weaker, the local nobles became more powerful. Within their lands, they made laws, levied taxes, dispensed justice, and offered protection. They became supreme rulers over their own lands.

The feudal lord enjoyed a life of privilege while the serf faced poverty, ignorance, class distinction, and feudal dues. The decline of feudalism in Europe began around the 12th century when the Crusades began to broaden the outlook of people, stimulated trade, weakened the nobility, and weakened serfdom. In the 14th and 15th centuries, the rise of nation-states and stronger central govern-ments in England, France, Spain, Russia, and Prussia resulted in the weakened power of feudal lords. In 1789, the French Revolution led to the decline of nobility and class distinction. Increased trade and industry revived towns, and serfs found new ways of making a living. However, in many less-developed countries such as Pakistan, feudalism is still alive, and strong even today.

Pakistan's Feudal System

Feudalism is one of the major features of Pakistan. Feudalism is alive and well in Punjab, as it is in Sindh, Baloachistan, and Frontier provinces. The extent of feudalism may vary but the *waderas* of Sindh, the *chaudhris* of Punjab, the *maliks* of Frontier, and the *sardars* of Baloachistan are power-ful feudal lords. Almost all feudal lords of today have inherited their lands from their ancestors. They in turn got their lands in reward for services pro-vided to the British government in colonial times, particularly following the mutiny of 1857[111]. Sepoys loyal to the British were favored with land and government positions.

They evolved into feudal lords who prospered by providing some basic services to the government and by putting fear in the hearts of the peasants. Their power grew and by the time of independence in 1947 they represented

---

[111] Aqeel Abbas Jafri, *Pakistan Ki Siyasi Wadere* (in Urdu) (Karachi: Gord Books, 1995).

a significant element in the country who could demand and receive considerable privileges from the government.

The feudal lords think in terms quite different from the "rational" thinking that urban citizens are used to. They respect only physical power and feel that weaker people have been created to serve them. They provide some services for their "peasants," but expect total loyalty in return.

Government funds provided for rural development are often used for the personal benefit of the landlord without any shame. Kidnapping of young girls for pleasure by younger feudal lords is acceptable and frequently practiced. Such kidnapping can lead to murder and suicide. Kidnapping of men and older women is also acceptable as a means of pressuring and negotiation. Some followers of feudal lords specialize in kidnapping and take pride in their specialization.

The landlords exercise their power through strong henchmen among the poor, using a carrot and stick approach. Those who obey are rewarded with money, praise, accessibility, power over others. Those who oppose are punished physically, monetarily, and emotionally. Landlords prefer to deal with one threat and person at a time. Mass protest or government action is threatening to them. They try to introduce frictions among the masses and practice divide and rule to the fullest extent possible.

The peasants accept their fate at the hands of their feudal lords as the will of Allah; they are very reluctant to challenge the status quo. They are too afraid to pay the price of any revolt. Police and other officials working in rural areas are in the regular pay of the local lord, and in return, are expected to take care of "the nuisances."

The feudal lords see education among the poor as a threat. Historically, they have discouraged education and the opening of schools in their areas of control. While most parts of Punjab may have passed this stage, most parts of Sindh and Baloachistan continue to experience this condition.

Education for children of the feudal lords is helpful in certain cases, but is totally wasted in others. Some of the educated ones are trying to improve the lives of people under their control. Others are using their education to tighten their grip on peasants further.

Several observations can be made:

- Feudal lords are greedy for ever more money, regardless of how much they have.
- The break up of large agriculture estates is a big threat to the feudal lords since fewer people will be directly dependent on them for a livelihood.
- Resettlement caused by construction of a dam, and subsequent flooding of lands is a great threat and concern to affected people.

- Children of the feudal lords are moving to urban areas and investing capital in urban properties and industries;
- The women of feudal lords are treated as their property who must be protected from outsiders at all cost.
- The educated women of feudal lords are fighting for a change, and are gradually succeeding.
- Guns are status symbols, a necessity for protection against others, effective tools for intimidation, and widely possessed and used.
- The break up of the feudal system appears to be very difficult. Looking back at history, it has been damaged by industrialization, urbanization, education among the peasants, compulsory abolition of large measures of lands, withdrawal of special subsidies, and tax exemptions to the agricultural sector.

53. *Rural Sindhis and Feudalism.* There exists a paradoxical coexistence between the rural Sindhis and the feudal lords which may be difficult to understand in modern terms.[112] The relationship is based on the rural Sindhis' desire for protection against local government officials such as police, revenue collection personnel, and engineering staff responsible for providing irrigation water. They also seek protection against other local feudal lords who threaten their employment and honor (by molesting their young children, particularly females). In addition, the feudal lord provides protection against local lawless elements such as robbers and thieves, is influential in obtaining infrastructure facilities such as roads, drinking water, electricity, schools, medical clinics in their villages, and in arranging education, employment, medical facilities, and legal services in the required urban areas for their families. Above all, they provide credit and financial support in times of need, such as the marriages of children, and purchase of livestock and seed or the failure of a crop.

The local feudal lords have much more to gain from the relationship, including:

- a cheap source of reliable labor to work on their lands, and in their households;
- enhancement of their reputation in the local area which can result in control over vote banks at times of local, provincial, and national elections; such prestige can lead to financial and other benefits;

---

[112] Rural Sindhis have slaved for and co-existed with feudal lords such as Chandio, Jatoi, Talpur, Bhutto, Mahar, Bijarnai, Pagaro, Unar, Jamot, Syed, Makhdoom, Wasan, and others.

- increase in their influence with local government officials based on their followers in the community; this gains them preferential treatment; mone-tary opportunities; and "honor," a highly valued commodity in feudal communities; and
- protection against opponents, be they political, commercial or criminal.

Generally there is an overlap between the needs of the rural peasants and the feudal lords. Feudal lords provide the needed protection and support to those who will work for them; the peasants provide cheap labor, votes and help them look good in the eyes of outsiders. There are some compassionate and humane feudal lords who work in the interests of the poor. Others are interested in perpetuating their influence and power. When they become elected officials, and even ministers, they are often accused of deliberately minimizing infrastructure development in their areas in order to keep the people poor, backward, and dependent. Whenever it is to their advantage, some feudal lords turn to modern automation to reduce their dependence on peasants' labor; contract labor is also used to reduce costs.

54. *Feudalism in Punjab.* The basic elements of the feudal lord and peasant relationship are the same in Sindh. However, relatively more industrialization, urbanization, and education in Punjab have reduced feudalism in that province, even though it still survives. However, the well-known feudal families of Piracha, Tiwana, Janjua, Chalta, Chaudhri, Cheema, Daultana, Abbasi, Qureshi, Khar, Khosa, Gilani, Laghari, Makhdoomada, Nawabzada and others continue to prosper. With money and connections, feudal lords have learned to take advantage of industrialization. They obtain licenses and either sell them for instant profits or become industrialists themselves, with large, low cost loans from the government. They get residential and commercial plots in urban areas and either sell them for profit or establish themselves as prominent urban citizens. Through their connections, they have been getting their children recruited into civil and military jobs for years. Already their children are well established in high positions. Their control and influence over all segments of the society continue to grow.

55. *Feudalism in Baloachistan.* A typical example is the Jamali family in Baloachistan. It holds large tracts of lands and a rural vote bank. In recent times, two members of the family have been chief ministers of the province; several have been members of national and provincial legislatures; one has been chief secretary of the province; they own industries and choice real estate properties. Other well-known feudal families include Bugti, Jam,

Khan of Kalat, Rind, Raisani, Khosa, Marri, Magsi and Mengal. The have-nots are crying for a level playing field. Long-term action programs are needed to eliminate undue advantage and benefits to feudal lords and other similar groups of people.

56. *Meeting the Needs of the Rural Poor.* In order to supplant the archaic feudal system prevailing in rural Pakistan, particularly in Sindhi and Baloachistan, it is necessary to satisfy the needs and services now being provided by feudal lords. Who can provide the rural poor with the benefits and advantages being provided by the feudal lords? In modern societies, federal and local governments (often elected officials) should provide most of the feudal lords' activities:

- Protection against local officials such as police, revenue collectors, irrigation engineers, etc., should not ever be necessary when the laws of the land are working properly. It is the role of government to protect; there should be no need for protection against government officials themselves. Honest and sincere government should be responsible.
- Protection against threats to their employment and honor can be provided by government or quasi-government organizations established for and by local citizens.
- Protection against robbers and criminals should be provided by honest government; there should also be united resistance by the peasants.
- Support and influence for obtaining infrastructure facilities should come from local elected officials and a sincere government planning ministry.
- Education, employment, medical facilities, legal services, etc. in the nearby urban areas for their families should be provided by the government, often under programs already promulgated.
- Financial support in times of need such as marriages of children, purchase of livestock or seed should be provided by a rural banking system.

Once the society begins to function the way it is supposed to function, the feudal lord–peasant relationship will begin to be normalized and become more human.

Land Ownership and Reform

At the time of independence, Pakistan had a large number of small farms and a small number of very large estates. Less than one percent of the farms consisted of more than 25% of the total agricultural land. Farm laborers and tenants were very poor, uneducated, and undernourished, in sharp contrast to the wealth, status, and political power of the landed elite. Following independence, the political leaders recognized the need for more equitable distribution of the land and security of tenure.

In January 1959, the government of General Ayub Khan promulgated land reform regulations that aimed to boost agricultural output, promote social justice, and ensure security of tenure. A ceiling was placed on individual ownership and compensation was paid for the surrendered land. However, the impact was very limited. Slightly fewer than one million hectares of land were surrendered, of which a little more than 250,000 hectares were sold to about 50,000 tenants.[113]

In March, 1972, the government of Zulfiqar Ali Bhutto reduced the landownership ceiling. Owners of the expropriated land received no compensation and beneficiaries were not charged for land distributed. The new legislation required landlords to pay all taxes, water charges, seed costs, and one half of the cost of fertilizer and other inputs. Official statistics show that by 1977 (i.e., by the time of the Bhutto government overthrow) only about 520,000 hectares had been surrendered, and nearly 285,000 hectares had been redistributed to about 71,000 farmers. In 1977, just before its overthrow, the Bhutto government further reduced the ceilings. However, the Zia regime neglected to implement these reforms.

The whole effort has had relatively little impact. Data shows that between 1960 and 1980, the number of farms decreased by 17%, and the farms decreased in area by 4%, resulting in slightly larger farms. The number of marginal farms of two hectares or less has declined while those of between two and ten hectares have increased. The number of very large farms remained unchanged at about 14,000. However, the average size of the biggest farms was smaller in 1980. There have been no major changes since then. Large landowners retain their power over small farmers and tenants specially in the interior of Sindh, southern Punjab, and Baloachistan.

Human Rights Violations

The federal and provincial governments of Pakistan have a very poor record of human rights violations. People are routinely arrested without charges filed, not brought before judges for extended periods, and tortured. During 1995, there were several reports of detainees being shot in fake encounters while attempting to escape. People living near police stations have often heard screams of people in custody being tortured. Severe

---

[113] Blood, pp. 177-179.

beatings, pulling out of nails, lying naked on blocks of ice in winter, hanging upside down, and electric shocks to the genitals are just a few of the routine police interrogation methods. Deaths in police custody have increased. An ever larger number of people are dying in police encounters. Cruelty by the police in rural areas is legendary. Police brutality in urban areas is a relatively new phenomenon but has reportedly increased at a fast rate in Karachi. For the last two or three years, it regularly has made headlines.

Almost every politician, including Prime Minister Benazir Bhutto, has been a victim at one time or another. Nevertheless, the problem continues even after the victimized politicians gain power themselves. They feel confident and secure and continue to use the same methods against their enemies.

> **When trouble toucheth a man, he crieth unto Us (in all postures) - lying down on his side, or sitting, or standing. But when We have solved his trouble, he passeth on his way as if he had never cried to Us for a trouble that touched him! Thus do the deeds of transgressors seem fair in their eyes! (Qur'an 10:12)**

57. *Fearful Citizens.* The fear of arbitrary arrest, forced separation from loved ones, isolation from civil society, inaccessibility to due process of law, or of being locked up in some police station, military camp or jail in unsanitary conditions can be extremely depressing. The thought of arrest and its implication has persuaded many would-be activists and reformers to stop thinking about the national welfare and focus on personal survival.

When the author asked some individual politicians about why they retired from politics prematurely or why they supported the government in rather inexplicable situations, they cited fear of going to jail. They did not wish to lose their freedom, family, standing in their community or material possessions. In other situations, aspiring politicians who have little to lose, have become extremist and radical and taken immoderate positions assuming that they will be put behind the bars in any case. In any event, the society has lost much human talent.

Then there are relatively "more polite" ways of victimization by the government. Famous cricket player, Imran Khan, constructed and operates a cancer hospital in Lahore. Based on the press reports, "92 percent of the patients out of the 22,000 who visited the hospital in 1995" were provided free treatment. Imran has made this possible through continual fund raising at home and abroad. However, the hospital has also been a vehicle for promoting him as a possible future leader of Pakistan.

The sitting government has not been impressed. Imran has accused the government of personal harassment and active opposition to the hospital. He has accused the government of (a) wrongful inquiries concerning his wealth, income, and taxes, (b) banning any public television advertisement relating to the hospital which has made his fund raising efforts much more difficult, and (c) unwarranted investigation by the Federal Investigation Agency (FIA), and (d) a bomb blast which killed and injured many in the hospital.[114] Regardless of the facts, the incidents reinforce the perception of victimization. A lesser mortal would have withdrawn from public life by now. Instead, Imran, who is married to a wealthy British "heiress" has launched a "movement for justice" and is expected to convert it into a political party.

The political field is thus left open to those who will either tow the government line, those who are not afraid of arrest and whatever else comes with it, or those who have the backing of higher powers than the government itself. In a democratic country, the higher powers should be the people themselves. Some brave politicians and newspaper personalities have been saved from arrest or let out early due to public support. However, in the past, the enormous popularity of Zulfiqar Ali Bhutto, Benazir Bhutto, Maulana Maududi, Shaikh Mujib-ur-Rahman and others have not saved them from jail in Pakistan. However, few seem to learn even from their own experiences.

Foreign influence and power can be a savior. People whose arrest will raise trouble from abroad may find a deterrent in some cases. In fact, some have been released on the basis of persistent protest from abroad. However, it does not always work. The easiest way around for political survival and staying out of jail in Pakistan is not to upset the rulers of the day and to cooperate with them.

From the point of view of the sitting governments, there is a general feeling that Pakistan's people are "bad" and cannot be controlled without threat and use of excessive force. Such behavior by the Sindh government is often sighted as an excuse by the federal government to justify cruelty to Sindhis at the hands of the army. The Sindh local government must show that they respect the human rights of their own people before demanding others to do the same.

On the international front, it has been argued by some "Muslim governments" among others, at a June, 1993 United Nations conference, that "human rights " is a Western concept, and that different regions, religions, and cultures require substantially different standards. This gives credence to

---

[114] *Pakistan Link* (5 January 1996), p. 15.

an imperial colonial approach namely, "Give them a full belly, a strong hand, and an occasional boot and they are happy; that is their nature and culture."

As some Muslim and Asian block countries have argued, economic development is the most fundamental human right. However, the rights of society as a whole are important, too. [Violation of individual human rights cannot be essential for economic development or for the protection of society as a whole.] Islam stands for equal human rights for all. Each country is free to set punishments for individual crimes. However, punishment should be given only after conviction through due process of law.

58. *Needed Rights at the National Level.* In principle, the United Nations charter on human rights has much that can be implemented in Pakistan. All citizens desire to ensure the following rights for all Pakistanis:
- equality before the law;
- protection against arbitrary arrest;
- right to a fair, speedy, and public trial by an impartial judge/jury; right to be informed of the nature and cause of the accusation; right to be confronted with the accusing witnesses; right to have compulsory process to obtain witnesses in one's own favor; right to have assistance of counsel for defense;
- freedom from ex-post facto criminal law;
- freedom of thought, conscience, culture, and religion;
- freedom of opinion and expression;
- freedom of peaceful assembly and association;
- equal pay for equal work;
- the right to education (implying elimination of illiteracy);
- the right to enjoy own culture;
- the right to use one's own language;
- the prohibition of discrimination because of language, sex, or color; political or other opinion; origin, property or other status;
- the prohibition of discrimination in employment in civilian and military jobs;
- the prohibition of discrimination in education or in the admission of pupils to educational institutions;
- the obligation of government to ensure equitable regional economic development;
- the obligation of the government not to engage in any act or practice of discrimination; and to amend, rescind, or nullify any laws, regulations, and practices at all levels of government that have the effect of creating or perpetuating discrimination;

- the prohibition of ideas based on racial, ethnic, and cultural superiority or hatred;
- the right of the persons to be secure in their persons, houses, papers, and effects, against unreasonable searches and seizures;
- the prohibition against excessive bail, excessive fines, and cruel and unusual punishment; and
- the right of people previously neglected and discriminated to receive compensatory accelerated development in order to ensure speedy recovery for subsequent effective participation in equal development opportunities.

59. *First Investigation Report.* One method of keeping political opponents (particularly crooked ones) behind bars is the blind FIR (First Investigation Report).

> For example, "A" lodges an FIR in a police station that his scooter has been stolen by "persons unknown." The police, unable to find the thief, file the FIR in a dormant FIR file. When needed in the per-secution of a particular man, one of these dormant FIR's is removed from the file and taken to the magistrate by the police, with the information that the suspect in the crime is [the same man]. The police ask that he be remanded to their custody for fourteen days (the maximum allowable) while they investigate. Before the fourteen days lapse, another dormant "blind FIR" is produced and [the same man] is remanded for further fourteen days, and so it goes on and on *infinitum.*[115]

60. *Human Rights Ministry.* The federal government has even set up a new Human Rights Ministry.[116] The Secretary has conceded that:
- Roughly half of thirty-eight million children of Pakistan aged five to fourteen were not going to school.
- There are a large number of human rights violation complaints. These largely concerned women, child labor, religious minorities, and ethnic minorities.

---

[115] Ardeshir Cowasjee, "Fascism," in *Pakistan Link*, (10 November 1995), Section 2, p. 9.

[116] "Pakistan Activates Ministry for Human Rights," in *Pakistan Link*, (19 January 1996), p. 24.

- In Punjab alone, some 1200 cases of child labor abuse were before the courts but processing them was difficult because of the work load on the judiciary.
- There are allegations of victimization by police and abuse by authorities. The government will set up a tribunal to deal with cases of underprivileged people.
- There are allegations of kidnapping, rape, police encounters, arrest of women, extrajudicial deaths and torture. The Ministry will provide relief funds for legal and financial assistance.

The Ministry is reportedly working closely with local and international agencies to inquire into human rights violations and to take corrective action.

Corrective Action

Most of the human rights enumerated above are theoretically assured under the constitution and legislation in Pakistan. Practice is something else. Each strong person who decides to violate these laws—a feudal lord, a terrorist organization, a local police inspector, a chief minister, or an army general—claims to have a "higher purpose" in mind at the time of doing so. If Pakistan's citizens decide to accord high priority to human rights for all, then the "higher purpose," no matter how important or sacred, will have to take a back seat.

Corrective action is available if a sincere commitment is undertaken. Such action must focus on

- additional legislation covering areas which are not addressed by the constitution and existing laws to close loopholes in order to ensure effective implementation;
- accelerating the process for dispensation of justice;
- repealing laws or parts thereof which offend fundamental human rights (e.g., Maintenance of Public Order, Frontier Crime Regulations);
- stopping use of state machinery to suppress political dissent or cause state-sponsored terrorism;
- establishing independent and honest judiciary;
- vigilant action by citizen groups including creating/strengthening human rights monitoring agencies at local, provincial, and national levels; and
- coordinating and supporting human rights organizations at the international level.

CHAPTER 7

POVERTY AND UNEMPLOYMENT

Satan threatens you with poverty and bids you to conduct unseemly. Allah promises you His forgiveness and bounties. And Allah careth for all and He knoweth all things. (Qur'an 2:268)

Large Population

Pakistan has one of the highest population growth rates in the world. Today Pakistan's population is greater than that of combined East and West Pakistan at the time of secession of the East and independence of Bangladesh. Aside from continued heavy immigration from Afghanistan, India, Bangladesh, and other countries, the large increase is "caused by a falling death rate combined with a continuing high birth rate. In 1950 the mortality rate was twenty-seven per 1000 population; by 1990 the rate had dropped to twelve (estimated) per 1000. Yet throughout this period, the birth rate was forty-four per 1000 population. On average, in 1990 each family had 6.2 children, and only 11 percent of couples were regularly practicing contraception." [117]

Based on a report from the United Nation population division, Pakistan's largest city, Karachi has been growing at a rate of 6.7 percent a year between 1970 and 1990. Even though the future growth rate is expected to moderate, Karachi's population is expected to grow from about eight million in 1990 to twenty-one million in year 2015. Karachi which was the twenty-first largest city in the world in 1990 is expected to become seventh largest in 2015. Lahore, the second largest city of Pakistan, is expected to become the twenty-second largest with a population of 10.5 million in year 2015. [118]

Wars and domestic civil strife do continue to take many lives. However, population planning policies have not been successful to date for social, economic, and religious reasons. As in most Islamic nations, social and eco-

---

[117] Blood, p. 92.

[118] "UN Report Says Karachi, Lahore to Emerge as 7th, 22nd Largest Cities By 2015", *Pakistan Link*, (17 May 1996), p. A14.

nomic safety nets for Pakistanis are provided by the extended family and by adult male offspring. While Pakistanis are familiar with the strong economic arguments in favor of population control, nevertheless, most Muslims believe that Allah has promised sustenance for all creatures. The Qur'an is frequently quoted to point this out:

> **Kill not your children for fear of want: We shall provide sustenance for them as well as for you. Verily killing of them is a great sin. (Qur'an 17:31).**

Some Pakistanis argue that there is little justification to curtail the size of affluent families deliberately. Such families can more than afford to provide adequate education and sustenance for their children. These families need not place a heavy emphasis on birth control. Many assert that, after they have grown older and their children have moved on in pursuit of their own careers, they wish they had had more children.

With a population of more than 130 million and a land area of about 0.8 million square kilometers, Pakistan has about 2.3 percent of the world population on 0.6 percent of the land. At a current growth rate of more than 3 percent, the population is expected to double to about 260 million within twenty-three years or by 2020. How will a small country like Pakistan accommodate nearly the total current population size of the United States?

Some approach has to be found. Social, economic, and spiritual aspects of population planning must be reconciled. It is generally agreed that natural reduction in population growth rates through educational programs, improved economic status, and health care for women is justified. It is already a priority on the national agenda. However, much more needs to be done to deal with this urgent and explosive issue.

Income Distribution

Based on a World Bank Report, Pakistan Poverty Assessment, the highest 20% of the population receives almost half of the household income. The wealthy have a disproportionately large share of the income. Over the years, the wealthy have continually increased their share.

Table 4: Pakistani Household Income Distribution[119]

Year	Lowest 20%	Middle 60%	Highest 20%	Ratio of Highest To Lowest 20%
1971/72	7.9	49.1	43.0	5.4
1979	7.4	47.6	45.0	6.1
1985/86	7.6	48.4	44.0	5.8
1990/91	7.3	48.2	44.5	6.1

The household income share of the lowest 20% of the population has decreased from 7.9% in 1971/72 to 7.3% in 1990/91. Poverty in Pakistan is widespread. Despite some past success in reducing poverty, about one third of the total population lives below the poverty line. Rural areas which contain 70% of the total population, contain 74% of the country's poor.

Compared to the average for all low-income economies, Pakistan fares very poorly. Total fertility rate is 65% higher; infant mortality rate is 30% higher; adult literacy rate is 25 percentage points lower; gross primary and secondary education ratios are about half of the average.

Table 5: Pakistan - Poverty [120]

	Poverty Ratio (%)	Income Gap	Population (000's)	Poor (000's)
National Level				
1984/85	46.0	24.1	94,733	43,577
1990/91	34.0	20.9	113,787	38,688

---

[119] World Bank, *Pakistan Poverty Assessment* (Washington, D.C.: World Bank, 1995), p. 50, Table 1.2.

[120] Poverty line of Rp 296 per capita per month in 1991/92 rural prices. The poverty ratio (head count ratio) measures the proportion of individuals in the total population with consumption below poverty line. The income gap measures the average shortfall of consumption of the poor relative to poverty line, as a percentage of the poverty line. It has been adjusted for the number of adults and children and differences in the cost of living between the urban and rural populations. Source: World Bank, *Pakistan Poverty Assessment,* (1995), Table 1.4, p. 52.

Rural Areas		
1984/85	49.3	24.1
1990/91	36.9	21.1

Urban Areas		
1984/85	38.2	24.1
1990/91	28.0	20.3

The report goes on to recommend that the nation should:
- continue addressing poverty in a more effective way until human development indicators improve significantly;
- sustain a minimum annual growth rate of 6%;
- enhance the efficiency of resource use in industry and agriculture
- deepen economic reform programs;
- improve governance and public administration;
- strengthen social safety nets by better targeting the poor through its two main income transfer programs, the *Zakat* and *Ushr,* and the Pakistan *Bait-ul-Maal*; and
- shift expenditure away from government subsidies that are not for the poor to programs targeted for the poor.

Reducing Poverty

61. *Reduction of Poverty.* Reducing poverty is a long and complex matter. In spite of persistent pockets of shocking poverty, the high income countries of the Americas and Europe have significantly reduced poverty. Many of the oil-exporting countries also have made considerable progress. In Asia, Singapore, Malaysia, Hong Kong, Korea, and Indonesia have made notable progress in the last few years. Based on the World Bank methodology, Pakistan must analyze its policy, public expenditure, and institutions from a poverty reduction point of view.

Each meaningful action by the government must be judged from the point of view of its impact on reduction of poverty. The focus must be on the efficiency of incentive policies (e.g., tariff and trade restrictions, price controls, agriculture pricing, wage and employment policies, industrial regulations, etc.). There must also be concern for cost effectiveness in public expenditures, in particular for developing the human capital of the poor and reducing of wastage or leakage (e.g., corruption, theft of public goods and services such as losses of electricity, water, gas etc.).

Governments and private sectors must increase allocations for financing programs and projects that support and enhance poverty reduction. Policies for each sector (agriculture, rural and urban infrastructures, health, education, etc.) must focus on poverty reduction. The design and implementation of each project must involve the poor directly. Targets must be clearly set.

Pakistan's performance must be monitored at the highest levels of the government to ensure achievement of targeted improvement in social and economic indicators. The federal and local government must coordinate their efforts and cooperate with supporting poverty reduction agencies and other interested groups at home and abroad.

62. *Removal of Hunger*

> **It is not righteousness that ye turn your faces towards East or West; but it is righteousness—to believe in Allah and the last day, and the angels, and the Book, and the messengers; to spend of your substance, out of love for Him, for your kin, for orphans, for the needy, for the wayfarer, for those who ask, and for the ransom of slaves . . . . (Qur'an 2:177)**

The Qur'an requires all Muslims to help the needy ones. Nevertheless, many people in Pakistan continue to go hungry. Action is required at international, national, and household levels. Muslims as a group in cooperation with others need to (a) increase the supply of food through more research, extension work, and conservation of natural resources, (b) stabilize supply through maintaining sufficient stocks, paying attention to early warning signals, and doing more research in relevant areas, and (c) accelerate shared growth in Muslim economies which empower all to get the needed quantity of food. If per capita consumption of poor people can be increased, poverty will be reduced. The larger the increase in consumption, the larger the decrease in poverty.[121]

63. *The Conference on "Overcoming Global Hunger"* held in Washington in late 1993 emphasized the following points, which are applicable to Pakistan, too:

- Each country and its people are ultimately responsible for overcoming hunger. International agencies can only help.

---

[121] Ibid., Table 2.2, p. 67.

- Too many international agencies are involved in hunger issues. Each has its own prescription. They must increase coordination among themselves, and be prepared to change policies as needed to meet the requirements of the poor in each specific country.
- Many poor countries have weak governments. International agencies wishing to help must assess and understand the capacity of the country involved and its leadership, and provide practical advice. Programs must be specific to each country and the situation. There must be hands-on support ensuring that capacity is built within the country. Special attention should be given to ensuring the involvement of women.
- International agencies must ensure that none of their actions harms the poor. In the past some structural adjustment schemes may have harmed the poor. They should listen to the poor and their representatives, and provide incentives to their staff for helping the poor through their operations.

Poor Medical Facilities

While urban areas have both public and private sector medical facilities, most rural areas have almost none. The rural citizens must somehow survive without an accessible hospital, doctor, or drugs. With limited or often non-existing financial resources, they are not likely to be taken to the available facilities in urban areas unless they are suffering from prolonged illness and are literally near the end of their life.

Once they reach the public hospitals in the nearest urban area, they find the doctors in the public hospitals to be absent, medical equipment to be non-functional, and drugs to be out of stock. Unless, they sold some land or borrowed a large sum of money (from their feudal lords or loan sharks) before reaching the hospital, they are unable to "buy the services" which the government facilities are expected to provide at a nominal charge. In simple terms, government doctors have to be paid by the patients directly in order for patients to get the required service.

Emergency facilities are lacking even in the urban areas. If someone is having a heart attack, it is difficult to find a doctor, oxygen, equipment for EKG, or emergency medicines even in the best of public hospitals. People relate horror stories even about Combined Military Hospitals which are known to be the best funded and best staffed among all public facilities.[122] Medical facilities in the public sector of Pakistan are in dire need of reform.

Improving Education and Scientific Research

The large number of illiterate citizens and the poorly trained workforce was discussed in an earlier chapter. The World Bank's sector report, issued in 1992, has addressed some of the serious issues requiring corrective action:[123]

- There are several institutional deficiencies including ambiguous assignment of power, coordination, and oversight resulting in defused ultimate responsibility; bureaucratic rigidities; minimal roles of the unit managers in recruitment or dismissal of staff, pay scales, and promotions, and in establishing or changing fees or academic standards.
- There is inefficiency in higher education and the scientific research sector, resulting in a low caliber of graduates and leading to difficulties in their being absorbed at home or abroad.
- The 'sector is under-funded compared to spending in other countries around the world and even in the region.
- The resources available to the sector are improperly deployed.
- Higher education generally results in degrees regardless of interest, aptitude, and subject, resulting in dissatisfaction on the part of the graduates and the community. The quality graduates are compromised due to (a) the centralized imposition of inflexible, insensitive, and often, inappropriate entry requirements; (b) credit accumulation without real learning, skill training, or innovation; (c) the absence of incentives or accountability for quality control; (d) the procedure for appointing and appraising academic and support staff that militates against establishing and maintaining high standards; (e) inadequate provision, maintenance, and use of instructional resources, especially computers, books, and materials; and (f) the lack of any effective input from the world of work into the curriculum design.

---

[122] M. Tamton, "My Horrible Experience at the CMH," in *Pakistan Link,* Lahore (10 November 1995), p. 5. The article describes the lack of equipment and poor service given by the medical staff leading to the death of Lt. Col (R) Abdul Hameed Tamton.

[123] The World Bank, *Islamic Republic of Pakistan, Higher Education and Scientific Research: Strategy for Development and Reform,* (22 July 1992). (Report No. 10884-PAK), pp. I-V.

There is a lack of clearly stated and understood targets and priorities in research resulting in difficulties of rewarding success and avoiding waste. There is also a lack of an overall plan for research, including collaborative roles for various institutions and funding bodies. Accordingly, research activities are planned and carried out without an overall perception of the problem.

Low Per Capita Income

During the 1985-94 period the per capita GNP of Pakistan grew at the rate of 1.3%. All low-income countries, excluding China and India, grew at an average rate of 3.4 percent per year. The middle income countries experienced a slightly negative growth. The high income countries, Switzerland, and the world as a whole grew at 1.9%, 0.5%, and 0.9, respectively.

Assuming similar growth in the future, their projected data are shown below.[124]

Table 6

Country	Per capita 1994 ($)	Per Capita Annual Growth % (1985-94)	Per capita 2000 ($)	Per capita 2050 ($)
Pakistan	430	1.3	465	886
India	320	2.9	380	1,586
Low Income Countries (av.)	380	3.4	464	2,471
Middle Income Countries (av.)	2,520	-0.1	2,505	2,382
High Income Countries (av.)	23,420	1.92	6,505	67,196
Switzerland	37,930	0.5 3	9,505	50,151
World (av.)	4,470	0.9	4,717	7,383

Obviously, if the current patterns of economic development continue, the gap between rich countries and poor countries will increase. Even India and low income countries who as a group have a lower per capita income than

[124] Based on the World Development Report of 1996.

Pakistan could overtake Pakistan in view of their higher growth rates. High income countries as a group and individual countries such as Switzerland will leave Pakistan far behind. Pakistan must grow at a much higher rate or else she will never be able to catch up.

Incidently, it has been possible for neighboring countries in East Asia to achieve much higher rates of growth. During the 1985-94 period, China achieved an average annual growth rate of 7.8% and has already overtaken Pakistan in terms of per capita income of $530. Thailand has achieved an 8.6% growth and $2,410 in per capita; Korea 7.8% and $8,260; Hong Kong 5.3% and $21,650; and Singapore 6.1% and $22,500.

Unless drastic improvements occur in the development policies of Pakistan which will result in increased per capita income (after adjustment for population growth rates), there is no reason to expect any major improvements. If Pakistan could achieve an annual growth rate in per capita income comparable to China (i.e., 7.8% per year), its per capita income could reach $29,000 by the year 2050. Accordingly, all major factors affecting economic development, including revenue mobilization, expenditures, borrowing, human resource development, and defense, must be reconsidered to improve the outlook. Ways must be found to increase the productivity of the least productive and therefore the poorest element of the society, namely, the rural laborer. Modern technology such as television must be used to provide education. Better agricultural methodology must be applied to double and triple agricultural productivity. All permissible methods must be used to stabilize the size of the population.

The government must use all possible diplomacy and ingenuity to reduce its debt repayment burden, get as much of the foreign debt forgiven at the international level as possible, and renegotiate the rest. Interest rates for productive uses of money must be kept as low as possible so that people can start and remain in their own businesses.

People of Pakistan must initiate and demand a dialogue with their counterparts in India for a better relationship. With improved relations, the cost of defense can be reduced and more resources can be devoted to economic development. After adjusting for population increases, maximum economic growth at rates of 2 percent or 3 percent loom ominously over Pakistan. There must be much higher rates of return (as in China and Korea) in order to raise the living standards of people and narrow the gap with the West. Pakistani leaders and citizens must agree to implement ambitious five-, ten-, twenty-, and fifty-year plans of development.

Unemployment

With the exception of a few rich oil exporting countries, all Muslim countries face very serious unemployment problems. Lack of employment opportunities is the single most important economic issue in countries such as Bangladesh, Pakistan, Egypt, and almost all of the Muslim countries in Africa.

Given low employment rates for women outside their homes in Muslim countries, each job provides sustenance for at least one family. In spite of the family support system, without that job, it is difficult for that family to survive. Related problems of underemployment, inadequate wages, and lack of economic safety nets for the poor, are secondary. The first need of everyone is to have a job.

Pakistan is already facing several consequences from lacking sufficient productive jobs. In addition to a relatively low standard of living for a vast majority of its citizens, there are widespread political unrest and large-scale emigration of the educated. It is common to pay bribes for getting and keeping jobs. Many fear losing their job and accept illegalities and corruption from superior officials.

The system has given rise to quotas based on urban or rural domiciles of the population. There is pressure for "quotas" from rural citizens who feel that they do not have adequate educational facilities and that they cannot compete in an open market. There is also pressure for removal of quotas from urban citizens who feel that they are denied jobs in spite of their merit.

The World Bank has assessed the situation in Pakistan and the region as follows:

> Expanding employment and increasing the wages of workers are crucial for poverty elimination, which is the overarching objective of all countries in the region . . . South Asian workers have made some gains over the past thirty years. Nevertheless, the growth has been slow, poverty is still pervasive, and social and human indicators are too low. This performance reflects a development strategy that turned out to be biased against labor. High protection and inward orientation failed to achieve rapid growth in industrial employment, productivity and wages. Most workers remained in the rural and informal sectors, where they are underemployed and poorly paid. Except for Sri Lanka, South Asian countries did not invest ade-

quately in their workers to equip them with the skills needed to compete in the world market better and raise their living standards.[125]

64. *Economic Solutions.* In order to combat unemployment and to create jobs, the current economic wisdom emphasizes the need for:
- high economic growth policies;
- low population growth;
- accelerating rural development in order to discourage large scale movement of labor to already congested urban areas;
- well-designed and directed public works projects;
- support for schemes which maximize labor utilization;
- discouragement of high minimum wages;
- incentives for self employment;
- incentives for a large scale employment generation in the private sector through reforms of trade policies, the financial sector, investment regulations, taxation, and public enterprises;
- well-directed educational policy matching skills with job opportunities; and
- removal of discrimination against ethnic, racial, tribal, and gender groups.

Pakistan has tried most of the above to some extent. However, the results have been largely inadequate. Under one successful effort, passport rules were relaxed during Z. A. Bhutto's regime to encourage workers to find better jobs abroad. As a result, millions of workers have gone abroad and succeeded in improving their economic lots. Those who have gone to the Western countries have generally stayed there and obtained citizenship or permanent residence. Those who have gone to the Middle East have generally returned after a few years. Their places have often been taken by other Pakistanis. Even today, there are a large number of Pakistani workers to be found in every part of the world, particularly the Middle East.

Different governments have provided special incentives for self-employment. Qualified professionals were offered cheap loans to start their own businesses. Others were allowed to buy imported taxis or tractors at preferential rates to provide a needed service and to earn a living. However, in view of the increasing population and the size of the labor force, the overall impact has been minimal. Unemployment continues to be a serious problem.

---

[125] World Bank, "Jobs, Poverty, and Working Conditions in South Asia", *Regional Perspectives on World Development Report 1995* (Washington D.C.: The World Bank, 1995), p. v.

Employment Creation Schemes

Pakistan has experimented with several programs in its efforts to improve economic conditions:[126]

65. *Small Business Finance Scheme.* This ongoing program was created in 1972 in order to finance cottage and small-scale private sector industries, individual transporters, small businessmen, traders, and professionals. Funds of up to Rp 1.5 million per loan have been provided. Loan recovery of 42-63% has been experienced in the past five years.

66. *Youth Investment Promotion Society.* This is also an ongoing program. It was created in 1987 to provide financial assistance to unemployed, educated youth to enable them to set up small businesses of their own.

67. *Provincial Small Industries Corporations (Punjab and Sindh).* These continuing programs were created to provide loans to qualified professionals to help them start their own businesses. Nearly six thousand loans have been made in Punjab. Forty-five loans have been made in Sindh. An estimated 50,000 jobs have been created in Punjab while 229 have been created in Sindh.

68. *Self Employment Program.* This program was started in April 1992 and ended in June 1994. It was created to provide loans to unemployed persons, as individuals or in groups, for self employment within a list of 115 economic activities. The program disbursed 44,577 loans amounting to Rp 4.7 billion. There has been a recovery of 70%.

69. *Public Transport Revamping Scheme (Yellow Cab Scheme).* This effort was started in February 1992 and ended in October 1993. It provided loans for purchase of public transport vehicles by educated youth. Vehicles were exempted from import duty and sales tax. 90% debt financing was provided. There has been loan recovery of 65%.

70. *First Women's Bank Loan Scheme.* This continuing scheme was started in 1991 to provide loans to lower income women interested in starting any

---

[126] Source: The World Bank, based on data provided by participating financial institutions. Ibid., Table 4.8.

income generating activity. Loans of up to Rp 25,000 are made. There has been a 97% recovery.

71. *National Self-Employment Program.* This has been an ongoing program since it was started in July 1994 to replace the Self-Employment Program mentioned above.

72. *Awami Tractor Scheme.* This project was started in 1994 and is an ongoing one. The purpose is to provide loans to purchase tractors by farmers. More than 120,000 applications have been received.

These programs and projects have resulted in some success but they have not produced the required number of jobs. The reform programs for trade liberalization, simplification of investment regulations, taxation, and privatization of public enterprises are relatively new. These should lead to a greater flow of goods, services, and capital. In turn, opportunities for labor and employment should increase. The government however, will need to intervene in selective cases to protect workers who may be adversely affected.

Pakistan's government will still need to pay special attention to generation and maintenance of productive jobs for its citizens. In fact, all Muslim governments need to accord high priority to reduction of unemployment. As a group, they can plan and implement a well-coordinated action program.

Creating a Middle Class

With the decline of feudalism, a significant middle class emerged in Europe several centuries ago. A middle class has already emerged in Pakistan, too. About half of the middle sixty percent of the population referred to above is truly middle class. The goal is to have as many people in the middle or upper income brackets as possible. This means moving as many people out of the lower income brackets into higher income brackets as soon as possible. One can look at it from the point of reducing poverty, meeting basic needs, doing the Islamic duty or achieving economic development.

Improved education, better paying jobs, improved incomes from family farms, manageable family size, increased rates of personal savings and improved availability of credit for investment in home ownership and small business, and the resulting self-confidence will all lead to the induction of more people in the middle class. The society's economic policies should therefore be directed at providing minimum safety nets to families who are unable to care for themselves, and providing maximum incentives to move out of poverty and dependence into improved economic conditions.

The emphasis should be on the family unit rather than on individuals in order to preserve the current tradition of family safety nets for children, the elderly, and the handicapped, and to reduce the burden on the public treasury. Unlike some Western welfare policies where people become accustomed to receiving public charity, incentives for moving out of poverty should be made so obvious that everyone receiving outside assistance will recognize their transitional nature, take advantage of it, and rush to move out of "poverty" into the middle class. Economic, social, and moral incentives must be provided to that end.

Overall Economic Performance

During the early 1960s, Pakistan was a model of economic development. Economists from Korea, Thailand, Malaysia, Indonesia, and Africa flocked to Pakistan to study the techniques being applied there. Since then, several of its Asian neighbors have left Pakistan far behind.

73. *Cause of Poor Performance.* The former caretaker Prime Minister of Pakistan, Moeen Qureshi, identified the following causes of poor economic performance by his country in a speech in December, 1990:
- inadequate economic management; economic policies without a clear long term course;
- low social investment resulting in inadequate development of human resources;
- low investment in physical capital which is partly a result of a declining investment rate as a percentage of gross domestic product;
- weak competition and a weak incentive system;
- a complex and anomalous tax system which discourages exports; and
- an absence of political and social institutions capable of mobilizing the nation for development.

Mr. Qureshi suggested the following corrective actions:
- double the size of the economy in ten years, which translates into 7% annual growth for the economy or about 4% growth in per capita income, after allowing for the population growth;
- sharply increase the investment rate through reform of the tax system and administration;
- obtain a national consensus on resource mobilization and priorities of expenditure in the various sectors of the economy (e.g., defense) and regional spending;

- creation of an open economy with the government assuming the role of regulator rather than manager, promotion of the private sector, and liberalization of the trade and exchange system;
- set up programs of social development which emphasize basic health coverage and education for all; and
- grant greater freedom to financial institutions in the conduct of their affairs.

These corrective steps offer useful suggestions. However, some of the other basic problems will still remain and need to be addressed by the society. These include:

- greed on the part of the policymakers, administrators, teachers, and researchers;
- refusal by college students to devote time to classes and homework, while preferring to rely on cheating during exams and using influence to obtain the required degrees;
- need, for jobs on the part of the students (supported by their parents) which can lead to personal power, money, and prestige without necessarily working for it;
- an acute shortage of jobs of all kinds; and
- both the demand for quotas by people of the less developed areas who have not yet entered the higher education and higher level jobs, and the demand for abolition of quotas by those who are already highly educated and hold good jobs within the system and wish to maintain open access for their children. This will mean increasing access to students throughout the country to higher education. However, an equitable way will have to be found to give preference to the best qualified in each part of the country.

Continuing Action

Knowledgeable economic experts have correctly recommended:
- renewed commitment by the government to economic reforms, including fiscal, monetary, and banking reforms;
- creation and maintenance of an enabling political environment that is accountable to the people and economic in terms of being open, competitive, and responsive to local and international changes and that has a well-defined financial regulatory system;
- reducing fiscal deficits by higher charges, tapping private sectors, increasing public funding for the sector, exploring other potential opportunities and more efficient use of available resources; and

- developing sustainable municipal systems which will supply the needs of citizens at the local level.

In the area of education, a new policy statement for higher education is recommended, including the following:

- creating an apex body responsible for macro-policy formulation and oversight; and creation of a support structure for the apex body;
- ensuring efficient use of all resources available through improved accountability, creation of incentives for faculty performance, establishing a system for measuring institutional performance, establishing balance between teaching and research, restructuring institutional budgets to reach a balance between capital and recurrent costs, consolidating institutions and programs to reap economies of scale; and
- improving the quality of higher education and research through translating national goals into institutional goals, improving access and selection of all students—with particular emphasis on female students, enriching the educational experience, improving the selection and training process for academic staff, improving efficiency and effectiveness of support staff.

74. *In Summary.* Pakistan must devote its energies and resources to finding better and faster ways, and implementing them to achieve removal of hunger, reduction of poverty, human resource development, raising the standard of living, and reduction of underemployment and unemployment. Without success at a much accelerated rate in these areas, Pakistan is doomed to remain an unhappy place for its citizens.

CHAPTER 8

INCREASING WEALTH

Current Situation

Based on World Bank data, Pakistan has one of the lowest income economies of the world. Based on the 1994 data, it had per capita income of USA $430. [127] In terms of per capita income, it is ranked 34th lowest among 209 economies of the world for which data is provided in the World Development Report of 1996. Accordingly, approximately 175 economies have higher per capita income than Pakistan. From a purchasing power point of view, Pakistan may be better off than that; Pakistan's per capita income in 1994 was estimated at about 8.2% of that of the United States or $2130.[128]

Large bungalows and mansions in housing societies in Karachi, Lahore, Islamabad, Peshawar, Quetta, and other large and medium size towns indicate great wealth in some sectors. Similarly, the roads are packed with relatively new model imported cars, and shops are full of imported luxury goods. All these are associated with considerably richer economies. This has led many to comment that Pakistanis are richer than what the country data shows. Slums in urban areas and widespread poverty among rural peasants provide another side of the same coin. Of course, a far larger number of people belong to this category. The difference in the living standards is so significant that Pakistan may be called a "Land of Few Rich and Many Poor." The problem relates to wealth distribution, as discussed in an earlier chapter, rather than the wealth itself.

Sources of Wealth

Where does any increase in wealth come from? It comes largely from savings, although Pakistanis save relatively little. Gross domestic savings as a percentage of gross domestic product (GDP) is about 14% for Pakistan as

---

[127] The World Bank, *World Bank Development Report 1995* (Oxford: Oxford University Press, 1996), Table 1, Basic Indicators.

[128] Ibid., Table 30.

compared to 22% for India; 29% for Hongkong; and 41% for Singapore.[129] Another main source of investment in Pakistan is borrowing and "other unaccounted for sources." An underground economy in the form of drug trade, smuggling, mafia activities, and income from bribery may provide a part of the answer.

Many people feel that most of Pakistan's problems can be traced to its relative national poverty. In addition, ethnic tensions, lack of infrastructure, illiteracy, unemployment, and corruption are all directly related to economic fortunes. Many of these problems can be solved if $100 billion or so were quickly infused into the economy.

Others argue that Pakistan's problems run much deeper. The richest people are often the most corrupt. Religious intolerance will certainly not go away with economic development alone. One can list many problems which money alone cannot solve, but there are many others which money can indeed solve.

Prosperity and Islam

Some of Pakistan's religious leaders point out that emphasis on economic development should not receive such high attention. Allah has put us on this earth to worship Him and therefore the emphasis should be worship. They wonder if the emphasis on economic development indicates too much love for and attachment to the material world. They even question whether economic development or prosperity is Islamic.

> **And when the prayer is finished, then may ye disperse through the land, and seek the bounty of Allah: and celebrate the praises of Allah often (and without stint): that ye may prosper. (Qur'an 62:10)**

As the above quotation indicates, seeking of Allah's bounty is perfectly consistent with Islam.

75. *Business is Islamic.* Islam has encouraged honest trade, science and technology, and commercial endeavors and travel. The Prophet (PBUH) was a merchant by trade. He married a businesswoman. The Qur'an deals explicitly with a number of business issues:

---

[129] The World Bank, *World Bank Development Report 1994* (Oxford: Oxford University Press, Table 9, pp. 178-79.

- Private property is protected (Qur'an 2:188).
- The fulfillment of obligations is commended (Qur'an 2:177 and Qur'an 5:1).
- Details of contract law are presented (Qur'an 2:282-283).
- There is prohibition of fraud (Qur'an 26:181).
- Islam requires the establishment and maintenance of fair standards of weights and measures (Qur'an 55:9).[130]

Welfare of People Is Islamic

... For Allah loveth not ... those who are niggardly, enjoin niggardliness on others, hide the bounties which Allah hath bestowed ... (Qur'an 4:36-37)

In his presidential address to the Constituent Assembly on 11 August 1947, Jinnah said, "Pakistan could be made happy and prosperous if the government were to concentrate on the well-being of the people and especially of the masses and the poor." [131]

Article 3 of the Constitution of Pakistan states, "The state shall ensure the elimination of all forms of exploitation and the gradual fulfillment of the fundamental principle, from each according to his ability to each according to his work."

Article 38 states: The State shall:

(a) secure the well-being of the people, irrespective of sex, caste, creed or race, by raising their standard of living, by preventing the concentration of wealth and means of production and distribution in the hands of a few to the detriment of the general interest and by ensuring equitable adjustment of rights between employers and employees, and landlords and tenants;
(b) provide all the citizens, within the available resources of the country, facilities for work and adequate livelihood with reasonable rest and leisure ...

---

[130] Dr. Imad A. Ahmad, "An Islamic Perspective on the Wealth of Nations" presented at the International Conference on Comprehensive Development of Muslim Countries from an Islamic Perspective (Subang Jaza, Malaysia, August, 1994).

[131]*Jinnah Speeches*, (Lahore: Sang-e-Meel Publications, 1989), p.14.

It is the duty of all Muslims and their governments to (a) increase opportunities for all people, (b) establish an environment conducive to prosperity, and (c) help those who cannot help themselves—the disadvantaged and orphans.

Wealth of Nations

The wealth of nations increases in the same way that the wealth of individuals does. It requires net increase in wealth. It can happen through increase in revenue, decrease in expense, wise investments, and more efficient management of existing assets or a combination thereof. For the government of Pakistan, it can come through some of the following ways:

76. *Increase in National Revenue.* This implies an increase in (a) tax revenues through more efficient collection of existing taxes, an increase in the tax base (i.e., increase in citizens' wealth), or introduction of higher tax rates or new taxation, and (b) user charges for services provided by the government, e.g., electricity, water, telecommunications, etc.

77. *Decrease in National Expenditure.* This implies decreases in defense spending, debt service, and operating costs of civilian departments, which constitute the largest categories of the national expenditure, and/or decreases in subsidies and less productive investments.

78. *Increase in Investment.* This implies investment by the private or public sectors which will yield high returns and result in increased revenue. The investment may be in human capital, physical infrastructure, domestic peace and international harmony (resulting in reduced expenditure on law and order and national defense), industrial capacity for import substitution, export promotion, and improvement of government efficiency.

79. *Efficient Operation of Assets.* This implies such things as reduction in unaccounted uses of electricity and treated water, improvement in irrigation efficiency for agriculture, improved use of industrial capacity, and cost control.

The increase in wealth of the nation can be used to make the lives of citizens easier. They need income to meet basic needs of family and savings which can be used for improving the living standards or as surplus for rainy days, luxuries, and investments.

Privatization

80. *Reduce Reliance on Government.* Reduction of reliance on government or increased citizen self-reliance and increased private sector development are important ingredients in the formula for increasing the wealth of Pakistan. There are numerous examples of self-help schemes where people in urban and rural areas have undertaken to improve their life. In the Orangi part of Karachi, under the leadership of Akhtar Hamid Khan, people have largely financed and operated their own sewage and sanitation, an employment generation program, and a cooperative for marketing local women's handicrafts. Many villages around the country have built their own small water supply schemes and improved road access. The examples need to be replicated throughout the country.

81. *Privatization.* In developed countries, the private sector is the main producer of goods and provider of employment. While it is happening in Pakistan at an increasing pace, the reliance on government for provision of services and jobs remains excessive. Private sector participation can happen in the form of new investment by the private sector or "privatization" (i.e., transfer of public investments into private hands). New investments from the private sector continue to be welcomed in most sectors of the Pakistani economy.

While there were some questionable practices of the Nawaz Sharif government, they took several steps to liberalize the economy in order to increase private investment. Through removal of government controls on industrial investment, liberalization of foreign exchange controls, abolishing the system of import licensing, and reducing discretionary powers of the tax officials, the investment climate appeared to have been significantly improved.

While the agenda remains the same under the new government, some have claimed that "government intervention has reappeared in every important sector of the economy partly for political patronage and partly for corruption."[132] The private sector is unwilling to pay any more taxes. The relatively poor law and order situation in the country has further dampened the investment atmosphere. There have been many confrontations, including the one between MQM and the government in Karachi, *dacoits* and kidnapping in interior Sindh, and robberies and bombings in Punjab. Private

---

[132] Senator Sartaj Aziz, "State of Economy After Two Years of PPP Rule," in *Pakistan Link,* (10 November 1995), p. 6.

funds seem to be moving back into real estate or abroad. The government needs to provide a new push to accelerate investment from both domestic and foreign sources in the country. Without substantial new private investment, the country will not be able to grow and meet its many needs.

All agree that privatization will benefit the nation if there is:

- net generation of new financial resources for the purchase. Use of the government's own resources or already available capital inflows for transfer of ownership into private hands do not generate new resources;
- demonstrable increase in operational efficiency, e.g., through elimination of losses or operating subsidies;
- transparency of the negotiations and contracting which maximizes the proceeds for the government;
- equitable sharing of costs and benefits arising from the transaction; and
- use of the proceeds from the sale of assets, for high priority purposes.

On the other hand, bloated work forces, antiquated equipment, bureaucratic resistance, fear of layoffs, and social dislocation have all conspired against the sale of government-owned companies. Potential buyers want to be able to reduce the size of the work force, while the workers do not wish to lose their jobs.

The privatization of public sector resources initiated by the Nawaz Sharif government resulted in several questions about the transparency of the process. Critics also doubt whether the government received the maximum amount for the assets transferred, including the Muslim Commercial and Allied Banks. Whether the proceeds were wisely used is also questioned.

In the case of privatization of the Muslim Commercial Bank (MCB), Abdul Qadir Tawwakul was the highest bidder for the controlling share, at Rp. 56 per share. His bid was followed by those of Adamjees, then Crescent. The Mansha group was fourth with a bid of Rp 43.49 per share. "Nawaz Sharif wanted Mansha to have the bank, so his government maneuvered a bid rise for Mansha to match the highest, and he was given control." Tawwakul wanted to fight for his cause and petitioned the court. In his affidavit he stated, "Let it be stated that in his (Finance Minister Sartaj Aziz's) office ... the petitioners were bullied and threatened with dire consequences if they challenged the government decision."[133]

The Human Rights Commission of Pakistan indicated in its 1993 interim report that the performance of the units already privatized was uneven, and there was strong criticism from the unions. Privatization of many units was

---

[133] Ardeshir Cowasjee, "Corruption", in *Pakistan Link*, (5 January 1996), p. 9.

challenged in the courts. Some of the alleged wrongdoings were as follows:[134]

- The sugar mill in Larkana was sold to Ghulam Mohammed Mehr, adviser to the Prime Minister at the time.

- After one year of operations, the new owners of the National Motors Ltd. Karachi failed to make good on the golden handshake agreed with 500 out of the 686 employees. The Privatization Commission could not help the workers.

- The country's largest antibiotics manufacturers, spread more than 100 kanals of land, including workers' housing colony, with machinery worth billions of rupees, and Rp. 20 million in stocks of medicine was sold off on paper for Rp. 24 million; but the amount actually realized was only 9.6 million.

The Benazir government reportedly followed a more transparent process. However, questions are being raised about (a) increased efficiency and costs of power to be purchased later as a result of privatization of profitable thermal power plants at Kot Addou and Jamshoro, (b) national security in the case of the privatization of the Oil and Gas Development Corporation, (c) and use of proceeds in the case of almost all projects. What happens to the labor of the privatized projects is a key concern and has to be handled in an equitable manner.

Many Pakistanis, both outside and inside the government, see privatization as a way of handing over large chunks of publicly-owned assets to the favorites of the sitting governments at a fraction of the cost or far below fair market value. The favorites may be local political allies who are branching out into business, or they may be businesses from the Western countries, which the Pakistan government is eager to please.

The President of Pakistan, Farooq Laghari, confessed that the privatization effort suffered a bad image in Pakistan. While addressing delegates from Asia-Pacific countries at a regional conference on privatization in Islamabad on 7 November 1995, he said:

If the perception is that the country's silver is being sold at throw-away prices, that is bad; it discredits the privatization process . . . The cynicism against the manner of privatization has to go. The government has to ensure that this cynicism is replaced by full

---

[134] Human Rights Commission of Pakistan, *State of Human Rights 1993, An Interim Report*; (Lahore), p. 44.

understanding of the manner in which state assets are being privatized.[135]

82. *Privatization of Electric Power Sector.* Pakistan has been faced with a severe electric power shortage for years. The government-owned energy companies have been unable to keep up with the increasing demand of the rapidly growing population. Accordingly, the government has signed a number of agreements for independently-owned Power Projects with investors from a number of countries. The idea is grand. However, some elements of the agreements will come to haunt the country. For example, "government guarantees of revenue in foreign exchange and a fixed offtake price of 6.5 cents per kilowatt hour" may be too generous. Some sources have indicated that a part of the price will be subject to adjustment, e.g., on the basis of the cost of fuel. Given the cost of transmission, distribution, and large power losses, it will result in a substantial rise in overall electricity tariffs. Once the new bills start coming, the consumers will be extremely unhappy.

Secondly, most of the new plants are based on burning of oil. It would mean a large increase in bills for imported oil. Given the current levels of foreign exchange availability, the economic situation could become difficult unless the new electricity translates into a substantial increase in exports and foreign exchange. The oil prices have been maintained at a relatively low level since the end of the Gulf War. If there is a significant rise in price of oil, it could mean additional cost and trouble.

83. *Use of Proceeds from Sale of Assets.* Use of the resources obtained through sale of the assets is another area of concern. The money could be used for some worthy cause in order to strengthen the national economy, e.g., investment in sectors which remain the direct responsibility of the federal government, investments which could not be tackled previously due to shortage of funds, retiring national debt, or setting up reserves. Instead, the money may become a part of the national revenue and spent with the usual carelessness. It may simply be used to reduce the current year's budget deficit. Pakistanis need to be assured by their government that privatization is a worthwhile exercise in the national interest.

84. *The Federal Budget Deficit.* The federal revenue is barely sufficient to pay for national defense and make debt service payments. A good part of

---

[135] *Pakistan Link,* Inglewood Ca., (10 November 1995), p. 14.

regular establishment costs and all counterpart funding for development schemes have to be funded through additional domestic borrowing. The rest of development expenditures are met from foreign borrowing and aid.

The national budget of Pakistan for 1993-94 indicates revenue of US$7.227 billion; debt service payments of $4.96 billion (69% of revenue); and defense spending of $3.3 billion (46% of revenue). Much of the cost of establishment (employees and routine operations) and practically all development costs have to be borrowed, at home or abroad. How Pakistan has reached this level of deficits and almost total dependence on others for development expenditures is a tale of great sadness.

Domestic Debt

Domestic debt has been rising even at a faster rate than the budget. It increased from Rp 602 billion on July 1, 1993 to Rp 800 billion on July 1, 1995. The outstanding foreign debt on the same date amounted to about $22 billion or Rp 700 million. The annual debt service of Rp 157 in 1995-96 (compared to 97 billion in 1992-93) is expected to account for more than 60% of the national budget revenue.

Together with defense expenditure of Rp 115 billion, the debt service and defense expenditures are expected to consume Rp 272 billion against total projected revenue of Rp 265. All other expenditures, e.g., establishment and admin-istrative costs of Rp 40 billion, and the development budget of Rp 96 billion will have to be funded entirely from borrowing. Given the poor prospect of collecting the projected revenue, the deficit will be probably even larger during 1995-96.[136] The situation looks even worse for the future. The government will have to borrow to finance an increasing part of defense and debt service.

85. *Temporary Measures.* In order to close the large gap between the federal government expenditure and revenue, Prime Minister Benazir Bhutto's govern-ment announced a "mini budget" on 28 October 1995. The measures included 7% devaluation of the Pakistan rupee, 7% increase in fuel prices, a temporary 10% additional levy on imports subject to duty, and a 5% tariff on industrial raw materials that were previously duty-free.

An increased level of revenue has been needed for a number of years in order to put the national budget on a sound footing. It was urgently needed

---

[136] Senator Sartaj Aziz, "State of Economy After Two Years of PPP Rule," in *Pakistan Link,* (10 November 1995), p. 6.

for obtaining of IMF endorsement of the government's economic policies which, in turn, was needed to maintain international financial confidence and to ensure sufficient loan financing for the next hydroelectric project.

On the negative side, the "mini budget" has resulted in an immediate increase in the cost of living which may lead to an annual inflation rate of over 15%. There was an immediate outcry from opposition parties and the public.

86. *Tax Exemptions.* The fiscal policy essentially continues to exempt agriculture landlords from taxation. The agriculture sector which accounts for about 27% of Pakistan GDP[137] reportedly contributed only about 2.5 million rupees ($73,000) per year in taxes. Nevertheless, neither the government nor the main opposition parties are willing aggressively to push for income tax on the agricultural sector because of the overwhelming number of feudal lords in the national and provincial assemblies. They remain largely unaffected by the national belt-tightening. [138]

As indicated in the 1993-94 Tax Payer's Directory,[139] noted landowners of the nation, including President Farooq Laghari, former Governor Nawab Akbar Bugti, former Prime Minister Balakh Sher Mazari, Chief Minister Nawab Zulfikar Magsi, former Chief Minister Muzafar Husain Shah and others, paid zero income tax. Prime Minister Benazir Bhutto paid Rp 32,647 or about $1000.

The industrial barons seem to have found a large number of loopholes too. Former Prime Minister, and successful industrialist, Nawaz Sharif paid Rp 2680, i.e., less than $100 in income tax. His brother, Shahbaz Sharif, paid Rp 897 or about $30.

The bulk of the taxes seems to be paid by salaried people who are concentrated in the urban areas of the country. Why doesn't the tax system change and become more equitable? While the leaders of the government and the opposition attack each other on all kinds of issues, they are "in full agreement on ways to rob the country."[140] Reform of the income tax for purpose of making it more equitable ought to be a high priority for all.

---

[137] The World Bank, *World Development Report 1994*, Table 3, p. 166.

[138] *Far Eastern Economic Review*, (16 November 1995), p. 38.

[139] "Politicians Misuse Their Position to Evade Taxes," in *Pakistan Link*, (10 November 1995), p. 12.

[140] An article in Urdu by Dr. Hasan Ali Shahzeb in *The Pakistan Post*, (New York, 17 November 1995), p. 3.

Dependence on Foreign Aid

All agree that dependence on foreign aid should be reduced. This does not imply closing doors to mutually beneficial assistance without undue strings. Based on past experience, Pakistan has benefitted from assistance from the multinational organizations such as the World Bank, Asian Development Bank, and other specialized agencies of the United Nations. These agencies have tried to protect their member countries from undue risks and extravagance. The conditionality of the assistance has helped to keep Pakistani leaders on the path of institutional reform and economic conservatism.

The benefits of some of the bilateral aid have been more questionable in view of tied procurement and political strings. However, even in those cases, aid from Japan and some others has been invaluable in financial terms and with relatively minor conditionality. Foreign assistance deemed to be in Pakistan's interest must obviously be continued.

Nevertheless, self-reliance must be increased. Lessons in self-reliance may be partly learned from the experience of (a) China from the 1940's through the1970's, (b) Iraq since the end of Gulf war, and (c) Iran since the revolution. It will mean hardship and lowering already low living standards. However, eventually Pakistan will emerge stronger, and will be able to deal with the rest of the world on equal terms.

Increasing Revenue

87. *Tax Reform*. There are some obvious solutions which need to be implemented. In terms of taxation, (a) the existing taxes must be collected. The high and mighty should not be allowed to escape from paying their tax as specified under law, (b) existing loopholes in tax laws must be closed, (c) tax admin-istration must be made more efficient, while the corrupt tax officials must be punished, and (d) all income must be equally taxed—including agricultural income.

88. *Agricultural Taxation*

It is He who produceth Gardens, with trellises and without, and dates, and tilth with produce of all kinds, and olives and pomegranates, similar (in kind) and different (in variety); eat of their fruit in their season, but render the dues that are proper on the day that the harvest is gathered. But waste not by excess; for Allah loveth not the wasters. (Qur'an 6:141)

Agriculture employs more than half of the labor force and accounts for one quarter of the gross domestic product (GDP). However, the agricultural sector was exempt from income tax until 1993, when a temporary levy on large landowners was introduced by the Qureshi government. Since then, the measure has received limited support from the elected government. The sector remains largely exempt. However, it is undergoing belt-tightening because of reductions in subsidies, increases in income and wealth taxes, and price increases of inputs such as electric power and diesel fuel.[141]

It may be noted that farm incomes for the poor may be experiencing a long term decline, and millions of farm jobs are in jeopardy because of stagnating agricultural output. This situation may worsen unless agricultural reforms are made. The suggested reforms include: (a) improvements in the water irrigation system, (b) educating farmers to use the latest agricultural technology, and (c) redistributing large land holdings among more farmers so that smaller and more productive farms are created.

The government is reluctant to privatize irrigation systems. Powerful agriculturists who dominate the national assembly will not permit land reform. An urgent reform of the sector is needed in order to ensure that agricultural productivity and incomes will continue to rise and that the sector will contribute its share of tax revenue.

89. *Borrowing.* In terms of borrowing, the average cost of foreign loans is about 3% per year. However, the domestic borrowing is being done at about 17% per year. While efforts must be made to reduce all debt, it is more important to reduce the domestic debt. Proceeds of the privatization process must be used to pay off domestic debt.

90. *Collected Debts.* While the government must pay its debts, it is neglecting to collect debts from its favorite citizens. The banking system has a huge bad debt portfolio. The banks are unable to recover their loans, resulting in their financial ruin. The outstanding loans must be collected.

91. *Tax Avoidance.* Customs duties account for a major part of the federal revenue. Smuggling of goods across the borders reduces the national revenue. Experience has shown that reduction of customs duties does not always reduce smuggling because the smugglers do not wish to become official importers; they wish to remain anonymous in order to avoid payment of

---

[141] "World Bank Urges Reforms", *Financial Times*, (London; 9 April 1996), p. v.

income taxes. Improved law-and-order administration would obviously increase collection of all taxes.

92. *Transit Trade.* The transit trade for neighboring landlocked Afghanistan has been significant in volume and value. Banning of this transit trade in certain products which were not needed by Afghanistan was attempted. This was meant to reduce smuggling back into Pakistan but has backfired by angering the Afghan government and Afghan traders. It has meant reduction of transit fees collected in Karachi and related income.

The smuggling itself has not stopped because the smugglers have found alternative landing facilities by air in Jalalabad in Afghanistan and a seaport at Bandar Abbas in Iran.[142] The solution again lies in stronger enforcement of all laws, regarding customs as well as income tax.

93. *Savings Schemes.* The domestic borrowing of the government includes a number of savings schemes guaranteed by the government of Pakistan. An advertisement by the Central Directorate of National Savings[143] indicated the following possibilities:
- savings account with 11% profit per annum,
- special savings certificates (bearer) 12% to 14% pa,
- special saving certificates (registered) 12.7% to 15% pa,
- regular income certificates 13.8% pa,
- mahana (monthly) amadani (income) account 20% pa on maturity,
- defense saving certificates 34.1% profit pa on maturity, and
- prize bonds.

These high interest rates mean a large payment for interest. Is this the optimum way to raise the needed money? In view of its large amount of deficit financing, the government needs to raise a large amount annually. It must compete with the private sector in the credit market. Periodic and almost continuous depreciation of the rupee, in relation to Western currencies, adds to a need for greater compensation to the savers than planned. Does Pakistan need to pay as much in interest rates as it is doing? A review is warranted.

94. *Impact of Payment of Zakat.* Payment of zakat (alms tax) is one of the most fundamental rules of Islam. It is estimated to be about 2.5 % of the

---

[142] *The Herald,* (Karachi; March, 1995), pp. 101-4.

[143] *The Herald,* (Karachi; March, 1995).

value of one's assets. It is supposed to be paid annually. Some important exemptions are allowed. Priorities for the payment in terms of recipients are also indicated with first preference being given to needy relatives.

Attend to your prayers and pay the alms tax. Whatever good you do shall be rewarded by Allah. He is watching over all your actions. (Qur'an 2:110)

They will ask you about almsgiving. Say: "Whatever you bestow in charity must go to your parents and to your kinfolks, to the orphans and to the poor man and to the wayfarer. Allah is aware of whatever good you do." (Qur'an 2:215)

. . . They ask thee how much they are to spend; say: "What is beyond your needs . . ." (Qur'an 2:219)

Data is not available about either the total value of assets of Pakistani Muslims on which zakat could be levied, or how much the zakat will amount to, if all Muslims paid their due share. However, based on 1993 data, the gross national product (GNP) of Pakistan for year 1993 amounted to USA $52,804 million equivalent. 2.5% of GNP alone would amount to about USA $ 1.32 billion. Normally, total value of accumulated assets on which zakat will be levied will be several times larger than GNP of one year alone.

It can be safely assumed that the zakat will amount to a very large amount. For comparison purposes, it may be noted that the total amount of net disbursement of all official development assistance to Pakistan in 1993 amounted to $1.065 billion.[144] The zakat amount would be certainly sufficient to provide a safety net for needy Muslims and would exceed total foreign aid received by Pakistan.

However, there are some other unresolved issues. Under the Islamic rule in effect during the days of the Prophet (PBUH), zakat was reportedly the only tax on Muslims. Today, Muslim governments already levy several taxes on their Muslim citizens, income tax, property tax, sales tax, customs duty, etc. Are the Muslim governments supposed to abolish all other taxes, and simply collect zakat? Muslims should study taxation options, including zakat, and improved arrangements for collection. An improved taxation system, and

---

[144] The World Bank, *World Development Report 1995*, (Washington, D.C.: The World Bank, 1995), Table 19, p. 198.

its efficient collection, could greatly reduce fiscal deficits, and the need for foreign aid from non-Muslims.

It may be noted that payments for community development played a very important part in strengthening Islam in the early days. The Jewish community, as well as some Muslim sects (e.g., Ismailis), have improved their lot greatly through mandated payments as well as individual generosity.

Budget Review

One way of reviewing the budget is to ask if people's priorities are reflected in it. One needs to look at the budget statement of national values, budget myths and facts, the budget process, public input in the budget process, and provincial and local government issues and concerns. Subsequently, one needs to look at allocations for each category of expense, e.g., military, international affairs, education, science and technology, agriculture, community and regional development, health, justice, central government operations, provincial government subsidies, and the interest and repayment on national debt.

In the context of policy, one needs to see what the share of each of these functions should be, and then compare it with the actual expenditures. One will be amazed at the substantive changes which are needed in the budgetary allocations.

Debt servicing and military spending are the two largest items of expenditure and they are also the most inflexible. International realities demand that debts must be serviced on time. Armed forces of Pakistan remain powerful within the government structure and insist that they need to remain strong to counter security threats from India. They demand and get their share of budget allocations.

On the revenue side, easily collected import tariffs are being reduced in line with liberalization policies. As far as income taxes, not only are the feudal lords paying little tax, but even town dwellers are continually discovering new loopholes to avoid payment. They buy a barren piece of land in the countryside and claim that their total income is exempt because it is entirely derived from the barren agricultural land. The government's next priority seems to be to broaden the sales tax and eventually introduce a value added tax. The government is also thinking about withdrawing all exemptions in exchange for lower rates of income tax which everyone will be required to pay. Recommendations from the World Bank and the IMF continue to carry weight and are generally followed.

Other Measures

95. *Gaps in Life of the People.* Millions of people in Pakistan have the basic ingredients for being successful. They have the education, desire for success, and even access to some capital. But they do not know how to put it all together to be financially successful. They need to be guided toward "the areas of demand." Someone needs to stay in touch with the marketplace to identify where the demand is, and then (a) inform the people, (b) set up advanced schools for bridging gaps between what the people have and what the market needs, (c) help in preparation of appropriate projects, and (d) help in such implementation of projects. There are current needs for:

- coaching centers for passing school and college examinations,
- centers for passing CSS (Central Superior Service) examinations for very bright students,
- placement bureaus for jobs in Pakistan (including interview skills),
- centers for gaining admission into colleges abroad and arranging financial assistance,
- centers for helping with emigration to foreign countries, and
- centers for finding employment abroad.

There is also a need for:
- courses in self-improvement, computers, real estate management, the stock market, and financial management;
- help in developing concepts for projects, preparation of feasibility studies, discussion with investors; and
- help to newcomers in planning and implementing projects; contracting; construction management; relations with lenders, government, and other interested parties; operation and maintenance of projects; and marketing of goods and services at home and abroad.

96. *Keeping Hope Alive.* There is a need for keeping the people motivated. There are too many educated people in Pakistan with postgraduate degrees, who have given up on their futures. Years of underemployment or outright unemployment and fruitlessness from many attempts to make something of themselves has led to a sense of failure and worthlessness among many educated Pakistanis. There are cases of young and highly educated people committing suicide for lack of economic opportunities. They must be shown examples of success and be made hopeful again. With some guidance in a growing economy, these people can be net contributors to the society. They should not be wasted.

Whether liked or not, the government is a powerful force in Pakistan. People look to the government for many things, including provision of the best possible and relevant education to meet the times and the needs of people. The government is very important in terms of its setting and implementing work ethics, its method of dealings with the private sector, and its determination and collection of taxes.

A government dedicated to the prosperity of its citizens must:
- be stable and reliable;
- be dedicated to solving outstanding domestic and international problems;
- ensure safety, security, and law and order on domestic and international fronts;
- follow internationally accepted laws and traditions in relation to safety of capital, be able to create and transfer money, create goodwill and good relations around the world;
- demonstrate respect for business, develop a well-trained and motivated work force, and be dedicated to making life easier for business;
- implement measures to increase productivity in all important sectors of its economy;
- establish an honest tax system while minimizing non-productive expenditures on military, corruption, etc.; and
- use taxes for improving the life of its people, with the objective of making them an effective partner in national development.

97. *Need for Simpler Procedures.* People understand the need of government to collect taxes and to maintain lawful control over the society. However, they resent wasted time, having to bribe officials, or having to seek favors from middle men simply to meet their obligations to the government. It adds insult to the injury. The need for obligatory contacts between the government and the people should be minimized to (a) registration of birth which in turn should result in issue of the national identity card for future entitlement from and obligations to the government (e.g., passports, taxes, social security payments, health and education entitlements); and (b) registration of death.

There is also a need to simplify procedures for getting things done, such as establishing a business, running it, and even closing it; and for many aspects of conducting one's own daily life. People are willing to pay the automobile tax every year but are unhappy about spending the whole day standing in lines to pay it. It should be possible to send the payment directly through the mail.

Much of the world looks at the United States as the model country in terms of democratic form of government, efficiency, technology, prosperity, freedom, and power for good around the world. Many countries around the world are trying to copy the good features. Pakistanis who live in America should enjoy the facilities, but also help develop others who are already there, and legally help bring more loved ones over. At the same time, they should help replicate all the good features of the United States in Pakistan.

98. *Export of Manpower.* A large number of Pakistanis have been going abroad largely in search of better economic life. Most succeed. They take care of their own needs as well as send money back home to support their families. Net current private transfers of money from abroad are shown below.[145]

Table 7

Year	Net Transfer Million $	Transfer as % GDP	Per Capita US $/year
1972/73	145	2.2	2.2
1982/83	3083	10.7	34.6
1992/93	2327	4.5	19.3
1993/94	2375	4.6	19.1

The export of manpower increased substantially in the early seventies as the demand for labor in the Middle East increased and the Bhutto government made obtaining passports and travel easier. The remittance per capita reached their peak in 1982-83—in terms of share of GDP, as well as inflow per capita. It is currently in decline. However, it continues to play a very important role in the economic life of Pakistan.

Millions of more Pakistanis are dreaming of going abroad. The government of Pakistan can help its citizens wanting to go abroad or already living abroad by ensuring that they have the opportunities for the best education and the required help in job searching, establishing small business, getting the needed loans and credits, and minimizing discrimination against them. Such action would enhance their opportunities and security in America, Europe, the Middle East or wherever they might be. Much of this can be done through establishment and community development sections of

[145] Source: Ministry of Finance, Pakistan. As shown in The World Bank, "Pakistan Poverty Assessment," (1995), Table 2.1.

Pakistani embassies abroad, channeling resources of Pakistanis who are already well-established abroad, and using national economic and diplomatic resources directly.

In turn, the homeland can expect to receive a share of the riches through
- direct support to relatives in Pakistan;
- investments in agriculture, commerce, and industry by the nonresident Pakistanis;
- deposit of foreign currency in Pakistani financial institutions; and
- economic and political support of well-established and well-connected people for their homeland

The relationship between the American Jewish community and Israel provides a working model.

99. *Obstacles to Prosperity.* The obstacles which must be minimized include:
- unstable government,
- lack of law and order,
- ethnic problems, and
- external threats.

The complexity of bureaucratic rules is perhaps the single most critical factor in preventing Pakistanis from becoming prosperous. Improving the processing of required permits for starting and running business for the local citizens, and obtaining visas for foreign workers can go a long way.

100. *Opportunities for Prosperity.* Pakistan's government and citizens must exploit all available opportunities. For example, the proximity to Central Asia provides opportunities in transportation routes and vehicles, contacts and agents, the supply of required labor. The country has scenery and a healthy climate which offers the development of hotels, restaurants, transportation, handicrafts, and the many benefits which accompany a tourist industry. In addition, there are the natural resources which are waiting to be exploited.

101. *Investment Counseling.* A major source of money is return on investment. If one seeks higher growth, one has to invest wisely. Creation of investment opportunities is important. Therefore, the availability of expert investment advice is often critical. There is a need for wide-scale availability of such advice. In order to be able to judge the potential risks and reward

wisely, one has to have access to and read business news, magazines, and books and be updated in investment ideas.

Financial Success of Some Countries

102. *Japan.* At the time of its surrender to General Douglas MacArthur in August 1945, and for years thereafter, Japan was a devastated country. Yet within thirty years, i.e., by 1975, it had become a highly developed country. Based on the latest data available, during 1993 Japan had a per capita income of $31,490 as compared to $24,740 for the United States.[146] Its economic miracle has been attributed to a number of factors including:

- the benevolent and wise leadership of General MacArthur ,who gave a new constitution, direction, and hope;
- military protection by the United States resulting in no defense budget for decades;
- a government dedicated to the welfare of its people and the pursuit of economic growth;
- high quality, hard working manpower with a commitment to education[147]; and
- the desire to succeed in the world marketplace through devotion to its companies and an endless zeal to improve its products.

Throughout the reconstruction and development process, Japan, for the most part, managed to protect its religion, traditions, culture, and language. None of it had to be sacrificed. Pakistan can learn lessons from Japan in terms of wise leadership, reducing defense budget, dedication to economic development, and qualities of manpower.

103. *Switzerland.* This country also enjoys some high value-added products—Rolex watches rather than cheap ones. It enjoys a scenery and healthy climate which are an attraction for tourists. Swiss banks provide great benefits to their nation: good reputation in finances, safety of deposits, large income from service fees, earnings on deposits, and unclaimed deposits in numbered accounts. At one time, the banking sector in Pakistan also had great promise. The failure of BCCI and the plundering of local banks have

---

[146] The World Bank, *World Development Report 1995,* (Oxford: Oxford University Press, 1995), Table 1, pp. 162-63.

[147] *The Washington Post,* (15 August 1995), p. A14.

hurt the prospects of this vital sector. However, banking talent remains available and can again be developed.

104. *Singapore*. During the mid-1960s, Singapore was on the brink of disaster. It had just separated from Malaysia. Britain, facing tight financial conditions, was in the process of reducing budget expenditures and had decided to reduce its military presence in Singapore significantly. This in turn meant less protection from Britain against internal disorder or external aggression; it also meant less revenue from the British treasury. Singapore was lucky to find a good sincere leader in Prime Minister Lee Kuan Yew.

Looking at his government in retrospect, it appears that he looked at all peoples of Singapore as members of his extended family. He was there to look after their long-term interests and needs. They needed tranquility at home, jobs for income and self-respect, adequate housing, and education for their children. Lee understood that and addressed those issues directly. He provided:

- a democratically elected, stable government which has continued to this day with regular elections;
- correct assessment of national strengths and weaknessses;
- focus on employment generation which increased employment opportunities for the citizens with practically full employment for the last several years;
- focus on production of goods and services in which the country and the people had a comparative advantage; they began to develop banking, insurance, and electronics from the start;
- solutions to housing problems through massive and large scale construction of flats to be made available to citizens for purchase at very reasonable rates;
- large investment in manpower development through education and on-the-job training, leading to an almost 100% literacy rate;
- cleanliness through strict fines for people who threw garbage on public property; beautification through establishment of public and private facilities;
- communal harmony for the diverse communities of Chinese, Malay Muslims, Hindus and Muslims from the subcontinent, and Westerners;
- an almost totally honest government which was unheard off in that part of the world;
- strict law and order with speedy punishment for the guilty;
- good habit of saving for the future, including compulsory savings and investment; and

- peace with all neighbors resulting in minimal defense needs while relying on Britain and others for external security; this, in turn, minimized threats of coups d'etat from the nation's armed forces.

The above policies made Singapore attractive to its citizens and made the country hospitable to foreign investors, too. They admired the political stability, law and order, trained manpower, adequate infrastructure, and good banking. Foreigners living there enjoyed excellent health, education, and travel facilities for themselves and their families. They came in hordes and have stayed on to make themselves and Singapore richer. Many governments, including Pakistan, can benefit from emulating the example of Singapore.

105. *Hong Kong* has attracted the attention of business for its open economy and relatively few rules and regulations. Its proximity and access to China have attracted everyone who wants to do business with China. Unfortunately, Pakistan has not been able to benefit fully from its proximity to the large markets in the Middle East and Central Asia.

106. *Saudi Arabia.* In earlier times, Makkah and Madinah were the only attractions Saudi Arabia held for the outside world. These holy sites attracted pilgrims from all over the world. When oil was discovered, and it became a very valuable commodity, investors and businessmen from all over the world flocked there. They were followed by contractors, managers, and workers. Some kings had to make concessions and compromises in order to preserve their thrones. The Saudi government has tried to maintain its peace and prosperity by keeping everyone happy. They have (a) shared wealth with Saudi citizens, (b) given aid to poorer Muslim countries, and (c) made transfers to their powerful military backers through bank deposits, awards of contracts, and by keeping oil prices low.

107. *Industrial Revolution.* A review of the industrial revolution indicates that it started in England in the middle of the 18th century and was successful because England had (a) a large market for manufactured goods, both at home and throughout her widespread empire, (b) skilled workers capable of inventing complex machines and operating them, (c) wealthy capitalists willing to invest large sums of money in expensive machines and factories, (d) the natural resources essential for industrialization, including coal, iron and other raw materials such as lumber, cotton and wool within her colonies plus labor at home, (e) avoided being a battleground for the many 18th-

century wars because she was an island, and (f) political unity under a competent government ready to further the interests of the middle class.[148]

Similar ingredients are needed for an industrial revolution even today. If Pakistan hopes for large-scale industrialization, it must acquire large markets through export promotion; skilled labor through education and practical training; wealthy investors, native or from abroad; natural resources, preferably from home; and avoid battles on its home ground, particularly domestic strife and external attack; and weld political unity under a competent government dedicated to advancement of the citizens.

108. *The Great Depression and Revival of America.* The great depression, which began with the stock market crash of October 1929, produced widespread economic misery. It also led to a series of fundamental reforms, notably in the role of the American government. This has helped sustain the American system to this date. Between 1929 and 1932, the great depression manifested itself in:

- a drop in stock prices—stock in many companies became virtually worthless;
- a large number of banks failing at home and abroad;
- construction activity and production of durable goods such as automobiles being reduced greatly;
- increasing unemployment (by 1932, about 25% of the total American work force was unemployed; industrial cities suffered most, e.g., Cleveland, Ohio had an unemployment rate of 50%; Akron 60%; and Toledo 80%);
- farm income declining by more than 60% (about one third of American farmers lost their land through mortgage foreclosure or eviction. Combined with drought, vast agricultural areas turned into a dust bowl. Efforts to protect farmers through controlled imports of foodstuffs from abroad failed); and
- local governments and private relief and charitable organizations being unable to cope with the suffering and needs of the people.

The relatively modest efforts of President Hoover failed to restore national confidence or the economy. On taking office in March 1933, President Roosevelt initiated measures which turned the country around. These included:

- a sense and manifestation of confidence in the people and country;

---

[148] Gordon, p. 259.

- banking reforms allowing the federal government a regulatory and monitoring role, curbing of irresponsible speculation by the banks, establishment of the Federal Deposit Insurance Corporation which guaranteed bank deposits to a certain level, overhaul of the Federal Reserve System with some control over interest rates and money supply;
- reform of the stock market through establishment of the Securities and Exchange Commission (SEC) to police the stock market and prevent fraud;
- active government support of farm prices even if it resulted in destruction of "excessive" crops and limited the areas to be cultivated;
- industrial recovery through a major program of public works designed to pump needed funds into the economy, establishing a minimum wage and maximum work week, abolishing of child labor, minimizing cutthroat competition;
- creation of the Tennessee Valley Authority (TVA) which improved five existing dams, constructed twenty new ones, and constructed an extensive system of inland water ways resulting in abundant electricity at cheap rates, reduction of floods, and improvement of agricultural productivity; and
- provision of federal relief to citizens through emergency grants, jobs through public works programs, refinancing home and land mortgages to minimize evictions and bankruptcies, and provision of funds for small business development.

The government was able to deal with each of the specific problems of the great depression. The process was not easy. There was much trial and error and criticism. Many adjustments had to be made along the way in programs and the personnel who manned them. Nevertheless, the United States emerged as a stronger world power. Pakistan has been passing through a great depression, too. It must address each of its specific problems.

109. *The Marshall Plan for the Reconstruction of Europe.* In 1947, U.S. Secretary of State Marshall extended an offer of economic assistance to all Euro-pean nations to help them recover from the destruction of World War II. Great Britain, France, Austria, Belgium Denmark, Greece, Iceland, Ireland, Italy, Luxembourg, the Netherlands, Norway, Portugal, Sweden, Switzerland, and Turkey participated in the Marshall Plan. Officially known as the European Recovery Plan (ERP), it provided foodstuffs, raw materials, and machinery. During the 1948-52 period, it promoted economic develop-

ment, raised standards of living, and contributed to about 50% increase in production. The cost was about $12.5 billion.

The Marshall Plan helped bring political stability to Europe and stopped the growth of communism in that area. As a follow-up, the U.S. urged the nations to move toward economic unity by eliminating tariffs, and establishing a uniform currency. The ideas lead to the European Coal and Steel Community, the European Common Market, and today's European Economic Union.[149]

110. *The East Asian Miracle.* The success of economic development policies in East Asia is legendary. Japan followed by Korea, Taiwan, mainland China, Singapore, Hong Kong, Thailand, and Malaysia have done extremely well. They all experienced above average growth rates in the 1970s and high rates since the 1980s. They have not followed uniform policies. Each has been impacted by their initial endowments of natural resources, human resources, and foreign aid. The presence of "visionary leadership," political stability, strong bureaucracy, and strong economic ministries has been helpful. To a varying degree, they have maintained macroeconomic stability, export drive, large investment in human resources, import openness, directed credit, industrial policies based on market signals, and a balance between privately owned and state-owned enterprise. The most common themes have been (a) macroeconomic discipline, (b) outward orientation in search of locally produced goods, (c) human resource development, and (d) a national consensus on priority for economic development.[150]

111. *Pakistan.* Pakistan itself can be an example. The leadership of Ayub, Z. A. Bhutto, Nawaz Shariff and Benazir Bhutto all contributed to move Pakistan in the right direction. Each offered policies and plans which brought progress and improvements. Their positive contributions, however, have been largely offset by compromised values, lost ideals and forgotten promises. Pakistan's leaders must again assert the highest ideals and practice complete integrity to elevate Pakistan to new heights and improve the condition of all its citizens.

---

[149] Gordon, pp. 497-500.

[150] Danny M. Leipziger and Vinod Thomas, "The Lessons of East Asia, and Overview of Country Experience", in *The World Development Report*, (Washington D.C.: The World Bank,1993).

CHAPTER 9

RELIGIOUS INTOLERANCE

As for those who divide their religion and break up into sects, thou has no part in them in the least: Their affair is with Allah: He will in the end tell them the truth of all that they did. (Qur'an 6:159)

Religion and Its Role

Based on official documents, about 97% of all Pakistanis are Muslims; 77% are Sunnis and 20% are Shias. Christians, Hindus, and other religious groups account for about 1% each.

As previously discussed, it was the recognition of two distinct groups, Hindu and Muslims, in the subcontinent that led to creation of a separate homeland for Muslims, i.e., Pakistan. The founder of the nation, Mohammad Ali Jinnah had hoped, that after its creation, Pakistan would become a secular state. In his inaugural address, he stated:

"You will find that in the course of time Hindus will cease to be Hindus and Muslims would cease to be Muslims, not in the religious sense, because that is the personal faith of each individual, but in the political sense as citizens of the State."

However, his secular vision was challenged from almost the start. Even though the Muslim majority was never deeply religious, it has been unwilling to discard religion. Under Islam, politics and religion have always been intertwined. Islam is a way of life and the Qur'an is a comprehensive guide to spiritual, ethical, social, and political life. Accordingly, Islam plays a pivotal role in Pakistan.

From the very start of the constitution writing process, the Objectives Resolution of March 1949 specified that Pakistan would be Islamic, democratic, and federal. The first constitution, adopted in 1956, proclaimed Pakistan an Islamic Republic and contained directives for the establishment of an Islamic state. The 1973 constitution contained several provisions relating to Islam. For example, Article 227 (1) states:

> All existing laws shall be brought in conformity with the Injunctions of Islam as laid down in the Holy Qur'an and Sunnah, in this Part referred to as the Injunctions of Islam, and no law shall be enacted which is repugnant to such injunctions.

In 1977, the government of Zulfiqar Ali Bhutto—who was one of the most secular leaders in the nation's history—outlawed alcohol and changed the official weekly holiday from Sunday to Friday. The Zia regime initiated a large Islamization program. Regardless of their personal inclinations, each of the subsequent governments has reaffirmed Islamic law and related constitutional provisions. In addition, whenever there is a political or security problem of any significance, leaders of the government and opposition rush to the holy city of Mecca for *'Umra* (visitation) and special prayers.

In spite of repeated reluctance of Pakistani voters to elect candidates of Islamic political parties, Islam is a basic part of the psyche of a majority of Pakistanis. While Pakistanis have allowed their political leaders to adapt secular ideas on the personal level, they remain religious and whenever secular ideas fail, the people look to Islam for solutions.

Accordingly, the solutions to Pakistan's problems as discussed in this book cannot be oblivious to Islam. While the solutions must be developed in a modern context, they must not be "repugnant" to Islam. Otherwise, the people will just not accept them. Solutions which are consistent with the complexities of current times and are fully consistent with Islamic principles have a far greater chance for success.

Differing Interpretations of Islamic Teachings

112. *Islam Means Submission to Allah.* Dedicated followers of Islam are willing and able to sacrifice all for the pleasure of Allah. The Qur'an is available to anyone who wishes to understand the message of Allah. Even though there is agreement among the scholars on the duties of a Muslim toward Allah and mankind, unity of opinion does not exist regarding many other specific points. Differing religious leaders believe their own interpretation to be the correct one. Quotes from *hadith* and the Qur'an are offered in support of conflicting opinions. Some Muslims are willing to go to extremes to achieve acceptance of their interpretation.

Many civil wars between Muslims have taken place during the centuries since the death of Prophet Muhammad (PBUH). In modern times, Muslim countries continue to disagree over their religion and over secular issues as well. Their leaders simply consider the others to be misguided; they do not hesitate to declare war against other Muslims. Military action in Bangladesh, the current massacre in Afghanistan, annual riots on the 10th day of the month of Muharram in several Muslim countries, and other conflicts continue to be justified on the basis of Islam. The essential teachings of the Qur'an regarding Muslim unity have for the most part been ignored.

If two parties of believers take up arms against each other, make peace between them. If either of them commits aggression against the other, fight against the aggressors till they submit to Allah's judgement. When they submit, make peace between them in equity and justice; Allah loves the equitable. The believers are brethren. Make peace among your brethren and for Allah, so that you may be shown mercy. (Qur'an 49:9-10)

113. *Lack of Religious Leadership*. Pakistani Muslims (particularly the Sunni majority) do not have established religious leadership. In the early days of Islam, the *khalifah* (successor to the Prophet PBUH) was the religious leader as well as the head of the government. This leadership, though only nominal at its end, terminated when Turkey was defeated in World War I. Since then, there has been no titular leader who speaks for all Muslims.

A *khalifah,* supported by a suitable organizational structure, could deal with the world powers in regards to the religious issues just as the Pope does for Catholics. If the person was respected and accepted by Muslims, he could prevent many conflicts among Muslims and clarify disputed interpretations of the religious teachings. Such a leadership is urgently needed. Attempts by religious scholars, leaders of individual countries, and the Organization of Islamic Conference have produced little results in cases of conflicts in Pakistan, Afghanistan, and Somalia and elsewhere in the Muslim world.

In the 1920s, when the office of *khalifah* was abolished, there was much protest among the Muslims. For example, Muslims of the Indian subcontinent launched a movement to restore this office. In the last several years, there has been discussion about reestablishment of the *khilafah*. The International Muslim *Khilafah* Conference, held in London in August 1994 focused on this subject. Questions about how, when, where, and who are controversial.

114. *Low Education Level of Religious Leaders.* Religious leadership is frequently left to *imams,* leaders of the local mosques, most of whom have little education. Religious leaders, particularly in rural areas where the majority of Pakistanis reside, may not even be high school graduates. Memorization of some verses from Qur'an, often without even understanding the meaning, can be sufficient qualification for becoming the *imam* of a mosque. The Friday sermons, which are the dominant means of religious communications, are often repetitive and uninspiring, focusing on rituals and dogma while neglecting the plight of the citizens.

The communication between common Pakistanis and *imams* is a one-way lecture on basic rules. The tradition of Muslims questioning the Prophet (PBUH) and his rightly-guided successors in the mosques are hardly in practice today. This is one of the main reasons given by many educated Pakistani Muslims of today for absenting themselves from the mosque and neglecting the full practice of Islam. There is urgent need for upgrading, training, and broadening the education of imams.

115. *Difficulty of Understanding Arabic.*

> **Had We sent this as a Qur'an (in a language) other than Arabic, They would have said: "Why are not its verses explained in detail? What! (a book) not in Arabic? And (a Messenger) an Arab?" Say: "It is a guide and a healing to those who believe; and for those who believe not, there is a deafness in their ears ..."** **(Qur'an 41:44)**

Based on the above, the Qur'an was revealed in Arabic partly because the Prophet (PBUH) was an Arab and was initially dealing with Arab people. Today, about three out of four Muslims are non-Arab. Some non-Arab Muslims learn Arabic. The majority of Muslims do not read or speak Arabic. For them, the Qur'an is a holy book, to be touched, recited, and listened to in a state of reverence. However, reading, understanding and, subsequently, acting on what the Qur'an teaches remains outside the reach of most believers. As a result, religious education is usually limited to instructions on commonly known duties and rituals. In other words, the fact that Qur'an and daily prayers are in the Arabic language, has prevented many non-Arab Muslims from studying Islam in depth. Mosques are often full of worshipers who do not understand what has been said in the prayers, which are always recited in Arabic.

Muslims believe that Arabic is a very rich language with multiple meanings. Accordingly the Qur'an cannot be fully translated. It has to be read in Arabic in order to be fully understood. This leaves most non-Arab Muslims with a sense of inadequacy. Turkey's attempt to hold prayers in their own language has not been well received by most Muslims.

Some have proposed compulsory study of the Arabic language while others have emphasized greater use of local languages. In any case, there is a need for making Islamic knowledge more accessible to common Muslims in Pakistan. There is an urgent need to deal with the language issue in order to ensure wider understanding of the Qur'an. As a result of *ijma* (collective thinking) and *ijtihad* (individual scholarship), Muslims may consider several options, including compulsory study of Arabic in all Muslim countries and greater use of their local languages in religious matters.

116. *Partial Practice of Islam.* The practice of Islam as a complete way of life is rare. A vast majority of professed Muslims in Pakistan ignore many practices. "Traditionalists " have largely restricted Islam to the rituals of prayers, fasting, and pilgrimage. "Modern Muslims " who are motivated to increase human rights and welfare de-emphasize the "rituals" and focus on general conduct in day-to-day life only. The traditionalists and the modern Muslims look at each other with some contempt; each feeling a sense of superiority over the other.

Increasing Religious Tolerance

117. *Non-Muslim Minorities.* The historic evidence shows that Muslims have generally been tolerant of the non-Muslim minorities within their boundaries. For example, Jews lived under Muslim protection for years after being expelled from Spain in the sixteenth century. Nevertheless, non-Muslims have often com-plained of feeling as second class citizens. Accordingly, they are the most vocal proponents of secular governments in Muslim-majority countries.

In Lebanon, non-Muslims maintained their identity and continued in power by constitutionally dividing the Muslims into two groups (Sunnis and Shiahs) with the help of the French colonial masters. Subsequently, they used military power and an alliance with Israel to avoid Muslim rule.

What can be done to build confidence and protect the interests of minorities within Muslim countries deserves further study. Nevertheless, the current laws relating to religious minorities in Pakistan need to be reassessed. For example, many, including representatives of international organizations, believe that the death sentence under the blasphemy laws of Pakistan is disproportionate and excessive.

118. *The Case of Gul Masih*. Gul Masih, a 41-year-old Christian was arrested in December, 1991 for blasphemy against Prophet Muhammad (PBUH). The presiding judge disregarded a long history of personal enmity and political rivalry between the families of the complainant and the accused. In addition, two of the three eye witnesses refused to implicate the accused. The accused was convicted in November, 1992 on the basis of the sole testimony of the complainant. The penalty under Section 295-C PPC is death.

An appeal was lodged before the Lahore High Court. "The High Court observed in its ruling that it was not prepared to accept the plea of the complainant that Gul Masih continued committing blasphemy against the Holy Prophet (PBUH) for an hour and a half with no public reaction till the first information report (FIR) was lodged two days later when the complainant approached the superintendent police of Sargodha."[151]

The court set aside the conviction and the sentence and Gul Masih was acquitted. He immediately went into hiding for fear of reprisals at the hands of an enraged religious community which strongly protested his acquittal. It may be a long time before Gul Masih can really be free.

119. *Forced Conversions?* There are periodic reports of forced conversion, particularly of young Hindu girls. For example, *DAWN*, of 7 May 1995, Lahore headlined: "Landlord Blamed for Abducting Girl." It related how a 14-year-old Hindu girl disappeared while male members of her family were sent to the fields by the landlord. *The Muslim*, dated 14 May 1995, Islamabad headlined: "Hindu Girl Embraces Islam." The story related to the same girl. She was produced before a civil court and stated that she had freely embraced Islam and married a Muslim. The newspaper reported that her Hindu parents and a large number of relatives had gathered to catch a glance of the girl. They were "wailing and lamenting the authorities for their oppression . . . There were moving scenes of parental affection and depravity mixed with humility and helplessness before feudal power . . . ."

This was not an isolated incident. Based on other similar stories, this sort of event carries a number of possible messages: a teenage girl is kidnapped, sexually molested by some important person, forcibly married to a servant or someone else as a cover, forced to change her religion, separated from her parents and family for the rest of her life, and condemned to a life of illicit

---

[151] *The Newsline*, (December, 1994), p. 51.

sex and even prostitution. If genuine religious conversion is the objective, there are better ways of achieving the objective as detailed in Islamic history.

Sunni-Shiite Conflict.

Be not like those who are divided amongst themselves and fall into disputations after receiving clear signs: For them is a dreadful penalty. (Qur'an 3:105)

But people have cut off their affair (of unity), between them, into sects; each party rejoices in that which is with itself. But leave them in their confused ignorance for a time. (Qur'an 23:53-54)

120. *Sectarian Violence.* The Sunni-Shiite disagreement is centuries old. In Punjab, the cities of Jhang and Shorkot where Sunnis and Shiahs had co-existed for centuries, have become centers of sectarian violence. Traditional scholarly *munaziras* (religious debates) have been replaced by death and destruction. More than a hundred Muslims of different sects have been killed during the last few years. Each community has declared their opponents to be *kafirs,* disbelievers. Sunnis and Shiites are reluctant to walk into each other's neighborhoods for fear of being shot.

The traditional emphasis of the religious leaders on the unity of Allah, the prophethood of Muhammad (PBUH), prayer, pilgrimage, and alms-giving have taken a back seat. Many are focusing on love for *sahaba* (companions of the Prophet) and hatred for those "who do not love them," namely Shiites. The strong feeling on this point has focused on writings of extremist writers and speakers within both Shiites, who abuse the *sahaba*, and Sunnis, who malign Imam Hussain's (hero of the Shiah) historic struggle.

It has resulted in sectarian war which (a) identifies each person as either a Sunni or Shiah; (b) has separated and scares the community; (c) has led to labeling of each other as *kafir* and, therefore, promises heaven to the one who kills the opponent; (d) started a boom in construction of sectarian mosques with their names clearly identifying their affiliation; (e) initiated an economic boycott of each other; (f) has led to the purchase of arms on both sides and the shooting of partisans outside and inside the mosques; and (h) is claiming lives each day. The violent struggle which has its roots in events which took place 1,400 years ago, and which cannot be changed today in any case, has repelled many away from the religion and its leaders.

Maulana Azim Tariq, Chief of Sipah-e-Sahaba (SSP), feels that the problem lies with Shiites who openly curse the *sahaba* and the wives of the

Prophet (PBUH) especially. He told *Newsline* (September 1994, pages 28-29) that there are more than 300 books written by Shiahs which contain insults of the *sahaba*. He claims that some of those books are printed at the official press of Iran and some were written by Imam Khomeini himself. The Maulana feels that Shiite leaders should have disowned these books but they have not. He has argued that while there is a law protecting the honor of national poet and philosopher Allama Iqbal and founding father Qaid-e-Azam, there is none for the *sahaba*, the companions of Prophet Muhammad (PBUH). He feels that enactment of such a law would ensure *namoos-e-sahaba* and therefore prohibit offensive books and statements, removing the main cause for the Sunni-Shiite violence.

The brotherly relations between Pakistan and Iran have already suffered. Iran has taken serious note of the murder of an Iranian diplomat, the burning of the Iranian flag and photos of Imam Khomeini, and the denigration of Imam Mahdi. The Iranian Parliament has already warned Pakistan. [152] There is an urgent need for dialogue and mutual understanding.

Limited Role of Women

The believers, men and women, are protectors, one of another: they enjoin what is just, and forbid what is evil ... (Qur'an 9:71)

In spite of Islamic injunctions to treat women as equal partners, discussion about the restricted role of women under Islam continues in Pakistan and elsewhere in the Islamic Nation. There have been various attempts at social and legal reforms aimed at improving women's lives in Pakistan. The Muslim Personal Law of Sharia in 1948 recognized a woman's right to inherit all forms of property. The 1961 Muslim Family Law Ordinance covers marriage and divorce and is widely regarded as empowering women. However, women feared a backward movement and therefore protested against the 1979 Enforcement of Hudood Ordinances, which failed to distinguish between adultery and rape adequately.

A number of diverse groups such as the All Pakistan Women's Association, Women's Action Forum, the Pakistan Women Lawyer's Association, and the Business and Professional Women's Association are working hard to address special issues faced by women. Nevertheless, Pakistani women face four important challenges: increasing literacy, gaining access to employment

---

[152] Interview with Allama Sajid Naqvi, Chief Tehrik-e-Jafria Pakistan, *The Newsline* (September, 1994), p. 30.

opportunities at all levels in the economy, promoting change in the perception of women's roles and status, and gaining a public voice both within and outside of the political process.[153] Much has been expected from Prime Minister Benazir Bhutto who has experienced first hand many of the problems faced by Pakistani women and has managed to overcome enormous odds in achieving political power.

There is an urgent need for greater empowerment of women in Pakistan. Their political struggle will undoubtedly continue. However, in order for a permanent change to occur, "it must be based on a definitive interpretation of what the Qur'an and Hadith command regarding women. Islamic scholars need to discuss the issue with all interested parties (historians, sociologists, representatives of women, etc.); they must reach a consensus and adopt it."[154]

Role of Government

121. *Who is responsible?* Some blame Z. A. Bhutto government for yielding to the street power of *mullahs* by catering to their demands in declaring one minority sect, the Ahmadiyya, as non-Muslim. Others blame the Zia government for greatly enlarging the position and power of the *mullahs* by rewarding them for their struggle against Bhutto. Zia gave them high-level official positions and granted concessions: cabinet assignments, support for *deeni madrassahs* (religious schools), treatment of *madrassah* graduates at par with university graduates, allotment of thousands of jobs within the bureaucracy, establishment of the *Zakat* fund with mullahs holding control over finances.

The revolution in Iran resulted in much support for the Shiite clergy everywhere, including Pakistan. Saudi Arabian money has supported the Sunni clergy. The Afghan war has provided training and weapons to both sides. Enemies of Pakistan and of Islam have exacerbated the conflict to keep Pakistanis and Muslims occupied with internal conflict.

The primary blame for the violence must go to those who perpetrate it. Some argue that the secular governments and their intelligence agencies are encouraging the violence in order to discredit religious parties, and to keep citizens divided. Some feel that there is an Indian government and even Western hands in it. India gains from it because of the violence and disharmony in an "enemy state." It sours relations between Pakistan and Iran which has been one of the main supporters of Pakistan on the Kashmir issue.

---

[153] Blood, pp. 120-24.

[154] Memon, p. 50.

The West gains by reducing the positive impact of the Iranian revolution, by dividing Sunnis and Shiahs and sowing seeds of mistrust between Pakistan and Iran. Others see the hand of some domestic intelligence agencies who may do it for the purpose of undermining the civilian government. The general view prevailing is that Saudi Arabia and Iran are supporting Sunnis and Shiites respectively.

Much more trouble may be forthcoming as the sectarian differences grow. The SSP is reportedly building a large training center for its cadre in Baloachistan, only 50 miles from the Iran border. It may lead to a direct confrontation. On the other hand, following their disagreement with Jamat Islami over the Gulf war, Saudis have reportedly shifted their support to the Ahl-e-Hadith group. There have been some incidents of violence between Sunni sects. The government, supporters of a united Muslim nation, and the public are either too weak or unwilling to confront the sectarian forces and their foreign sponsors.

122. *Action by Government Needed.* The government of the day cannot stay aloof from religious issues, even if it claims to be a secular one. Religion is a very important part of the life of Pakistani citizens. Even the secular Muslims wish to ensure that their children receive some sound Islamic education and eventually turn out to be good human beings. In view of the problems experienced to date, the government cannot afford to leave spiritual elements in the life of its citizens entirely in the hands of clergy. A Ministry of Religious Affairs already exists. The staff, budget, powers, and influence of this Ministry must be utilized to ensure that:

- there is no compulsion in religion and that citizens are free to choose the religion or sect of their choice;
- current controversies relating to religion are resolved in an orderly manner, and facilities must be provided for conflict resolution;
- facilities must be provided for sound education and training of imams and religious scholars;
- teaching of Arabic on a wider scale must be incorporated in the educational curriculum to facilitate understanding of the Qur'an and Traditions among the masses; and
- required protection and facilities must be provided for religious minorities.

123. *Sunni-Shiite Leadership Cooperation in Karachi.* Following a string of murderous attacks and counterattacks on each other's mosques in Karachi during the holy month of Ramadan in 1995, the Sunni and Shiite violence

could have accelerated. However, both Sunni and Shiite religious leaders came to the conclusion that someone else was causing the violence and trying to start a religious war. They publicly absolved the followers of each other and thus stopped the violence from spreading. It was cooperation in the true sense of Islamic teachings. It has saved lives and stopped further attacks, at least for now. Such cooperation must be encouraged.

124. *Milli Yakjehti (Unity) Council.* The religious violence in Karachi and elsewhere led to the arrest of many religious fanatics and to restrictions on some religious schools. Western governments applauded the action. Even some external supporters of the religious groups did not object. This led to a realization that it was time for the religious groups to put their house in order. As a result, an alliance of all major and many minor groups was formed, the Milli Yakjehti Council. It had three basic objectives: the end of sectarianism in the country; improvement of the law and order situation, and revival of the positive image of the religious parties. The result was a relatively peaceful Muharram in 1995. [155]

Based on the success of such cooperation, the alliance has been encouraged and is showing political and electoral ambitions. The lukewarm support of Pakistanis to its call for a general strike in early 1996 in Karachi is leading to some reassessment. Given alliances of individual religious groups with different political parties, a unity of political purpose is difficult to envisage. However, there have been other occasions in which the leaders have found ways to reach agreement on critical issues.

As far back as the early days of independence, it was frequently argued that there were so many sects among Muslims that it was hard to prepare an Islamic constitution which would be acceptable to all religious leaders *(Ulama)*. In response to such an argument, a meeting of *Ulama* representing all schools of thought was convened in Karachi from 21-24 January 1952 under the leadership of Syed Suleyman Nadvi in which "they agreed upon the twenty-two funda-mental principles of an Islamic State."[156] If a similar spirit can be demonstrated, and if leaders of the various religious sects can agree on fundamental points of day-to-day concern to all Muslims, the population will certainly reward them with support.

---

[155] *The Herald,* (Karachi; June, 1995), pp. 48-50.

[156] Sarwat Saulat, *Maulana Maududi* (Karachi: International Islamic Publishers, 1979), p. 41.

125. *The Malakand Uprising.* When two civilian judges arrived to hold a camp court in Malakand subdivision, the local religious leaders saw it as an extension of the civil law in the Provincial Tribal Area (PATA). The religious leaders, organized under the Tanzim Nifaz Shariat-e-Mohammadi (TNSM), wanted the rule of Qur'an rather than the civil law.

The religious leaders sent out calls to the faithful to resist. They responded in force. With the support of other anti-government groups, they were able to obtain Soviet made heavy guns, rocket-launchers, Kalashinkov submachine guns, and other weapons. They blocked roads, dug trenches, and took hostages. They occupied Saidu Sharif airport, police stations, and several government buildings. People were killed and injured on both sides.

The government accepted the main demand and agreed to use Qur'anic law in the region. It convinced the TNSM chief to tour the area in military helicopters and government transport to convince his followers to stop the insurrection and go back home. Most of them did. Those who did not (particularly in Bajaur) paid a heavy price. The government forces demolished and burned the houses of defiant TNSM leaders. Following the tribal custom of collective punishment, whole villages were punished. People were rounded up for interrogation, their houses were searched and weapons were confiscated. Eventually heavy fines were levied against some.

Malakand's holy war provided many lessons. It showed that:

- many people have become disenchanted with the current corrupt system of government. Many favor introduction of Qur'anic laws;
- the state's ability to decide and impose its will can be successfully challenged;
- it is possible for all anti-government elements to cooperate even if the cause is not of common interest; in this case drug barons joined hands with and supplied arms to TNSM;
- sophisticated heavy weapons are easily available; Afghan *mujahideen* and retired army officials are available to provide training in their use;
- regular civilian authority, including the police and the judiciary melted in front of the insurgents;
- it took acceptance of demands and the cooperation of the TNSM leader to restore law and order;
- acceptance of Islamic (*Shari'ah*) laws in Malakand through the use of force by TNSM is likely to encourage Islamists in other parts of the country to seek the same through the same unconstitutional means; more acts of a militant nature in favor of Islamic law can be expected in Punjab and other parts of the country;

- Shiite groups did not support the holy war in Malakand and will resist similar demands elsewhere; it is likely to lead to increased tension between Sunnis and Shiites;
- the division between secularists and Islamists is real; the secularists are afraid of the increasing power of Islamists and want the government to become firm in dealing with them;
- journalists have been threatened by both Sunni and Shiite groups and are mortally afraid to annoy either one;
- opposition groups seeking other types of changes are likely to feel confident about gaining concessions through force; and
- it is questionable whether members of the armed forces would be willing to use serious force against their own kith and kin in the frontier province on a sustained basis, as they have done in Sindh Province.

The Solution

Solutions to the problems of religious intolerance discussed above include:

- return to the basic tenants of Islam namely, unity of Allah, prophethood of Muhammad (PBUH), prayer, *Hajj, Zakat,* belief in the Day of Judgment, and moral and just living;
- firm action at local, national and international level to prevent future violence;
- withdrawal of official patronage to all sectarian organizations;
- stopping of any instigation of discord among people by government agencies based on religious differences;
- stating clearly to Iran, Saudi Arabia, and other interested countries that their patronage of different sects is un welcome and will not be tolerated;
- critically reviewing transfer of funds from abroad to sectarian organizations;
- the government has to find ways to ensure that religious beliefs are protected by each side, e.g., give public recognition and reward for dialogue among the religious leaders as tried in Karachi; actively promote communal harmony; and publicize instances and events of mutual cooperation;
- strict punishment should be given to those convicted of crimes regardless of the sect involved; and
- finding appropriate legal action against extremist organizations and individuals who are fanning sectarian fires is needed.

CHAPTER 10

POWERLESS PEOPLE

No matter who comes to power, they are not going to favor us. Once they come to power they kick us around. They think they are everything and we are nothing. (A voter).

An Alien System

126. *British Influence.* Pakistan inherited the British form of parliamentary democracy. People are surprised that it has not worked equally well in Pakistan. Others have argued that Pakistan did not inherit pure British democracy but one made by Britain for its colonies. The former was meant for the welfare of the British citizens while the later was meant for implementing its "imperial purpose." On top of this, critics assert that powerful interest groups in Pakistan have tried their best to twist and turn democracy for their own benefit.

> The electoral process was controlled and manipulated by the officials. The people were exposed for the first time to political harangues, bribes, and threats, all intended to secure their support in elections. Every local rift, sectarian difference and family dispute was exploited by the candidates to advance their prospects. There was corruption at every step, from the recording of names in the electoral rolls to the counting of votes. Forgery, impersonation, and casting of bogus votes were all part of the game. Politics soon became a profession of skill and strategy and only losers talked of principles and programs. [157]

127. *Undemocratic Concentration of Power.* The consensus heard in discussions with politicians, bureaucrats, journalists, businessmen, and with common people is that there exists a group of "elders" and king makers who control the political process. They include a few current and retired high

---

[157]Altaf Gauhar, *Ayub Khan* (Lahore, 1993), pp. 83-84.

officials of the civilian government and the armed forces. They instigate major changes. At the top, there is the army chief, the president, and prime minister. They make all the policy decisions. The day-to-day army related matters are left to the army itself. The day to day civilian matters are in the hands of the Prime Minister.

The chief ministers of the respective provinces are responsible for running the provinces, but someone from the central government keeps close watch over each province. Under Prime Minister Benazir Bhutto, her husband Asif Zardari is supposed to watch over Sindh and reportedly makes all major decisions. It is also reported that all key decisions (e.g., relating to appointments and expenditure) are made at the top, by local officials. Government ministers and top bureaucrats often complain that they have no real authority.

Whether such centralized power exists or is only the perception of outsiders needs to be clarified. It is not possible effectively to garner the confidence of the people when suspicions persist that the government is run by an elite group and not by the elected officials.

Decentralization

128. *Need for Decentralization.* Whatever limited resources are available to Muslim countries, they generally are controlled by the central governments. Pakistan is no exception. Given widespread non-representative governments, even under the appearance of "democratically elected governments," the national resources are often concentrated in the hands of a few people resulting in the poor distribution of resources.

An effective way of dealing with this problem is decentralization. This means exercising authority and responsibility at as low a level of government as possible. The people at village, municipal, district, division, and provincial levels believe that they best understand their own problems. If allowed by the overly centralized governments to do so, they can find the solutions.

Under such an arrangement, provision of local services such as water supply, sanitation, local transport, area development, etc., is left in local government hands. Some political parties, proponents of decentralization, have gone as far as limiting the central government powers to defense, foreign affairs, and currency.

The poor in urban and rural areas often wish to increase economic opportunities for themselves. They wish to have power over essential aspects of local government in order to accomplish this. They seek to:

- expel all non-local people, reserve employment opportunities for local citizens, and introduce a system of work permits for the exceptional cases of non-local workers;
- give high priority to provision of basic nutrition, clothing, shelter, health, and justice to local citizens at as low cost as possible;
- actively promote the local language and culture;
- curb special rights and privileges enjoyed by a few local citizens unfairly received for services rendered to the colonial masters or local dictators;
- provide technical assistance and credits to local citizens in order to enable them to become entrepreneurs;
- reform the educational system with the aim of reaching full literacy and employment;
- collect and keep all taxes locally and pay only the budgeted amounts for agreed functions of the central government; and
- control local law and order with assistance from the local police or militia.

Many Pakistani Muslims would object to reservation of opportunities to local citizens to the exclusion of Muslims from abroad. Under the concept of one Muslim ummah, the door to all opportunities has to be open to all Muslims. In this case particular reference is made to Muslims of India, Bangladesh, Nepal, Burma, Afghanistan, etc., who wish to have open doors for migration to Pakistan.

This argument sounds very convincing at first glance. However, given the limited resources of the country, including poor education and high unemploy-ment, the weaker, poorer, and relatively disadvantaged locals have been left further behind as a result of the open door policy. Free competition among equals is healthy and produces good results. However, free license to the strong to exploit the weak in the name of competition cannot be Islamic.

Some regulation is essential. Fear of being ruled by the Hindus who had become relatively more advanced was one of the main reasons why Muslims demanded and obtained partition of the Indian subcontinent. If people are allowed to develop and prosper in their own area, the chances for exploita-tion will be reduced.

Full decentralization will solve many of the current problems facing Pakistan, but not all. For example, on the financial side, it would badly hurt less developed areas including rural areas of all the provinces which do not make significant contribution to the national treasury. Currently the national treasury collects almost all of its revenue from customs duties, excise taxes, and income taxes. It spends a significant chunk on centralized activities such as the military, debt service, and the federal bureaucracy. It passes the rest to each province largely based on population. Hardly any of the revenue is generated in rural areas because most agricultural income is exempt from income tax.

Based on financial decentralization, NWFP wants revenue from hydro power. Baloachistan wants revenue from exploitation of its gas reserves. Karachi wants revenue from customs duties collected from seaports and airports, local industry, commerce, and income tax. If their demands are fully accepted and they are simply invited to make a contribution for agreed federal government expenditure, there would be little for development of the weaker areas where most of the population lives. Of course, the less developed areas have to begin to generate their own revenue through taxation on agriculture and small business. However, in the meantime, some equitable sharing of the national revenue has to continue. By the way, the hydro schemes, gas fields, seaports, airports, and industries which currently generate revenue have been funded by the overall national treasury.

Decentralization and the best division of powers among central, provincial, and local governments require considerable compromise. Each government must determine the optimal arrangement for itself. However, there is merit in the concept of decentralization and it should be seriously considered by Pakistan.

Constitutional Provisions

129. *Proportional Representation.* Some have argued that elections based on a national list rather than on individual constituencies will help reform the electoral process. Under such a system, the political parties would receive proportional representation based on the total number of votes received nationally. Election of a particular candidate would not be dependent on local feudal lords and therefore the party would be able to offer candidates on the basis of merit. Similarly, each party, as well as the national electorate, would be able to take a broad view of the national priorities. It could lead to better formulated and focused party platforms and voting for a better quality of candidates.

On the other hand, people argue that (a) local citizens would not be able to identify their local representative and therefore make them responsible for local development and other specific activities; (b) the process would put too much power in the hands of party leadership which can deny nomination to locally popular candidates; and (c) overall power would shift to areas of population concentration (e.g., even greater focus on Punjab, which has the largest population among the provinces, at the expense and neglect of Baloachistan) and urban areas where traditionally larger number of voters turn out to vote; rural areas would therefore suffer.

To some extent, the current system of direct elections for the national assembly and indirect polls for the senate can provide the balance. However, it has not worked effectively. Since the feudal lords constitute a majority of the electoral college for the senate (members of the provincial and national assemblies), and also control leadership positions in most parties, they have managed to bring a majority of feudal lords into the senate, too.

At least one political party has demanded that elections for a minimum of 50% of the national assembly seats should be on the basis of a national list. The other 50% can be elected on the basis of individual constituencies. The idea deserves serious consideration. Turkey and Israel already use the model. Their experience should be studied in the context of Pakistani conditions. There is a need to find ways to improve the quality of the elected representatives.

130. *Make Politics Affordable.* The cost of elections is very high. In order to get a desirable party ticket, the candidate must demonstrate an ability to win. There must be a vote bank and money. The vote bank comes about through years of work by someone, either the party or the candidate and his family. To keep a large group of people happy over a long period of time costs money. Money is also needed for cultivating the party leadership, nomination fees to the party, campaigning, and "buying" support of a sufficient number of elected representatives to form a government. Ways must be found to reduce the cost at each step in order to attract qualified candidates.

131. *Campaign Cost.* The election campaign costs include transportation (vehicles, fuel), food, and general expenses for the candidate, VIPs visiting the constituency, and campaign workers. These are incurred during months of campaigning. Advertisement and publicity are a relatively smaller cost. While exact data is not available, the average successful candidate for the national assembly spends approximately one crore rupee or about $300,000. The provincial assembly candidates spend 50% to 70% of this amount. It is a huge sum for a poor country where the average citizen has per capita income of only $430 per year. As mentioned earlier, a way must be found to reduce the cost of elections and the financial burden on the candidates themselves.

Politicians have come to realize that they need to raise and save money during their tenure in power in order to get ready for the next elections. This is often accomplished through illegal means. They feel that they have no choice. Since other politicians, bureaucrats, and even the military have come to the same conclusions, nobody is really eager to stop it.

132. *Fund Raising.* Pakistan does not have a tradition of fund raising on an individual basis. Most candidates would consider it demeaning to ask for campaign contributions. Candidates must have their own money. As a result, only the very rich can think about becoming a candidate.

Most candidates end up incurring large debts. After the elections, successful candidates cannot expect to recover election costs from honest remuneration. Even though salary, allowances, and benefits for members of Punjab and Sindh assemblies have been substantially increased recently, many believe that they are still inadequate.[158] They amount to a few hundred dollars per month, barely sufficient to cover even day-to-day expenses. The salary for fortunate members of the assemblies who become ministers amounts to a few more hundred dollars per month. Most successful candidates, however, turn to bribery to repay past election debts, save money for the next campaign, and meet living costs.

133. *Public Financing.* The government and people of Pakistan should consider other forms of financing for election campaigns. In the United States, taxpayers allow the government to pay for a part of the election campaigns. Individual citizens, political action groups, and corporations contribute the rest of election expenses. The solution may lie either in direct contributions by the people as practiced in the United States or full financing through tax revenue.

Immunity

134. *Reduction of Excessive Immunity to Public Officials.* Under British colonial rule, Section 306 of the Government of India Act of 1935 stated:

(1) No proceedings whatsoever shall lie in, and no process whatsoever shall issue from, any court in India against the Governor General, against the Governor of a province, or against the Secretary

---

[158] "Salaries of Sindh CM, MPAs Raised," in *The Frontier Post*, (Lahore; 26 March 1995).

of State, whether in a personal capacity or otherwise and, except with the sanction of His Majesty in Council, no proceedings whatsoever shall lie in any court in India against any person who has been the Governor General, the Governor of any province, or the Secretary of State in respect of anything done or committed to be done by any of them during his term in office in performance or purported performance of the duties . . .

The modern elected officials of Pakistan want nothing less than what the British master employed. Article 248 of the Constitution of the Islamic Republic of Pakistan, 1973, has even extended the protection to a larger number of persons. It states:

(1) The President, a Governor, the Prime Minister, a Federal Minister, a Minister of State, the Chief Minister and a Provincial Minister shall not be answerable to any court for the exercise of powers and performance of functions of their respective offices or for any other act done or purported to be done in the exercise of these powers and performance of these functions . . .

During the subsequent period of military rule, similar blanket amnesty was granted to a large number of military personnel. This has put the rulers above the law. No wonder that Pakistan's elected officials (and military officials during martial law) become so corrupt. Once they are in office, they cannot be punished for breaking the law. They use their powers to the full extent for personal benefit, fully realizing that they cannot be legally touched. Even the opposition party keeps quiet. They recognize that when their turn comes, they will be able to use the same laws for their own benefit.

Muslim governments in particular should review and modify the laws relating to blanket amnesty provided to officials in order to minimize corruption. Provision of amnesty should be minimized while ensuring efficient operation of government. The concept has been elaborated by Abdul Fatah Memon in an unpublished note on *Protection of High Executives in Pakistan*.

135. *In Summary.* The people of Pakistan feel powerless. They have little ability to reward or punish their representatives on the basis of performance. There are many reasons for this:
- lack of trust in leaders, because many of them are perceived by citizens to lack honesty, competence, vision, ability to inspire, and genuine commitment to the welfare of the citizens;

- lack of a sense of participation in government;
- immunity provided to the rulers under the law;
- a relatively less developed state of the local press which limits honesty in reporting; and
- international communications such as television and the Internet allow citizens to see vast changes in the economic status of their leaders and others, but little real change in their own lives.

In order to restore power to the citizenry, there is a need for:
- minimizing concentration of power and maximizing decentralization;
- amending the constitution and relevant laws to give meaningful options to the people during elections;
- reducing excessive immunity to public officials; and
- making reelection difficult for representatives who fail to keep their promises to the electorate.

CHAPTER 11

LAW AND ORDER

Do not mischief on the earth, after it hath been set in order, but call on Him with fear and longing . . . (Qur'an 7:56).

. . . for persecution is worse than slaughter . . . (Qur'an 2:191)

Breakdown of Law and Order

136. *Violence.* Incidents of violence in Pakistan are occurring in record numbers. In Karachi, more than 400 persons were murdered in cold blood during 1994. The number increased to 2,100 in 1995. Bombs are exploding frequently in major cities of Punjab. There are murders and other violent crimes related to property, passions, and personal issues occurring all over the country. In addition, based on press reports, there are political and religious murders relating to (a) ethnic and linguistic differences; (b) sectarian differences among Muslims; (c) religious differences between Muslims, Hindus, and Christians; and (d) political differences among the followers of different parties. The press and the government have pointed to foreign involvement.

And remember We took your covenant (to this effect): shed no blood amongst you, nor turn out your own people from your homes: and this ye solemnly ratified. (Qur'an 2:84)

. . . And make not your own hands contribute to your destruction . . . (Qur'an 2:195)

137. *Extortion.* Extortion of money (*bhatta*) from shopkeepers and industrialists has reached new heights, particularly in Karachi. In previous times, some business people paid some money to a powerful group or police in return for protection. Now powerful groups, often associated with political parties, demand large sums of money from businessmen, threatening them with death and the burning down of their businesses if they refuse.

The Herald magazine of March 1995 reported that criminals with political patronage were demanding and receiving significant amounts of money. Shop-keepers at the Nazimabad market in Karachi were asked to pay Rp 1.6 million. Hyderi market owners were asked to pay one million. Tariq Road shopkeepers were asked to pay five million. The shopkeepers hold meetings, go to the authorities, and negotiate with the extortionists. In the end, they end up paying. Some who have refused have been promptly and severely punished.

138. *Kidnapping.* Kidnapping at gun point is not new. However, the numbers are reaching new highs. Businessmen, professional doctors and engineers, government officials and their children, foreigner—no one is safe. Everyone has to pay. Even the governments of the day have to negotiate and eventually pay in order to get "VIPs" released.

139. *Robberies.* Robbery has become a common occurrence. During earlier times, the robbers came in the dark of the night, quickly committed their crime and hurried away. Now they come openly in daylight., stay for hours, even have a meal, collect the loot in a leisurely manner, and drive away in full sight of neighbors and others who care to watch. Often, they stop the targeted person's car on the road, ride with him to his house, collect whatever they wish to, and then drive away. No one has the courage to face the guns. People have lost faith in the police. The robberies continue to increase.

Causes of Violence

As for those who divide their religion and break up into sects, you have no part in them in the least: Their affair is with God: He will in the end tell them the truth of all that they did. (Qur'an 6:159)

140. *Divided People.* Muslims of today are generally a divided people. They are divided in terms of national origin, ethnic origin, religious sect, language, race, and economic condition. Muslims do not hesitate to fight among themselves or question each others' "true faith" on the basis of any of these factors. Pakistani Muslims are no different.

At the time of independence, "expectations were high that Pakistan would flourish and that its citizens would be unified by their sense of social contract . . . The failure to forge a widely understood social contract is reflected in increased tensions among ethnic groups, social classes, extended families, and religious factions."[159]

Ethnic Warfare

Recently completed research shows that, in the last decade, there have been thirty-four conflicts around the world based on linguistic differences. Twenty-three of them had been supported by various leaders to advance their political objectives. People should be careful about leaders who blame others for their miseries.

Ethnic problems are not new in Pakistan and have been around in different forms for a long time. Former princely states, including Bahawalpur, were not happy to become an integral part of Pakistan. Many Pathans of the Frontier Province have sought provincial autonomy and closer alliance with Afghanistan. Tribal areas have always been restive. Baloachistan has been tamed with periodic shows of force by the central government. Some nationalist groups in Sindh have demanded the right of self-determination.

The largest ethnic warfare in Pakistan, of course, occurred in East Pakistan. The civil war in Pakistan resulted in brutal action by the Pakistani army against East Pakistan. After India's intervention, Muslim fought with Hindus against Muslims. More than 90,000 Pakistani soldiers were captured. Eventually, the Islamic Republic of Pakistan was divided into two separate Muslim countries. Some suggest the cause to be a "feeling of superiority among the martial ethnic group" of West Pakistan. The leadership in Bangladesh has publicly accused their Muslim brethren in the Pakistani armed forces of having committed a large number of rapes.

Ethnic strife in what remained of Pakistan continued after the civil war, based on differences in language, religious views, culture, and "degree of education." There has been ethnic violence between Mohajirs and Sindhis and between Mohajirs and Pathans. The Sunni-Shiite violence also continues. Successive governments have chosen to use the army in Sindh and Baloachistan provinces, at great expense in money and loss of good will by local people. They have failed to solve genuine local grievances.

Many people believe that cultural differences among the Muslims are quite significant and cannot be overcome. Arab Muslims, South Asian Muslims, African Muslims, and European Muslims are all very different from each other. To refute the reports or deny the differences would be folly. The differences need to be recognized. The economic standard of living,

---

[159] Blood, pp. 142-45.

including standards of cleanliness, degree of flexibility and tolerance in spiritual practice, and degree of political freedoms, are some of the factors which make the cultural composite. Some ways will have to be found to accept and minimize the differences.

141. *Kalashinkov Culture.* [160] The Kalashinkov Culture is named after AK-47 and similar rifles that were used to oust the Soviet army from neighboring Afghanistan. The war ended in 1989, but the guns continue to enter Pakistan. Initially, the Mujaheddin (Islamic warriors) captured the weapons from the Soviet troops or received them from supplies provided by the Americans and the Saudis. Since then, Afghan soldiers are reportedly bringing them into Pakistan and selling them in order to supplement their income.

Over the years, it has been a status symbol to own the weapons. At one time MQM leadership urged its followers to sell televisions and consumer appliances and buy the guns. The price of the gun has declined over the years, from about $3,000 in the early 1980s to between $375 and $500 currently. Since then, the ethnic and sectarian conflicts in Karachi, Hyderabad, Lahore, Jhang, and elsewhere have resulted in ever-increasing numbers of deaths. Karachi suffered about 2,100 deaths in 1995; Lahore had 450.

Permissive Society

A closer look will indicate that Pakistani society has all the ills which are normally attributed to more advanced Western nations. Pornographic literature in English as well as Urdu is easily obtainable in bookstores and privately-owned lending libraries. Pornographic movies have become available in every video shop. Drugs of all kinds are sold from open fields and market places and by pharmacists. Villagers concoct their own brews which make them high.

Homosexuality is widespread; certain parts of the country are notorious for it. Students and adults often joke about homosexuality. Prostitution is banned but common. Most towns have a legally operated separate area for singing and dancing girls; the next step is easily arranged. The higher income people have access to girls from all parts of Pakistan and other countries such as Bangladesh, Nepal, Burma, Sri Lanka, Eastern Europe, and even Russia; they are housed in the best parts of the large cities. Alcohol is prohibited for Muslims but is openly available to local and visiting non-Muslims. At the right price, it is available to everyone.

---

[160] "A Kalashnikov Culture," *The Washington Post* (14 March 1996), p. A17.

The permissive nature of the society exposes young Pakistanis at a very young age to whatever excites them. As the availability of perverted opportunities grow, so do the perversions. The situation is made worse by widespread disapproval of sports. Parents prefer that their children study. They feel that organized sports and the regular practice sessions take students away from "study time" and expose them to bad influences; therefore, sports are often discouraged. Lack of respect and even ridicule for the local *imams* often prevent emphasis on religion and encourage channeling of energy into unproductive and even destructive activities.

Pakistani society has been a double-faced society for a long time. There is a clear need to reassess private and public values.

142. *Narcotics.* Opium and heroin production and distribution have become a serious problem since the late 1970s and early 1980s. The Soviet invasion of Afghanistan interrupted the drug pipeline from Afghanistan to the West and made Pakistan an attractive alternative. In addition, the Iranian revolution and the subsequent crackdown on illegal drug traffic by the Islamic Republic made shipment of drugs through Iran more difficult.

Pakistan has been able to reduce opium poppy yields, estimated at 800 tons in 1979, to about 140 tons in 1993. However, use of heroin has affected a significant part of the population. The Pakistan Narcotics Control Board estimates that although there were no known heroin addicts in Pakistan in 1980, the figure had reached 1.2 million in 1989. There were more than two million drug addicts of all types in 1991. There were only thirty drug treatment centers in Pakistan in 1991, with a cure rate of about 20%.

143. *Corrupt Police.* Pakistanis have always regarded their police with distrust and fear. In the earlier days of independence, corruption was assumed to be limited to lower level personnel. The senior officials who were a part of the police service of Pakistan (PSP) were generally considered to be incorruptible. However, this started to change in the mid-1950s. During the early period of martial law, General Ayub Khan investigated many officials in the Police Service of Pakistan and punished them for corruption, misconduct, inefficiency, or subversive activities. The situation has progressively worsened.

Presently, with few exceptions, personnel involved in corruption range from low level employees to top management. Low salaries are certainly a cause for the pervasive bribery at lower levels of the police. Senior officials have fewer excuses. The income generated from bribery is ten to twenty times that of the salary earned. Accordingly, no realistic amount of salary increases can possibly prevent police officials from taking bribes.

Police frequently act without warrants or other proper authorization, and individuals disappear into the criminal justice process for weeks before they can be found and, through writs of habeas corpus, be brought into regular judicial channels. Rape of prisoners, both male and female, is common. Prisoners often die in detention but are reported as killed in the course of armed encounters.[161]

Such practices provide ample opportunities for extorting money from those in fear of arrest or the relatives of those under arrest. People will pay any amount to avoid arrest or treatment after arrest. Amnesty International and other human rights groups have collected considerable evidence but it has resulted in little government action against the responsible police officials.

144. *Weak Judiciary.* Critics argue that the judiciary is neither independent nor fair. They complain of:[162]
- lack of autonomy and undue control by the executive branch of government over the judiciary;
- a heavy backlog of cases—more than sixty thousand cases were pending before twenty judges of the Lahore high court in 1993;
- undue delay in dispensation of justice. People are in jails for years without trial. During 1993, at least three defendants were freed after being in jail for ten or more years without the hearing of their cases;
- leniency toward the powerful, e.g., General Aslam Beg was found guilty of contempt of court in 1993 but was not punished, while a journalist was jailed for reporting the case against court instructions. A police official convicted of putting a nail through the nose of a political detainee was sentenced to a few hours of detention until the court rose and a Sessions Judge gave him a fine;
- unfair and arbitrary practices of special tribunals; and
- accusations of widespread bribery among many judges and their staff;

Recently, the judges of the Supreme Court and some provincial high courts have asserted their independence. It is not clear if this represents a permanent move toward autonomy of the judiciary or personal rebellion by some judges against high-handed pressures from the executive branch.

---

[161] Blood, pp. 306-7.

[162] Partly based on *The State of Human Rights 1993:* An Interim Report, (The Human Rights Commission of Pakistan, Lahore), pp. 13-17.

145. *Powerful Intelligence Agencies.* As discussed in the earlier chapter "Who Controls Pakistan?" the intelligence agencies have been used by different regimes to perpetuate their own power. These agencies have been accused of encouraging the civil unrest which led to the fall of Zulfiqar Ali Bhutto. Following the death of General Zia, ISI was accused of trying to determine who the next ruler of Pakistan should be. They have been accused of creating MQM in order to undermine the power of PPP and JI in Karachi, and of subsequently undermining the first government of Prime Minister Benazir Bhutto. Observers have speculated that the agencies have been involved in much more. Some observers have accused the intelligence agencies of involvement in almost every law-and-order problem. The desire to keep the nation divided is cited as the reason for such activities.

146. *Economic Issues.* Lack of adequate economic opportunities is a big factor in the breakdown of the law and order in Pakistan. The ethnic and linguistic violence is explained in terms of lack of economic opportunities, a sense of deprivation, and a limited prospect of success through legal means. The extortions are explained in terms of raising money for party activities which in turn are aimed at obtaining equal economic opportunities. Kidnapping and robbery is a means of earning a living for many.

147. *Conspiracy Theories.* Pakistanis tend to see enemies of Islam and Pakistan everywhere. Allegations are made all the time. To make a theory stick, drop a name of a Hindu or a Jew in the story. To spice it further, mention the name of a woman and an Ahmadi too. Everyone will be convinced that it is a true story and the enemies of the nation are hard at work. Nevertheless, conspiracies and foreign hands are not completely missing.

148. *Indian Hand.* Even government officials have repeatedly stated that India is behind the Karachi violence in order to get even for Pakistan's role in the Khalistan and Kashmir rebellions. The enmity between India and Pakistan has not been exploited by the government to unite Pakistanis. Instead, it appears that India is using the internal divisions of its enemy to keep it unstable and disunited.

149. *American Hand.* Many trace the breakdown of law and order to the influx of American weapons from the Afghan war. Some argue that the United States wants to keep Pakistan politically weak as long as it (a) has an active nuclear program, (b) promotes Islamic rule in Afghanistan, (c) supports Islamic unity in international affairs, (d) provides moral or political

support to Iran, and   (e) fails to promote actively the Middle East peace process (for example, Pakistan has not recognized Israel).

The Trend in Violence Continues

A widespread perception that justice cannot be obtained through the police and the judiciary has led people either to shy away and withdraw from the society, or take matters into their own hands. An ever-increasing cycle of revenge and counter-revenge is leading to collective punishment and arbitrary victimization. It is likely that the violence in Karachi and other parts of Pakistan will continue and probably escalate. More and more people are being killed and injured, families are being destroyed, and the desire for revenge is multiplying. Cycles of violence are increasing. As this rate, violence will continue to have significant adverse impact on all aspects of Pakistani life.

Spiritually, Pakistanis are becoming weaker and weaker. Divisions among Muslims are increasing. The Sunni-Shiah split at the local level continues to accentuate the similar split at the international level. Relations between Pakistan and Iran are beginning to suffer. It is becoming increasingly difficult to bring the Muslims closer.

The Pakistani economy is suffering due to lack of security and stability. Investors are becoming reluctant to invest. Even the existing ones are considering withdrawing. As economic conditions worsen, social strife is sure to increase.

Politically, there is continued dissatisfaction with the elected government, both domestically and abroad. People continue to look for alternate solutions. Political instability and frequent changes in government can be foreseen. This can lead to a takeover by the armed forces.

The law-and-order situation is worsening. Police officials are often afraid to pursue criminals. This was demonstrated during the attack on U.S. embassy employees. The army has already withdrawn from Karachi and conceded its inability to stop violence unless it is given addition powers.

Action Taken

150. *Army Called In.* The army, which had been directly involved in policing Karachi for more than two years, has decided to withdraw. Some feel that it was due to their conclusion that the situation was helpless. Nevertheless, the army has been replaced by paramilitary rangers. In addition, the police have been greatly strengthened with more manpower, equipment, and training.

151. *Political Settlement with MQM.* It is conceded by most that affected parts of Karachi remain politically affiliated with and controlled by MQM. The government contends that the violence is caused by MQM in order to achieve their goals. On the other hand, MQM feels that the government and its agencies are the cause of violence and it is simply defending itself. It is clear that whenever the MQM leadership declares strikes and demands agitation, violence in Karachi increases. Some political understanding and compromise between the government, MQM, and natives of Sindh are necessary in order to stop or at least reduce the violence in Karachi. Negotiations have been underway for a long time but an acceptable settlement has not been attained.

Some, including, General Aslam Beg, have suggested that even if there is an accord between MQM and PPP, there will many who will sabotage it.[163] The saboteurs may include India-supported groups who wish to promote instability in Karachi, MQM splinter groups, the drug mafia, and others who feel that they will lose due to "undesirable concessions" by the PPP.

Action Needed

The robberies, kidnappings, extortions, destruction of public property, and killings have become common in many parts of Pakistan, particularly in Karachi and some other parts of Sindh. Gradually, they have spread to Punjab and become common in Lahore and other towns. There are a variety of reasons for the breakdown of the law and order. The nation must address all of them and work on several fronts in parallel, including:

- Reforming the police and the judiciary;
- finding political solutions for political conflicts, particularly the demands for decentralization and distribution of national resources, two of the most important issues generating political agitation resulting in the breakdown of law-and-order;
- gaining control over terrorist organizations, including feudal lords;
- controlling ownership and flow of weapons;
- supporting organizations, groups, and citizens who confront lawless elements; and
- empowering common citizens through more representative government.

---

[163] General Aslam Beg's speech to the Washington Policy Analysis Group at Kabab Masala Restaurant in Alexandria, Virginia on 30 July 1995.

152. *Dialogue with MQM.* The political solution for Karachi must be pursued through political dialogue until it reaches a satisfactory conclusion. Political commentators have sighted a lack of sincerity on both sides. If true, there is an urgent need for improved dialogue.

153. *Physically Defeat the Guilty.* This can be done through private and public resources. On the public side, the government can and should further strengthen law enforcement agencies. The government, including the army, has claimed that 10,000 rangers and 6,000 police, almost all of whom have been trained by the army, are needed to maintain law-and-order there.

On the private side, citizens need to confront those who cause the law-and-order problem. They need to identify them, report them to the authorities, be witnesses against them in courts of law, and advocate strong punishment for them. In some cases, people have already formed neighborhood watch groups and even vigilante groups to protect their area. The concept needs to be spread to all of the affected areas.

In some cases, people use fasting to dramatize their causes. Fasting for peace has helped achieve objectives in many cases. It needs to be applied to influence the government, public opinion, and the guilty ones. In any case, citizens and the government have to ensure that the guilty ones are caught and punished.

154. *Remove Basic Causes.* In the long run, the law-and-order problem can be improved by removing the basic causes for its existence. This means focusing on political, economic, moral, and physical causes. It means listening to the people. Some understanding between native and new Sindhis is urgent. Many people refer to the country's declining moral values, lack of fear of Allah, and neglect of the Day of Judgment. Disregard for human life and welfare has reached an alarming level. There is a little fear of accountability in this world or the next.

There is a sense of hopelessness among young people. The economy is not growing fast enough to absorb them into lawful job markets. Frustration and unemployment causes many youths to turn to crime. Focusing attention on making Pakistanis richer will help in improving law-and-order too.

155. *Contain Influence of Outside Forces.* The ability of outside forces to undermine law and order in Pakistan should be clearly analyzed and understood. For example, the United States has considerable influence over almost every element of Pakistani government. The United States can easily facilitate or sabotage a political solution if it is interested in the outcome. The

United States can help bring parties together and help resolve conflicts or it can generate mis-trust and jealousies further alienating opposing sides. Accordingly, maintaining cordial relations with the United States is important for law-and-order in Pakistan. It requires a delicate handling.

In view of Pakistan's support for the freedom fighters in Kashmir, it is unrealistic to expect that India will sit quietly and not retaliate through intervention in Pakistani affairs. Peace with India is essential to stop sabotage activities within Pakistan. Positive signals from the India government must be fully pursued.

Peace within Afghanistan is also critical to stop the flow of arms and immigration into Pakistan, which is one of the causes of the law-and-order problem. Such a peace is difficult while Afghanistan itself is embroiled in civil war. It therefore is in the interest of Pakistan—and Muslims—to assist in the peace process in that country.

156. *Improve Social Environment*. There must be increased understanding and cooperation between the citizens and the government of Pakistan. Ways must be found to improve the adversarial atmosphere. Arbitrary arrests and torture in jails must be stopped. Jail administration must be improved. Human rights as guaranteed by the constitution must be respected and sectarian and ethnic issues must be addressed.

Some argue that solution to the law-and-order problem, particularly in Karachi is simple—just accept the demands of MQM. Unfortunately, much of what is demanded by MQM is at the expense of others. The other parties to the conflict will not accept such an accord. Many argue that an uneven compromise would lead to equally or even worse violent protest. Efforts must be made on all fronts. However, the long-term solution lies in multi-faceted action to address all key causes for the breakdown of the law-and-order.

CHAPTER 12

ETHNIC STRIFE IN SINDH

It may be that Allah will establish friendship between you and those whom ye (now) hold as enemies. For Allah has power (over all things); and Allah is Oft-forgiving, Most Merciful. (Qur'an 60:7)

Introduction

Thje objective of this chapter is to understand some key causes of discontent in Sindh, and to explore ways for promoting peace, prosperity, and Pakistani unity. Nevertheless, this is the most difficult chapter to write, partly because the author is a native Sindhi. No matter what is said, one or the other powerful group is likely to be offended which in turn may diminish in value the whole book. On the other hand, there is little hope of a change without understanding some of the causes of the current dilemma. It is hoped that the readers will ultimately understand the need for cooperation among all Sindhis (natives and immigrants) for betterment of themselves and the nation.

157. *Background.* Historically, Sindh was the first province to accept Islam in the subcontinent and is known as the gateway of Islam. Sindhis are devoted Muslims and very proud of the role they played in the creation of Pakistan, being also the first province to vote for creation of Pakistan.

158. *The Mohajirs.* The first Mohajirs (refugees) in Islamic history were those who left their homes, property, and members of their families in Mecca. They migrated so that they could be with the Holy Prophet (PBUH) in Medina. The people of Medina who accepted Islam and played host to the Mohajirs were the Ansars (helpers). The migration was made possible by the generosity of the Ansar. They entertained the Mohajirs, helped to house them, fed them, and took care of their needs. The new government in Medina under the leadership of the Prophet (PBUH) made special efforts to settle them. There are a number of references in the Qur'an regarding obligations

to the refugee and the kindness shown by the Ansars. This led to the building of the Islamic brotherhood.

On their part, the Mohajirs realized that they had the special status for a relatively short period. They had to and did integrate into the local society. Having been close to the Prophet (PBUH), they had greater knowledge of Islam which they readily shared with their hosts. Within a short period, as they found their feet in Medina, they stopped calling themselves Muhajirs and became a part of the Medina society. From then on, the basic principles applied equally to everyone—all actions must be for the pleasure of Allah, all resources belong to Allah and must be shared, do not eat a full meal if your neighbors have not done so, etc.

In the case of the Mohajirs in Sindh, starting in 1947, when Pakistan became independent, the local Ansars (native Sindhis) received them with open arms. The local government and people took special actions to help settle them to the point that on the whole, they are much more prosperous than the local Ansars. Yet when the Ansars have begun to demand their rights, the Muhajirs are very upset.

Sindhis feel that they have been treated as second-class citizens of Pakistan ever since then.

A whole generation of Sindhi youth and intellectuals is smarting under a sense of great betrayal. They have lost their lands; they have lost their language; they have lost their autonomy; and they have lost their individuality. They are confronted with an imminent threat of losing their demographic edge over others in Sindh. They hear insistent calls for division of their homeland every day. Besieged by demons of domination and extinction, they are producing abundant resistance literature in Sindhi language every year. But other Pakistanis neither know nor care about it. Only when an explosion like the 1983 MRD agitation or a madness like that of September 30, 1988 occurs does Pakistan or the world condescend to take fleeting notice of the tragedy of Sindh.[164]

Most Sindhis believe that they have not received an equitable share of Pakistan's economic resources, in terms of physical infrastructure, human resource development, commerce and industry. Above all, they feel short-charged in terms of civilian and military jobs.

[164] Abdullah J. Memon, "Facing Facts in Sindh-II", in *The Dawn,* (Karachi; November, 1995).

Many small towns and villages in Sindh lack electricity, water, health facilities, schools, and adequate housing. A million Sindhis continue to live in huts made out of mud and thatch with no windows. Inside, there are dirt floors with straw on it. Rarely does one find any furniture. There may be a cot or two for sleeping. There are pots and pans, and a crude stove for cooking.

Unsanitary conditions are common. Sewage runs through the villages. There are ponds of dirty water everywhere during the rainy season, full of mosquitos. They have few if any public facilities. By contrast, almost every Muslim refugee who migrated to Pakistan in 1947 now has a solid house or apartment. It is not difficult to understand why most Sindhis feel that their plight is the direct result of unfair treatment at the hand of the government.

Sindhi people love their language and culture. However, instead of receiving facilities and support for development of their language and culture (such as Urdu, Punjabi, and Pushtu speaking people have received), people taking interest in the Sindhi language and culture are often harassed and suspected of anti-Pakistan activities.

People of Sindh

159. *Composition of People of Sindh*. The population of the Sindh province can be divided on the basis of:
* ORIGIN. Among all possible divisions in the province, the main one is among Mohajirs (Muslim immigrants from India) and native Sindhis. In addition, a large number of Punjabis, Pathans, and Baloachs have settled in Sindh, particularly in urban areas.
* RELIGION. Muslims (Sunnis, Shiites, Ismailis), Hindus, Christians, Parsis.
* LANGUAGE. The Sindhi language spoken by Sindhis, Urdu spoken by Mohajirs, Punjabi spoken by Punjabis, and Pushtu spoken by Pathans;
* ECONOMIC STATUS. Large landholders; bureaucrats, industrialists, middle class landholders; low-level government and private sector laborers, shopkeepers and small businessmen, the poor without land or education.

160. *Powerful Groups*. There are several powerful groups in Sindh. These include (a) the PPP which enjoys broad-based political support; (b) the MQM, due to widespread support of the Urdu speakers; (c) Sindhi landlords, including *pirs* and *syeds* (descendants of Prophet Muhammad PBUH), who enjoy significant representation in the legislative assemblies and influence over the bureaucracy, the army, and landlords in other parts of the country;

(d) and Sindhi nationalists including the Jiai Sindhi movement. PPP, MQM and the major land–owners have been discussed in earlier chapters.

161. *Pirs and other Syeds*. People of Sindh have a special love for descendants of the Holy Prophet and other saints who have lived and died in their midst. Most of the rural and many of the urban Sindhis have a special affinity for one or other pir or saint. Sindhis visit their *dargah* (place where a saint lived or is buried) and give voluntary *nazrana* (gifts), or make payments on demand. The followers are generally afraid to do anything important without receiving blessings from their pirs. Come election time, the followers provide a very large vote bank for them. As a result, the pirs and their nominees enjoy large political clout and often sit in the provincial and national assembly chambers. At any given time, one can find several of them in the Sindh cabinet. Pir Pagaro, Pir of Hala, and Pir of Ranipur are just a few of them.

Pir Pagaro has hundreds of thousands of followers in Sindh and on the other side of the border in India. Because of his many followers, he enjoys considerable power within private and official circles in Pakistan. During the 1965 war against India, he was able to provide manpower for defense of the Pakistan border. The army remains grateful to him. He and his nominees have been rewarded in many ways, including appointment of his nominee, Mohammed Khan Junejo, as a Prime Minister of Pakistan, and Jam Sadiq Ali as Chief Minister of Sindh.

On the other hand, his common *murids* (followers) have suffered much and have made many sacrifices at the behest of the current Pir and his father. Yet, unlike Agha Khan, who is well-known and respected around the world for his philanthropic activities and efforts to advance his community, Pir Pagaro has been criticized for doing relatively little to improve the economic conditions of the majority of his followers.[165]

Rural Sindhis

Given the low rate of literacy in Pakistan, particularly in rural areas, Sindhis can be divided into educated and uneducated ones. The latter ones generally live in rural areas. They live from hand to mouth, with little knowledge of the world outside their immediate area. Most are sustained by meager earnings earned as sharecroppers or farm laborers, and by their profound faith in Allah and submission to their ordained fate. They pray and hope that

---

[165] *The Newsline*, (Karachi; February, 1995), pp. 66-78

tomorrow will be better for them. On top of poverty, they face serious law-and-order problems. They are generally at the mercy of their feudal lords.

The educated ones among them have been to schools, read some books, and done some traveling outside their hometown. Only a few of the educated choose to reside permanently in their rural areas. Most of them manage to get a job and a primary residence in the urban areas, where they keep their school age children. They travel to their rural home during holidays or at times of need.

The majority of rural Sindhis want to have what others have, despite the many problems urban Sindhis and non-Sindhis face. They demonstrate their liking and admiration for the urban populace by wanting to:

- come to Karachi, Hyderabad, and other urban areas;
- live there on a long term basis;
- educate their children in schools, and colleges there;
- train their children in the urban organizations after their formal education rather than returning to the rural areas;
- replicate the urban facilities in their respective villages, if possible; and
- have the relative freedom of speech, human rights, economic growth, etc. as enjoyed by the urban people.

The almost total lack of economic development in rural Sindh and insufficient economic opportunities in nearby urban areas are of great concern to Sindhis. The issue of feudal control in Sindhi politics and in the economic life of rural Sindhis is another critical issue.

There is no reason that just demands of rural Sindhis should not be met.[166] Sindhi leaders have the votes and the required political muscle to emphasize their needs through their representatives. However, Sindhi voters have not been able to pressure their leaders to focus on the common good. With some reordering of priorities, the government and private sector have the resources to meet the needs. There are earlier precedents of comparable national action in support of Mohajirs. The experience of other countries shows that it is far cheaper to provide basic facilities to people in rural areas than to let them migrate and then provide the same facilities in urban slums.

Sindhi peasants should seek and the nation should consider a special action program for rural development, including construction of educational, health, and transport facilities; provision of home construction facilities and

---

[166] Former Prime Minister Moeen Qureshi discussed the issue of providing basic infrastructure to rural Sindhis and expressed his view that the financial cost of such an effort would be relatively small.

financing; and programs for generation of employment. Sindhis should demand and obtain greater freedom of speech, human rights, and protection for their language and culture as enjoyed by the urban people.

162. *Can Feudal Lords Be Made Accountable?* Feudal lords can be made accountable. However, local peasants at a particular village cannot do it by themselves, but organized peasants can achieve a lot. A well-organized peasant organization can give guidance on how to achieve the objectives. The peasants need to use political power in terms of captive votes without which the feudal lords will lose their social standing, social and economic power, and access to government power. In addition, as producers of goods and services essential to the feudal lords for maintaining their position, peasants hold economic power which can be mobilized for their own benefit.

If government officials realize that feudal lords are in danger of losing their voter banks, and that the peasants are taking their fate into their own hands, the political leaders will switch sides. They will expedite implementation of the land reform legislation and possibly introduce additional laws. The national leadership wants votes—if feudal lords cannot deliver them, the leaders will court whoever has the power to deliver them.

163. *Party of the Poor.* Most mainstream political parties claim to have taken up the cause of the rural poor. In fact, the PPP and others have successfully maintained educational and job quotas for rural Sindhis and initiated several rural infrastructure projects. However, the mainstream parties are so dominated by feudal lords that these programs are channeled through them and end up favoring them, their immediate families, and supporters. Others remain unaffected and largely at the mercy of these people.

There is a great need for a group of people who can perform the functions which are currently performed by the feudal lords at a lesser cost to the rural population. The ultimate responsibility lies with the peasants themselves. There are many examples of how the rural workers have improved themselves—within Pakistan in Punjab; in capitalist countries like Britain, France, and the United States; and in socialist countries like China and the former Soviet Union.

Under the Chinese model, peasant associations were created which were able to smash the political power and prestige of the landlord class. They moved on to break traditional authority—clan authority, religious authority, and even husband authority. They eventually succeeded in obtaining land reform which abolished all rent on land—the farmers became owners of whatever land they were actually cultivating. Landowners were able to keep only those lands that they cultivated themselves. Though extreme and accomplished under the auspices of a communist government, the model is a valid one for oppressed peasants. Sindhi peasants can achieve reform through their unity and voting power in a democratic system.

In the past, attempts have been made to organize and empower the rural peasants. The Sindh Hari (farmer) party was established by a dedicated former bureaucrat named Haider Bux Jatoi. It did not amount to much. He attempted to get elected but lost.

Educated children of rural Sindhis have established several nationalist organizations. They have tied rights of rural Sindhis to autonomy of Sindh. The later issue has been viewed suspiciously by the central government and armed forces. These organizations may have better luck if they were to concentrate on the economic rights of the rural areas.

Urban social and political workers visit rural areas, but it is often as guests of the local feudal lord, and/or for a specific project of a relatively short duration. They complete their research or initiate a limited philanthropic project. However, they avoid extended political or social activity in the rural areas without sponsorship of the feudal lord because of several factors including lack of law-and-order, specially for those who will be a threat to the existing feudal lord; and lack of infrastructure facilities such as clean water, health facilities, and places to live and buy food.

164. *Is Revolution An Option?* If a peaceful change in peasant and feudal lord relationships cannot be achieved, revolution is the last option. World history is full of instances where the weak are woven together by common objectives to overcome powerful oppressors. It is relatively easy to throw out the old, but relatively difficult to find a new system and institutions which can work better. Revolution often replaces one kind of tyranny with another. That is why moderate leaders often try to improve the existing one by reforming it.

The West has gone through the French Revolution, the Bolshevik Revolution, and others of smaller magnitude. However, the reform approach has been more viable because of the relatively successful functioning of the democratic-capitalistic process. People have become more educated and better understand their interests. They have the vote and know how to use it to achieve their objectives.

There has been limited reform for the good of Pakistan in Sindh because they have had neither revolution nor working democracy. The weak who should benefit from proposed reform are illiterate, do not understand the options available to them, cannot distinguish between their friends and enemies, and are easy to manipulate and divide. On the other hand, those in power have held all the cards, education, political power, financial resources, the media, and the support of most of the international community.

Urban Sindhis

All district headquarters of Sindh can be considered urban areas. Outside Karachi, there are sixteen district headquarters, namely, Hyderabad, Jacobabad, Shikarpur, Ghotki, Larkana, Sukkur, Khairpur, Naushero Feroz, Nawabshah, Umerkot, Mirpurkhas, Sanghar, Badin, Thatta (Thar), and Dadu. Even though Karachi has a majority of non-Sindhi speaking people, there are several hundred thousands Sindhis who live there. In addition to Sindhis, there are a large number of Pathans, Punjabis, and Gujratis-speaking immigrants from India.

Lacking recent census data and considering the conflicting claims by the government, Mohajirs, and Sindhis, it is not clear whether Urdu-speaking people have a majority in Karachi. Leaders of Punjabi and Pathan groups have claimed that, together with Sindhis and Baloachs, they constitute 55% of the population of Karachi. Hyderabad is virtually divided along ethnic lines with half of its population being Sindhi. The rest of urban areas mentioned above have a clear majority of Sindhis as demonstrated by various election results and census reports.

The issues faced by urban Sindhis are similar to urban people everywhere in the developing countries: inadequate infrastructures (electricity, water, roads, sanitation, housing, educational facilities); a high cost of living; inadequate law-and-order; and, above all, unemployment. The urban areas are inhabited by civil servants, businessmen, small shopkeepers, and professionals. The people wish their towns to have all the facilities that the larger cities such as Karachi, Lahore, and Islamabad have. They want peace and economic development.

Politically, the urban native Sindhis have been a confused lot. They produce many capable social and political leaders, but rarely vote for them. They tend to vote for the neighboring feudal lords who generally maintain homes in the urban areas, too. They seek leadership which can protect their own interests, but have not found it. They see the MQM model of middle class control as the one most promising for them. Non-Sindhis are always hoping for political splits among the Sindhis so that a candidate relying on non-Sindhi support can be elected.

On the other hand, Mohajirs who filled the power vacuum at the time of partition and filled most government jobs after independence are angry over losing their dominant position. They have lost much to Punjabis and Pathans who have increased their position of power in Sindh. With rising levels of education, Sindhis have increasingly claimed their share of power, also.

The Sindh martial law government, under Governor General Rakhman Gul, introduced a quota system for the rural areas where most Sindhis live, and in urban areas where most Mohajirs live.[167] Even though Mohajirs are among the most advanced ethnic group in the country in terms of material possessions (housing, automobiles, telephones, foreign travel, etc.), they sense that their overall share is declining. They are feeling the impact of 20% plus unemployment which Sindhis and Baloach people have known for decades.

165. *Urban and Rural Divide.* There is a significant urban/rural rift between native Sindhis themselves. The urbanites, regardless of their urban background, tend to look at the rural population as illiterate, irrational/unpredictable, unsanitary, and violent. The rural ones look at the urbanites as greedy, selfish exploiters who have essentially sold their souls. The urban Sindhis generally speak the Sindhi language at home, while rural Sindhis tend to speak Sindhi as well as Siraiki. While the urban and rural Sindhis join hands in times of common threats, there is little cooperation between them.

Sindh Issues

166. *Poverty.* A review of poverty conditions in Sindh indicates:
- The number of poor remains high. A large number remain in absolute poverty. A larger number live only slightly above the poverty line.
- Benefits of the economic development to date have not been evenly distributed. The regional variation in poverty is striking, being particularly striking in rural areas of Sindh.
- With the expected increase in the labor force, the situation is likely to get worse.
- Experiences indicate that a high rate of sustained economic development is required for poverty reduction; the two go hand in hand.
- Economic and political management committed to reducing poverty is required. This includes increased sharing of funds and establishing suitable institutions to implement the programs.
- Targeted programs are needed to reach and help the poor and disadvantaged.

[167] Ibid.

- An integrated approach is required under which the government and private sector work together to combat poverty.

During nearly fifty years of independence, many heads of government in Pakistan have been Sindhis: Messrs./Ms. Jinnah, Z. A. Bhutto, Junejo, B. Bhutto, Jatoi, and again B. Bhutto. Still Sindhis appear to have benefitted or progressed little. Even today, outside Karachi, Sindh is one of the least developed areas of Pakistan which happens to be one of the least developed countries of the world. Accordingly, Sindh leaders, past and present, must share a large part of the blame for the poverty of Sindhis.

167. *Government Response.* Often, government officials sympathetic to Sindhis do not know what to do or how to achieve the economic goals. Many steps are possible to ameliorate the situation. Some helpful steps are given below.

- Sindhi people who want to make the government more responsive should either join the government or actively lobby for change.
- Decision-makers in Pakistan (e.g., army officials, heads of political parties, bankers, investors) should be exposed to the problems of the peasants and poor urbanites.
- Sindhi government officials interested in helping Sindhis (e.g., those who support the Sindh Graduate Association) or those who are known to be sincere to the cause of peasants should be identified and supported
- Officials who openly are opposed to the interest of peasants should be identified and identified and held accountable.
- Cooperation should be encouraged with those non-Sindhis who are sincerely eager to help peasants (e.g., peasant organizations all over the country).

Above all, economic development projects should be accelerated.

Ethnic Warfare

Ethnic conflicts and bloodletting have become a prominent feature of many developing countries. Ethnic warfare in Rwanda and Burundi caught the attention of the world in 1994."In the heart of sub-Sahara Africa, Hutus and Tutsis—the ethnic groups in Rwanda and Burundi—share the same language and culture, the same tortured colonial history, the same dependence on land and livestock. Yet, for much of this century, the two groups in these small Central African countries have battled each other, resulting in millions of their people dying or being displaced . . . Yet the physical and cultural differences between Hutus and Tutsis are largely superficial . . . Indeed, Rwandans were not officially identified as Tutsis and Hutus until the Belgians created an identity card system that forced citizens to choose ethnic groups."[168]

Ethnicity is alive and well in Pakistan too. It is often linked to the very pervasive provincialism. People of each province and ethnic group take pride in their own language and culture, and are willing to make sacrifices to protect them. In addition, there are legitimate grievances which need to be recognized and addressed before the situation worsens.

168. *Current Turbulence.* The province Sindh has been going through considerable turbulence of late. In 1983, the Sindhi dominated areas actively participated in the Movement for Restoration of Democracy (MRD), a political protest against the regime of General Zia which resulted in military action; the Sindhi suffered heavily. Karachi has been going through political violence since the 1992 military invention initiated by the Nawaz Sharif government and continued under the Bhutto regime. The turbulence in Karachi, the capital of Sindh, has reached such a level that the entire country is talking of the Sindh issue and demanding a solution.

> **. . . the areas in which the Muslims are numerically in majority, as in the northwestern and eastern zones of India, should be grouped to constitute independent states in which the constituent units shall be autonomous and sovereign . . . (Pakistan Resolution, 1940)**

169. *Resolution of 1940.* Denial of provincial sovereignty and even autonomy as promised under the Pakistan Resolution of 1940 was a sore point with the people of East Pakistan. If they had received their due, probably the original Pakistan would be intact today. It is a significant issue with people of Sindh, Baloachistan, and the NWFP. People of the smaller provinces have continually complained of oppression. On the other hand, people of the largest province have maintained that the smaller provinces are themselves to be blamed for their backwardness and relative lack of progress; if they would get an education and leave their villages in search of livelihood and progress, they would be better off.

Mutual distrust is another aspect. It goes deep into the culture and history of the area:

---

[168] *The Washington Post* (27 January 1996), pp. A1 and A15.

Provincial conflict and mistrust, ancient geo-historic fears, taboos
and terrors; the sources long forgotten, but with legacies of pain ever
green in hearts brimful of parochial prejudice. Punjabi distrusting
Sindhi, Baloachi suspicious of both, and half the tribesmen along the
North-West Frontier holding rifles loaded at the ready, cocked to fire
at the other half. [169]

Some will say that "The whole history of mankind is a struggle of the
oppressed against exploitation and domination."[170] Under the surface, however, the smaller provinces of Pakistan, particularly Sindh and Baloachistan,
are seeking something more basic and fundamental. They are extremely
underdeveloped outside their main towns and face special problems. Their
people have a higher degree of poverty, unemployment, helplessness, and
nationalism which deserve close attention and special action to resolve them.
There is a feeling of both social and economic deprivation.

170. *Sindh vs. Pakistan?* Following the denial of autonomy promised under
the 1940 Resolution, some Sindhi intellectuals and political leaders, led by
the late G.M. Syed, have advocated "self-determination" and implied independence of Sindh.[171] The vast majority of Sindhis are frustrated by their
condition in Pakistan but oppose the idea of independence. The revolt by
East Pakistan and eventual establishment of Bangladesh showed that despite
physical separation of the two wings of the country by about 1500 miles, the
declaration of independence had huge costs in destruction of life and
property. By contrast, Sindh is a contiguous part of the remaining country.
The Pakistan army will be in a position to inflict much higher damage if
there is a conflict over breaking up the remaining country.
    The population of Sindh is already in conflict with each other. The Urdu,
Punjabi, and Pushtu speaking people dominate the main commercial, financial, and communications centers of Sindh, i.e., Karachi. While they have
severe conflicts among themselves, they would not join hands with Sindhis
in a separate Sindhu Desh. They would also want separation of Karachi.
Rebelling Sindhis would be divided themselves and simply be committing

---

[169] Stanley Wolpert, *Zulfi Bhutto of Pakistan* (Oxford: Oxford University Press,
1993), p. 326.

[170] Zulfikar Ali Bhutto, *The Myth of Independence* (Oxford: Oxford University
Press, 1969), p. 188.

[171] G.M. Syed, *Sindhu Desh,* (G.M. Academy, Karachi).

suicide by confronting the Pakistan army. In addition, the resources of Sindh outside Karachi are limited. It is questionable if a landlocked Sindh can be a viable independent country.

Separation would likely provoke hostility from the northern neighbor, Punjab. Sindh will continue to rely on that area's water supplies and therefore Sindh agriculture would be dependent on Punjab. In case of separation of the Sindh, Punjab would be able to build projects like the Kalabagh dam. Without an appropriate water distribution agreement, these projects can severely damage Sindh agriculture and its economy.

There is a question about who will rule an independent Sindh. Based on their economic and political power, it is likely that the same feudal lords and pirs of Sindh who currently dominate the province would comprise the leadership. It is doubtful if they will prove to be better rulers than they are today. Without some moderating influence and the fear of the current central government, they would probably prove even worse dictators. The people of Sindh would be hesitant to make all the sacrifices for the sake of giving even greater power to the same despots.

In order to weaken Pakistan, India may provide some military support to Sindhis. However, in the long run, it is unrealistic to expect positive input from India which has a large Urdu-speaking Muslim population. An independent Sindh would have to expect increased influence by Indian Muslims. Sindhis would be back to square one.

It is also unrealistic to expect substantive support from Sindhi Hindus in India, those who left Sindh about fifty years ago. Some prominent Sindhi Hindus of India such as Advani, President of BJP, would be likely to lend support, however only a few such individual leaders exist. Those Hindus who were twenty years old at the time of partition are about seventy now; most of them have passed away. The new generation has little first hand knowledge of or love for Sindh. While some of them speak the language, the Sindhi that they write is in Sanskrit rather than Arabic script. If they returned to Sindh, while they may invest some of their money, they would also likely demand the return of their ancestral property, part of which is occupied by Sindhi Muslims.

Through their votes in numerous elections, Sindhis have already rejected secessionist groups. It is time to close that part of the debate. Like most of their Sindhi brethren, the remaining nationalists should work within the framework of Pakistan to achieve their genuine goals for economic development of their people.

Based on the experience of modern times in the developing countries of Asia, Africa, and South America, this is the right time to be a part of greater unions and not separate from them. Even the mighty Europeans have elected to form the European Union. Accordingly, Sindh should always remain a part of Pakistan, and struggle to obtain its rights within Pakistan. In fact, Pakistan should be actively promoting the cause of the greater Islamic Nation.

Changing the Ethnic Balance in Sindh

Many Sindhis who have neglected to participate in previous national censuses, have recently become much more interested. They have come to realize that political power and distribution of economic resources depends on their share in national and provincial power. They aim to be counted at each opportunity. Similarly, they have become determined not to give an unfair advantage to their competitors. Immigration of non-Sindhis from other parts of Pakistan or from other countries into Sindh is, accordingly, a very sensitive subject.

171. *Effects of Immigration into Sindh.* All agree that Sindh has received more than its share of immigrants. Karachi is already home to more than two million illegal immigrants from India, Bangladesh, Nepal, Burma, and the Middle East. Limited economic resources cannot sustain additional immigration, particularly in light of current ethnic tensions. During October and November, 1995, the Government began to send illegal immigrants back home. Only time will tell if the efforts will succeed.

Another question is that of repatriation of the Biharis, who had migrated from the Indian province of Bihar and settled in East Pakistan at the time of partition. They wish to resettle in Pakistan and this remains an emotional issue. There has been speculation in the press that Biharis have not been repatriated because the Pakistan government is convinced that a large number of Indian agents and other undesirable people have infiltrated the Bihari camps. Their repatriation to Pakistan would lead to a security problem for Pakistan. Accordingly, none of the several governments which have come into power since 1971 has allowed a significant number to enter Pakistan.

Nevertheless, whenever the Sindh-based PPP government comes into power, the issue is raised. Each time Sindhis oppose the proposal because they fear that the Biharis will end up settling in Sindh since the previous efforts to settle them in Punjab were not successful. They feel that the arrival of several hundred thousand additional Urdu-speaking people will lead to

• an overall increase in the number of Urdu-speaking people in Sindh, leading to (a) additional claims about the majority of non-Sindhis in the province, (b) momentum for division of Sindh, (c) and actual division of Sindh; and

- redirection of already limited financial resources to provide jobs and shelter to newcomers while a majority of Sindhis suffer a lack of the same.

From the point of view of Sindhis, it is a fight for survival of their home land, language, and culture. The second objection listed relates to economic issue. Economic development of the region could lead to adequate opportunities for all including the newcomers. The confidence of Sindhis can be enhanced by first giving them the jobs and shelter that they lack. If they can see that there is enough to go around, they will have little economic reason for trying to block repatriation of Biharis to Sindh.

Mohajir Demands

The two prominent parties in Sindh are the PPP and the MQM. The PPP is a national party with strong support in rural Sindh. MQM champions Mohajir concerns and has considerable support from Mohajirs in Sindh.

The MQM demands a greater share of power. After several years of violence and military/police action, they demand[172]

- discontinuation of operations against Mohajirs and withdrawal of all military and paramilitary forces from civilian areas;
- representation proportionate to their population in the national and provincial assemblies and the Senate;
- increase in urban quotas in federal and provincial services;
- sharing of the posts of governor and chief minister of Sindh in rotation by Mohajirs and Sindhis;
- repatriation of Pakistanis stranded in Bangladesh without further delay.
- compensation for MQM workers killed or injured and for their loss of property; and
- unconditional withdrawal of cases against MQM leaders.

Unofficially, they demand creation of a separate province from parts of Sindh, including Karachi. Native Sindhis, who have felt neglected since independence, are unwilling to acquiesce to what they believe to be exaggerated demands of a vocal minority. Prospects for peace are dim and additional violence appears almost inevitable. There is visible distrust and even hatred

---

[172] *India Today* (North America's Special Edition); (15 July 1995), p. 39.

among the two groups. Nevertheless, some solution has to be found. Neglecting genuine needs of citizens at home, while talking of the ideals of a Muslim ummah across fifty countries, is not going to work. Some effective mechanisms have to be found for balanced regional and ethnic development.

172. *MQM Claims—Sindhi Response.* Dr. Feroz Ahmed, a prominent Sindhi scholar, has evaluated several claims of MQM.[173] These are: (a) that Mohajirs have made great sacrifices for Pakistan, (b) that Mohajirs created Pakistan, (c) that Mohajirs have been treated unjustly, (d) that the demands of MQM (and Mohajirs) are genuine, and (e) that MQM is the sole representative of urban Sindhis.

These claims are to some extent exaggerated. Sindh and Sindhis also have made sacrifices in the creation of Pakistan and particularly in the resettlement of Mohajirs. Sindh was the first province to opt for Pakistan. The implication that Mohajirs should be treated as more equal than others is questionable. In terms of material progress, Mohajirs are far ahead of any other ethnic group in Pakistan. However, many of the past achievements have been at the expense of local Sindhis. The expectations of Mohajirs are so high that they feel that they are being persecuted.

MQM has received a large number of votes in the two urban areas due to its ability to register the votes and get them out on the polling day. Other groups are also becoming more active politically and MQM's current advantage may not be permanent. Karachi and Hyderabad, where MQM is dominant, are not the only urban areas in Sindh. Even in Karachi and Hyderabad, there are a large number of Sindhis, Punjabis, Pathans, and other ethnic groups who have serious differences with MQM.

It is true that MQM is a force to reckon with and sincerity is needed in negotiating with them. There can be no peace in Karachi without MQM. Their claims are correct in that respect, but there are other forces in the province and the country too. After all, MQM supported the provincial government led by Jam Sadiq Ali in keeping PPP out of the government in Sindh after 1990 elections. PPP was and is a force too.

In spite of an earlier agreement, MQM betrayed PPP in 1990 and helped to bring about the fall of the PPP government. Then, they cooperated with the Jam government to persecute PPP leaders and workers. MQM needs to demonstrate its sincerity by denouncing ethnic hatred from its political platform. It is argued that if the Agartala conspiracy case against Awani

---

[173] *The Daily Dawn,* (Karachi; 3 January 1995).

League leader Mujibur Rahman could be dropped, then the criminal cases against Altaf can be also withdrawn.

Dropping criminal cases would be harmful to the democratic process and would encourage law-breaking and violence. It should not be encouraged. Benazir Bhutto and Asif Zardari have gone through the court cases. Murtaza Bhutto is going through one now. Altaf should do the same.

Partition of Sindh?

Many Mohajirs are asking for division of Sindh into two or more provinces. There are two arguments for division: increased efficiency of administration and provision of a home for the "refugee nation."

As for as the administration of the province is concerned, it needs vast improvements. As pointed out elsewhere in the book, people hunger for increased efficiency, decentralization of powers to the provincial, divisional, district, local, and even the village/neighborhood level. Native Sindhis prefer to achieve administrative efficiency while keeping Sindh Province intact.

Those seeking division of the province on efficiency grounds wish to have the smaller provinces resemble the current divisions. The objective can be served by delegating the necessary powers from the federal government down to governments of each province, division, district, or local government as the case may be. Increased cost of administration under a decentralized system has been cited also as the main constraint in the past. Such costs are insignificant in comparison to the cost of lawlessness currently being incurred. If the money can be made available, the current divisions of Sindh (i.e., Karachi, Hyderabad, Sukkur, Larkana) can function as subprovinces of Sindh.

173. *Partition and Violence.* If the province is divided for political reasons to provide a separate province for refugees, most native Sindhis would resist for historical, economic, political, cultural, and security reasons. They would con-sider it a further betrayal of the promises made to Sindhi people under the Pakistan Resolution of 1940. Such a division would alienate Sindhis against Mohajirs and all others who would implement such a division.

Pakistan's short-lived "One Unit" experiment should be remembered. In the mid-fifties, the government abolished the provinces of then West Pakistan and formed a "One Unit" government. Much discontent and political violence ensued and the historical provinces were restored. Most observers agree that dividing Sindh would lead to more conflict and bloodshed. All sides appear well-armed and capable of inflicting considerable damage.

It is also argued that the breakup of Sindh and creation of a new province for Mohajirs would not meet the full expectations of Mohajirs either. Critics of division assert that there would inevitably be differences and conflicts between Urdu and Gujrati speaking people who have a different language, culture, and interests. Mohajirs would still have to face large Pathan and Punjabi communities who are economically and politically powerful on their own and would be supported by their representatives in the federal government.

A review of the past violence between Mohajirs and Pathans indicates that existence of a united Sindh province was never an issue. Accordingly, there would be more violence between Mohajirs and other communities unless the fundamental causes, particularly the economic ones, were addressed. Water supply, agriculture, railways, the bulk of electrical power and telephone networks—all pass through rural Sindh. The division would affect a large number of Mohajirs in the interior of Sindhi and also Sindhis in Karachi, or require a massive transfer of population.

If the migrant community succeeds in getting a province of their own, including Karachi and access to the ocean, they would facilitate the flow of Indian Muslims into the new province. More than a hundred million Muslims in India feel as second class citizens. Many of them, particularly the poor and the unskilled, would consider this a second opportunity to migrate. The new provincial government would find a way to ease the migration through the vast seashore using its budgetary powers. Given the explosive population problem in Pakistan, the consequences of yet another flow of refugees into Pakistan have to be assessed for the rest of Pakistan in general and Sindh in particular.

There are also intelligence reports of MQM's desire to establish the new province and eventually declare independence. India and even some in the West are likely to support such a policy. The implications for the national security of Pakistan are likely to lead to resistance by the Pakistan armed forces and people of other provinces.

174. *Cooperation among Old and New Sindhis.* The answer lies in a need for all the Sindhis, new and old, to try harder to (a) understand each other, (b) respect each other's language and culture, (c) help each other in raising the standard of living, (d) work together to make peace throughout the province, and (e) put joint pressure on the federal government to resolve their grievances and oversee the equitable sharing of resources. If they took a longer term view instead of fighting over short term goals, Sindh could become a most pleasant paradise on earth for its inhabitants.

175. *Political Compromise*. The deal between MQM and PPP should try to give a political role to all members of the community including Mohajirs.
- No concession should be made at the expense of the legitimate rights of Sindhis.
- No false claim should be accepted.
- No concession should be given for reasons of terrorism and blackmail.

176. *Genuine Compromise*. Mohajirs as well as Sindhis are citizens of Pakistan. Their genuine demands have to be met. However, it must not be at the expense of anyone else. A genuine compromise must be fair to all and must include:
- INTEGRATION—greater effort by public and private means to integrate the native and new Sindhis in the province.
- LOCAL ELECTIONS—holding local government elections throughout the country including Karachi and Hyderabad as demanded by Mohajirs as well as other communities.
- DECENTRALIZATION of the government and giving as many powers to the local governments as possible—local governments of Karachi and Hyderabad should receive the same powers and responsibilities as others on the basis of their population size and other relevant criteria.
- FOCUSED AND PHASED QUOTAS—a well-focused quota for the deserving should be limited to residents of areas without adequate higher educational facilities. Within a short period after the requisite facilities are producing graduates, the quota should be phased out.
- JOINT STRUGGLE for increased federal allocation—joint efforts by Mohajirs and natives should be exerted for full rights and for equitable distribution of the national budget for education, jobs, investments, and other facilities.
- MUTUAL RECOGNITION of Urdu and Sindhi—recognition of Urdu as well as Sindhi language and culture and their protection through educational institutions, public administration, and official media as has been done for other groups in Pakistan.

Future of Sindh

Sindh as a whole is experiencing a very high growth of population due to natural fertility in rural areas and migration into urban area from within Pakistan and overseas, India, Bangladesh, Iran, Afghanistan, Burma, etc. Effective measures must be taken to stop migration into Sindh. Education and hygiene which tend to slow the natural fertility must be promoted.

Sindhis should aim to be thriving, contented, and successful people who are (a) working hard in a competitive way to improve themselves individually and collectively, but without cutting each other's throats; (b) enjoying fruits of their labor in field of their own choice in public and private sectors; (c) controlling their own destiny, free of coercion, bullying, or dictation from anyone; (d) secure and safe in every way inside their homes, within the Sindh province, and within Pakistan; (e) free from compulsion in choice or practice of language and culture; and (f) free from discrimination and exclusion from every quarter.

Sindhis (old and new) should develop themselves and participate as equals in Pakistan. Development is equally urgent on moral, economic, political, and social fronts. They should be able to (a) meet basic needs of adequate food, shelter, education, and health care for all, principally through ensuring gainful employment based on their qualifications; (b) have stable and representative government in the province which cooperates closely with all segments of society; (c) stop the violence plaguing urban and rural areas, tolerate and if possible peacefully resolve differences among the Sindhi speaking people, among Urdu speaking people, and Sindhis as a group; (d) be strong enough to defend their own vital interests against all.

The above should help the Sindhis to emerge as a self-sufficient, self-confident, peaceful, and strong group of people in Pakistan. It would gain them self-respect, and the respect of others. They would be treated as equal partners, and full participants within Pakistan.

All well-wishers of Sindh and the Sindh government must coordinate their efforts with the federal government, other provinces, donors supporting poverty reduction, and other interested groups at home and abroad to maximize the assault on poverty. Every obstacle in the way of poverty reduction including those listed earlier, must be removed. Again, there will be trade-offs and sacrifices will be required if Sindhis are serious. Only with well-directed and sincere efforts can the federal and provincial governments expect to reduce poverty in Sindh.

CHAPTER 13

CONFLICT IN BALOACHISTAN

Overview

Baloachistan is the largest province of Pakistan in size and the smallest in population. It rises steadily from the coastal plain of the sea of Arabia to the lofty height of Quetta, the provincial capital. Mountainous and extremely dry, it has scarce water resources and faces rural poverty, feudal control, and lack of infrastructure outside major towns. As Sindh, Baloachistan faces major problems including:

- the sardari (feudal) system and tribal laws rather than Pakistan government laws outside its few urban settlements;
- the absolute authority of the tribal leaders over their people;
- the limited interest of the leaders in advancement of their people— almost a determination to keep people backward;
- the growing power of narcotics producers and/or dealers as a source of possible challenge to Sardars;
- a middle class which is smaller and weaker than that of any other province in Pakistan; and
- a dangerous mixture of ethnic groups and subgroups which often explodes into violence.

Baloachistan has been ruled by the British government and subsequently by Pakistan, indirectly through cash and other favors to the Sardars. There is violence under one pretext or another if the payments or other favors from the government are reduced or even delayed. "Clan militia find that token attacks on the province's infrastructure are a useful way of reminding Islamabad of the apparent limits of the center's powers." [174] Violence has suited the tribal chiefs because it leaves their authority at local levels intact. It also permits them to dispense central and local government patronage at will. However, it has left the common citizen backward. The people need to be educated and brought into the nation's mainstream.

---

[174] "On the border of Violence," *The Financial Times*, (London; April 9 1996), p. v.

There have been quotas for educational facilities and jobs designed to develop the backward people. However, they have been used primarily by the Sardars to advance their own families and a few loyal and close associates. The economic and job quotas in fact are needed by the backward communities and should be continued, but, as discussed in the case of Sindh, measures must be put in place to ensure that they reach those deserving within each community rather than nominees of Sardars.

The press within the province is limited and restrained too. They dare not point a finger at an important person without fear of physical violence.

177. *Family Feuds Among the Baloach Sardars.* Baloach society has traditionally been stratified and characterized as "feudal militarism." The significant social tie is between a leader, the *hakim,* and his retinue.[175] Tribal violence or clan warfare is a part of daily life. Historically, when the Sardars fought among each other, only their followers died. In recent times, the Sardars are getting killed themselves. In 1983, Nawab Ghous Bux Raisani, the powerful chief of Sarawan, was assassinated following clashes that had taken place during the "Local Bodies" elections that year. This led to a lasting enmity between the Raisanis and the Bugtis.

In 1992, Sardar Taj Muhammad Rind and Sardar Arif Jan Muhammad Hasni were killed. Both were former members of the National Assembly. The same year, Amir Hamza Bugti, son of a Kalpar landlord, Khan Muhammad, was killed during the Local Bodies polls at Dera Bugti. The Kalpars took revenge within weeks by gunning down Salal Bugti who was the favorite son and political heir to Sardar Akbar Bugti. [176]

On 27 August 1994, nine persons, including three grandchildren of Nawab Akbar Bugti, were killed and more than sixteen innocent bystanders were injured in crossfire between tribesmen from Bugti and Raisani tribes.[177] This was the largest incident of its kind in terms of tribal rivalries and is likely to lead to even more violence.

On 22 November 1995, a few men hiding in bushes killed Ayub Buledi, the Baloachistan Minister of Excise. He was not a Sardar but belonged to the middle class. Some speculate that it was an "attempt by the once politically powerful mafia, now losing ground to the enlightened and educated middle

[175] Blood, pp. 113-17.

[176] "Long Trail of Blood in Baloachistan," in *The Pakistan Link*, (22 December 1995), p. 5.

[177] *The Newsline,* (September, 1994), p. 59.

class, to regain their political position simply by eliminating their opponents."[178] Some attribute murders like these to trigger-happiness of one or the other party at a particular moment. Others attribute it to well-planned conspiracies.

The local government is often unable to control the Sardars. *Jirgas,* the tribal courts, which often work well for common people, usually work less effectively when the Sardars or other powerful people are involved themselves. The responsibility remains with the federal government to ensure law-an- order; to date, it has been ineffective for the most part.

178. *Division Among Baloach, Pashtun, and Punjabis.* The previous balance among the three communities has been upset by the influx of Afghan refugees. There are now about 400,000 Afghan refugees in Baloachistan. Many of the refugees have acquired Pakistani identity cards and registered on voters lists. The Baloachs who have been the majority in all censuses since 1901, are visibly concerned. They fear being converted into a minority in their own province. Fairness and transparency of the census, including checking identity cards and excluding the refugees may resolve the issue.

The southern part of the province has the vast majority of Baloach people, while the northern ones are primarily Pashtu-speaking Pathans. Given the ethnic divisions in other parts of the country, and cultural and linguistic differences among the two main groups, demand for division of the province can become an issue and may lead to conflict. Steps taken now to achieve integration of the various communities would prevent such conflict.

Conclusions

The grievances of the people have been underestimated and ignored. Their concerns and justified demands need to be fully understood and acted upon. The small provinces suffer from all of the problems that the country as a whole does. In addition, they suffer from issues peculiar to them.

The government must pay special attention to developing the small provinces which happen to be least developed. Special encouragement must be given to new industries, particularly those providing employment and future growth (e.g., electronics). Inter-provincial problems (e.g., allocation of water, and financial resources) must be resolved equitably. The federal government must consider special developmental priorities of the people of small provinces.

---

[178] *The Pakistan Link,* (22 December 1995), p. 5.

Feudalism must be eradicated and a middle class must be developed. The common people are particularly concerned about the relative lack of government efforts to preserve their languages and cultural heritage. Special encouragement and resources must be provided.

The Baloach and Sindhi leadership, including the politicians, the press, civil servants, intellectuals, and the military must reassess their cultural anomalies. They must discard archaic ideas which have decayed, leaving only remnants of their original value. The issues relating to a dowry at the time of marriage, "marriage to the Qur'an" in the case of non-availability of a suitable match within the family, murder in the case of the slightest suspicion of sexual misconduct, etc. must be reconsidered.

The central government and Pakistanis from all provinces must realize that an overwhelming portion of the population wishes to remain a part of Pakistan. This has been repeatedly demonstrated by the defeat of separatist parties in elections. The decision makers must therefore remove the cloud of suspicion regarding national loyalty which hangs over almost every Sindhi and Baloach.

A constitutional provision is needed to protect the rights of all ethnic minorities. It should include provisions for the protection and development of their language, culture, economy, and human rights. The need for provincial and local government autonomy is particularly strong in Sindh outside Karachi and Hyderabad and Baloachistan, where a large number of civil servants are not willing to transfer.

Steps must be taken to achieve a better integration of the various communities within Sindh and Baloachistan provinces so that a division of the provinces, which is sure to lead to great conflict and bloodshed, will not be necessary.

CHAPTER 14

CORRUPTION

**Do not usurp one another's property by unjust means, nor bribe
with it the judges in order that you knowingly and wrongfully
deprive others of a part of their possessions. (Qur'an 2:188)**

Souls For Sale

179. *Easy to Purchase.* For those who can see, there is a big "For Sale" sign
all around Pakistan. Almost everyone and almost everything is for sale—
state secrets, appointments to cabinet and senate posts, powerful positions in
the civil service, government lands, government assets in industry, banking,
new loans, and projects. From the top, the highest elected and appointed
public officials appear willing and able to sell everything for the sake of
keeping or enhancing the powers and positions that they have acquired.

The most senior opposition politicians are willing to sell whatever state
secrets and physical assets they have and to mortgage whatever they will
control in the future, provided they are brought into power. At the lowest
level, the common voters are ready to give away their votes for the jobs and
favors which are promised, either by the political parties and the candidates
directly, or through middle men. Almost everyone is willing and able to sell
their soul in the name of "survival."

For reasons of need, greed or insecurity, Pakistanis are easy to purchase.
It is commonly felt that most public officials at all levels can be made to look
at any issue from any point of view, if the right price is paid. It is particularly
easy for individuals, organizations, and governments from the West. Even
ministers and senior officials can be purchased by representatives of Western
countries with a smile, an invitation to a cocktail party, the companionship
of a pretty woman, a visa to the right country, etc. If nothing else works, one
can be easily threatened of dire consequences or blackmailed into submission
and treachery. National interests often have a secondary position in relation
to personal interests. Thanks to a relatively free press, hundreds of instances
of such corruption have been made public. Books written by former officials
from the Western countries have added to the exposé of prominent persons.

Corruption

180. *Definition*. Obtaining money illegally is the most common form of corruption. It happens in a wide range of activities ranging from cash bribery in exchange for illegal favors to loans from government banks without intention of repayment; sale of government lands at artificially low prices to those in power; purchase of private lands at low market price with prior knowledge of forthcoming government projects on the same land; and other real estate fraudulent transactions perceived to be legal.

Corruption can be found in all parts of the world. However, in developed countries, the common man does not need to pay extra money for obtaining routine services, the rich and powerful are often willing to pay to secure added benefits and extraordinary services. In Pakistan (and most developing countries), common people pay extra to obtain even the simplest and most routine services.

181. *Who Pays*. Many people pay. People pay for unjustifiable favors related to employment, contracts, prosecution, etc. People pay for accelerated action on justified works, e.g., driving license renewal, movement of a file in a government office, etc. From a broader perspective, all citizens who pay pass on the cost—shopkeepers pass on the cost to those who buy their product. Contractors simply increase the bid price of the next contract. Eventually, the nation as a whole pays.

There is a general notion that corruption is everywhere and nothing can be done to stop it. Every government has an anti-corruption department which catches many small fish. The big ones always seem to get away. Once a while, there are major purges of senior officials, however, corruption is growing. The 1993 interim government in Pakistan led by Moeen Qureshi initiated steps to force some powerful individuals to repay loans to the government treasury. The effort had limited success.

182. *Who Takes*. People with official authority to do things—power to move a file from one desk to another; or to make a final award of a multimillion dollar contract—can get paid. Not every official takes unjustifiable actions or refrains from doing their duty for pay. However, it is the public perception that more and more people are willing to receive the extra gratification. Thirty years ago, a majority of public officials did not accept payments. Now a majority does. Up to ten years ago, officials would not admit acceptance of bribes. Now, there is no shame or stigma. People demand payments and acknowledge them publicly.

183. *Where*. During private conversations, Pakistan government officials confirm that corruption exists in virtually every part of the government. There is no sacred territory or whistle-blowing haven.

184. *Bribes for Politicians*. Members of the national and provincial assemblies receive fund allocations for development works in their respective constituencies with few strings. It is widely reported that little of it is used for the benefit of the constituents. Most of it is pocketed. The rest is spent on schemes which personally benefit the members, e.g., roads connecting existing public highways to houses, farms, factories or other places of interest to members.

The members stand to make the most money in times of political instability. In case of unclear majorities, coalition governments mean huge cash payments and ministerial portfolios for members of small parties who get to play king makers. Threats of no-confidence votes against a government bring about vast rewards at the public expense. The need for this type of expenditure is asserted to be a main justification by each political party for "accumulating funds" while they are in power.

Government officials from the president on down are accused of taking unfair advantage of their official position. Press, common people, and, in some cases, the courts have accused them of misusing government property for personal use.

In a typical situation, young and dedicated party workers of PPP, MQM, or other parties have worked hard for years. They are poor and thin, and have sacrificed everything for the cause and the party. Then the party gets power. The lucky young worker becomes an MPA, MNA, or even a minister. In most cases, both the mental and physical personality changes.

The political and bureaucratic power brings about a new way of thinking which is not different from those of other feudal lords and other powerful people. The power changes the personality. The dedicated worker becomes arrogant, unapproachable, greedy, and abusive. Physically, he becomes fatter, acquires new social habits, including drinking, and is frequently lethargic and indifferent at work. He becomes dedicated to accumulation of wealth, satisfaction of personal pleasures, and perpetuation of power. He becomes one of those whom he despised and worked hard to replace a few short years ago. The nation must wait years to see if the next round of young and dedicated workers will be any better!

Investigations by the State Bank of Pakistan into the affairs of United Bank Limited in 1996 revealed another type of abuse. The labor union leadership allegedly took control of 180 to 190 vehicles of the bank "whose bills for petrol consumption and overtime payment of drivers were being collected at gun point." Similarly salaries were collected for "ghost workers" who never reported for work. Such activities resulted in a loss of Rp 680 million to 690 million or about $35 million per year to the bank.[179]

185. *Windfalls for the Bankers*. Bankers have control over allocation of the most scarce commodity namely, money. They have authority to approve investment loans, they can charge informal fees for guidance on loan processing, and they can charge varying degree of personal commissions on approval of almost every loan. They can also charge more for approving undeserving loans. They can charge for denying and then reconsidering and approving deserving projects. They can reap major windfalls when there is an opportunity for writing off unpaid loans. The large numbers of defaulted loans indicate that numerous projects were approved on the basis of deficient financial statements. Some people have obviously made a lot of money in the process.

186. *Over-invoicing of Equipment Purchased with Government Loans*. Influential individuals who wish to set up a new industry with government support can make a profit immediately. They can borrow up to seventy percent of the value of the investment from one of the government's financing institutions. If it is judged to be a "priority" industry, they can get another twenty percent from the institution in equity. By "over invoicing imported machinery, he can get the government to pay more than the cost of the whole investment, as well as stashing away some foreign exchange in London or Switzerland."[180]

187. *Land Allocation*. Officials often seek and receive payment in connection with legal transactions, e.g., transfer of titles or registration of property. A great deal of money is also pocketed through allotment of government land to favored people at below market rates. Many stories have been reported in the press since the time of independence. As an example, the *Newsline* of June, 1995 quoted an opposition leader complaining that two plots of land of 30 acres each in Karachi were initially allotted to former Revenue Minister Sibghatullah Shah and a builder Haji Adam Jokhio for one and a half crore

---

[179] *The Pakistan Link,* (17 May 1996), pp. A1 and A26.

[180] Emma Duncan, *Breaking the Curfew* (Arrow Books, 1989), p. 38.

each. They sold them to another builder Firoz Gitu for thirty crores each. Gitu resold to other builders and developers for sixty crores each. [181]

The government received a total of three crores (approximately one million dollars) for a property valued at one hundred twenty crores (approximately forty million dollars). Forty-fold profits resulted from allocation of land at a preferential rate. Thousands of such transactions take place under each government. The amounts run into billions of rupees, if not dollars. Favored politicians, bureaucrats, military officials, and businessmen have benefitted and continue to do so.

Officials dealing with land issues and control can make money in connection with encroachments on public or private lands; valuation of property —increasing the value so that sellers can get more or decreasing it so that the buyers can pay less or buy more. In each case the government is the victim because there are few who will protect its interest. Usually the person guarding it is the one giving away the government (and really public) assets in return for a small private gain.

188. *Purchase of Military Equipment.* Commissions on the purchase of military equipment are notoriously high. There have been frequent reports of huge commissions pocketed by senior politicians, bureaucrats, and military officials. Hundreds of millions of dollars in commissions are involved in the purchase of expensive military hardware such as aircrafts and submarines. The accused rarely bother to deny their guilt. The powerless citizens are unable to do anything about such abuse.

Dr. Mehboobul Haq, former finance minister of Pakistan, and others have alleged that top officials in the defense department of the country were involved in getting commissions for striking deals to purchase military hardware. "Pakistan may be the only country in the world where no system exists to decide on the purchase or import of equipment." In other countries, such decisions are taken by defense committees of the Parliament, but in Pakistan, it is done secretly.

"A country purchases a jet paying US $10 million to the producer, but at the same time gets another one paying $30 million." Why is it so? asked Dr. Mehboobul Haq. Because the vested interests of generals and dealers are involved, he added.[182]

---

[181] Ibid., p. 88.

[182] *The Pakistan Link,* (16 February 1996), p. 16.

189. *Police*. Police departments collect money from accused persons in exchange for delay in or avoidance of prosecution. They can collect from a complainant for speedy registrations of complaints, for actions against accused, or to prevent destruction of evidence or dismissal of the case. The jail administrators make a lot of money from goods and services provided to the accused or to convicted prisoners in jail.

Passport Office. The Passport Office collects money in many ways, including occasionally losing a large number of blank passports. Another common way is using the requirement of police reports. The report is meant to ensure that the applicant for a passport is not a criminal. However, in practice it is used to delay the issuance of a passport until a bribe is paid. Outside each passport office, agents are around to facilitate the police report for a fee of around Rp 500 per passport. Even Abdus Sattar Edhi, the well-known social worker and founder of Edhi Trust, was required to produce a similar certificate.[183]

190. *Judiciary*. Corrupt officials in the judiciary can obtain money for granting bail, acquittal of the accused or in determination of the sentence (length, location, facilities, etc.). Then there is *bakhsish* or "palm greasing" for lower level staff who want payment for issuing a copy of a legal document or expediting implementation of a legally binding order.

People with authority to provide employment to others in any and all departments have a great opportunity for pocketing money. Many charge for appointments to new jobs, transfers to more desirable positions or locations, promotions, and similar favorable job-related benefits.

191. *Public Works*. Payment rates are much larger in departments managing public funds and contracts. The public works department has always been notorious for kickbacks. The irrigation department responsible for dredging canals, may get to keep as much as 70% of the contract amount since it is hard to verify exactly how much volume of earth or silt was excavated. Some claim that little if any silt is excavated as evidenced by almost annual floods in the same canal systems. Other departments of public works may charge up to 40% on the contract amounts for road construction. The amounts pocketed are rumored to be even larger in the case of repaving of secondary and tertiary roads. The smallest quantity of rain seems conveniently to wash away the "recently completed" repair work.

---

[183] *The Pakistan Link,* (31 May 1996), p. 14.

192. *Public Utilities*. Officials of public utilities, e.g., telephone, electricity, and water departments, make money for themselves during awards of construction or maintenance contracts, and by provision of accelerated legal connections, overlooking illegal connections, arranging or accepting lower meter reading, etc. People with large telephone or electricity bills often make deals with the relevant staff to reduce the bill to a fraction in exchange for a monthly side payment.

193. *Ministry of Finance*. There are many ways of cheating on taxes. With the help of government officials the ways become innumerable. For example, an excise duty is levied on the basis of production in factories, seating capacity in cinemas, number of rooms in hotels, etc. People reportedly make deals with tax officials to declare lower capacity, lower production, or lower number. In turn, they may receive a percentage (as much as a third) of the value of the tax one would have paid. Businessmen or professionals declare only a fraction of their income by paying relatively small amounts to the tax officials. There is also money to be made in controlling legitimate payments. Officials may charge up to 10% for release of the money they have earned to the contractors.

194. *Customs*. Officials of customs departments are the most notorious for bribery. They collect pocket money for simply closing their eyes while a passenger coming from abroad passes through the green channel with his stuffed boxes and suitcases. They charge for favorable rulings on duty exemption on goods, valuation of goods, smuggling etc. The candidates seeking jobs in the customs department are willing to pay large amounts of money for appointments and transfers.

195. *Public Health*. Health officials are accused of making money through purchase of outdated medicines with large kickbacks; theft and sale of public equipment and medicines meant for poor patients; false certifications varying from sick leave to government employees to cause of death in cases of questionable deaths; and provision of false alibis. For a small fee, they can issue a false certificate about someone being sick in order to justify absence from work. For a larger amount, they can issue a certificate whether wounds in an assault or murder case were deep or superficial.

A doctor informed the author of how a very prominent local feudal lord walked into the office of the superintendent of a public hospital and demanded that he show in the hospital's official record that a particular person had his appendix removed the previous day. The superintendent obliged.

Later it turned out that "the patient" was accused of having committed three murders the previous evening. The "surgery" provided him a perfect alibi.

196. *Corruption in Educational Institutions.* Relatively speaking, teaching institutions have fewer chances of corruption. Yet the teachers and officials are accused of corruption in various forms: Inadequate preparation for classes; unauthorized use of lower level staff (for domestic work), vehicles, and other facilities (e.g., rental of servants quarters); commissions on contract awards for purchase/repairs of facilities and equipment; private tuition payment from students; allowing copying during examinations; unfair marking during exams; selling of examination halls—in some areas, examiners are paid a large amount of money to look the other way during the examinations.

The Human Rights Commission of Pakistan reported that corruption in examination boards was widely admitted. It was estimated to be in the region of Rp. 50 million in each of the boards of secondary and intermediate examinations. Other institutions like the Punjab Education Foundation also reveled in wrongful expenditures on massive scales.[184]

Civil servants are not embarrassed anymore about living beyond their means. Like businessmen, they ask for their percentage openly and up front.[185] In general, there is a culture of corruption. Those who do not pay will not get required services or approvals and will not be able to complete their transactions. Big and small companies will not be able to get approvals for their new projects, borrow money from the banks, get approvals for issue of new equity shares, get approvals for land acquisition; nonpayment will assure that tax authorities will start investigating your affairs.

Those who pay willingly find life to be much easier. Business opportunities and more money come their way. The same applies to common citizens who want admission in a school, a job, a driving license, a plot for house building, leniency from police, etc.

Size of Corruption

197. *Federal Government Spending.* It is believed that 20% to 40% of government expenditures are syphoned off in payoffs to government officials. Using gross national product (GNP) data, a rough estimate of the

[184] The Human Rights Commission of Pakistan, *State of Human Rights 1993:* An Interim Report; (Lahore), p. 6.

[185] Duncan, pp. 40-43.

payoffs on central government expenditures can be made in millions of U.S. dollars. Based on 1993 data, the central government of Pakistan spent 24% of GNP.[186] With $430 per capita for a population of 122.8 million, total GNP of Pakistan amounted to $52,804 million. The central government expenditure thus equaled $12,672 million.

Assuming that the payoff equaled only 20% of the expenditure, the total payoff would have amounted to more than $2,534 million in 1993. This figure does not include expenditures by provincial and local governments where the rate of bribery and corruption is known to be even higher, nor does it include many other types of payoffs mentioned above.

In comparison, during 1993, Pakistan received only $1,065 in official development assistance from all overseas sources. It must be noted that much of the receipts were in the form of loans, which have to be repaid. The foreign aid amounted to a fraction of potential savings from the bribery.

Table 8: Estimated Payoffs on Central Government Expenditures in 1993

Payoff Rate (%)	Bribery (million US dollars)	Bribery as % of Foreign Aid
20	2,534	237%
30	3,801	357%
40	5,068	476%

If the bribery on government expenditure can be eliminated or reduced, much of the foreign assistance will not be required.

198. *Theft of Electric Power.* During fiscal year 1994, the Water and Power Development Authority of Pakistan (WAPDA) lost more than 24% of its electricity. About half of it is assumed to have been due to theft, with or without knowledge and consent of WAPDA's employees. Based on audited financial statements, WAPDA had total operating revenue from electricity of about Rp 50 billion. WAPDA lost revenue of Rp 15.7 billion due to the loss of electricity. About a half of the loss amounting to Rp 7.88 billion or about $ 262 million at the prevailing exchange rate was due to theft.

WAPDA had an investment program of about Rp 25.5 billion in that year for which it borrowed a total of Rp 20 billion. Foreign loans amounted to Rp

---

[186] The World Bank, *World Development Report 1995*, Tables 1, 10, and 19.

14 billion which was less than the lost revenue. It may be noted that more than half of the foreign loans used in that year would not have been required if the theft of electricity was avoided.

There are hundreds of other items, such as kickbacks on government loans, and payments to police and other government officials for favors unrelated to the federal government contracts, which are difficult to quantify. In any case, the total loss to the economy is much higher than the foreign assistance received each year from all sources. If the economy could conserve the leakage of money caused by bribery, there would be no need for foreign assistance at current levels of investments.

Payoffs of 20 to 40% in provincial government contracts are also fairly common. The amounts are reportedly much higher in local governments. In Karachi, payoffs of up to 50% for Municipal Corporation and Karachi Development Authority contracts have been mentioned.

Consultancy contracts regularly include provisions for bribery through excessive rental amounts for offices, residences, automobiles, and other equipment. Recent reports charge that local consulting companies are expected to pay up to 40% of the contract value in kickbacks.

199. *Sharing of the Loot.* The public seems to feel that everyone is on the take. In fact, most are! Within public works and other departments, there are well-established formulas for sharing of the loot, e.g., the executive engineer, subdivisional officers (SDO), and overseers may each receive 5% of the contract payment. Of course, the higher-ups receive a much larger amount because they control a large number of officers and contracts. In recent times, those "closest to the throne" have been accused of getting the largest share of the loot. The son of a president, the brother of a prime minister, and the husband of another prime minister have been the most notorious.

200. *Pervasive Corruption.* There is a general notion that corruption is every where and nothing can be done to stop it. It is frightening not only for the common citizen who wishes to operate honestly but also horrifying for the remaining honest civil servants. They fear Allah and they fear the widespread web of the corrupt ones.

Those who refuse to accept bribery are often unwilling to allow others to do the same. They become thorns for their seniors as well as the juniors. The honest ones are a threat to the overall corrupt system. They are considered unaccommodating and are often denied important assignments and promotions. Some God-fearing citizens avoid powerful assignments lest they may be trapped.

Second Most Corrupt Nation in the World. Transparency International, an anti-corruption pressure group, ranks nations on the basis of prevalence of bribery, as perceived by businessmen. Nigeria has been ranked as the most corrupt. Pakistan is rated second followed by Kenya, Bangladesh, China, Cameroon, Venezuela, Russia, India, and Indonesia. On the other side, New Zealand has been rated as the least corrupt, followed by Denmark, Sweden, Finland, Canada, Norway, Singapore, Switzerland, the Netherlands, and Austria.[187]

Why Does It Continue?

Access to power now meant phenomenal fortunes—fortunes unimaginable to those located outside the state. The sword had always commanded its share of wealth ... Control of means of destruction had always paid off ... It was difficult to tell where public authority ended and personal plunder began.[188]

201. *Immunity Under the Constitution.* The president, prime minister, federal ministers, provincial governors, chief ministers, and ministers in Pakistan enjoy blanket amnesty under the Constitution for all acts performed during tenure in office. These officials often use their powers, particularly the discretionary ones, to benefit themselves without any fear of prosecution. They are openly accused in the press of making policy and contract decisions —based on bribes rather than on merits.

202. *Systems Do Not Function.* In Pakistan, systems and procedures of government often do not function well for routine things (police investigations, providing water for agriculture land, telephone billing, issuing driving license, etc.). The government officials are the gatekeepers. They want payment for performing the most routine functions. Honest officials are not always a blessing either. They are often proud of their honesty, sticklers for details, slower in performance and may make non-cash demands. Accordingly, many people are often willing to pay affordable amounts of money just to get things done. For business, it is a part of the cost of doing business.

---

[187]"Where Money Talks," in *Time,* (10 June 1996), p. 24.

[188] Fouad Ajami, *The Arab Predicament,* (Cambridge University Press, 1981), p. 183.

The failure of the system manifests itself in a number of ways:

- Declining faith in the working of the legal system. It results in cultivating contacts with those who can meet the needs of people. They charge money for the service. The legal system declines further.
- Monopoly on availability of development plans results in inside knowledge of land acquisition. People with the knowledge acquire land at cheap prices from unsuspecting peasants or small holders and then promptly resell the land to the government for inflated prices.
- Transfer of public assets for private use. For example, in the fifties and sixties, when irrigation was introduced to large tracts of virgin lands in the province of Sindh, a significant portion was given to government functionaries—mostly civil and military officers. This effectively resulted in the transfer of potential income from the province's indigenous population to new land colonizers.[189]

203. *Financial Need.* Some have argued that corruption takes place because of the low salaries of public employees. They simply need to supplement their salaries in order to survive at a reasonable standard of living. This may be particularly true for lower level officials. As mentioned above, party officials argue that they need bribery to pay debts from the past campaigns and get ready for the next one.

204. *Greed.* Evidence shows that many civil servants continue to amass wealth through illegal means well beyond a reasonable level of need. Some claim the needs of their children and other dependents. Others talk of keeping up with the living standards of their peers. Many in positions of power simply continue to loot because of greed.

205. *Absence of Fear of Punishment.* Government officials have found unique methods of protecting themselves. They leave perfect paper trails. Generally, the whole department shares the loot in a prescribed manner. The money really comes from the padded prices which contractors are encouraged to charge to the government. Senior officials provide protection for colleagues and subordinates. Once in a while there are major purges of senior officials. However, the corruption only tends to grow.

There has been some cleansing of civil service through group firing—about 300 were fired by General Ayub and about 1,200 fired by President Bhutto; however, there has been no consistent and fair action against

---

[189] Shahid Javed Burki, "Pakistan's Economy in the Year 2000."

corruption. Many officials against whom action has been taken feel that action was taken for political reasons rather than to fight corruption.

Why Do People Tolerate It?

People tolerate corruption because:
- It is so widespread that almost everyone is involved.
- They all benefit from it one way or the other.
- They are helpless and do not know how to stop it.
- Corruption lubricates the wheels of government; people will accept it until the government can be made more efficient.
- It is the only way to get something done.
- Most people who pay are able to pass on the cost; people who cannot pass it on are hurt, but they are relatively few and relatively powerless.

206. *Final Analysis.* Most of the money comes from the general government treasury, and not from individual pockets. Those who make the payments, consider it a part of doing business, add the charges to invoices, and are reimbursed through signatures of those who received the kickback and authorized the payment. Most of the "corruption money" is simply adding to the cost of goods and services procured by the government.

The government could invest in the country much more if savings from reduced corruption could be realized. If people realized how much more would be available for education, schools, hospitals, and infrastructure development, they would possibly demand firmer action against corruption. If, for example, the actual cost of constructing "roads" in a given year is only one half of the contracted price and the rest is going to bribery, then twice as many roads could be built with the same money if bribery were to be eliminated. The implications are significant.

Corrective Action

Corruption is an unnecessary burden on the people. Pakistan's government should work more diligently to stop it. Many solutions can be suggested. They are all obvious and simple, but difficult to implement without a serious commitment of people and government. The solutions include:
- Create an ethical environment.
- Set good examples at the top; higher-ups in government must set proper examples, must be held to a higher standard and should be subject to higher punishment for corruption.

- Review the government's cost structure to determine what the cost of different items ought to be, and make sure to have disincentives for padding those costs.
- Set and award exemplary punishment on a systematic and consistent basis. Many have told the author that despite outward appearances, many government servants are really insecure and timid. They are ready, willing, and able to do everything to protect their jobs. If they get a firm signal that bribery will lead to termination of employment, confiscation of property or jail, they will stop.
- Increase income of public officials to a reasonable level to allow them to survive honestly. Accordingly, salaries of all public officials must be reviewed and suitably revised.
- More education of citizens, transparency of government, and account-ability on individual basis will encourage reduction of corruption.
- Reform of the police, judiciary and anti-corruption apparatus.
- Fear of Allah and punishment right here in this world.
- Less emphasis on consumerism by the society.
- Financial insecurity is one of the main causes; introduction of economic safety nets for "have nots" will discourage corruption.

The above suggestions have been implemented in varying degrees, over a long period of time in the developed countries. There is some corruption everywhere. However, in most developed countries, common people are not harassed in day-to-day activities. A few unique solutions have emerged in recent times in some developing countries, too. South Korea's first civilian president in thirty-two years, Kim Young Sam, has made a dent by simply demanding that all bank accounts bear the names of their true owners. Former President Roh Tae Woo was arrested on charges that he collected bribes from companies to amass a $654 million political slush fund.[190] The Iranian Revolution has reportedly reduced corruption significanthy. Some unique and tailor-made solutions for Pakistan may also be needed. Corruption has to be considered a well-planned and organized theft. Comparable punishment has to be awarded. The people of Pakistan appear to want major changes in society, particularly regarding corruption in government.

---

[190] *The Washington Post,* (19 November 1995), p. A21.

CHAPTER 15

BORDERS AND NEIGHBORS

Truely Allah loves those who fight in His cause in the battle array, as if they were a solid cemented structure (Qur'an 61:4).

Policy Objectives

Pakistan's foreign policy has been marked by a complex balancing process—the result of its history, religious heritage, and geographic position. The primary objective of that policy has been to preserve Pakistan's territorial integrity and security, which have been in jeopardy since the state's inception.[191]

Key elements of the policy have included:
- the quest for security against India, which may not have reconciled itself to the existence of an independent Pakistan;
- seeking security through outside alliances or strategic relationships particularly with the United States and China;
- searching resolution of the Kashmir problem;
- close relations with all South Asian countries for purposes of improved trade, communication, addressing issues of mutual concern, and avoiding threats from India;
- close relations with Islamic countries for religious, economic, political, and strategic reasons; and
- reliance on the United Nations and its specialized agencies for developmental assistance and for resolution of issues such as Kashmir, Afghanistan, etc., in spite of the shortcomings and weaknesses of the UN itself.

President Ayub Khan stated Pakistan's foreign policy and defense objectives well:

---

[191] Blood, pp. 243-254.

Our relations with other countries would be determined by our requirements of national defense and development and must reflect geopolitical compulsions of our location.[192]

Pakistan and India

There have been four wars between India and Pakistan . . . More than five million lost their lives in those wars . . . Two of the poorest nations in the world—India and Pakistan—spent more than $11 billion a year for the purpose of waging a future war. The conflict has its roots in profound religious differences, but it has been exacerbated by the fact that the Soviet Union supported India, and China supported Pakistan. (Richard Nixon)[193]

207. *History.* India has been either the direct or indirect factor in formulation of Pakistan's foreign policy from the start. India and Pakistan share the same subcontinent. They share history, geography, culture, and roots of all kinds. Hindus and Muslims have lived together for centuries, at times struggling to overcome common enemies. Yet, there was partition based on differences of religion between Hindus and Muslims.

While Pakistanis feel that they should have gotten more territory as a result of the Partition of the subcontinent, they were relatively happy that the partition took place. Over the years, however, anger has been building. In a top secret memo to General Tikka Khan, Chief of Staff, Army, then President Zulfikar Ali Bhutto wrote on 23 June 1972 that:

We have always wanted peace—but peace with honor and freedom. India, on the other hand, at the very birth of our country, thrust upon us violence, tyranny and oppression. She occupied Hyderabad by force, annexed Junagadh unlawfully after its accession to us, and for twenty-three years denied to the Kashmiris the plebiscite pledged before the United Nations. In 1971, she committed unconcealed aggression against us . . . bisected our country . . . The threat from India keeps mounting . . . So neither a few years of arranged peace, nor the present situation can possibly

[192] Ayub Khan, *Friends Not Masters, A Political Biography,* (Karachi: 1967), p. 85.

[193] Richard Nixon, *Beyond Peace* (New York: Random House,1994).

permit us to ignore the reality that there must inevitably, sooner or later, come another war.[194]

Hindus of India and their government appear to resent the historic rule of Muslims extending over several centuries, and see the partition as uncalled for, a desecration of "mother India." Historically, India's area of influence extended far beyond the current borders. To Pakistanis, Indians wish to regain those borders. In that context, they see other neighbors, such as Nepal, Bhutan, Sri Lanka, Burma, and even Bangladesh, as having been "controlled" to some extent, but not Pakistan.

Pakistanis see India seeking to establish the Indian Ocean as truly "Indian" and believe that India wishes to be master of the area just as the United States is master of the Caribbean. To them, even the United States has historically wished to "bring Pakistan under Indian hegemony." [195] Of course the main objective of the United States has been to make India and Pakistan jointly face China.

The existence and certainly the strength of Pakistan have been a source of "irritation" to India. It is a miracle that the situation is not worse and that there have not been greater hostilities between the two countries.

208. *Current Status*. Pakistan and India have been looking at the world with different eyes for many years. They have differences of opinion on a number of critical issues. The most prominent of these relates to the future of Kashmir. However, other issues in contention relate to Siachin Glacier, nuclear proliferation, military size, budget and content, visa restrictions, trade policies, telecommunications, etc. From the Pakistani side, Kashmir is the number one issue. The Indians give priority to other subjects.

The implications of these problems are many. There has been an almost continuous state of war among the two neighbors resulting in three major wars to date. Probably both sides are making continued efforts to humiliate and destabilize the other. The animosity has resulted in mutual fear and hatred and huge annual outlays on intelligence and the military on both sides.

Many families which were divided as a result of the partition are kept apart as a result of the visa restrictions by both sides. "As New Delhi and Islamabad engage in a war of diplomatic one-upmanship, visa applicants on both sides of the border are being forced to undergo endless emotional and

---

[194]Wolpert, p. 186.

[195] Bhutto, *The Myth of Independence,* pp. 79-92.

financial hardship."[196] It may be noted that today India is the second largest home of Muslims in the world; only Indonesia has a larger Muslim population. Even the Indian government concedes that there are more Muslims in India than in Pakistan or Bangladesh.[197]

The state of affairs has meant a miserable life for the minorities on each side. Muslims who have chosen to stay in India, and Hindus in Pakistan are both suffering. Frequent communal riots make life even more miserable. The future for them does not appear to be bright. Tourism, which could be beneficial for both sides, remains a fraction of what it could be.

Trade and commerce which has existed between the two areas since long before the British conquest has been virtually stopped. Borders stretching more than 1400 kilometers and a well-developed network of communications including roads, railways, telephones, and telegraph which existed in 1947 has largely remained blocked and unused.

Each government of Pakistan has recognized the numerical, economic, and military superiority of India and has tried to resolve the Kashmir issue peacefully. Nevertheless, none has openly conceded Kashmir to India. India also has repeatedly talked of better relations. Even Prime Minister Nehru offered a "no-war pact" but without resolution of Kashmir.[198] Goodwill ends whenever the question of Kashmir comes to the table. Prime Minister H. D. Deve Gowda reportedly offered a no-war pact also.

Hindus and Muslims

> **Revile not ye those whom they call upon besides Allah, lest they out of spite revile Allah in their ignorance . . . (Qur'an 6:108)**

> **We did aforetime send Messengers before thee: of them there are some whose story We have related to thee, and some whose story We have not related to thee . . . (Qur'an 40:78)**

The average Muslim of the subcontinent believes that Hindus worship many gods in the form of several types of statues and cows. This is totally unacceptable to Muslims. However, study of the religion would show that in

[196] *India Today* (15 April 1995), pp. 84-87.

[197] Statement by Indian Ambassador to USA, Mr. Ray in a television interview on 19 August 1995.

[198] Altaf Gauhar, *Ayub Khan* (Lahore: Sang-e-meel Publications), p. 57.

Hinduism there is only one supreme God known as Permatma. He has been manifested to the followers in three forms, Brahma (the Creator), Vishnu (the Preserver), and Shiva (the destroyer). The Preserver is supposed to reappear from time to time to show the right way to the followers.

Hindus explain that they make statues of all physical appearances of God, as well as other important characters of their history and mythology. They show respect to all such manifestations including cows, but they worship only one God. Hindus feel that it is as unfair to think of destroying their statues, as it would be to destroy graves or shrines of holy men of Islam.

Just as Muslims await the coming of Imam Mahdi and/or Prophet Isa, son of Mariam (i.e., Jesus), and Christians await the second coming of Jesus, Hindus await the final appearance of Vishnu, the Preserver. On the day of judgement for Hindus, Shiva will destroy it all. Under different names, Hindus believe in one God and a Day of Judgment.

Hindus and Muslims have noted the differences among them, e.g., Muslims believe in equality of humans while Hindus have an elaborate caste system; Muslims pray relatively quietly, while Hindus sing and play music in their temples; Hindus do not eat beef while Muslims do not touch pork. However, they have either failed to see or chosen to ignore the common features of their faiths and their similar code of good human behavior.

In spite of centuries of misunderstandings and conflict in the name of religion, economics and national aspirations, Hindus and Muslims of the subcontinent (about 700 million Hindus and more than 350 million Muslims) should realize that they share a lot of common beliefs, behavior patterns, culture, history, and languages. This is recognized more clearly by Hindus and Muslims living abroad than those living in the subcontinent.

The horrors and tragedies witnessed at the time of the partition in 1947 focused attention on the differences. With three major wars in the last fifty years and the continuing possibility of a nuclear war, there is a need to research, understand, emphasize, and build on the common heritage of India and Pakistan. The welfare of more than one billion people in India, Pakistan, and Bangladesh depends on it.

Muslims in India

In the late 1930s, Gavalkar, founder of the BJP and RSS political parties of India, wrote about the superiority of Hindus and the need to purify India of all non-Hindus. He openly admired the example of ethnic purification being followed by Nazi Germany against Jews at that time. Muslims see his followers of today essentially pursuing the same objective, and argue that their public service at the community level is only a step to gain political power. They are said to consider Muslims less pure and clean.

In parallel, Hindus claim that several mosques were built on sites of Hindu temples several hundred years ago. The famous mosque in Ayodhia was first locked up for several years and then demolished in December 1992, against the order of the Supreme Court of India. Law enforcement officials merely looked on as a riotous mob razed the mosque.

In subsequent riots, hundreds of lives, primarily Muslims, were lost and considerable property was destroyed. About 150 million Muslims in India who already felt like second class citizens became extremely alarmed. They still fear for their future in terms of freedom to practice Islam, ability to live in security, and ability to progress economically. They dread the day when the BJP may gain power at the national level.

Press reports indicate that the Indian Muslims have begun to think. For example, a letter published in the *Saudi Gazette* (Riyadh) of February 26, 1993 showed that reactions to the demolition of the Ayodhia Mosque among Indian Muslims working in Saudi Arabia varied according to their economic and educational status. Unskilled and semiskilled workers wanted to retaliate, preferring the death of martyrs rather than passively dying. Militancy was freely advocated without any thought of consequences.

Skilled labor and non-executive office workers were advocating training in self-defense for men and women, and creation of "look-out squads." Disillusionment with the current Muslim leadership was mentioned.

Senior executives were also worried. They emphasized the need for self-defense. However, they put more emphasis on prevention. They advocated (a) educating and reminding Hindus that Muslims are as much Indians as they are; (b) cultivating close relationship with backward Hindus and emphasizing the classless nature of Islam and Muslim society; (c) patronizing the secular press and clarifying questions about Muslim personal laws which have been attacked in the Hindu press; (d) Increasing Muslim involvement in politics through support of secular parties, as well as personal participation in elections at various levels; and (e) helping needy Muslims in restarting their lives, and providing education (English and religious) for their children.

Muslims in all parts of the world should support their Muslim brethren in India. If 100 million plus Muslims in India are unable to defend themselves, it will be a great tragedy for all Muslims.

The results of regional elections in several Indian states in November, 1993 thwarted the efforts of BJP to advance its power and its platform of Hindu nationalism. BJP did much worse than expected. Political analysts interpreted the results to mean that the voters were not swayed by appeals to their religious emotions. The results were quite different in 1996 when BJP won the largest number of seats in the Indian Parliament. However, unable to form a coalition, they were forced to surrender the prime minister position.

Following its failure to win an absolute majority in 1996 elections, BJP is busy in evaluating the causes and working on a strategy to win the majority in the next elections. The party's success has been largely in the northern and western parts of the country. It won only one of 88 seats in the east and six out of 132 in the south.

Faced with a choice of maintaining its Hindu nationalist message or moving towards the political mainstream, the party leaders have decided to attempt both and in so doing, to cross both a regional and ideological divide. They are attempting the kind of artful ambiguity and balancing act that all big political coalitions must manage.[199]

Under the new approach, they will maintain the nationalist approach which is so popular with the upper castes of the north. In addition, they will (a) keep liberal and moderate Atal Bihari Vajpayee as the party's candidate for prime minister; (b) adapt the political language of the political left and emphasize social change and justice which are important to lower caste Hindus; and (c) emphasize major regional issues including states' rights, state finances and water, and power which are important in south and east.

209. *Implications of BJP's control of central government in India.* Whether or not BJP is able to rule at the center, their political influence has increased significantly. If BJP gains direct power over the central government of India, and keeps all its promises to its Hindu voters, one can expect to see a significant increase in tension with Pakistan and India's own Muslim population. The tension may be manifested through

- withdrawal of special status and autonomy granted to Kashmir under the Indian constitution, and increased military repression with the objective of destroying the liberation movement;
- construction of the Ram Temple on the site of the Babri Mosque in Ayodhya which was demolished by supporters of BJP;
- increased threats to other religious centers and mosques many of which have already been identified by the BJP leadership;

---

[199]"Hindu Nationalist Party Looks to South and East India for Future Majority," *The Washington Post* (24 June 1996), p. A12.

- increased economic pressure on Muslims in India through loss of employment and business opportunities; and
- increased pressure on Pakistan through an increased Indian military budget, accelerated development of a conventional and nuclear weapons system, an increasingly offensive posture, and more severe retaliatory actions.

Each of these situations will put increased pressure on Muslims in India and Kashmir. The Muslims will be able to view BJP with greater clarity. It will also put greater pressure on the government of Pakistan to respond through increased military preparedness, and eventually through covert and overt activities which can lead to a full scale war. In any case, BJP will taste power sooner or later. The Muslims of India and Pakistan better prepare themselves for the above eventualities.

On the other hand, it is argued that once in power, BJP will be more sensitive and sensible. As a party in power, it may have to consider the domestic and international implications of its actions. If BJP is convinced that confrontation with Pakistan will not lead to the increased welfare of its Hindu voters, then BJP may be restrained. In fact, if it chooses the path of peace, BJP is the party best able to make peace with Pakistan. While the negotiations will be very difficult, it is probably the only party in a position to make settlement of all outstanding issues and achieve a lasting compromise with Pakistan.

Kashmir

210. *Denial of Right of Self-determination in Kashmir.* In 1947, when the British were leaving India, each province and princely state was given a right to choose whether they wanted to join India or Pakistan. Muslim majority areas chose Pakistan. There were many injustices in the partition of Punjab and Bengal and in the decisions involving the fates of the states of Hyderabad and Junagarh. However, the case of Kashmir was the worst.

The overwhelming majority of the people of Kashmir wanted to join Pakistan. However, the ruler (a Hindu) was not sure and invited Indian troops for protection. A war between India and Pakistan left the state divided with about two-thirds of the territory occupied by India. Subsequently India promised to the United Nations that a plebescite would be held to determine the views and the fate of Kashmir and its people. That was in 1949.[200] The promise was never kept.

For the last few years Kashmiris have been in open rebellion. The Indian army is there in full force. At one time, even Israeli advisors were helping. Based on press and Amnesty International reports, thousands have been killed, permanently injured, and raped. Many more thousands remain in Indian jails. The beautiful valley has turned into rubble and hell for its inhabitants. "After six years of terror, killings, curfews, and military sieges, an estimated 20,000 deaths, and the resulting collapse of its tourist-based economy, the citizens of Kashmir are fed up."[201]

It may be noted that the relatively free Hindu press of India has failed to rally against the human rights violations in Kashmir. It has generally behaved in a nationalist manner and faithfully reported the official version of the events. Some observers have noted that since the Muslims are considered inferior in the Hindu's eyes, action against them is not considered critical.

The death of many Hindu soldiers in Kashmir has not mobilized anti-war sentiment either. This may be explained by the facts that (a) the soldiers generally belong to lower castes; their deaths do not have the same impact on the press and public sentiments that deaths of higher caste officers may have; (b) descendants of the soldiers are hopeful that the deceased will be reincarnated as higher caste Hindus; (c) descendants who are relatively poor receive generous compensation from the government which is financially sufficient to give them a new start in life.

In the international press, there has been relatively sympathetic coverage of the Kashmiri struggle, particularly in the context of violation of human rights. India has dampened the international support by labeling the Kashmiris "Islamic fundamentalists." The world powers have not reached a consensus on what to do about the solution. They prefer to focus on economic cooperation with India, and show little desire to get involved or to enforce implementation of this particular U.N. resolution. Kashmiris deserve an explicit opportunity to decide whether they wish to remain with India, join Pakistan, or become independent.

Kashmir has been the main cause of poor relations between India and Pakistan. They have been at war over Kashmir in 1948 and 1965. They

---

[200] Resolutions adapted by the United Nations Commission for India and Pakistan (UNCIP) on 13 August 1948 and 5 January 1949.

[201] "Kashmir in Flames: Why India Hides From the Truth," in *The Washington Post* (21 May 1995), p. C3.

fought again over East Pakistan and Kashmir in 1971. Whenever there is a threat of violence to Muslims in Kashmir, or any part of India, Muslims in Pakistan are concerned. Such violence increases the danger of new war between Pakistan and India.

Past agreements at the United Nations, Tashkent, and Simla have failed to bring peace. Reportedly, the two countries came close to a nuclear confrontation in 1990. As caretaker Prime Minister Moeen Qureshi stated, Kashmir and Pakistan's nuclear program are linked. It is widely recognized that both countries either have nuclear weapons or can assemble them on short notice. Recognition of this may prevent both from starting a major war.

211. *Possible Solutions.* There are five possible basic solutions to the Kashmir problem: (a) continuation of the current partition or status quo; (b) India should get it all; (c) Pakistan should get it all; (d) independence; and (e) a revised partition. Some interim solutions, such as making Kashmir a trust territory of the United Nations, have been mentioned. Some modalities for dealing with Kashmir as a part of Pakistan or India have been suggested, too. The people of Kashmir appear willing to listen to all suggestions.

Both India and Pakistan seek to possess all of Kashmir as part of their respective countries. Neither is keen about independence. If possession of all of Kashmir is not possible, Pakistan would prefer a new partition of Kashmir leaving non-Muslim areas with India.[202] India prefers possession of the full state including the Azad Kashmir, which is currently under the influence of Pakistan. Short of that, India would like to have international recognition of the current boundary. India is very reluctant even to discuss any other option.

By contrast, many Kashmiris prefer independence. As a second option, they prefer joining Pakistan. Through the struggle of the last several years, they have demonstrated that they do not wish to accept the status quo.

Recent Pakistani governments, including the military, have been convinced that while India cannot seriously harm Pakistan, Kashmir cannot be won militarily from India. In light of the results of the earlier wars with India, and the development of nuclear programs by both sides since then, most observers agree. Both sides have "resolved to settle their differences by peaceful means through bilateral negotiations or by any other peaceful means

---

[202] Wolpert, p. 78. Mr Bhutto was advised by Sheikh Abdullah that Jammu and Kashmir's partition below the river Chenab at a point called Pethlinot would be a realistic position. Then foreign Minister Bhutto was "elated" by the Sheikh's flexibility.

mutually agreed between them."[203] However, bilateral negotiations have been scarce and have not led to much progress since the Simla Agreement in 1972.

Kashmiri citizens have tried to awaken the two countries and the international community through peaceful demonstrations and violent rebellion. However, after several years of efforts on their part, significant results have not been achieved. If debates in the United Nations, Soviet diplomacy in Tashkant, wars between India and Pakistan, and armed struggle by Kashmiris themselves are not sufficient, the next best option is mediation under the auspices of the United States. Many Kashmiris hope that eventually the United States will assume a role similar to their mediation in Bosnia. The cost of fighting with Kashmiris and continued bad relations with Pakistan may convince India to accept a compromise.

India continues to hope that Kashmiris will accept increased autonomy rather than separation from India. As a next step, India prefers to have regular provincial elections in Kashmir. The United States has advised Pakistanis and Kashmiris not to reject them. The Kashmiri leadership is willing to accept the elections provided the Indian army is withdrawn, an oath of allegiance to India is not required from the voters, elections are held under international supervision, and the role of the newly elected representatives in the solution of Kashmir is agreed upon.[204] India has not accepted these conditions and is not likely to do so.

212. *Stalemate.* There is a stalemate. The situation on the ground is not improving for either side. Kashmiris have already sacrificed considerably. Unlike supply routes to Afghanistan during its war of liberation, the supply routes into Kashmir are generally closed or limited at best. India has initiated a large scale infiltration of the Kashmiris and has succeeded in anti-Kashmiri propaganda in the West (e.g., Kashmiris are convinced that kidnapping of foreigners during the summer of 1995 was carried out by Indian agents pretending to be freedom fighters). It is generally suspected that the United States and Western nations do not support having one more Muslim government in that part of the world.

---

[203] The Simla Agreement was signed on 2 July 1972 between Zulfikar Ali Bhutto, President of the Islamic Republic of Pakistan and Indira Gandhi, Prime Minister, the Republic of India.

[204] The conditions were enumerated by Sardar Abdul Qayyum, Prime Minister of Azad Jammu and Kashmir during a dinner meeting with the Washington Policy Analysis Group on 6 October 1995 in a Washington area restaurant. The author, a member of the Group, was present.

Many feel that Kashmiris have to make the struggle much more expensive for India in order to budge them from their current position. It may take a combination of several factors to permit a resolution: (a) a right wing government in India which has the confidence of its Hindu population; (b) a right wing government in Pakistan which has the support of the hardliners; (c) uncontrolled insurgency in Kashmir; and (d) a massive public relations campaign in the United States. The chances for such a combination of events are not good.

Pakistan's citizens have not accepted the fact that under current circumstances, the Kashmir issue is not likely to be resolved satisfactorily. They have invested so much energy, resources, and "emotional capital" in it, that they are unwilling to hear about anything short of "victory." Scenes of brutal action by India's army are visible to all through television. The reaction of Muslims throughout the world, and Pakistanis in particular, has been highly emotional. However, there is a need for Pakistani politicians in the government and in the opposition to face current political and military realities and to make a decision before false hopes of imminent victory destroy many more Kashmiris, economically bleed Pakistan to an irreparable level, or lead to a nuclear war.

213. *National Referendum.* The Pakistani government should continue to push for the right of Kashmiri self-determination through an international conference on Kashmir. Eventually, the government will have to initiate an open debate of all aspects of Kashmir policy.

Following two to three months of free debate, there should be a national referendum to decide Pakistan's future actions in this regard. All realistic options, including going to another war, continuation of the current bleeding, acceptance of the results of the international conference, if any, and formal acceptance of the status quo should be presented. All politicians should agree to accept and abide by the verdict of the people. If the military, politicians in power, and the politicians in opposition (who have been in power earlier) are courageous enough to tell people what they know, the people will probably accept "less than desired results." The population must recognize that Pakistan may be forced to accept the unacceptable. In any case, the minimum package must include (a) maximum autonomy for occupied Kashmir, (b) protection for all Muslims in India, and (c) renunciation of disruptive activities in each other's territories by India and Pakistan.

The Nuclear Issue

There are many proposals for peaceful coexistence between India and Pakistan. Under one proposal, Pakistan and India may be allowed to keep an agreed number of nuclear weapons each. However, India may also be allowed to keep additional weapons to counter threats from China. Each side would then be given full inspection rights over the facilities of the other.

Such a treaty would ensure that there will be no nuclear war in the subcontinent. Pakistan may be asked to provide guarantees that it will not pass on any nuclear weapons or technology to any other country. Israel would receive assurance that its neighbors would not receive nuclear technology from Pakistan. Presumably, India would want China to be a part of the agreement. However, it would not solve the problems of Kashmir and the threat felt by Indian Muslims. A comprehensive solution is required for long-term peace in the area.

214. *Parallel Diplomacy.* In addition to the government military and diplomatic efforts, there have also been efforts by private citizens on both sides. The citizens include prominent people from politics, the judiciary, the military, civil service, the press and the arts. They have been financed by interested parties at home and abroad, including the Henry Stimson Center in Washington, D.C.; the U.S. Information Agency; businessmen from Calcutta, Punjab, Haryana, and Delhi; the Frontier Post; and the Friedrich Ebert Stifung of Germany. The efforts have been going on for several years. The participants have clear access to the two governments and are often entertained by the host country government. However, the governments remain outside the discussions.

There has been relatively little tangible result. Citizens from each country usually remain wedded to the position of their own country. However, a statement released after the February, 1995 dialogue indicated that there is a consensus on some key points.

ON KASHMIR: There was a consensus that there should be a peaceful democratic solution in accordance with aspirations of the people in Kashmir. The statement also calls for the establishment of a democratic process in Kashmir and condemns human rights violations in the area.

ON NUCLEAR PROLIFERATION: Nuclear preparations should be restrained and there should be continuing negotiations toward regional disarmament; India and Pakistan should sign the Chemical Test Ban Treaty without linking it to the global treaty.

ON DEFENSE: There should be no resort to war for the solution of conflicts. There should also be a mutual and balanced reduction of defense forces.

GENERALLY: Visa restrictions should be withdrawn; communications and telecommunications barriers should be removed; there should be a revival of sports and cultural activities and the creation of citizens vigilance groups.

The Lahore Convention of Pakistan India Peoples' Forum for Peace and Democracy held in November, 1995 more or less repeated earlier positions with regards to war and peace between the two countries. In addition it urged steps to improve conditions of minorities and understanding between the citizens of the two countries (e.g., the writing of balanced books on history, monitoring of communal violence, improvement of human rights).

Minorities in India and Pakistan

While Kashmir is the main outstanding issue between India and Pakistan, the plight of minorities is each country is a serious cause of concern to both. India has repeatedly expressed concern about the safety and welfare of Hindus in Pakistan. On the other hand, Pakistanis feel that Muslims in India are treated as second-class citizens. To a large extent, minorities in both countries are deprived of full protection, economic opportunities, spiritual freedom, and political power. An ultimate compromise between the two countries will have to include measures to improve conditions of the minority communities.

Afghanistan

Afghanistan is another tragic example of civil war among Muslims. The current instability started after King Zahir Shah was overthrown by his cousin Daud in early seventies. A few coups later, Soviet forces arrived in support of their local communist partners. The West and most Muslims in Afghanistan and abroad united, struggling for years to defeat the communists. Pakistan was the main conduit for assistance to the freedom fighters and the new home for millions of refugees who fled the conflict. After thousands of casualties on both sides and destruction of much of the country, the Soviet forces withdrew. With the evacuation of the communist "superpower," the West and most of the Muslims from abroad also departed.

Left on their own, the Afghan freedom fighters are now unable to agree among themselves on their new government. All parties agree that Islam should be the state religion, however, there is a difference of opinion on whether the monarchy should be restored, the degree of Islamization that should be adopted, and the sharing of political power between the prominent leaders and their supporters. The ruinous use of heavy weapons to destroy the remaining parts of the cities, productive infrastructure, and life is unparalleled in the country's violent history. Unlike Somalia, the main groups are mostly led by religious leaders, each of whom claims to be fighting for the cause of Allah. If non-Muslims were inflicting this level of destruction, the whole Muslim *ummah* would be united in demanding that hostilities stop. Under the present circumstances, everyone is simply watching.

In recent times, all factions have expressed an interest in a peace settlement. They were all represented at a Washington meeting organized by Senator Hank Brown in 1996 to explore ways for peace and to get the United States interested in the process. However, few leaders are willing to make the compromises needed.

It is sad to note that:

The most compelling reason for renewed U.S. efforts to resolve the conflict may have been offered by Marty F. Miller, vice president of Unocal Corp. He said his firm plans to build mammoth pipelines across Afghanistan to carry oil and gas from Turkmenistan to Pakistan, but all potential sources of finance "have consistently advised us that there will have to be a single entity governing Afghanistan that has international recognition" before they will put up any money.[205]

China

Since the time of independence, Pakistan has sought to have good relations with all its neighbors, including China. These relations became closer in 1959 following China's occupation of Tibet and the resulting end of Chinese-Indian friendship. The Chinese closeness to Pakistan grew as her hostility to India increased leading to a border war with India in 1962. Since then, the informal alliance has become a cornerstone of Pakistan's foreign and military policy. It has led to a border agreement in March, 1963, high-

---

[205]"Afghani Factions Say They Want Peace," in *The Washington Post*, (1 July 1996), p. A14.

way construction connecting the two countries at the Karakoram Pass, agreements on trade, Chinese grant of economic assistance and military equipment, including nuclear technology. China provided significant military assistance during the 1965 war with India and diplomatic influence after the 1971 war over the independence of Bangladesh. For its part, Pakistan served as a window to the world for China during its years of self-imposed isolation. Pakistan played a useful role in bringing the United States and China closer. The warm relationship between the two countries continues to date. During 1996, the United States accused China of continuing to provide nuclear technology and equipment to Pakistan.

Russia

The Pakistan government has, in the past, tried to improve relations with the Soviet Union and its successors. There has been little success, principally due to Pakistan's perennial competition with India. Somehow, Pakistan has been closer to the United States while India has been closer to Russia.

Pakistan's close relationship with China has contributed to cold relations with Russia. Also, Pakistan's role in the Afghan–Soviet war widened the gap between the two nations even farther. Nevertheless, the Soviet Union agreed to provide the Karachi Steel Mill to Pakistan. Also, following the 1965 war, Pakistan was close enough to the Soviet Union to accept its mediation effort which resulted in the Tashkent Agreement.

Despite these few moments of cooperation, there remains a definite pro-India tilt in Russia. The feeling is even shared by some of the opposition leaders in Russia. Russian opposition leader Vladimir Zhirinovsky made a number of anti-Pakistan and anti-Muslim comments while visiting India in March, 1995. *The Washington Post* of 8 March 1995 reported that he would:

- return Pakistan and Bangladesh to India;
- donate a vast portion of dismantled Russian military arsenals to India free of charge;
- ask Afghanistan to give a part of its territory to Russia so that India and Russia can have a common border; and
- have "Russian soldiers to wash their boots in the Indian ocean"; Russian policy apparently would be to overrun nations other than India to make that possible.

Pakistan needs to keep good relations with Russia for at least the following reasons:

- to deny India the advantage of having the exclusive patronage of a major international power;
- to have an alternative source of supply of science and technology;
- to discourage hostile action from a powerful neighbor;
- to encourage better treatment of millions of Muslims under the Russian government's direct or indirect controls; and
- to encourage an equitable solution to the Kashmir issue.

Solidarity with Muslims

Solidarity and therefore a close working relationship with other Muslim governments of the world has been an important policy of the government of Pakistan. However, Pakistan has been often disappointed by the indifferent response of some Muslims nations (i.e., Egypt, Syria, and Iraq), particularly when a Muslim government is not willing or able to support it on the Kashmir issue; even worse some have even sided with India at the cost of Pakistan. In accordance with the dictates of its avowed faith, and the desire of most of its citizens, the Pakistan government must

- work hard to strengthen the Organization of Islamic Conference (OIC);
- help needy Muslim countries, particularly in Africa, in economic, political, and military areas to the fullest extent possible;
- recognize current constraints and work with other members of OIC to resolve outstanding military, economic, political, and other matters of dispute among the Muslim governments;
- encourage and support closer coordination of all policies with important Muslim countries such as Indonesia, Malaysia, Iran, Turkey, Egypt, Saudi Arabia, etc.; and
- support all steps which would lead to creation of a single Muslim government in the long run.

Given the number of Muslims in areas west, north, and east of Pakistan, closer and friendlier relations with other Muslims would not only be in keeping with the tenets of Islam but would also provide security and help establish peace on Pakistan's borders.

CHAPTER 16

RELATIONS WITH THE WEST

Not all of them are alike: of the People of the Book are a portion that stand (for the right); they rehearse the signs of Allah all night long, and they prostrate themselves in adoration. They believe in Allah and the Last Day; they enjoin what is right and forbid what is wrong; and they hasten (in emulation) in (all) good works; they are in the ranks of the righteous. Of the good they do, nothing will be rejected of them; for Allah knoweth well those who do right (Qur'a 3:113-115).

Allah only forbids you, with regard to those who fight you for (your) faith, and drive you out of your homes, and support (others) in driving you out, from turning to them (for friendship and protection). It is such as turn to them (in these circumstances), that do wrong (Qur'an 60:9).

Pakistan and the West

The twentieth century has been a period of conflict between the West and the Muslim world. If we work together we can make the twenty-first century not just a time of peace in the Middle East and the Persian Gulf, but a century in which, beyond peace, two great civilizations will enrich each other and the rest of the world—not just by their arms and their wealth but by the eternal appeal of their ideals (Richard Nixon).[206]

Clearly, Pakistanis are not sure how to deal with the West, particularly the United States. It is also evident that the United States has not been able to establish a comprehensive policy towards Islamic nations. For example, the United States has
- a policy of hostility and confrontation against Iraq;

---

[206] Nixon, pp. 155-156.

- ideological confrontation with Iran and Sudan;
- alignment of policy with Algeria, Egypt, and Turkey, primarily with the objective of keeping Islamic political groups out of power; and
- undertaken to protect the security of the monarchs of the Gulf countries, at the expense of representative governments, largely to secure oil supply.

Muslim activists are suspicious of the intentions and policies of the United States. While the posture of the United States toward Muslim countries cannot be compared with that toward its old arch enemy, the Soviet Union, it is interesting to note that the sentiments expressed by communist leaders of the collapsed Soviet Union echo that of the Islamists. Russian presidential candidate, Grennady Zyuganov, declared that " . . . the West conspired to deform the Soviet economy . . . ignited nationalism . . . to destroy the country from inside . . . and used agents provocateurs . . . to take the mass media hostage . . . ruin the Soviet collective lifestyle . . . and strip the country of its future."[207]

215. *Excessive Privileges for the West.* Some argue that Pakistan's politicians and high officials are willing to bare all to win American support and patronage. Politicians regularly approach U.S. embassy officials for a sympathetic hearing. Even the government allows local civilian and military officials to meet the embassy staff and visiting dignitaries to discuss strictly domestic issues such as law and order.

Many feel that the government has allowed excessive facilities to the foreign powers. Permission for opening embassies and having required staff housing are normal. However, sovereign states usually do not allow foreign powers to open military bases, post a large military staff and equipment, and gather intelligence about it and friendly neighboring powers. Pakistan has reportedly allowed the United States to do all that and more. Members of NATO allow the United States to have similar facilities as a part of the mutual defense treaty, but Pakistan and the United States do not have such a treaty. Colonial powers have maintained such facilities in the occupied territories, but then the colonized lands received something in return.

216. *New World Order.* Pakistanis recognize the importance of the United States in the new world order. They clearly do not want total, ideological, or any kind of confrontation. On the other hand, they do not want to surrender

---

[207] *The Washington Post,* (13 May 1996), p. A1.

their independence and live at the mercy of the United States as Kuwait and some other Gulf countries do. They would like to have a close working relationship and mutual understanding.

However, the United States does not appear eager for such a relationship. Despite Pakistani efforts, overall U.S. interests in the area, ethnic linkages, or popular support closer ties are unlikely. Pakistan would like to imitate the Turkish model in terms of U.S. relations. However, Turkey's relationship is explained by its proximity to Europe, relatively Western outlook, state of economic and military development, and above all membership in NATO.

217. *Varied Opinion.* There is a variety of opinions within Pakistan regarding the West. The Western-educated and oriented citizens want a close relationship with the West at almost all costs. By contrast, Islamists want a guarantee that the West will not interfere in their efforts to consolidate Muslims. Nevertheless, on the whole, Pakistanis want a warm relationship based on mutual strength, respect, help, and the protection of national interest.

It must also be recognized that the West has influence and interests all over the world. Pakistan is a small part of that world. With some exceptions, most of the 180 plus countries want the type of relationship with the West to which Pakistan aspires. In spite of its strategic importance and the close relations of prior years, the relationships of today and tomorrow have to be based on current realities and interests.

It must also be recognized that the West is not a static society, but rather a dynamic one. Changes in technology are rapidly producing updated information and analysis which are playing a significant role in decisionmaking. The emphasis is on rationalism whether it relates to political, economic, or military factors. There is a little room for emotionalism, especially when it comes a country like Pakistan which is clearly out of the primary area of interest as far as the West is concerned.

218. *Appeal of Western Way of Life.* Almost all Pakistanis, particularly the educated ones, are strongly attracted to the Western way of life. Most would like to have a Western education, job, income, home, and conveniences—if not for themselves, at least for their children. A majority of those who travel to Western countries, particularly the United States, for education or for a visit, wish to stay. This may be related to (a) poor economic conditions or a lack of political free-dom back home, (b) better economic opportunities or greater political freedom in the West, (c) hope for a better education and future for their children.

Whatever the reason may be, most people prefer and make an effort to stay in the West. It can be argued though that this may not be an "un-Islamic" appeal. Muslims note that desires to travel, explore the world, and have a comfortable life are perfectly Islamic, as long as all is earned through honest means.

219. *Help to Muslims in Other Countries.* The Western press often accuses Pakistani religious groups and even the government of helping Muslims who are fighting for their causes in Kashmir, Bosnia, Chechniya, Afghanistan, the Philippines, and India. *The Washington Post* of 8 March 1995 reported:

- Pakistan has been a haven for militant Islamic groups since the start of the Afghan war against the Soviet Union. Since the defeat of the Soviets, the groups have stayed on to help with causes of Muslims elsewhere. They continue to prosper because of the easy availability of weapons left over from the Afghan war, and donation of money from Muslims in and outside Pakistan. They have also benefitted from tolerance of the Pakistan government which is committed to support of the freedom fighters in Kashmir pending permanent resolution.
- Harkatul Ansar (Movement of Friends), headquartered in Islamabad, is sworn to fight for the global supremacy of Islam. Since 1987, it has trained more than 4,000 volunteers in making bombs, throwing hand grenades and shooting assault weapons. It believes that Muslims are one nation and that political frontiers cannot divide them. They claim to draw members from Pakistan, Afghanistan, Egypt, Algeria, Bangladesh, and other countries. They claim to be ready to fight in any part of the world where Muslims are victimized.
- Another organization, Markaz Dawatul Arshad, aims to establish "the rule of God" throughout the world. They claim that their members have fought and died in Tajikistan, the Philippines, Bosnia, and Kashmir.
- Pakistani citizens are donating money in response to the condition of Muslims around the world. Indian Muslim businessmen from the United Kingdom are donating in order to protect Muslims in their original homeland. Arabs who are unhappy with pro-Western policies of their governments are also contributing.

The government of Pakistan is generally apologetic for the existence and behavior of these groups. Each incident involving members of these groups has led to a greater scrutiny of their activities by the government. The bombing of the Egyptian Embassy in Islamabad was probably the last straw. Hundreds of foreign fighters have left Pakistan voluntarily or have been expelled. The remaining ones are either in hiding or under close watch by the authorities.

Opponents of the government policy have argued against yielding to Western influences. They assert that the right of self-determination is a fundamental human right recognized by the United Nations. Pakistanis, they feel, have a right and obligation to help their fellow Muslims in need anywhere in the world.[208]

The government should reevaluate their policy options. As a nation created on the basis of Islam, Pakistan has a moral duty to help all Muslims around the world who have a genuine cause. Pakistan's leaders are obliged to work with other Muslim governments to make clear to all offending nations that, while Muslims may be divided into "many tribes," they are one nation. It is often repeated that when one part of the Muslim community hurts, the whole Muslim nation hurts. Muslim governments should work together to find peaceful solutions to the problems within their own borders and outside.

Privatization

Privatization is a current economic buzzword. Some Pakistanis see it as allowing foreigners in, as the reentry of the East India Company that eventually led to British colonial rule. They feel everyone is being allowed to bid on national assets. With some exceptions, the Westerners are going to be the main bidders, buyers, and eventually operators of key assets on which the national economy depends. Such control will give excessive power to outsiders who can manipulate the national economy in directions which may or may not be conducive to Pakistan's best interest. Some feel it will lead to re-colonization by the West without firing a bullet or commitment of troops.

Eagerness to privatize around the world has made it a buyer's market. It may preclude sound judgment on whether privatization is the answer to the problems experienced in specific cases. Will the buyer bring in incremental resources without recourse to the Pakistan government? Will it bring improved efficiency in the long run? Will the cost and benefits be shared equitably? Transparency in decision-making is often missing. The personal interests of the decisionmakers in Pakistan in terms of earning money fast and making alliances for future jobs for self and family members may cause them to give assets away too cheaply.

---

[208] Presentation by Lieutenant General Hameed Gul (Retired) of the Pakistani Army at a gathering hosted by the American Muslim Council on 23 May 1996.

Acceptable Areas of Compromise

220. *Vital Interests of the West.* The West, particularly the United States has a number of interests around the world. There is irritation in Washington every time Pakistan expects the Unites States to sacrifice its other interests for the sake of Pakistan. The United States would like Pakistan to recognize that it is only one of many countries of interest and not the focus of priority attention. The United States is clearly unwilling to sacrifice its relations with India for the sake of Kashmir, or with Israel for the sake of Muslims. The United States is unhappy with Pakistan in terms of

- Pakistan's possession of nuclear or other weapons of mass destruction which can be used to threaten friends of the United States, particularly Israel;
- the supply of narcotics to the Western citizens through Pakistan;
- close relations with any Muslim country which is unfriendly to the West. Iran, Iraq, Libya are a few of those who have tested Western re-solve and are paying the price. The West would clearly like Pakistan to avoid them; and
- the unsatisfactory state of human rights in Pakistan, particularly those for women.

Historically, Pakistan has been an asset to U.S. foreign policy. It played a vital role in advancing the U.S. agenda in Southeast Asia through membership in SEATO. It helped in the Middle East through CENTO and numerous bilateral actions. It helped in opening the door for the United States in China. It played a decisive role in defeating the Soviet Union and communism through the war in Afghanistan. Pakistan periodically articulates its foreign policy objectives and generally assures the United States that while it cannot remove all irritating issues, it will be as helpful as possible in working out mutually satisfactory solutions. Pakistan continues to maintain extended cooperation with the U.S. State Department, armed forces, intelligence agencies, narcotic control agencies, etc. In fact, many Pakistanis feel that Pakistan has given much more than what it has received.

221. *Protection of Non-Muslims in Pakistan.* Muslims have a religious duty to protect the life and property of non-Muslim minorities in their countries. It is difficult to complain about the rights of Muslims in India on moral grounds, if Pakistan cannot protect Christian or Hindu minorities in Pakistan. It is the obligation of the government to do all in its power to ensure protection of non-Muslims.

222. *Islamic Fundamentalism vs. Political Issues.* The Western press and therefore the Western public is alarmed by Muslim "fundamentalism," which is equated with violence. An Islamic appearance (beard, head cover, or full body clothing) is suspect. For Muslims, fundamentalism means a return to the basics of Islam—belief in one Allah (God); authenticity of the Prophet Muhammad (PBUH) as the Messenger of Allah, regularity in prayers five times a day, charity (zakat) equal to 2.5% of assets (with specified exclusions), pilgrimage to Mecca once in a lifetime if affordable, and belief in the Day of Judgement.

In short, fundamentalism results in following the model of the Prophet in living life and being more devout. However, to the West, it means political violence for promotion of Islamic government. There is a great need to explain the difference between the two and remove the stigma against political Islam.

223. *Measures Supported by the West.* The world powers feel less threatened by governments in Muslim-majority countries which are democratic, capitalist in philosophy, support privatization, believe in cleaner environment, fight drugs, and support improved governance. More specifically, the West does not object to the countries whose principal objectives are to

- practice democracy on a continuing basis, at national, provincial, and local government level;
- practice decentralization by delegating authority and responsibility downwards to people;
- maximize their economic growth by focusing national energies and attention on economic development;
- allow private ownership to play a significant role in the economy;
- improve the economic well-being of their people through increased attention to and expenditure on education, food, and shelter;
- improve their judiciary with impartial and prompt justice, and emphasis on human rights for their citizens in general, and women in particular;
- settle domestic and international disputes peacefully leading to reduced expenditure on military;
- treat religion as a personal matter even if the ministry of religious affairs and private organizations are active in supporting Islamic eduation, construction of mosques, performance of Haj, payment of Zakat, fasting, offering of prayers, missionary activities based on freedom of choice;
- eliminate corrupt practices, e.g., bribery, food and drug adulteration, thievery and use of drugs;

- devote national resources to elimination of poverty, elimination of illiteracy, raising education and health standards, improving environmental conditions, and developing infrastructure; and
- fight production, distribution, and consumption of illegal drugs.

The activities which are non-threatening to the world powers also happen to be consistent with Islamic behavior, and very important for improving the life of common Muslims. Malaysia and Indonesia have been mentioned as examples of "good and non-threatening" Muslim countries. Pakistan can go a long way in protecting vital interests of the West on its own soil and trying to persuade other Muslim countries to do the same. However, there are limits to which any government of Pakistan can go to meet the desires of the West. There are some areas in which compromise is difficult.

224. *Wishes of Pakistan.* From the West, Pakistan seeks security, write-off of old debts, new financial assistance and investments, and access to science and technology. Pakistanis have been trading with the West for a long time. They will likely continue trading but are unlikely to sell themselves cheaply. They fully evaluate what they give and what they receive in return and negotiate carefully. They have noted the examples of those who appear to have received large compensation, e.g., Israel, Egypt, Jordan, and European nations.

Unacceptable Areas of Compromise

If the West asked Pakistan to abandon Islam, no political leader would be able to oblige. If Pakistan were asked to keep Islam out of politics, the secularists would be pleased to oblige. They would also ask for Western support in terms of money, ideas, and even force to achieve the objective. However, most other politicians would not separate their religious affirmations from politics.

Pakistan is reluctant to help the West against "Muslim antagonists," including Iran and Sudan. The issue of Iran is particularly sensitive for Pakistan. It is a neighbor, a close friend and an ally of long standing. However, if Shiite–Sunni hostilities continue to accelerate at the current pace, the two countries may become hostile to each other.

Similarly, the West is reluctant to compromise their foreign policy goals for the sake of Pakistan. They are unlikely to modify relations with Russia over the conflict in Chechniya, their relations with Europe because of Bosnia, relations with India over Kashmir, or their relations with Israel because of

Palestinians. Pakistani leaders must recognize the nature of the interests the United States and the West have in the Middle East and South Asia, including Pakistan, and balance their demands accordingly.

Role of Pakistanis in the West

American citizens of Pakistani origins are slowly getting acquainted with and increasingly becoming involved in the American political process. They have established good relations within both political parties (Republican and Democrat) through participation in political campaigns, voter registration drives, financial contributions, and regular follow-up activities. Many of them have access to senators, congressmen, and governors. Some have even direct access to the president of the United States. They are lobbying on behalf of Kashmir, the sale of U.S. weapons to Pakistan, and improved relations with the Pakistani government. Within the legal framework they can and should do even more, including lobbying for improved U.S. relations with all Muslims, particularly Pakistanis.

Pakistani citizens living abroad should also join Pakistani political parties. They should become active in their local branches and lobby for desirable policies in Pakistan. Due to the frequent visits of Pakistani politicians in the Western countries, they can be approached and even influenced relatively easily during their visits.

People of Pakistani origin should join and even form think tanks. They should help formulate policy options on issues of importance to Pakistan, provide options and ideas to the government of Pakistan, and lobby for desirable ends.

CHAPTER 17

NATIONAL DEFENSE

Fight in the cause of Allah those who fight you, but do not transgress limits; for Allah loveth not transgressors (Qur'an 2:190).

Fighting is prescribed upon you, and ye dislike it. [209] But it is possible that ye dislike a thing which is good for you, and that ye love a thing which is bad for you. But Allah knoweth, and ye know not (Qur'an 2:216).

State of Affairs

225. *Objectives*. The purpose of writing this chapter is to recognize the facts of Pakistan's situation and to analyze which strategies will provide the required national defense at an affordable cost.

The ability to carry out national defense depends on national strength. No one denies the justification for having national military and police forces which are suitably manned and equipped to defend the nation within and at the borders. There has been a failure to achieve many of Pakistan's defense objectives to date, e.g., failure to defend East Pakistan; liberate Kashmir; and maintain law and order at home. Accordingly, the nation is striving to strengthen its national defense. However, given the existence of many high priority objectives in other areas and its limited resources, Pakistan is seeking to maximize its military efficiency.

There is an urgent need to reduce the expenditure on the military without sacrificing essential defense needs. General Schwarzkopf has explained in the case of size of the United States armed forces:

> The purpose of our armed forces is to protect our national interests and defend our country . . . We should be sure that we have made a

---

[209] If one is a mere brawler, or a selfish aggressive person, or a bully, then fighting is strictly forbidden.

thorough analysis of what our national interests will be for the next twenty years and where and how we might be required to commit our forces. Only then can we honestly assess what size our armed forces should be. [210]

It is not clear whether Pakistani military leaders approach the issue of national defense in a similar manner. However, based on other evidence, experts have suggested (a) substantial reduction in permanent standing armies, (b) universal military training for all citizens with increasing reliance on national draft or conscription, (c) accelerated development of the defense armament industry, and (d) extreme selectivity in acquisition of advanced conventional equipment from abroad which is expensive and tends to get obsolete quickly. Under all circumstances the overall cost has to be affordable. Pakistan citizens and leaders ought to consider their options carefully.

226. *Acquisition of Advanced Weapons.* The military history of the world suggests that access to advanced weaponry has been a critical factor in winning almost all wars. The access can come through acquisition of the weapons from others or by development at home.

The Western world has achieved military supremacy over the rest of the world and maintained its superiority with the help of continued research and development of the most advanced weapons. While continually developing and improving their weapons since World War II, they have used their diplomatic and economic power to ensure that no one else is able to outstrip them, particularly in the nuclear or biological fields.

Developing countries, including India and Pakistan, are allowed to obtain simpler weapons which are no threat to the West or its allies. Nevertheless, both countries have been eager to acquire whatever they can. Both also have been trying to develop the "forbidden" areas as much as they can.

Comparative Military Strength

India and Pakistan have been competitors in military fields since the early days of independence. Their military strength in terms of personnel, tanks, air force fighters, ships, and submarines is shown below.

[210] General H. Norman Schwarzkopf, *It Doesn't Take a Hero* (New York: Bantam Books, 1992), p. 502.

Table 9

Country	Personnel	Tanks	Fighters	Ships	Submarines
Pakistan	577,000	1890 (40)	336 (160)	11 (8)	6 (6)
India	1,100,000	3500 (2700)	700 (374)	21 (14)	18 (12)

Personnel means all active military; tanks are mainly battle tanks and light tanks; fighters are air-to-air and ground attack aircraft; ships are carriers, cruisers, destroyers, and frigates; and submarines are all types. Advanced systems in each category are shown in brackets. Advanced systems are at least mid-1960s design with advanced technologies, such as laser range fighters for tanks.[211]

This competition has meant large budget allocations for defense. It has been particularly expensive for the smaller Pakistan which feels that it must maintain an effective deterrence for its survival.

Cost of Defense

Details of defense spending are not easily available and are not open for debate in the assemblies. Each successive government has gone out of its way to please the defense forces. The stated allocation of defense in the most recent budget vastly underestimates the actual cost. It does not include the cost of coast guards, the rangers or the frontier constabulary. It does not show the defense related debt service or pensions of the armed force personnel. In addition, there is funding for the army's welfare organizations. These organizations almost guarantee jobs for any retired officer who wants one. Even the lower ranked ones can get substantial help. Current expenditure for defense alone has consumed about one third of the national budget revenue.

---

[211] *The Washington Post;* Monday (24 July 1995), p. A16. Source: General Accounting Office report, "Impact of China's Military Modernization in the Pacific Region", June, 1995.

Pakistan Defense Budget [212]

Year	1990	1991	1992	1993
Total Revenue (Billion Rupees)	158.8	163.9	222.6	261.9
Defense (Billion Rupees)	58.7	64.6	75.8	82.2
Defense as % of Total Revenue	37%	39%	34%	31%

Pakistan must keep up with India. However, it has not been able to do so in modern times. A roughly 3:1 ratio has been acceptable over a period of time in order to maintain deterrence against India. However, given the fact that India is roughly six times larger than Pakistan in population, the defense budget amounts to a much larger burden in per capita cost terms on the average Pakistani than it is on the average Indian.

227. *High Cost.* Standing armies use the lion's portion of the national budget. Pakistan continues to spend a large part of its national budgets on defense equipment and personnel. This results in an enormous sacrifice for other urgently needed expenditures for health, education, and welfare.

India is reportedly spending $9.00 per person per year on defense, while Pakistan is spending three times as much or $27.00 per person per year. India and Pakistan are reportedly spending one million dollars a day on maintaining their armed forces in Siachin Glaciers alone. There is ample justification for both sides to withdraw their forces from the Glaciers, hold talks, and come to an amicable solution. [213]

Since the end of the Cold war, global military expenditures have gone down by four percent per year. However, it continues to increase in the Subcontinent by about ten percent per year. "If SARC countries cut defense spending by five percent per year, they can give universal [health] coverage to everyone. Everyone will have social services that are a necessary condi-

---

[212] Blood, Appendix Table 4, p. 323.

[213] Dr. Mehboobul Haq as quoted in *The Pakistan Link,* February 16, p. 16.

tion of being a human being . . . "[214] Political leaders feel obligated to increase their military funding year after year, with little chance of ever cutting it or even reducing the rate of growth.

Many analysts have noted that given the fact that the army has come to depend on hostility with India to justify its spending, will any government be able to get away with making peace with India? [215] Many feel that only a bloody revolution at home or a strong directive from the United States can have a major influence on the army. Civilian politicians are too weak to have a major impact on the army.

228. *Profiteering.* Commissions on purchase of military equipment sales are notoriously high. The press has reported huge commissions pocketed by politicians, bureaucrats, and senior military officials. In recent times, there were allegations that the Pakistan government was no longer pressing for delivery of the F-16 planes purchased from the United States because it had the more lucrative option of buying the French Mirages at a much higher cost. "Those who were looking for kickbacks and commissions would not find a better opportunity and a better deal than dumping F-16s and buying the Mirages."[216]

229. *Pensions.* Soldiers retire young. Accordingly, army pension is one of the largest expense items in many national budgets. In addition, tradition has been established in some countries to award valuable land, licenses, and assets to retired army personnel on an individual basis. Additional large resources are periodically made available through foundations and trusts for the welfare of "soldiers."

Few dare to question the volume of resources allocated to military. They will be immediately labeled as unpatriotic, enemies of Pakistan and of Islam, and foreign agents. Given the performance of the Pakistan military on the battlefield, Pakistanis are well justified to review and evaluate the cost and benefits of their national defense. Sometimes it appears that the people hired to defend the nation have forcibly taken control of the national wealth, leaving many citizens living in poverty.

---

[214] Former federal minister Mahbubul Haq as reported in *The Pakistan Link,* (2 February 1996), p. 8.

[215] Talat Asalm, "The Changing Face of the Army," in *The Herald*, July, 1989, p. 74.

[216] Shaheen Sehbai, "Assef's Desperate Dash to Washington," in *The Pakistan Link*, (9 February 1996), p. 5.

Avoiding Reimposition of Martial Law [217]

Several generals have acknowledged that martial law is not a good form of government. Technically, it is simply the law of the military commander and is therefore not permitted under the constitution. The martial law periods of 1958 through 1969 and 1977 through 1988 were imposed despite constitutional restrictions. Experts continue to discuss differences between them and debate whether the martial laws were intentional on the part of the armed forces leadership or consequential as a result of the prevailing situation in the country. Nevertheless, the imposition of martial law in 1958 and 1977 were welcomed by a large segment of the population. In each case, the politicians appeared to have lost control. They appeared unable to settle quarrels among themselves on the basis of the democratic process. Many of the politicians were openly demanding martial law. Eventually, the 1977 martial law was upheld by the Supreme Court under the law of necessity.

Will there be another period of martial law? Mere laws and constitutions can never be a guarantee against a military takeover. The martial law will be imposed again if

- the civil administration and machinery fail,
- the political institutions become weaker and more unstable,
- the politicians fail to protect democratic institutions even at the cost of their personal interest,
- the politicians are willing and able to resort to irregularities to perpetuate their own rule,
- people demonstrate publicly their dissatisfaction with existing conditions and demand martial law,
- the economy deteriorates and investment becomes scarce,
- law and order disintegrates, conditions of civil war appear imminent, and
- people are unable or unwilling to defend the political process.

On the other hand, chances for another period of martial law will be reduced if

- elections are held regularly,
- good people come forward in elective offices,
- democratic institutions are nourished and made fully functional,

---

[217] "View From the Top," *The Herald*, (July, 1989), pp. 76-79. Based on interviews with six retired army generals (Fazle Haq, Ejaz Azeem, Amir Abdullah Niazi, Faiz Ali Chishti, Akbar Khan, and K.M. Arif) and two air marshals (Zafar Chaudhry and Asghar Khan).

- there is political and economic stability and progress,
- people are more aware of their rights and can see the benefits of democracy over martial law,
- the role of the armed forces, particularly that of Army Chief of Staff, is reassessed and limited to safeguarding the territorial integrity of the country,
- the civilian governments assert true control over the appointment, promotions, and posting of the senior officers of the armed forces, and
- the army diversifies its leadership and is made a national army through representation of all provinces and ethnic groups, as is the case in India.

There will always be ambitious and conceited generals who feel that they can save the country from disaster by assuming power. They will be prepared to impose martial law and rule the land unchallenged. However, they must not be tempted through direct or indirect invitation.

Universal Military Training

Universal military training has been supported in different forms by many political and military leaders in Pakistan. Mr. Bhutto stated:

> Pakistan's best deterrent would be a national militia, trained and led by professional officers, to support the standing forces in the event of total war. Military training in the universities should be obligatory; in every village there should be created a cadre of active and courageous young men well trained in the use of primary weapons. In Switzerland every household has to maintain a firearm in good order.
> The people must defend themselves, and the prospect of a whole nation armed and trained is as powerful deterrent as an under-developed country can hope to possess.[218]

Mr. Bhutto went on to say that a victory cannot be won against a nation which is fully armed. Devastation may happen, but not victory. The traditional argument against such a policy is that crime would increase due to widespread distribution of legal arms. The criticism has been countered by the argument that criminals already possess weapons. If law-abiding citizens also have arms and some safeguards, the crime rate would actually decline.

[218] Bhutto, p. 154.

230. *Questionable Professionalism.* The military is largely beyond public reproach in Pakistan despite demonstrated deficiencies. It is mostly controlled by certain ethnic groups, at the cost of total or partial exclusion of others. It attempts to play the role of king makers through undue interference in politics. Corruption of many under martial law often accompanied monetary benefits and excessive power. There is little control by civilian elected officials over the management of military affairs. A civilian defense minister is often there to rubber-stamp decisions of the military itself.

Military Balance

Ideally speaking, Pakistan should seek military balance vis-à-vis India. While Pakistan already has a sufficient deterrent force, achievement of superiority or even parity appears impossible in the foreseeable future. Pakistan is substantially behind India and does not have resources for much more than a defensive war. However, some suggest that if there was sufficient Muslim unity, a Muslim–Indian balance would be quite possible.

Now that the cold war is over and the Soviets have gone from Afghanistan, Pakistan is no longer a front-line state defending the free world. Unless the situation changes, Pakistan cannot expect to get military assistance on a grant basis. Neither can they expect to buy much advanced equipment without cash. The solution lies in being alert to all opportunities, but also increasingly to relying on research and development of its own armament industry. While this effort must continue, Pakistanis must not lose heart if they are true faithful. Allah has stated:

> **Prophet, rouse the faithful to arms. If there are twenty steadfast men among you, you shall vanquish two hundred; and if there are hundred, they shall route a thousand unbelievers, for they are devoid of understanding. (Qur'an 8:65)**

Technology and Manpower Development

The technology gap and inadequate manpower development are the most important causes for the domination of Pakistan (and Muslims in general) by others. Muslims owe a good part of their historic successes to superior technology. Of course, Muslims fell behind in technology after they became conquered people. The superior technology of the West kept them as colonies until economic and political factors arising out of World War II led to their freedom.

Pakistanis have acquired much technology and developed much manpower since then. However, there has also been a quantum leap in the knowledge of the West since then. While Pakistan has learned to make basic consumer goods and small conventional weapons, others have mastered the technology of nuclear weapons, missiles, space, oceans, biological and chemical warfare, laser surgery, etc. Pakistanis just have to move faster in order to narrow the gap. They should accord high priority to technology and related manpower development in the context of national as well as personal budgets. Technical education and practical experience for interested and promising youth should be supported. The experience of nations that have narrowed the gap should be studied carefully, e.g., Japan, China, India, Korea, and Singapore.

Nuclear Weapons

Non-Muslim nations have almost total control over nuclear technology and weapons. The United States, France, the United Kingdom, China, and four republics of the old Soviet Union (Russia, Ukraine, Kazakhistan, and Georgia) have publicly acknowledged possession of nuclear weapons. Israel, South Africa, and India are rumored to possess weapons and the technology. The South African capability has been reportedly dismantled since power was handed over to the Black majority.

Most industrialized nations of Europe (particularly Germany), Japan, and Canada are likely to be able to put together some weapons quickly, if needed. Several developing countries including India, Pakistan, South Korea, North Korea, Argentina, and Brazil, are presumed to have some nuclear capability too, even though the quantity and quality of their weapons and delivery systems are in doubt.

In the Subcontinent, India has successfully tested a bomb. In Pakistan, former Presidents Bhutto and even Zia, might have lost their lives in trying to acquire nuclear technology. Former President Ghulam Ishaque has confirmed many threats that he had received for the same reason.

Pakistan has lost hundreds of millions of dollars a year in aid from the United States and remains a candidate for declaration as a terrorist state mainly for the same reason. Iraq continues to pay heavily for its alleged interest in a nuclear program. Iran will face even greater opposition unless it renounces its desire to compete in the nuclear field.

Nuclear non-proliferation is a cornerstone of foreign policy of all Western countries because it will ensure continued military superiority and therefore security of the West. Only "responsible" new members will be accepted in the nuclear club. All other non-nuclear countries, particularly the Muslims, are watched carefully.

Pakistan's Dilemma

Some Pakistanis have argued that if Pakistan does have the capability, then like India, it should publicly test a small nuclear device. Such a move would demonstrate its capability and deter aggression. Pakistan should announce possession of a small arsenal, if true. It is thought that such a policy would earn the respect of many, even while earning the wrath of the West and the loss of economic assistance.

Based on suspicions about Pakistan's possession of a nuclear device, the United States has stopped direct economic and military assistance to Pakistan since 1990, under the Pressler amendment. Pakistan has not yet suffered considerably because the United States has chosen not to assess penalties fully. In fact, what is important is not just the direct military or economic aid of the United States, but the total financial resources, trade, and military power which it influences, such as:

- loans and assistance from international financial institutions such as the World Bank, International Monetary Fund (IMF), Asian Development Bank (ADB) and other UN agencies;
- bilateral aid from European countries and Japan;
- bilateral aid from pro-American Arab countries;
- international private investment;
- investment by Pakistanis living at home and abroad who may be concerned by U.S. hostility to Pakistan;
- U.S. signal to India, Israel, and others to go ahead and undermine the Pakistani government; and
- the supply of military parts for equipment purchased from the West.

Based on disclosures of high level officials, "a low level nuclear deterrence exists between India and Pakistan."[219] Some observers doubt whether Pakistan in fact has a nuclear capability. The policy issue is whether it is to Pakistan's advantage simply to maintain the "perception" of having a nuclear bomb or whether actually to conduct tests? The assumption that Pakistan has an adequate delivery system against its traditional enemy, India, is repeatedly

---

[219] General Mirza Aslam Beg, "Conflict Resolution in the South Asian Region." The paper was presented to the Carnegi Endowment for International Peace meeting in Washington, D.C. in July, 1995.

supported by Indian and U.S. accusations that China has been providing technical assistance and hardware support to Pakistan.

The renowned Pakistani nuclear scientist, Dr. Abdul Qadeer Khan, who is the head of the Qadeer Khan Research Laboratories of the Armed Forces has supported speculation about the existence of the nuclear deterrent by asserting that Pakistan has never capped its nuclear program. "No President or Prime Minister can take a step against the interests of the country . . . sometimes we slowed down our production but that does not mean that we have compromised on the security of the country." Speaking of the delivery systems, he has said, "We have developed many missiles for the army at low cost in comparison with international prices . . . We have also produced multiple rocket-launchers . . . and other warfare equipment which are very effective and cheaper."[220]

The potential costs of actually demonstrating the capability include:

- the immediate wrath of the United States resulting in condemnation and strained diplomatic relations;
- total U.S. hostility resulting in substantial reduction of the economic assistance mentioned above and additional sanctions;
- further hostile action in the economic, political, or military field by India; and
- the heightening of tensions and increase in the arms race between India and Pakistan.

The potential benefits of demonstrating nuclear capability include:

- the "respect" of the United States and other members of the nuclear club;
- improved relationship with the West within a "relatively short" period of time based on a reassessment of the Western interests;
- possible resumption of sustained aid from the West, and consultation on world affairs particularly relating to Muslim affairs;
- immediate respect of Arab and other Muslim countries, which can result in increased self-confidence of Muslims;
- increased financial assistance from some rich Arabs nations;
- the establishment of an effective deterrent in the mind of the Indian government (which may already exist), and Indian citizens (which may not exist now); and

---

[220] "Pakistan Never Capped N. Program, Says Dr. Qadeer", in *The Pakistan Link*, (17 May 1996), p. A13.

- an improved attitude of non-Muslim Indians toward Muslim Indians, resulting in less communal violence and better treatment of Kashmiri Muslims.

Some have speculated that Pakistan has already tested its device in China. Others have indicated that controlled laboratory tests have proven Pakistan's capability. On the whole, there is no urgency for Pakistan to test a nuclear weapon.

In early 1996, U.S. agencies reported that India was preparing a new nuclear test. If India carries it out, Pakistan will be forced to prove its capability. Pakistan will also have to carry out a test. It may mean a high price for Pakistan and its people in terms of international denials of aid. However, the Indian action will leave no option for Pakistan.

In any case, the West may accept at least one Muslim country as a de facto member of the nuclear club if it becomes a *fait accompli*. If Israel or other close allies of the United States are threatened by the Pakistani bomb, The United States will do its best to stop Pakistan and may take military action. However, given the peace movement in the Middle East, the potential threat felt by Israel will be minimal.

Defense Strategy

> **O ye who believe! If ye will aid (the cause) of Allah, He will aid you, and plant your feet firmly (Qur'an 47:7).**

Pakistan should consider a new defense strategy consisting of several elements. The purpose would be to (a) remove the cause of the main conflict with India in consultation with and support of other Muslim countries and the West, and hopefully usher an area of peace and trust in the Subcontinent; (b) reduce excessive amount of money being spent on defense—particularly conventional weapons; (c) prove to all concerned that Pakistan is a powerful country to be respected; and (d) have sustained defensive capability.

The policy would include the following elements:
- finding solutions to the main cause of conflict,
- seeking cooperation and protection from the remaining superpower against future threats,
- receiving simultaneous support from the Muslim countries,
- establishing Pakistan's own position of power,
- cost savings, and
- establishing sustained defensive capability.

The process can only start with the support of the people of Pakistan. It should be initiated with extensive consultation between Pakistan and India. Pakistan should also involve the United States and Muslim countries (directly or indirectly through OIC). The negotiations would probably continue for some time. With goodwill and compromise on each side, such a package could be negotiated.

231. *Removing the Main Cause of Conflict.* As discussed in an earlier chapter, Pakistani politicians in government and in the opposition should initiate an open debate on all aspects of the Kashmir issue followed by a well-supervised secret referendum to decide Pakistan's future actions in this regard. All politicians should agree to accept and abide by the verdict of the people. If the military, politicians in power, and the politicians in opposition (who have been in power earlier) are courageous enough to reveal publicly what they know, the people will probably accept continuance of the status quo, maximum autonomy for occupied Kashmir, and protection for Muslims in India.

Parallel discussion should be held with India to determine if they will accept the *quid pro quo.* Guarantees of peace in the Subcontinent by the Western powers, as done in the Middle East, must also be assured. Key members of OIC must give assurances of complete support for Pakistan's security. Following the referendum, Pakistan can finalize a peace treaty with India on the basis of full autonomy of Kashmir and protection of Muslims in India.

232. *U.S. Assurances Against Future Threats*: An agreement or treaty with the United States would be essential to ensure that, following resolution of the Kashmir conflict, other issues would not reignite threats of war. In exchange Pakistan can give assurance that the nuclear technology will not be shared with others and religious tolerance will be officially encouraged. Despite the popular perception in Pakistan that the United States is not a reliable partner for Pakistan, the citizens would welcome improved relationship with the United States. There is a feeling that the United States may consider playing such a role only if Pakistan is more helpful in the Middle East and recognizes Israel.

Recognition of Israel. Pakistan has been periodically under pressure from the United States to recognize the State of Israel and establish normal diplomatic relations. The main argument is that most of the direct parties to the quarrel, namely the Palestinians, Egyptians, and Jordanians, have already done so.

Several other Muslim states have followed suit. Why is Pakistan refusing, especially when continued enmity toward Israel is costly to Pakistan in terms of U.S. and Western aid, and encourages closer cooperation between Israel with India? It is a serious issue which deserves serious consideration.

Pakistan has close ties with Saudi Arabia and Iran. Saudi Arabia cannot recognize Israel until there is a satisfactory agreement on the status of Jerusalem. Iran cannot do so unless a comprehensive peace is in sight and direct threats to Iran are withdrawn, or at least become muted.

Pakistan should make clear to the United States that it is not against diplomatic relations with Israel as long as genuine concerns of Muslim are addressed. In fact, Pakistan can promise to take a lead in lobbying for overall recognition of Israel by all members of the Organization of Islamic Countries (OIC) provided (a) the peace process with the Palestinians remains on the agreed schedule; (b) agreement is reached with Syria concerning Golan and a security zone in Lebanon; (c) dialogue on the future status of Jerusalem appears to be on track; and (d) Iran is brought into the peace process.

Peace and recognition will be good for all concerned. It will remove the nagging fear of sabotage from Israel, remove hesitation within the United States about improving relations with Pakistan, and will be good for long-term peace and prosperity in the Middle East.

233. *Establishing Pakistan's Position of Power.* A sure way to demonstrate power is detonation of a nuclear device or diplomatically to confirm nuclear capability. Further development of its defense industry would also enhance international stature. The cost of both of these policies is extremely high and must be reconciled with their conflicting objectives. Wise leadership, lofty objectives, and sincerity of intentions may bring success.

234. *Cost savings:* Cuts in the purchase of high-tech conventional equipment are an essential aspect of any new defense policy. Cuts in size of standing army are also necessary. Their defense budgets are burdens to Pakistan and India. Both would appreciate the opportunity to reduce their defense budgets and devote increased funds to the welfare of their citizens.

235. *Establishing Sustained Defensive Capability*: Introduction of universal military training for adult citizens would improve the nation's confidence. Maintenance of a military balance between the forces of India and Pakistan would deter both sides. Improved cooperation with Muslim nations and with China would result in better connecting roads, railways, and pipelines providing new economic links and protection in times of embargo. Trade, travel,

and cultural links with friendly nations would increase under the umbrella of peace.

236. *Other Muslim Countries*. Pakistanis would welcome the involvement of and improved relations with fellow Muslims, e.g., members of the Organization of Islamic Conference. Some doubt the value of such assurances. However, Saudi Arabia, Iran, and Turkey have provided valuable assistance to Pakistan in past conflicts. Similar help in the future from the same and other Islamic countries would be most encouraging. Special efforts must be made to establish closer cooperation with Malaysia and Indonesia. It is in the long-term interest of Muslims, particularly Pakistanis, to have endorsement of the defense package from OIC. It would strengthen solidarity which would be helpful in case of future conflict.

237. *Likely Opposition*. The Pakistani army would object to a reduction in the standing army or to reduced acquisition of foreign equipment. They would be supported in the opposition by powerful arms merchants who make huge profits from such sales. Pakistani politicians, bureaucrats, and others who get commissions on such acquisitions will also resist. However, the army should be reassured by the protection provided by the nuclear option. In addition, they would look forward to increased development of the Pakistani defense industry, the large number of trainees, and the long-term supply of trained citizens. There is much for them to gain.

238. *Kashmiris*. The Pakistani army and citizens are not going to like giving up their claim on Kashmir for autonomy under Indian control. However, Pakistan has not been able to wrest control of Kashmir from India during the last fifty years. It is not fair of them to continue to give false hope to Kashmiris. In addition, in case of a plebescite, if Kashmiris choose to be independent, Pakistan will have to be ready to relinquish control over Azad (free) Kashmir, and even some other northern areas which may prefer to join Kashmir. Neither Pakistan nor India is going to like it. While Pakistan may be persuaded in the long run, India is going to fight it. Under current circumstances, the Kashmiris are unlikely to persuade or force India. Autonomy may be the best possible option for Kashmiris.

The brave Kashmiris who have fought long and hard want independence or merger with Pakistan, rather than increased autonomy within India. However, they also want an end of repression in Kashmir. Their struggle also would have resulted in improved conditions for over to 100 million Muslims who live in other parts of India.

239. *Other Conclusions.* The following additional points will help to strengthen Pakistan's national defense:

- Stop subversive activity against India and reduce involvement in military action of other countries which can adversely affect Pakistan.
- Continue and strengthen the current "crisis control arrangements" with India, e.g., the "hot line" between the two army headquarters, agreement "not to attack each other's nuclear facilities, and timely exchange of information on military exercises and movements. [221]
- Pakistan citizens must exert influence on their government to encourage it to resolve outstanding issues with India and other adversaries. They must resist powerful lobbies who benefit from continued conflict.
- Review internal administration of armed forces and take corrective actions in order to reduce internal corruption, introduce cost controls, and make the military more efficient.
- Stop official bribes to the military through lavish housing schemes, allocation of land for personal use, gifts to persons in the higher echelons, (e.g., BMW cars to generals during Nawaz Sharif regime).
- Pakistanis living abroad must support a suitable defense package through use of their personal influence and that of their adopted homelands.

[221] Ibid.

PART THREE

MECHANISM FOR CHANGE

CHAPTER 18

OPTIONS FOR CHANGE

Present Trend

The vast majority of Pakistanis hope that the nation's moral, economic, political, military, and judicial conditions will improve. All want Pakistan and Pakistanis to be successful and prosperous. Pakistan has already gone through a civil war in East Pakistan. It resulted in more than one hundred thousand casualties among civilian and military personnel. It provoked a war with India which cost hundreds of millions of dollars. Pakistan lost of half of the country. More than ninety thousand soldiers were made prisoners of war. It forced compromise on Kashmir under the Simla Accord. Many predict much worse for Pakistan and Pakistanis, if the moral, economic, political, and military problems continue.

Another civil war would bring the specter of East Pakistan to the soil of present-day Pakistan. Recent civil wars in Afghanistan, Somalia, Rwanda, Lebanon, and Yugoslavia should demonstrate what can happen to people and a country when civil war occurs. Hundreds of thousands of lives are lost. Properties are destroyed. Misery and sorrow prevail. The tragedies capture attention and headlines for a while, then the nation is left to cope with its tragedy. Those who die quickly prove to be the fortunate.

Who Can Bring Change?

240. *The Government.* The federal government has tremendous power which has been given by the people through the constitution to improve their welfare. In practice, power has been transferred outside the constitutional establishment to an elite group of politicians and civil and military officials. The constitutional power of the state includes the military; police and civil administration; foreign relations; financial resources directly owned and controlled by the people, e.g., state lands, state-owned industries, banks, and infrastructure; taxation power; the judicial system, including appointments; and regulatory powers over assets jointly owned with private citizens or those totally owned by private citizens.

There are of course limits to what the state can do. It is constrained by stronger international powers and opponents at home. However, it is still left free to do or not to do many things. Without doubt, the Pakistani state has a great deal of power. It can enrich or impoverish a great many people. Big landlords of today exist because most of the lands were given to their ancestors by previous governments, British, Indian, or even Pakistani. All the commercial and industrial giants of today enjoy their power and status because of licenses/permits, concessions and loans from the government of Pakistan. The state has the power to do much good or much evil. Many people are aspiring to be a part of the state apparatus. Those who are already a part of it are trying to maintain and enhance their role.

Change in control must happen democratically. It means going to the people directly for the purpose of gaining their confidence by explaining an alternative vision and action program. The change of control is not easy. It assumes that

- a majority of the voters can be convinced that the suggestions are valid and must be implemented,
- people controlling the state are neither willing nor able to implement them. Therefore a change in government is required,
- people vote for alternate candidates committed to bringing about the change,
- new people win the elections and are allowed to make a new government, and
- the new government is willing and able to implement the new program and does not back away from the promises as the others have.

There are many intermediate steps and hurdles. The people in power are going to resist change and will create difficulties for those who want it. They will use the powers of the state to remain in power. It is very easy to be discouraged and to give up the struggle. History is full of instances where people have compromised their principles.

The author himself does not expect to live long enough to see the implementation of the changes and transformation of the society for the better. However, the suggestions are meant for enhancing the welfare of the people. If they judge them to be valid, they must accept the lengthy process and many hardships involved and make the changes happen.

241. *Reforming Civil Servants.* Many argue that an ineffective and corrupt civil service has been one of the main causes of the relative lack of progress in developing countries, including Pakistan. A job in civil service has be-

come synonymous with a contract to rob the citizens within the jurisdiction. The public and the military, business, and political leaders are aware of it. International organizations have taken note of it for the last two decades. For example, the World Bank focused on the issue through Structural Adjustment and Technical Assistance loans. It emphasized retrenchment of personnel to reduce the wage bill. It recommended reforms of payment and employment policy as incentives to reduced corruption, and improve efficiency and productivity.

While there has been some downsizing, qualitative fiscal improvement and increased efficiency have been less than expected. Technical assistance through consultants has provided technical inputs; however, it has been rather ineffective in long-lasting and self-sustaining reform.

The main reason for the failure is attributed to lack of a supportive environment within the society, particularly in government. Independence from colonial rule has resulted in strong central governments which can presumably ensure economic development and equity for all citizens. In reality, independence has led to powerful states characterized by lack of accountability, disabling regulatory burdens on private sector development, distorted resource mobilization with exemptions and evasions for the powerful, and budgets dominated by the military and powerful interest groups who disregard important economic programs.[222]

The World Bank and other assistance donors recognize the need to address these issues. The governments in power pay lip service to the need for change, but rarely come forward with practical solutions. International donors are attempting piecemeal reforms through individual projects and policy dialogue. However, the impact is often limited to the projects which they fund directly. They are trying to sharpen their analytical tools and testing new approaches based on past experience. These efforts are continuing.

The staffs of international institutions, such as the World Bank, possess considerable technical skills and are bright and sincere. Many of them are from developing countries. With leverage from their institutions, they oftenare often able to achieve reform where the nationals themselves could not. However, several factors preclude a large scale, institutional reform by international assistance agencies: the limited scope of their mandate; priorities of their own management and shareholders; complexities and mag-

---

[222] Mamadou Dia, "A Governance Approach to Civil Service Reform in Sub-Saharan Africa," in World Bank Technical Paper Number 225, Africa Technical Department Series (Washington, D.C.: The World Bank, 1993), pp. 1-4.

nitude of the required change; and powerful domestic groups whose interests would be hurt by reform.

242. *Politically Active Citizens*. Citizens must try positively to influence their government in whatever manner possible. This applies to Muslims and non-Muslims alike. The Pakistani governments have eagerly demonstrated secular behavior. Pakistani Muslims, particularly Islamic political parties, have a responsibility to demonstrate Islam principles inside their own lines, parties, and the government. The Islamic leaders and parties claim that they know Islam and that they would bring Islamic ideals to government if given the power. However, when in power, Islamists in Pakistan (e.g., Jamat Islami, Jamiat Ulmai Islam, and General Zia) have simply put more emphasis on rituals, separation of sexes, and stern punishment for those who do not follow them. As a result, many people, including the more educated citizens, women and the non-Muslim citizens are skeptical.

243. *Powerful Individuals*. Powerful people who have specific projects can usually get them done, provided they are not going to threaten someone more powerful. For example:

- Gauher Ayub and other relatives could build an industrial empire when General Ayub was in power.
- The husband of Benazir Bhutto could wield immense influence during the tenure of his wife.
- The former governor of Sindh, Hakim Saeed, supervised the Hamdard University project. He could get it implemented when he was the governor of Sindh.
- Former minister, Kazi Abid, who owned the Ibrat group of newspapers and magazines, could develop business when he was Minister of Information or had equivalent power.
- Former Prime Minister Nawaz Sharif could expand the Itfaq group of industries when he was in power.
- All ministers and senior officials have been able to implement their personal projects on a priority basis.

By contrast, common people are too busy with their day-to-day struggle for food, shelter, and employment to be able to accomplish anything substantial. They moan and groan continuously but their energies are not pooled or channeled effectively to change the society. If the average citizens pooled their energies and/or the powerful individuals offered their support, the required changes would become feasible.

244. *Intellectuals and Would-be Reformers.* There are intellectual people who have a vague desire to change the world. They do not know exactly what needs to be done but perceive the need for change. They lose valuable time in conceptualizing actions, often arousing fear and opposition, simply for lack of clarity. Such would-be reformers must work out the details of exactly what they want to do. They must initiate national debate and obtain the people's support before seeking power.

245. *Persistence for Change.* Almost everyone who discusses Pakistan feels helpless in terms of improving the nation. Common people feel that no one listens to them. Political candidates make some interesting noises at the time of elections, but little if anything happens thereafter. Bureaucrats feel that they are not the policymakers. They are there to carry out the laws of the land and instructions of their superiors.

The politicians in power are charged with policymaking. In practice, the power is concentrated in the prime minister, the president, and the army chief. Even heads of ministries feel that they have little power. Their own bureaucratic staff ignores them, often not implementing even routine instructions. They are in no position to bring about any fundamental changes.

At the prime ministerial level, Benazir Bhutto has reportedly been forced to avoid certain key defense areas, e.g., military appointments, military operations, and the military budget; conduct of war in Afghanistan; and accountability of past favorites. She has argued that her majority in the National Assembly is so small that she cannot make any significant change in the society.

People who wish to change the society must persist in demanding and working for change.

Objectives of Change

The main objectives of bringing change to Pakistan can be summarized as
- establish a government of the common people, for the common people, and by the common people,
- maximum employment,
- raise the standard of living of common people,
- remove corruption,
- freedom of religion and its practice based on consistency with basic teachings of Islam,
- restore law and order,

- provide peaceful borders at affordable cost,
- accelerate rate of economic development, and
- demand demonstratioons of moral behavior by public servants.

There is a widespread desire to improve life in Pakistan. The general perception is that politicians have kept the power within an elite group. Common people have not received significant benefits from the politicians. Military rule has been corrupt and inefficient, too. Some have even recommended that all officials presently in power should be dismissed because they are perpetuating and benefiting from British colonial-type rule. The Soviet bloc and Iran have tried such an extreme approach. There is a question whether it helped them in making much progress.

A part of the solution lies in an improved incentive system. Incentives are relative. Groups of people require different incentives, e.g., for the truly poor, food, shelter, and clothing are sufficient incentives. For the unemployed, the promise of a job is sufficient. For shopkeepers, the ability to keep their shop open in a peaceful environment without interference of others is sufficient. For an industrialist, the ability to develop an industry and enjoy the fruits thereof is sufficient. Every citizen wishes to have security and a helpful government, but most want minimum interference.

Options for Changes

A. FOREIGN INTERVENTION. One of the most frequently mentioned solutions appears to be foreign intervention. There are, at least, three options. Some, particularly older citizens nostalgic of the British colonial days of relative peace, equal treatment of citizens under the law, and less corruption, go as far as wishing that the United States or the United Kingdom would simply take over Pakistan and run it. They equate the return of colonialism with "benevolent rulers," law and order, financial resources of the West, technology, and improved infrastructure. They dream of peace and prosperity but not necessarily independent existence. Many wish that the United States would force Pakistan's leaders to act in the interest of Pakistani people.

Some nationalist groups in less developed provinces have hoped for Indian support in resolving their problems within and without Pakistan. The law-and-order problem in Karachi has made many immigrants from India wonder whether they did the right thing in coming to Pakistan. Some even look to India for salvation. Many politicians have been accused of seeking Indian help, even though hardly anyone has admitted it.

Those who have worked hard for Islamic rule in Pakistan wish for closer relations with Muslim countries and a more active role in Islamic causes. The Sunnis have traditionally looked to Saudi Arabia. Following the revolution in Iran, many Shiites look to Iran. They all wish that the language of the Qur'an, Arabic, was the national language and that there was greater Arab influence. They seek help from other Islamic sources whenever they are in difficulties. Most Pakistanis look favorably on the Pan-Islamic movement.

Those in power or aspiring to it have recognized the emotional links of people to different foreign powers. They want to gain or hold on to power while maintaining the support of foreign powers. All political parties try to gain such foreign support.

The ambassadors of the United States, the United Kingdom, and Saudi Arabia seem to be the most sought after people in Pakistan. Leaders of all political parties and even ordinary citizens love to take their complaints to them and seek to get their problems resolved. Others, particularly among the educated, simply wish to migrate abroad to get away from the problems facing the country.

Foreign governments continue to absorb labor from Pakistan and continue to play prominent roles in policy formulation and provision of moral, financial, and other types of assistance to their favorite groups in Pakistan. They are eager to expand their influence in the country. Some wish to have military bases inside it. However, no one appears to be keen to take over the country, provide "benevolent leadership," and be responsibile for its affairs.

B. LIMITING PROPERTY AND INCOME. Many citizens feel that greed is the main problem of the country. They think of structuring the society in such a way that excess income will be impossible to accumulate and use. Under the new rules:
- Property and income beyond an agreed limit would be taxed away.
- Everyone would be assured of agreed minimum income and basic needs.
- Bribery would be of no use because of heavy punishment coupled with income limitation.
- Landlords would share with peasants because they would not be able to keep or use the excess property or income.

This solution is similar to that advocated by Senator Huey Long of Louisiana to deal with the great depression in the United States. It gained him much popularity in his time. However, it removes all incentive—neither productive nor lazy people would have any incentive to produce. Overall productivity would decline, and the society would become even poorer.

C. SLAUGHTERING CRIMINALS. Slaughter 100,000 or more crooks to set an example for those who have robbed the country monetarily. So propose hardline reformers. They demand that dacoits, robbers, smugglers, and crooked businessmen, politician, military official, and bureaucrats all be included.

Shehzad Amjad, in-charge of the economy section of *The News on Friday* has gone much farther. He wrote in the *Newsline* of November, 1994 that "The Establishment Must Die." He argued that some adjustments to the current system of government or even application of force without restructuring of the state and society will not be sufficient. "Unless the establishment along with its agents in civil society die, we cannot even begin to think of rational solutions to our problems."

Such solutions bypass constitutional rule and introduce disorder and lawlessness. They propose another packaging of violent *dictatorship* and introduce fear. They do not necessarily encourage people to stop their criminal activities and become better humans. Under the first martial law government in Pakistan, bribery rates went up, perhaps due to greater fear of getting caught; but bribery did not stop.

To some extent such solutions have been followed in Pakistan for some time. "Known criminals or enemies of the nation" are picked up by the army and/or police, interrogated, tortured, and eventually killed. A subsequent press notification would state that the person committed suicide while in detention or died in an "encounter" while attempting to escape from custody. When such violations of human rights occur, there are public outcries against the government along with continued complaints of corruption.

How much, if any good, this hard line approach has accomplished is difficult to measure. However, the problems of law and order have certainly not been solved. Similarly, trust and respect for government in Pakistan has probably not increased in the minds of people. At times, even though they were acknowledged criminals, some victims have been made martyrs in the public's eye simply because of the circumstances surrounding their deaths. In addition, it is probable that other criminals have not been deterred.

A better approach would be to have criminals arrested and prosecuted in courts of law and convicted after due process. It is true that witnesses are often afraid and are, therefore, difficult to produce before the court. However, with a few well-publicized convictions and public support, confidence of the witnesses can be gained. There are well-established methods of witness protection in the United States and elsewhere which should be considered.

Even Altaf Gauhar, one of the key players of the first military rule in Pakistan, under President Ayub Khan, has come to the conclusion that:

. . . military rule is a wasteful and oppressive form of government. It cannot lead a country to political growth and economic development regardless of the qualities of the military ruler. No individual, however accomplished, can replace the people who represent the supreme political reality to which a government must remain subservient and accountable at all times.[223]

D. POPULAR REVOLUTION. Almost everyone in Pakistan is fed up with the present system. Even the rulers complain about the failure of the system. They all talk of "an imminent explosion." In reality, they are praying for a revolution. "Pakistan Ripe for Revolution" is a common theme.[224] The "Khomeini style" revolution is often mentioned. People talk of expelling the current and previous rulers—throwing them out of jobs, jailing them, or even slaughtering them. They know it will mean a change without really knowing what it will be. They know they will start with fresh and probably inexperienced managers at all levels. Many hope "true Islam" will prevail with full implementation of religious teachings, despite the fact that religious parties are not supported politically. Others are just looking for a drastic change.

246. *Supporters of Revolution.* A revolution is likely to have many supporters, including:
- urban poor who feel left out by the current system, have little to lose, and look at revolution with romantic optimism;
- middle class who have tried to play by the rules, but have become fed up with law-and-order problems, a declining standard of education, and reduced opportunities of employment for their children;
- landless rural peasants who live under the tyranny of feudal lords and corrupt public officials, toiling year around, with little hope of progress;
- educated and uneducated unemployed who hope for drastic changes; and
- law and order proponents who have been victims or are afraid of the current lawlessness.

247. *Enemies of the Revolution.* A revolution would have many opponents, too. These are likely to include:

---

[223] Gauhar, p. 63.

[224] Commentary by Dr. Ghulam M. Haniff, Professor and Director of the International Relations Program at St. Cloud State University, St. Cloud, MN, published in *The Pakistan Link,* (26 July 1996), p. 4.

- feudal landlords, who have great power under the current system, and are likely to lose the most under a revolution;
- corrupt people—bureaucrats, businessmen, etc., who enjoy the benefits of the current system;
- proponents of sectarian or ethnic supremacy, who cannot be sure of the outcome of a revolution;
- beneficiaries of the domestic drug and weapon trade;
- leaders of the government in power; and
- king makers under the current system.

248. *People Sitting on the Sidelines.* There are people who do not have fixed views for or against a revolution. These include:
- honest bureaucrats (who are needed to carry out change);
- honest producers (who are needed to run the economy—small and medium sized businessmen, agriculturists, and industrialists);
- a majority of the armed forces; and
- citizens who hope to reform the system peacefully, or those who are too busy with their day-to-day affairs to worry about anything else.

The active proponents of a revolution in Pakistan have yet to become vocal. They have not organized current and potential supporters nor sought to weaken opponents. They would have to convince a large group that such a drastic change is necessary.

Objectives of the Revolution

If a revolution takes place in Pakistan, it would have to achieve a number of objectives in political, economic, military, spiritual, and judicial fields.

249. *Political Development.* The objectives in the political arena would include:
- effective civilian supremacy over the military, which would be reviewed and reorganized as required;
- trial and punishment of significant numbers of powerful leaders who have weakened the nation through corruption, including military officials, politicians, bureaucrats, and businessmen. Punishment would include removal from jobs, confiscation of property, long jail sentences, and death where appropriate;
- establishment and enforcement of rules for political and bureaucratic morality;

- effective equality of all citizens regardless of ethnic, racial, and religious origins;
- exemplary demonstration of Islamic principles and practices by Muslim public officials;
- high priority for law and order, speedy trials and punishment for violators; and
- enforcement of human rights; prosecution of violators within the government or outside.

250. *Economic Measures.* The economic measures will probably include:
- free economy with minimum rules and governmental impediments and removal of obstacles in the way of investment and business activity,
- generation of jobs through private and public sectors programs,
- severe economic penalty for any sort of corruption,
- honest collection of taxes and user charges,
- an affirmative action program for balanced regional development, and
- strict enforcement of laws relating to land reform.

251. *Spiritual Changes.* Islam remains the moral basis for creation and continued existence of Pakistan. The conflict between extremist and indulgent factions would have to be resolved on the basis that duties toward Allah are the responsibility of each individual. The government would provide facilities where it can, but would not interfere in performance. By contrast, performance of Islamic duties toward mankind would be overseen by the government and would probably include:
- effective freedom of religion and its practice. Those who compel others or curb the freedom of others would be punished,
- rules for personal religion observances would be minimized,
- training of imams would be implemented, and
- duties toward mankind would be emphasized.

252. *Military Changes.* In the military field, there will be a critical review of the mission of the armed forces, adjustment in its size and structure, and a significant cut in its budget. Full-time use of military forces in war as well as in peacetime would be recommended, and personnel and appropriate equipment would be fully utilized on civilian projects during peacetime.

253. *Consequences of a Revolution.* Violence is the worst part of any revolution. Many, sometimes hundreds and thousands of people are killed and maimed; families are destroyed; children are orphaned. Some of the most

creative and productive people under the previous system are destroyed; entrepreneurs and managers who know how to make things work are often killed or leave the country. Valuable physical assets which have taken years and vast resources to build are destroyed, such as roads, water supply, electricity, and industry.

Long after the revolution is over, emotional scars remain with those who were touched by the violence and the loss. New and untried leaders emerge who take years to learn the art of governing, let alone governing well. Many agree that if the same changes can be made in a peaceful way within the existing constitution, there is no need to go through the turmoil and violence of a revolution.

Once a revolution takes place, people are likely to realize that all their expectations have not come true. Those who benefit from the actual revolution will remain supporters. Others will become enemies. In fact, there will be almost certain realignment of friends and foes of the revolution after it has taken place.

If the abovementioned agenda is implemented, many will remain supporters of the revolution, such as the urban poor who benefit from increased social security and economic prospects and the rural poor who gain land and power. Similarly, enemies of the revolution will emerge, such as top military officials who will become subservient to civilians, soldiers who have to work even in peace time, conservative religious leaders who wish the state to be purely theocratic, and middle class members who may initially lose benefits.

A revolution would, by definition, have an impact on all aspects of life. Most of the desirable changes have been enumerated in this book and elsewhere. One can only hope and pray that the change which emerges is better than what now exists. Ironically, most of the required changes can be made peacefully within the existing constitution and existing laws. Ironically, the revolution is not needed for enactment of new law but rather for enforcement of the current law.

E. SINGAPORE MODEL. Pakistan need not reinvent progressive government. Effective models exist almost right next door. Singapore has been praised for its development from a colonial state to a modern economic power. Many Pakistanis wish to learn from the experience of Singapore and to emulate its success.

Four factors promoted the phenomenal economic growth and expansion of Singapore. They were: its location at the center of the vital sea lanes of South and East Asia; a free trade policy that imposed no taxes on trade or industry; a sincere, stable, and predictable leadership; and a hardworking and enterprising population.

254. *Performance of Leadership.* A study of Singapore's ruling People's Action Party (PAP) and its leaders indicates that from the early days of its formation, the leaders dedicated themselves to the interests and well-being of the country as a whole, taking into consideration all various ethnic segments of the population. Their concept of political management included not only retention of political power but also the viability of the policy and its institutions, an effective and honest administration, multi-racialism and the well-being and prosperity of its people.[225]

During the pre-independence period, when a PAP candidate was elected mayor of Singapore, the mayor set the tone of the government by:
- dispensing with traditional pomp and glory and making surprise visits to various departments to ensure efficient service and staff commitment to the people;
- establishing an Information Bureau, a Complaints Bureau, and weekly open meetings with people;
- serving notice on colonial-oriented administrators that they had to act as servants of the people;
- starting to carry out the promised programs with zeal and fanfare; and
- placing special emphasis on rooting out corruption, ensuring an efficient people-oriented administration, and establishing a multiracial and multi-lingual local government.

This initial performance and its repetition over the years, has been the basis of continued electoral success for PAP. Following independence in 1965, the leaders continued to act rationally and equitably:[226]
- They realized that there was *ethnic diversity of the population*—Chinese 75.4%; Malays 13.6%; Indians 8.5%; others 2.3% (based on 1957 data) —and went about establishing a multiracial society. The vast Chinese majority could have simply insisted on their dominance and required others to adapt, but they did not. They emphasized peaceful coexistence and tried for social cohesion. Opposing politicians were prevented from exploiting ethnic differences, and protection of minorities was assured.

---

[225] Ibid., p. 23.

[226] Ibid., pp. 1-24.

- Anti-colonialism was an important unifying force. However, it was a negative one which was minimized in favor of positive aspects of their common culture, consciousness, language, etc., to *transcend communal prejudices and interests.*

- As pragmatic politicians, they recognized that "there was no escape from the fact that, in the long run, the Chinese, the Malays and the Indians were substantially to retain their separate and distinctive identities . . . The only sure way the various segments could be made to feel and act as an integral part of a collective was to ensure for them an *improving standard of living* and expanding opportunities for business and employment."

- "In no way could one entirely satisfy the aspiration of the existing population in a Third World country while at the same time lay the foundation for future prosperity and well-being. The existing generation had first to be persuaded to pay a price and deprive itself to ensure continuing prosperity for the generations to come." However, the approach was difficult to promote. They started by *focusing on the immediate needs* of the people based on *realistic* political, social, and economic conditions.

- *Strengths of the community had to be recognized* and used beneficially, e.g., a hardworking, resourceful, and enterprising populace; easy availability of raw materials from the countries around Singapore; substantial capital availability with existing business infrastructures—business enterprises, banks, public authorities; existence of traditional markets nearby.

- *Guarantees for security of capital* investments and transfer of profits had to be provided.

- They saw social and economic rights as very important and placed the *highest priority on rights to a job, housing, and education*; they devised practical means to provide these rights to their citizens.

- The government effectively decided that "harmful elements" which included communal parties as well as communists would not be provided "freedom to use the democratic machinery to win and take over . . ." However, the *power of the state was not to be used for protection of the personal vested interests of the ruling class.*

- They placed considerable emphasis on education of the people. Educational facilities, particularly in scientific and technological fields, were expanded at all levels.

255. *Application to Pakistan.* Like their counterparts in Singapore, Pakistani leaders should accept the multi-ethnic and multilingual composition of the

nation. In spite of the unifying force of nationalism and of Islam, the people wish to retain their culture and language and will not part with it for a long time to come. Their desires must be respected. Pakistani leaders must display a dedication to long-term interests of the people as if all were members of an extended family. The government and its officials should prove that they are servants and not rulers.

The above type of policy has made Singapore meaningful to its citizens, and can do the same for Pakistan. These policies can make the country attractive to foreign investors too. The investors love the political stability, law and order, trained manpower, an adequate infrastructure, and good banking. The foreigners love the health, education, and travel facilities for themselves and their families too. They can come in large numbers and stay in Pakistan as they have done elsewhere when similar policies have been followed.

F. ISLAMIC MODEL. Despite all the mosques and Islamic schools, life in Pakistan is not much different from that of non-Muslim countries in the same stage of development. There are some good people and some bad ones. Falsehood, arrogance, hypocrisy, deception, and tyranny are common. There is a widespread system of bribery within the administration and the judiciary; ethnic, linguistic, and tribal disparity and injustice exist; violence is used for achieving political objectives; power is concentrated in unrepresentative hands; crimes of theft, rape, kidnapping, and prostitution are common; and use of drugs is increasing. Obviously, many Muslims of Pakistan have not been touched by the spirit of Islam.

Muhammad Iqbal, the philosopher and poet considered to be the spiritual founder of Pakistan, described the plight of Muslims in his famous *Complaint and Answer*. He pointed out the many social evils of Muslim societies: idol-breakers have been replaced by idol-makers; faith has been lost; one's native home is spurned; alien customs are adored; greed is everywhere; only a few aspire to Paradise; sectarianism, class, and caste prejudices are common; the examples of the Prophet (PBUH) have been abandoned; only the poor remain sincere; the rich refuse to give their share for good; and brotherhood has been abandoned. He felt that Muslims could get back on track only if faith and sacrifice returned.

The Qur'an clearly distinguishes the difference between the conduct of believers and nonbelievers:

> **. . . the un-believers follow falsehood, while the faithful follow the truth from their Lord. Thus Allah sets forth for mankind their examples (Qur'an 47:3).**

One can question whether, in practice, the majority of Muslims living in Pakistan are any different from the nonbeliever. Many Muslims feel that others have adopted the Islamic way of human behavior, while the Muslims have ignored it. Islam appears to be confined to the mosques. Islam appears to be missing from the hearts of Muslims.

Good examples at the top levels of the governments will, of course, help. Fair and just implementation of existing laws (or new ones, if needed) will help too. Government officials convicted of crimes deserve exemplary punishments. People must be convinced that the government is there to solve their problems and not just rule them. *Dawa'* (propagation) on a massive scale has been recommended. However, the question is asked, how do you invite someone to a religion to which they already adhere?

256. *Role of Muslims.* Individual Muslims are eager to play a role in strengthening Islam. Most want "drastic surgery" and immediate implementation of "true Islam." Many want to wake up the next morning with revolutions under way. They wish to see elimination of all oppressors and "enemies of God."

Sincere Muslims should become part of the Islamic movement in their own town, district, and province by becoming better Muslims. They should strengthen their practice of Islam and emphasize their duties toward God or their duties toward mankind. They must become politically active, joining Islamic groups of their choice. Through dedication and hard work, the policy-making levels of Islamic groups must present their vision.

Muslims have to work hard to bring like-minded groups to power through the democratic elective process. Once in power at the national level, they should use their power for the welfare of Muslims at home and abroad. If unable to provide a better performing government at home, they should recognize how difficult it would be at the international level (*ummah*).

Muslims, particularly Pakistanis, often talk about introducing the Islamic model of government. It is important to understand the Islamic model, examine the historical and current experience of Islamic governments, and point out some of the issues which remain outstanding and need to be addressed.[227]

257. *The Ideal Model.* The government established by the Prophet (PBUH) in Medina is accepted by all Muslims to be a model one. The Holy Qur'an

---

[227] Memon, *The Islamic Nation,* pp. 145-154. See also, Qutubuddin Aziz, *The Prophet and the Islamic State.*

was accepted as the eternal constitution. Shari'ah law based on teachings and practice of the Prophet (PBUH) was the law of the state. The government used the Prophet's mosque as the state's secretariat. Education of the people was considered as a duty to God. Science and discovery were highly valued and played a key role in advancement of Muslims. As a ruler, the Prophet (PBUH) demonstrated qualities of honesty, patience, tolerance, humility, diplomacy, and sacrifice.

The new Muslim state paid special attention to the well-being of non-Muslims with emphasis on religious tolerance, persuasion, and exchange. The economy supported a welfare state, social justice, and care for all. The administration was based on full accountability, with no corruption or bribes.

The Prophet (PBUH) was opposed to racism and slavery, and emphasized brotherhood. Human rights were highly valued under the new state, and respect for dignity of human beings was encouraged. Exploitation of fellow citizens was denounced. The importance and status of women were greatly enhanced. Under the new state, high priority was accorded to inter-faith dialogue with emphasis on increasing mutual understanding and communication.

Shi'ite Muslims believe that the state ceased to be Islamic after passing of the Prophet (PBUH) since Hazrat Ali did not succeed in forming the new government. Sunnis feel that the four rightly guided *khulafa'i* did their best to maintain the ideal government. Subsequent governments became monarchies.

Both groups feel that the original Islamic state ceased to exist in year 650 CE when the Umayyad dynasty came into power. While the monarchs followed many teachings of Islam, it is assumed that their primary objective was preservation of their own dynasty. The Muslim *ummah* accepted the monarchs largely because they had no choice. As a minimum, the Muslims expected justice and fair play from their rulers. Sometimes they got it, sometimes they did not.

History gives credit to Muslim rulers, including monarchs, for advancing architecture, higher education, science and technology, literature, etc. However, few Muslims wish to replicate these monarchies. Muslims around the world wish to replicate the model government set up by the Prophet (PBUH).

258. *Islam Today.* Compared to Muslims under the new Medina government, Muslims of today are much stronger in terms of the number, size of territory, acceptance of Islam as one of the world's great religions, financial and other material resources, etc. However Muslims lack leadership and a working model on how Muslim government should function in modern times.

In the opinion of Dr. Umar Chapra of the Saudi Monetary Agency, Islam has clearly set out four basic criteria of legitimate government:

- The government should be accountable to Allah, who is the sovereign and the source of *Shari'ah*. Since one of the primary objectives of *Shari'ah* is the well-being of people, the government must ensure it through "the adoption of all necessary measures, including the efficient and equitable use of the resources."
- The government is a trust, and must be accountable to people for meeting the terms of the trust. It must be open to people's suggestions and criticisms.
- There must be a general atmosphere of consultation. It demands the widest possible participation of people, either directly or indirectly.
- There must be justice and equality for all before the law.

These four criteria for legitimacy may not be satisfied unless those in political power derive their authority from the people and are answerable to the people for the quality of their performance. This demands a system of free and fair elections. Without such elections, people cannot fulfil the Qur'anic imperative of giving "the trust to those who deserve it" (Surah 4:58).[228] In recent times, Imam Hasan al-Banna, and Maulana Maududi have come to similar conclusions about the need for democracy.

Retired Air Marshal Asghar Khan of Pakistan wrote: "A fusion of religion and political power was and remains an ideal in the Muslim tradition. But the absence of such a fusion is a historically experienced and recognized reality. The tradition of statecraft and the history of Muslim peoples have been shaped by this fact."[229] He has shown that separation of religion and state has existed for at least eleven out of the last fourteen centuries. Nevertheless, attempts have been made to replicate the ideal model.

Existing Islamic Governments

Iran, Saudi Arabia, Sudan, and Bangladesh, along with Pakistan, claim to have Islamic governments. Their experiences are different, and worth studying.

---

[228] M. Umar Chapra, *Islam and the Economic Challenge* (Herndon: The Islamic Foundation, The International Institute of Islamic Thought, 1992), p. 244.

[229] Asghar Khan, *Islam, Politics and the State - The Pakistan Experience,* p. 19.

259. *Experience of Iran*. Following the Revolution, Iran started as the most promising Islamic government in modern times. It enjoyed support of virtually 99% of its people, many of whom had lived under poverty under the Shah and had sacrificed much for success of the revolution. As expected, differences with the West emerged quickly, leading to the taking of American hostages, freezing of Iranian assets, and a virtual economic boycott by the West. This followed an eight-year war with Iraq resulting in a million or more Muslim casualties on both sides. Even though Iraq was generally considered to be the aggressor, all efforts by other Muslims to restore peace were fruitless for eight long years.

The war ended in 1988. However, the suffering of Iranian Muslims has not. In presidential elections of June, 1993, President Rafsanjani won a second term with 63% vote, against two other relatively unknown but "approved "candidates. According to Reuters reports, a journalist candidate, who had attacked economic mismanagement of the regime, received a surprising 24% of the vote. Virtually every voter questioned complained about housing, low wages, and high inflation rates of 20 to 40% per year. All complained about declining living standards and the ruling clergy's isolation from the common people.

No doubt, many Islamic laws have been passed, however the life of common Muslim has reportedly improved little. Western conspirators have undoubtedly made considerable effort to sabotage the revolution but that was to be expected. The West, led by the United States, continues to make life difficult for the Islamic Republic. There are restrictions on investment and new penalties for supplying arms. Covert policies to disrupt the government are becoming ever more open. To what extent the Iranian model can be replicated in Pakistan has not been fully answered.

260. *Experience of Saudi Arabia*. As the custodian of Islamic holy places, and the provider of aid to many Muslim countries, Saudi Arabia is admired and looked up to by many Muslims around the world. The government has established Islamic laws for citizens and visitors. With great oil wealth, the kingdom has wisely spent much on the economic wealth on its citizens.

The Saudis, however, have their critics. They point to the "Western" lifestyle of many powerful people who appear to ignore Islamic laws; the protective measures enacted to secure the royal regime; excessive dependence on Western powers; and limited political participation of common people in government.

The positive and negative aspects of the Saudi experienceneed to be studied and improved to develop a better Islamic model of government.

261. *Experience of Sudan.* Around 1989, General Omar Hasan Bashir and other military officials seized power in a coup that gave control to their Islamic party. The attempts to introduce strict Islamic law has alarmed many Western powers, including the United States. Widespread human rights violations including arbitrary detention, torture, executions without trial, rape, forced migration, and starvation of thousands of citizens are loudly alleged by the Western media and governments. A visit in 1991 by Iran's President led to allegations of close cooperation between the two countries for the overthrow of pro-West regimes in Egypt, Tunisia, and Algeria.

Sudan's policy of allowing free entry to all Muslims has led to charges that the country is a haven for terrorists and used for their training. The arrest of some Sudanese citizens on charges of planning bombings in New York led to Sudan being declared a terrorist state by the U.S. government in 1993.

Sudan is another example of an Islamic government irritating the West. According to *The Washington Post*, Hassan al-Turabi, the "Islamic guiding light" of Sudan, sends shivers from behind the scenes.[230]

262. *Experience of Egypt.* Egypt has not proclaimed itself an Islamic form of government. However, Egyptian proponents of the Islamic model are actively working for it. News reports suggest that among other things, the "fundamentalists" are seeking to[231]

- denounce all foreign art and culture, particularly from the West, including paintings showing any nudity, plays, ballets, movie festivals, and translations of Western literature;
- denounce writings of secular writers of Egyptian origin;
- deny high positions in government to atheists or people with secular views;
- declare "secularists" as "apostates" who should be put to death;
- avoid contact with Christians, including shaking their hands, wishing them well on their religious holidays, or walking on the same sidewalks with them;
- introduce wearing veils in villages for girls starting at age six; and
- modify school books to emphasize Islam.

Clearly, Egypt is in the middle of a serious national crisis. People are being forced to take extreme positions in order to make their point. Many

---

[230] *The Washington Post,* (9 May 1995), p. A14.

[231] *The International Herald Tribune,* (4 February 1994).

Muslim citizens are worried about the current trend. There is a need to clarify just what the Islamic position is on the issues in question.

In the meantime, the secular and self-protective government continues to rule. Many Muslim citizens as well as the Western powers are concerned about the corruption, human rights violations, and "power at all costs approach" of the Mubarak regime. The Muslim groups have been trying to win the hearts of the citizens and improving their images by working with the poor and "have nots" in urban slums and rural areas. Through reported force and manipulation, the government won an overwhelming majority in the elections held in late 1995. The Islamic parties won very little representation in the new assembly.

Even though there are many dedicated Muslims in Egypt who want Islamic rule, they are unable to achieve it because (a) the current government wants to continue in power and has gone to extreme lengths to prevent its opponents from succeeding; (b) the West supports the government and prefers to have them in power rather than an Islamic government which they fear; (c) the people either are against Islamic rule or have been intimidated not to support the Islamic parties. There has been no effective challenge of the government on a massive popular scale.

263. *Experience of Pakistan.* Islam is the reason for creation of Pakistan. It was created to provide a homeland for Muslims of the Subcontinent who wished to live according to the laws of Islam. As summarized in an unpublished research paper by Asmah Tareen of Concordia College, the founder, Mohammed Ali Jinnah embraced liberal Islam even though he did little to incorporate it into the new state's government and politics.[232]

The subsequent governments supported the passive role for Islam until approval of the first constitution in 1956 under which Pakistan became an Islamic republic. The rule of Field Marshall Ayub Khan from 1958 to 1969 attempted to assert "developmental Islam":

> With capitalist policies, and no *Shari'ah* in effect, Ayub Khan responded to pressure from religious groups and rural *ulema* by cloaking his political agenda in Islamic garb. He created the Auqaf Department . . . and the Central Institute of Islamic Research,

---

[232] Asmah Tareen, "Islamic Identity in Pakistan's National Politics: Can the Government Continue to Walk the Line between Institutional Islam and Secularism?" Research Project, Fall, 1995, pp. 17-23.

composed of scholars to determine how Islam should be "modernly" incorporated into existing laws and government structure.

General Yahya Khan, the next ruler (1969-71), "promoted a 'nationalist Islam' to keep East and West Pakistan, with all their ethnic and economic differences, together under the common banner of Islam."

Zulfiqar Ali Bhutto (1971-77) followed. During his rule Islam reached a new level of official endorsement. Bhutto termed his agenda *Islamic Socialism* and promoted Islam as Pakistan's religion, socialism as its economic system, and democracy as its political system. Bhutto did little to promote Islamic policies until the new elections in 1977 when the Pakistan National Alliance (PNA) consisting of nine opposition parties combined and opted for incorporation of *Shari'ah* law. Bhutto responded by prohibiting alcoholic consumption, gambling, and even imposed non-Muslim status on a minority Muslim sect, the Ahmadis.

Mr. Bhutto was overthrown through a military coup led by General Zia-ul-Haq. Since he could not justify accession to power via democratic means, Islam became Zia's claim to legitimacy. Rather than wipe out the current economic and legal systems, Zia opted for symbolic change by trying to develop parallel Islamic banking and court systems. Nevertheless, Zia's Islamization policies had an ideological impact, making people more conscious of their Islamic identity. The *ulama* got their first taste of power and legitimacy as Zia appointed them to national and provincial government positions.

Zia's death in a mysterious plane crash led to a new round of elections which Benazir Bhutto won. Benazir campaigned on secular and anti-Zia platforms. She promised to undo the Hudud Ordinance which discriminated against women. However, she has not been able to do that during her two terms in office because of the substantial representation of conservative members in the National Assembly.

Nawaz Sharif who succeeded Benazir (1990-93) had a greater obligation to promote political Islam, but substantively, his policies have differed little from Bhutto's. As his concession to the *ulema,* Sharif passed a watered-down version of a *Shariat* bill the *ulama* had written, requiring that Pakistan's laws be in accordance with Islam. The *Shariat* bill is purely symbolic in that it declares an Islamic intent, but has no enforceable provisions to implement it.[233]

In short, Pakistan has been an Islamic Republic for some forty years. Islamization of the society has received much attention. High level councils

---

[233] Ibid., pp. 17-23.

have been created; many conferences have been held; some Islamic laws and punishments focusing on criminal and social acts have been introduced; and a parallel system of Islamic courts has been established to enforce the Islamic laws.

Islam is quite visible in Pakistan with a large number of mosques everywhere in the country; large number of people attend these mosques; Muslim women cover their faces in small towns and rural areas; there is an official ban on the sale of alcoholic drinks to Muslims; and there are frequent official calls for Muslim unity.

Yet, Islam is rarely visible in day-to-day government, business activities, or common dealings of Pakistanis with each other. Religious spokesmen are somehow more vocal and firm when it comes to punishing the weak and poor than holding the rich and powerful accountable. Islamic obligations toward fellow humans are rarely considered.

Pakistan has many Islamic political parties with many dedicated workers who regularly call for full Islamization. At least one ruler, President Zia ul Haq, fully supported their cause. However, Pakistani voters have repeatedly chosen to give little support to them and have preferred secular parties.

The October, 1993 elections proved the point again. Jamait-I-Islami, the largest and the most powerful religious group, made an election alliance with a number of other like-minded groups and formed the Pakistan Islamic Front (PIF). Acknowledged as the best organized Islamic party and having run a very efficient campaign, PIF won only three out of 103 seats it contested in a total national assembly of 217 seats. Its leader Qazi Husain Ahmed lost all three seats that he personally contested.

PIF parties had pushed for a hard line on Kashmir, opposed women entering politics, and pushed for the introduction of an Islamic economic and judicial system. The population chose to favor secular political parties in the freest elections held to date.

The causes of PIF's defeat include:
- disagreements and divisions among the Islamic parties,
- historic gaps between the pronouncements and actions of the Pakistani religious leaders,
- lack of faith in the abilities of the current party leaders,
- rejection of elements of their election platform,
- large influence of powerful local interests, e.g., feudal lords,
- preoccupation with local bread and butter issues,
- fears on the part of "moderate Muslims" and non-Muslims,
- stated "anti-fundamentalist" policies of the super power, and
- desire to keep religion and politics separated.

Regardless of the causes, the voters stayed away from PIF candidates in spite of their emotional attachment to Islamic causes. Islam will always be important in Pakistan. However, PIF's election defeat has reduced prospects for Islamization in Pakistan and it is likely to strengthen those who wish economic and social reform on secular lines. In any case, as long as the causes of PIF's defeat remain, religious parties will have limited political success.

Feasibility of Islamic Government in Pakistan

264. *Economic Concerns*. Will Islamic taxes such as *zakat* and *usher* be sufficient to meet the financial needs of the nation? If not, how will the financial needs will be met? How much can be produced by zakat and usher under different assumptions must be projected. Which of the current forms of taxes including personal and business taxes, excise and customs duties are Islamic and therefore can be retained?

The government meets a part of its budgetary needs through borrowing at home and abroad. Will there be a sufficient amount of money without payment of interest? If not, how will the gap be filled?

Similarly, business and industry finance their short, medium, and long term financial needs through borrowing? Will there be sufficient financing without interest? Some scholars have held that *riba* means excessive interest and does not apply to transactions based on reasonable rates of interest. There is a need for *ijtihad* on this subject to determine what is lawful today within Islam.

The Islamic system favors private ownership. Accordingly, the feudal lords and other rich interest groups expect to be able to keep their possession. However, does this apply to the lands and benefits awarded to individuals on the basis of their services to the British empire and other un-Islamic regimes to date. How will this be handled? There is a need for some data collection and analysis.

The traditional interpretation of Islam preaches assistance to the poor. How will such social justice promised by Islam be achieved? Obviously, the Islamic teachings have to be taken in total. Teachings about equality and social justice cannot be discarded. There is a clear need for resolving how economic development of the nation as a whole and the deprived class will be achieved.

265. *Present Situation*. Islamization is always a part of the political debate. On the positive side: (a) it is consistent with the religion of a vast majority

of people; (b) Pakistan was obtained in its name; and (c) if successfully implemented, it would provide a model for many other Muslim countries.

On the negative side: (a) it has not been successfully implemented in modern times with many aspects needing work before it can be operational; (b) women believe the role of women, particularly that of educated ones, will be jeopardized; (c) minority sects of Islam (Shiahs, Ahmadis, Agha Khanis, Zikris, etc.) oppose domination by the Sunni sect and its religious scholars; (d) educated men fear domination by poorly educated religious leaders who have been manipulated by politicians and who do not understand government; and (f) the current powers of the world will oppose it and sabotage it.

Because of President Zia's regime and policies of earlier rulers, many Pakistanis, particularly among the educated middle class, have, today, become allergic to the thought of an Islamic government. They do not want Zia's Islam and do not feel that introduction of the Medina model is practical.

The ruling class is of course content with the current establishment. It is clear that even the middle class does not take the discussion of an Islamic government seriously. They smile politely and keep quiet or even walk away. However, supporters of Islamization feel a "silent majority" of Pakistanis still think of the Islamic model with great affection. They acknowledge past failures in introducing the model and making it work and confess that they do not know how it can be introduced. Nevertheless, they remain convinced that only an Islamic government can bring prosperity to Pakistan.

Implementing the Islamic Model

Establishing a Muslim state in modern times along the lines of the ideal model has been difficult. Muslims continually debate the form of Islamic government suited to current times. Some feel that a return to fundamentalism, i.e., both the letter and spirit of the Medina model are essential. Others feel that Islam with the modern interpretation given by progressive and liberal Muslim scholars is the answer.

According to the latter, a modern interpretation of Islam would (a) remove Western nations' misunderstandings created by the fundamentalists; (b) remove obstacles erected by fundamentalism to the emancipation of weak and backward sections of Muslim societies; and (c) modernize the Muslim nation to suit the needs of the 21st century. This group wishes to follow the spirit of the first Muslim government, while adapting details based on needs of the modern times.

As long as one conforms to the teachings of Qur'an, there is room for diversity in Islam. It may be noted that even Christians have several hundred churches based on different schools of thought. Nevertheless, Muslims continue to search for a common path which Muslim scholars of different schools of thought can travel together. The sad part is that much acrimony and even violence has continued for several centuries among dedicated Muslims in the name of "the ultimate truth." All are quick to declare each other "*kafir*," or nonbeliever, and declare holy war. Non-Muslims have taken advantage of this division from the start.

266. *Pakistani Muslims.* At a minimum, Pakistanis appear to feel that (a) the constitution of every Muslim country must be based on the Qur'an and Sunnah; (b) the constitution must ensure that laws repugnant to the basic principles of Islam cannot be enforced; (c) people must choose their leaders on the basis of democracy which is mandated by Islam; [234] (d) the democratic process should not be stopped (by armed forces or powerful minorities) on any excuse; and (e) systematic and periodic elections will give confidence and experience to the people who will eventually learn to choose the right leaders.

As mentioned above, the people of Pakistan want to have an "Islamic" government. They have rejected religious parties and religious leaders but they have not rejected Islam. They have rejected political and legalistic concepts and interpretations but not the spirit of Islam. Many believe that with *Ijma* (collective thinking and consensus) and *Ijtihad* (individual effort), teachings of Islam and demands of modern times can be reconciled. The result would be an ideal government for Pakistan and a renaissance for Muslims everywhere. Such a new government would have to solve all of the major problems identified confronting Pakistan in order to be meaningful.

G. WESTERN DEMOCRACY. Western democracy is known to Pakistanis, mentioned in their constitution, and, to some extent, practiced. In its ideal form, as practiced in some countries of the West, it relies on eligible citizens periodically voting on basic policy issues. It provides sufficient incentives for producers of the society. It provides welfare for those who are unable to look after themselves (if people pay sufficient taxes). It is advocated by the powers of the world and has minimum opposition. It provides punishment for cheaters.

On the negative side, the majority is not always right. Elections can be manipulated by relatively few individuals or groups based on emotion and empty slogans. People have seen it operate and have, at times, lost faith in

---

[234] Chapra, p. 244.

it. It can degenerate to low levels of moral and ethical values. It does not affirm a spiritual base.

On the whole, as discussed in different parts of this book, democracy can be improved and made to work in Pakistan by sincere people. In order for it to be a viable option, at least the following changes need to be made in the current system:

- Democracy and free market policies must work hand in hand—the free market provides incentives and creative energy while sustained democracy provides for periodic approval by the general population.
- Public financing of elections must be introduced and private financing must be banned in order to give opportunities to all qualified candidates.
- Maximum possible number of seats must be allocated on the basis of party programs and votes rather than individual constituencies, which appear to be controlled by individual feudal lords.
- Elections must be held on fixed schedules, regularly and freely, under international supervision.
- Equal media access must be provided to all candidates and parties.

267. *Continued Trial of the Present "Democratic" System.* Is the existing "democratic" system worth continuing? It would be far better if the needed changes in Pakistan were made in a democratic and peaceful manner. It would be wonderful to have new ideas and progress come without destroying the old. In fully democratic systems, it is possible to have drastic change.

Americans are continually talking of changes in the government's scope, policies, and budget. They are able to make many types of changes through the existing legislative, executive, and judicial branches of the government. The checks and balances of the constitution provide some relief to the disgruntled citizens, too. On the basis of their Contract with America, the Republican Party leadership claims to be making revolutionary changes in a peaceful way, largely through Congress.

Is that scenario realistic in a country like Pakistan? Many argue that if democracy is given a chance to take root through several elections, people will learn how to distinguish between good and bad candidates. The system will improve. Others argue that the democratic process has been hijacked by the privileged class for their own benefit. Greed has overtaken the country. The current leadership will not allow more progressive people to move forward. They argue that the violence and loss of assets which have been continuing for years are more destructive and expensive than the one-time loss caused by drastic change. They wish to cut their losses and make the change now.

Private Efforts at Reform

There are plenty of examples of people and organizations within and outside Pakistan, who have made a substantial contribution to the life of others from outside the government. The Edhi Foundation and Imran Khan's cancer hospital have been mentioned earlier. The recently formed Awami Qiadat Party has laid out a welfare program. Jamat Islami and other religious parties in Pakistan have adopted a similar approach.[235]

The new party will not wait until it comes into power in order to start making its contribution. It will set up social welfare and community help projects from the start and will help implement them through its members at each level of society starting with villages in rural areas and neighborhoods *(mohallas)* in urban areas. The projects will help all needy people regardless of their party affiliation. The schemes may focus on:[236]

- education, e.g., literacy campaigns, training of teachers, establishment of libraries, vocational training, establishment of private schools;
- health care, e.g., low cost heath care through existing clinics, improved sanitation, clean water supply, population control;
- employment generation, e.g., provision of loans; establishing individual or collective enterprises; supply of seeds, fertilizers, and other farm supplies; network of cooperative stores; and
- general welfare, e.g., reduction of drug addiction, violence, child labor, bonded labor; elimination of litigation through the Punchayat system, legal assistance committees; promotion of healthy social environment through sports and debating competitions, and house/street/neighborhood/village cleaning competitions.

An Interim Conclusion

The people of Pakistan appear to want a major change in society in general and government in particular. Without realizing the unity of purpose, practically everyone would like to achieve the demands outlined in this book. However, most of the people have found a way to operate within the existing system. They do not appear to be ready to make major sacrifices for the

---

[235] The Muslim Brotherhood in Egypt and Hammas in Palestine are also following a similar approach.

[236] Awami Qiadat Party, *AQP's Welfare Program (AQPWP)*, (Islamabad: Central Secretariat: 1994/95).

change. They are hopelessly divided on ethnic, linguistic, and religious grounds. There is no leader in sight to unite them to fight for the major changes for which they all seem to yearn.

The key centers of power—the military, politicians, religious leaders, bureaucrats, and the business community are comfortable within the system, too. They feel that they can survive and prosper within the status quo. All they want is more power in their hands. A major shock of some kind—at home or abroad, e.g., a military defeat, a natural disaster, or an economic debacle can change the behavior of the public as well as the leaders of power centers. The scene can change rather quickly. In the meantime, the best option appears to be to strengthen the current democratic process.

At first glance, the Pakistani Constitution appears to include most of the required provisions for establishing and maintaining a good government of the people, by the people, and for the people. It guarantees essential rights and protection for all. Yet, it is amazingly impotent in meeting the essential demands of the people as outlined. It must be carefully reviewed by representatives of the people and suitably amended to ensure that the loopholes are closed and that people are able to achieve their reasonable demands within constitutional limits.

Special attention must be paid to reducing poverty and unemployment, provision of a basic infrastructure and services, making Pakistan richer, bringing back religious tolerance, restoring power to people, restoring law and order, stopping human rights violations, meeting basic concerns of the people of smaller provinces and relatively backward areas, stopping corruption, ensuring peace at the borders at an affordable price, and coexisting with the West.

268. *Promoting the Chosen Solution.* Whatever solution is chosen, it has to be promoted. Whether Pakistanis should aim at strengthening the existing political process or seek to bring about a major revolution, without concerted action to implement it, it will remain a theory. While some may read about it, not much is likely to happen. Of course, promotion is not an easy task. It will take hard work, time, money, media support, and efforts to convince others. Above all, it will take dedication of the proponents who are willing to make required sacrifices.

How have others done it? Intelligence agencies, government officials, and even large corporations of Pakistan and other countries promote policies and ideas through propaganda and manipulation of public opinion. Their resources include highly trained and specialized experts, money in required amounts and currencies, a cooperative media, weapons, and other appropriate equipment. They have the ability to arouse people to get the required emotional reaction— courage, fear, motivation for action or inaction. They offer continuing rewards or punishment to set the tone for the next program.

It is far easier to accomplish this when one is in power over a government which includes financial resources, intelligence agencies, the army, police, and an international network of connections and resources. This is quite difficult for individuals or a small group of people to accomplish.

How did the Prophet Muhammad (PBUH) achieve his mission? First, he had the direct inspiration of Allah, in the form of Qur'an. He also enjoyed the support of companions who believed in him and were prepared to sacrifice their lives and properties for him. Still he had to face years of persecution and wars before he was able to gain control of Mecca.

How did Gandhi achieve his objectives? He had a very powerful message in his demand for "independence of the motherland." There was a ready network of millions of supporters and dedicated workers who were willing and able to make sacrifices. For his own part, he sacrificed his lucrative legal practice, did not hesitate to go to jail a number of times, and chose to neglect his family life. Most important, he had a common enemy to unite his followers.

Similar approaches are used by political parties all over the world. Their platform is developed based on the needs of the people; their leaders accept the required inconveniences, sacrifices, and risks to present the ideas to local groups; they attempt to attract followers. They develop schemes and strategies to enhance their public image, then participate in scheduled elections or fight to get them scheduled. If they win, they try to implement what they promised in the platform.

Start of a Popular Movement

Popular movements for reform or even revolution can be started with relative ease, if a few dedicated people are willing to sacrifice their lives and other worldly possessions for it. Their success, the duration of their power, and the ultimate results of their movement is another matter. It is much more complex and too difficult to predict.

A relatively few Muslims in India started the movement for a separate Pakistan. It caught the imagination of the Muslims of the Subcontinent and led to creation of a new nation.

Zulfiqar Ali Bhutto, freshly out of power and with few friends willing to confront the government, started the People Party in late 1960s. It confronted the government of Field Marshal Ayub Khan and eventually brought it down;

it swept the elections in West Pakistan. His party has since continued to dominate the politics of Pakistan.

In the mid-seventies, people were able successfully to confront the govern-ment of Prime Minister Bhutto when they became disenchanted with it. Again Benazir Bhutto came to power and became prime minister on the basis of a popular anti-establishment movement. Of course, Allah sends help from expected and sometimes most unexpected sources.

If the people of Pakistan truly want a change, they can achieve it. Selfless leaders who can touch the hearts of the common people by focusing on basic issues of interest to them can gather enough support to initiate a major change. Almost everyone recognizes that the current crop of politicians, the majority of civil servants, most top officials of the armed forces, and most of the judiciary are dedicated to perpetuating their power and to self-enrichment.

Almost everyone recognizes that the country should be run in a better way; they want change. Who will start the mass movement? How will it start? What will eventually happen to those who start it? Will they remain steadfast and sincere to their cause until their goals are achieved?

Those wishing to take the lead should realize that they would

- be initially ignored by almost everybody—the people in power, people out of power, the media, the public;
- face hardships in getting their message to the people;
- be harassed in many different ways, if they are lucky enough to attract public attention;
- have their credentials, record and motivation scrutinized; and
- be distrusted and discredited by even those who stand to gain the most from the reform agenda.

One strategy is to work with those who are already in the field and who share, at least, some elements of the agenda. It would obviously be beneficial to join hands with those who seek similar change. It may be possible to influence and motivate an established group to work harder for the desired change. It may even be possible to win them over completely if they previously had poor leadership.

There also is the ultimate temptation to join the government and hope to reform the system from within. Those who have tried it have generally become part of it. It is possible that with good intentions, they achieved more from within the government than it would have been possible to do from outside. However, in the process, they often end up supporting and perpetuat-ing the existing system.

The most difficult way is to start from scratch. It takes a long time to achieve goals in that manner. On the positive side, one is totally free to mold the movement as one wishes.

In any case, all Pakistanis who share a common approach to government should join to make achievement possible. Those who support the reform agenda should not wait until they have gained full control of the government. They should start implementation to the extent they can within the areas of their own influence—inside their household; in their neighborhood; in their community; town; district, etc.

269. *Implementation.* Implementation of the reform agenda will require

- a clear and simple statement of objective, i.e., "a better and just Pakistan" which touches hearts of citizens by its correctness, and timeliness;
- an objective that people see as consistent with their religion and code of ethics;
- total dedication to the cause, including willingness of leaders and supporters to sacrifice; intellectual (and even physical) confrontation with supporters and beneficiaries of the existing system;
- wide dissemination of the ideas through free distribution of literature, meetings in drawing rooms, universities, and in public;
- debates leading to popular support for the platform;
- advocates for the ideas within the common people, students, the business community, politicians, the bureaucracy, and the military;
- support of people who can carry out the ideas (civil service and military); and
- eventual control of the government in order to implement the reforms promised to the people.

PART FOUR

CONCLUSIONS AND RECOMMENDATIONS

CHAPTER 19

VISION AND MANIFESTO FOR CHANGE

God does not change the condition of a people until they change their own inner selves (Qur'an 13:11).

Vision

Pakistan should be a country of prosperous and content citizens; at peace, and secure with itself; a country where citizens acknowledge, glorify, and benefit from their ethnic, cultural or spiritual diversity; and yet unite in the broader interests of the nation. Pakistan should be a part of the Islamic Nation and at peace with its neighbors, with each Muslim government, and with the West, particularly the the United States. Pakistan should continually develop, grow and blossom, and participate as an equal under the new world order.

Development is equally urgent on moral, economic, political, spiritual, and military fronts. Objectives in each of those areas have been discussed above. In summary, Pakistanis as a group should be able to

- meet their own basic needs of adequate food, shelter, education, and health care;
- have stable and representative government;
- tolerate, and if possible, peacefully resolve all differences among themselves, including those based on ethnicity and religious interpretations;
- devote maximum possible resources to education, science and technology in order to understand and effectively participate in today's world; and
- be strong enough to defend its own borders and to render help to other Muslims in defense of their vital interests.

Pakistanis should be thriving, contented, successful, and well-respected people who are:

- working hard in a noncompetitive way to improve themselves (individually and collectively), and the rest of the mankind;

- controlling their own destiny, free of coercion, bullying, or dictation from within or from abroad;
- resolving internal and external conflicts in a peaceful and harmonious way;
- free from compulsion in the choice or practice of religion;
- free from discrimination and exclusion from within and abroad; and
- enjoying their stay in this world while getting ready for the next one.

Pakistanis must emerge as a self-sufficient, peaceful, and strong group of people. It would gain them self-respect and the respect of others.

The Manifesto

270. *The Problems.* The rulers of Pakistan—politicians, feudal landlords, military officials, and bureaucracy have generally done well in promoting their personal interests. They have done poorly in advancing the national ones. The people have not done as well as expected either. As a result, there is general discontent and Pakistan faces many urgent problems.

About one-third of the population is poor by minimal international standards. Too many citizens are unemployed and are desperately searching for jobs. In daily life, the citizens are facing increasing levels of violence and intolerance. Law and order have nearly broken down. Average citizens in positions of power—from peon to the ministers—are willing and able to exploit the system for personal gain. Corruption is rampant. Human rights violations are a daily occurrence. Minorities and residents of small provinces feel exploited. The national borders are less then secure with frequent reports of violations. The cost of national defense has exceeded Pakistan's ability to pay. Constitutional lines of authority have become fuzzy. Almost all citizens doubt the sincerity of the leaders. People want change. Who can bring it about and how?

271. *Solution.* The extensive overhaul which is demanded suggests the need for a major revolution. The vested interests who benefit from the current system are likely to resist the change. The revolution, if and when it comes, is likely to be a violent one. However, noting the extent of destruction caused by revolutions elsewhere, and the uncertainty of its eventual outcome, there is a need to do everything possible to bring about the change peacefully.

Almost all existing political parties profess to seek a similar overhaul of the Pakistani government machinery. However, their performances during their tenures in office do not display the required commitment and action.

Unless the leadership of one or more parties rededicates itself, there is a need for a national party that differs from other parties in its zeal *to deliver on promises and devote itself to solution of the problems facing the people.* Whether within or outside the government, its members will dedicate themselves to finding and implementing solutions. The new party can surface either through restructuring an existing party or through creating a new one.

272. *Human Development.* The development of people is the most important task facing Pakistan. In human resource development, the party must continually remind the people of their own obligations to struggle and act individually and collectively to

- achieve whatever they wish to in private and public life;
- prove themselves vicegerents of Allah on this earth in terms of moral behavior;
- continually *upgrade themselves* intellectually, economically, and physically;
- be active in the political process and *vigilant over the government,* without obstructing its day-to-day functions;
- *Show tolerance* for differing beliefs of others and abide by the collective decision of the people;
- demonstrate *respect for the human rights* of others;
- provide special *opportunities to the weaker groups* within the society— the poor, women, children, the old; and
- increase *reliance on one's own action* and reduce dependence on government.

There is an urgent need to ensure human resource development at all levels of education and training.

273. *Politics.* In the political field, the party must work for continuation and strengthening of the democratic process with some basic structural changes. It must support the following policies:

- Make sure to look at the entire *population of Pakistan as members of one extended family* within the larger *ummah,* whose interests must be protected, and treat each one with respect as shareholders of Pakistan. Confrontational politics for the benefit of a few will be discouraged, and cooperative efforts for the benefit of the nation encouraged. Ethnic, regional, and sectarian tilts will be avoided at all costs.
- *Demonstrate practical benefits of the concept of one Pakistan* to all citizens, thereby inspiring loyalty.

- Find practical ways to give *meaningful roles in the political arena* to all—poor, middle class, and rich people from Baloachistan, Frontier, Kashmir, Punjab, and Sindh, regardless of language or ethnic group.
- Strive for *political and social development* of the people in parallel.
- *Award party tickets for elections on the basis of merit and ability* to solve the problems facing the particular constituency.
- *Practice preservation of human rights* as established by Pakistan's Constitution and reinforced by the United Nations.
- Practice genuine democracy within the party and the government with equal *opportunities for all citizens* for participation in the democratic process; negation of control or even advantage to the rich, ensuring that lack of personal wealth does not hinder participation in politics, e.g., through public financing of election expenditure, and adequate salaries for elected public officials.
- Ensure that elected representatives remain *in regular contact with their constituents* and sensitive to their genuine needs.
- Hold periodic *elections within the party* at all levels and for all offices, adhere to party policies once adopted, make periodic revisions in the platform if supported by at least two-thirds of the membership.
- *Support democratically elected stable government* with regular and honestly conducted elections every four years at agreed and announced times, restrict floor crossing (party-switching) by elected members, remove individual members of the government through well-established impeachment procedure rather than street violence.
- Help achieve the *legitimate vision of each ethnic group and minority* through decentralization, freedom to all ethnicgroups to develop their language and culture, well-targeted affirmative action programs to bring about balanced development of people throughout the country.
- Find ways to ensure that the political *leadership is sincere to the nation,* e.g., through reduction of current immunities, regular contact with con-stituents, and accountability to people and the party.
- Find ways to ensure that *"civil servants" stop being the "rulers for life,"* and become civil servants devoted to service of people.
- Find ways to *reduce concentration of power* in the hands of a few people in the federal government through maximum autonomy to each province; and decentralization of the government to the provincial and local level.
- *Support enhanced role for media* in terms of extending coverage to all parts of the country, opening competition in terms of ownership of media, insisting on responsible unbiased reporting, importing new tech-nology; and spreading education and knowledge.

- *Seek resolution of major issues* such as the Kashmir problem through debate on realistic options, discussion of each option's implications and costs, and a national referendum to determine government action.

274. *Economics.* In the economic field, the party must aim at *broad-based economic development at a significantly accelerated rate* and fight greed at all levels. Jobs for all those who want to work must be the prime economic objective. The party must

- *discourage* the practice of exploiting national authority and resources for the *benefit of a privileged few,* and work for economic development of all citizens;
- *weaken feudalism and help the rural population* through implementation of the existing land reform legislation, and provide those services for which peasants are normally dependent on their feudal lords;
- *ensure full payment of existing loans, taxes, and arrears* by all—including powerful and influential interests;
- *strengthen affirmative economic development* action programs in less-developed areas to achieve a degree of parity within the nation in an agreed period of time;
- *reduce poverty* through job creation, human resource development, provision of safety nets for the poor, development of women, strict controls over additional migration into the country, and provision of basic infrastructure;
- *focus on employment generation* which would result in increasing employment opportunities for the citizens, approaching full employment on a sustained basis;
- *focus on production of goods and services* in which the country and the people have a comparative advantage. Pakistan has a clear advantage in agriculture, some industries, banking, insurance, and export of trained manpower—more sectors must be discovered and developed;
- *make Pakistan financially viable* by significantly increasing revenue and controlling expenses, e.g., sound fiscal management through effective collection of current taxes and user charges, equitable ways to increase national revenue, and realistic ways to eliminate unproductive expenses;
- *increase private sector participation* by providing maximum opportunity for private investment based on transparent competition rather than favoritism;
- *dedicate the government to making each citizen prosperous* through encouraging excellence in professions of their choice, and freedom to enjoy benefits of lawfully acquired wealth;

- *solve the housing problem* of the citizens through large-scale provision of public lands and credits for housing, construction of flats in towns and cities and other suitable housing in small urban and rural areas; housing is to be made available to citizens for purchase at affordable prices and financing;
- *support large public and private investment in manpower development* by improving the quality of education, emphasizing the education of women, and on-the-job training leading to a universal literacy;
- *reduce economic disparities among* different regions through budgetary allocations and higher incentives for balanced regional development;
- *make agriculture efficient* and productive. Provide essential educational, health, market, and transportation facilities in small towns and villages in order to meet the needs of the majority of the population and discourage mass migration to urban areas;
- *provide equal opportunity for all citizens;* previously deprived communities to be given genuine opportunity to catch up within negotiated time frame and agreed allocation of resources;
- *increase national savings rate* through encouragement of good habits of saving for the future;
- *strengthen transparency in* order to assure citizens that privatization is a worthwhile exercise in the national interest; use resources generated from privatization for agreed purposes, including retirement of public debt;
- *encourage consultation* with and consent of the beneficiaries for each public and privately funded project; and
- *ensure sustainable environmental development* under each public and private project, cleanliness through strict fines for people who throw garbage on public property and pollute the environment, and beautification through establishment of public and private facilities.

275. *Judicial/Legal Issues.* In the judicial area and matters pertaining to law and order, the party must *support prompt and inexpensive justice for all citizens* in social, economic and legal matter. The party must stand for
- *enforcement of the laws* of the land in letter and, above all, in spirit;
- *full accountability for corruption* by civil servants, politicians, businessmen and military personnel. The punishment must be consistent and severe enough to make corruption unattractive;
- *independent judiciary* through secure tenure and other measures, so that it is an effective part of checks and balances within the constitution;

- *selection of the members of the judiciary for their competence*, experience, unquestionable honesty, integrity, and other good qualities, including social conscience and vision;
- *full protection of human rights*; violations must be stopped through existing laws and enactment of new ones if necessary;
- *special protection for minorities* and women and children through constitutional provisions;
- *restoration of law and order* in conformity with the law of the land; support measures which promote law and order, e.g., social justice; availability of basic goods and services at affordable prices; control over arms; communal and sectarian harmony; reduction of greed; active participation of the communities; and
- *Eeforcement of a ban on production and distribution of illegal drugs.* It must be made expensive and unrewarding.

Moral and Social Issues:

276. The platform for the party must contain strong affirmation of high moral spiritual ideals, including:
- the support of change in the society through an *end to the current emphasis on accumulation of wealth* by quick and generally illegal means, acquisition and control over power regardless of consequences for people and the country, exploitation of peasants and urban poor, and putting emphasis on long-term welfare of the people, elimination of poverty, achievement of full employment, control of the cost of living;
- *recognition of the Islam as faith of the majority* of the population, religious freedom for all sects among Muslims and non-Muslims, emphasis on religious tolerance partly through avoidance of special privileges or state sponsorship of any particular sect or group;
- *prevention of sectarian intolerance* through emphasis on the lack of compulsion under Islam; firm action at local, national, and international levels to prevent future violence; and strict punishment to those convicted of crimes regardless of the sect involved;
- *strengthening and the supporting family unit* and recognizing and honoring its role as the place of learning, and source of economic, social, and emotional safety nets for all members of the family;
- maximum *participation of the private sector in charitable* and social development *activities* through fiscal and other incentives for activities which do not generate sufficient revenue: community development, sup-

port for less privileged (orphanages, schools, clinics and hospitals, homes for the elderly and battered);
- *use of public and private resources for encouraging communal harmony* among the diverse communities of Punjabis, Pathans, Sindhis, Baloachs, Mohajirs etc.;
- *emphasis on pride in diversity* with a corresponding downplay of ethnic differences; freedom to all ethnic groups to develop their language and culture;
- *cleanliness* through strict fines for people who throw garbage on public property and pollute the environment, and beautification through establishment of public and private facilities;
- totally *honest government* with severe punishments for any form of corruption; accountability for politicians, businessmen, civil servants, and military personnel; wealth acquired through illegal means to be returned;
- *strict law and order* with speedy punishment for the violators; and
- *provision of moral examples* by the leaders of the country in order to encourage people to become more virtuous.

National Security

277. *National Defense.* In national defense, the party must support all measures to *ensure national security on a long-term, sustainable basis.* It must
- review and refine Pakistan's defense strategy;
- find ways to *make defense affordable*; review the military and civilian establishment to ensure that the objectives for which they exist are met;
- *stop involvement by "defense agencies" in civilian affairs*, e.g., creation or breakup of political parties; fueling differences in the communities, etc.; and
- *redefine the military's role* and make it accountable to the elected.

The defense package must address the following issues: Kashmir, U.S.–Pakistani relations, relations with other Muslim countries, nuclear policy, government efficiency and cost savings, and sustained defensive capability. Each of these is discussed below.

278. *Kashmir.* The government should continue to make an all-out effort for an international conference for peaceful resolution of the Kashmir issue. The government should also initiate an open debate of all aspects of Kashmiri

policy. Following two to three months of free debate, there should be a well-supervised secret referendum to decide Pakistan's future actions in this regard.

All realistic options including going to war again, continuation of the current bleeding, acceptance of the results of the international conference, if any, and formal acceptance of the status quo should be presented. All politicians should agree to accept and abide by the verdict of the people. If the military, the politicians in power, and the politicians in opposition (who have been in power earlier) are courageous enough to tell people what they know, the people will probably accept "less than desired results." The population must recognize that Pakistan may be forced to accept the "unacceptable" in its own and Kashmiri people's interest. In any case, the minimum package must include (a) maximum autonomy for the occupied Kashmir, (b) protection for all Muslims in India, and (c) renunciation of agitation in each other's territories by India and Pakistan.

279. *U.S.–Pakistan Relations.* Receiving effective assurances from the West against future threats is essential. A peace treaty/agreement should be negotiated with the United States to ensure that other issues will not reignite threats of war. In exchange, Pakistan should emphasize areas in which its views converge with the West (e.g., assurances that the nuclear technology will not be shared with others and religious tolerance will be ensured).

280. *Relations with Muslim Countries.* Pakistan should co-ordinate the foreing and defense policy with OIC. It should also work on measures to strengthen solidarity in case of future threats. Pakistan would be in the vanguard advocating Muslim unity in economic and military matters.

281. *Nuclear Policy.* Pakistan should establish its own position of power. It should detonate a nuclear device or give tactical confirmation of membership of the nuclear club. The availability of equipment for delivery of nuclear devices should be developed along with the rest of the national defense industry.

282. *Efficiency in Government.* The party should stand for cost savings through elimination of over-invoicing and payment of commissions to public officials directly or indirectly; reduction of high-cost loans, reduction in high-tech equipment purchase, reduction of the standing army, and gradual reduction in the national budgetary allocation for defense.

283. *Sustained Defensive Capability.* The party would advocate introduction of universal military training; maintenance of an overall balance of force with India; development of a close relationship with longstanding allies in the Muslim world and with China to connect roads, railways, and pipelines which can provide economic links and protection in times of embargo; and further development of trade, travel, and cultural links with friendly people.

Foreign Policy

284. *International affairs.* The party must strive *for protection of national interests,* and must stand for
- *peaceful coexistence* and friendly relations with the Western nations, giving priority to areas in which convergence of views exists;
- *resolution of the Kashmir issue* by means of an international conference organized by the world powers. A mandate should be obtained from the people as discussed above. Peaceful resolution of issues with India and all other nations of the world will result in reduced defense needs;
- *close working relations among Muslim states* in order to increase cooperation in the short run, and unite them in the long run. Develop capacity within the Muslim alliance to support each other against external threats. Attain equal partnership for Muslims under the new world order;
- *continued close relations with traditional allies* such as the United States and China, and improved relations with Russia;
- *close working relations with the United Nations* and its specialized agencies and maximum use of the facilities provided by them;
- *careful review of current and future international agreements* to ensure that the interests of Pakistan are not unjustly compromised;
- *development and maintenance of deterrent military power* in order to ensure peace; and
- *stop interference in affairs of Afghanistan,* encourage peace and prosperity, and maintain good relations with the government chosen by the Afghan people.

On the whole, these policies can make the citizens prosperous and proud and the country attractive to foreign investors. Investors seek political stability, law and order, trained manpower, adequate infrastructures, and good banking. Investors insist on health, education, and travel facilities for themselves and their families. They can come in large numbers and stay in Pakistan as they have done elsewhere when similar policies have been followed.

There are also many other goals to which the party can aspire. The community has many priorities in the linguistic, cultural, legal, and security fields. There is an economic agenda in agriculture, industry, education, science and technology, the environment, etc. Reduction of poverty and respect for human rights are fundamental for the welfare of Pakistanis, and the basic policies are clear. Nevertheless, specific targets have to be set by the people through the political process. Without clear vision, a set of priorities, and sincere dedication to those priorities, business will continue as usual. Pakistan will remain a relatively backward nation, and one of the low-income countries of the world.

All Pakistanis who share the above approach to running the society and government should join hearts and hands to make its implementation possible. The people who support the reform agenda should not wait until they have gained control of the government. They should start implementation to the extent they can within the areas of their own influence—in their household, in their neighborhood, in their community, town, district, etc.

There are plenty of examples of people and organizations, within and outside Pakistan, who have made a substantial contribution to the life of others from outside the government. The party (new or an existing reformed one) must not wait until it comes into power in order to start making its contribution. It must set up social welfare and community help projects from the start and must help implement them through its members at each level of society starting with villages in rural areas and neighborhoods (*mohallas*) in urban areas.

Unity Among Pakistanis

It appears that the disunity among people of Pakistan has permitted a few feudal families, many of whom were established by patronage from the British colonial government, to gain and retain control in alliance with leaders of the civil and military services. With the policy of divide-and-rule, they have appropriated the power of the state for themselves, and have rewarded or punished people at will. Without unity among the people, it will be impossible to wrest power from them and focus on the welfare of common citizens. Unity among Pakistanis is essential.

Unity Among Muslims

On the international front, with similar disunity among Muslim states, nothing short of surrender will be acceptable in respect of issues of importance to the West. Even with surrender, domination and harassment by the U.S.-led West may not stop. Given the current disunity among Muslims, those who do not obey, can expect personal and national threats, economic blackmail, attacks from third parties, sabotage, and eventually direct attack.

If Muslims, particularly the member governments of OIC, take a firm stand on a vital issue and convince the West that they are ready for any sacrifice, the West will take notice. The West is not ready to oppose fifty or more unified nations willing to sacrifice for a cause which is not vital to them. Al-Aqsa mosque in Jerusalem may be safe so far because Israel and the West sense that any damage to it will unite all Muslims. The moment Israel and the West sense a division of opinion about it, the mosque is sure to be attacked by some "fanatic" or "erased by an accident." The West has not observed similar unity in respect of Bosnia, Kashmir, Palestine, etc. The current efforts at peace in Bosnia and Palestine, among other things, recognized the growing Muslim frustration and movement toward unity.

Conquer Fear

Weapons of war can destroy years of economic development and kill and maim a very large number of individuals. Violence must, accordingly, be avoided. Pakistani citizens must regain power through political struggle. However, the people must demonstrate to the rulers that they are not afraid of sacrifice and are willing to fight for the cause, if needed.

On the international front, the change must be through peaceful means, too. However, violence for a just cause (and as the last resort) has been justifiably used by many nations. The United States, the United Kingdom, Germany, Israel, Vietnam, Iraq, Iran, Egypt, Syria, Pakistan, and Bangladesh have all lost large numbers of people in wars in order to continue to survive as nations. However, war should be avoided, if possible. Pakistanis should not provide any excuse to their opponents for initiating attack. The answer still lies in coexistence. If the enemy is presented with a united and determined combatant, damage, the futility of war, and the injustice of war, they will seek coexistence with honor, too.

Moral Government

What about the desire for having governments based on principles of Islam? For one thing, the ritualistic religion promoted by our typical *imams* at many mosques is not acceptable to most educated Pakistanis, particularly Pakistani women. Voters of Pakistan have repeatedly rejected the religious parties. People of Afghanistan continue to suffer due to the civil war among the religious groups.

Pakistanis are looking for establishment of a moral government and moral social structure. If possible, Pakistanis would wish to achieve this through implementation of the Islam brought through the Prophet Muhammad (PBUH). It would (a) emphasize duties to Allah as well as those to the mankind, (b) will make all Pakistanis better human beings, and (c) have no compulsion. This implies greater emphasis on implementation of responsibilities toward mankind.

The vested interests resist change. They include (a) narrow-minded religious leaders, (b) illiterate faithful who blindly follow them, (c) rulers who get and keep power through manipulating and controlling them, and (d) Western oil companies and governments who control most rulers of Muslim countries. They are more or less content with the status quo. Voters in Algeria, Iran, Sudan, Pakistan, and elsewhere in Muslim countries are looking for implementation of moral governments described above.

Accept Hardship

To achieve the desired objectives, Pakistanis have to work hard at reform. Many people and some countries are not going to be happy with Pakistani unity and progress for a variety of reasons, e.g., historic mistrust, fear, jealousy, and potential competition. Differences will be highlighted and divisions will be encouraged. Pressures are likely to be brought to discourage Pakistanis. The international boycotts, exclusion, and surveillance currently faced by Iran may be a preview of the future. Pakistanis can expect aid and assistance from the West to be critically reviewed and curtailed. However, pressure will hopefully be reduced when others are convinced of the reform's peaceful and constructive nature and see Pakistan as a force for good.

Work at the Personal Level

The Pakistanis who wish to strengthen the nation and the country, have to make their contribution in a number of ways according to their abilities. Some essential steps are:

- Be a part of the reform movement in your area by *becoming a better citizen*. Strengthen your day-to-day life in whatever way you can. Emphasize duties toward God and duties toward mankind.
- *Join a political party or reform movement* of your choice in your hometown and work with others in seeking reform.

- Through dedication and hard work, *rise to policy-making levels* of your group so that your own vision can receive a fair hearing in your own group.
- Work hard to bring your group and *like-minded groups to power* through the democratic process in your town, district, province, and the country.
- Once in power at the national level, *use power for the broader welfare of all Pakistanis.*
- Be prepared to delegate all national power or a part thereof in favor of the *ummah at the international level.*

In the long run, Pakistanis must be prepared to sacrifice for the development of Muslims and their effective participation in the new world order. The sacrifice can be in terms of time, money, relationships, or more. At all times, Pakistanis must work toward consolidating strengths; reducing weaknesses; and establishing solidarity.

Who Would Benefit by Reform?

285. Those who would benefit from the above agenda include:
- the poor everywhere—who would benefit from poverty reduction efforts;
- peasants would benefit from land reform, reduction in power of the landed aristocracy and therefore of tyranny, better rural development programs;
- women everywhere would benefit from the pro-women agenda;
- the unemployed would benefit from increased stress on employment;
- supporters of decentralization—people who work locally and would like to see more physical development in local areas;
- nationalist parties;
- all educated people, who can expect more direct input in government;
- military personnel, who can expect relatively more peace at home and on the national borders;
- businessmen, who can expect more emphasis on the private sector and peace and stability at home;
- religious leaders, who would like more emphasis on duties toward mankind and cordial relations among all Muslims;
- honest and dedicated bureaucrats, who have become "out of fashion" and are being ridiculed for being "old fashioned";
- minorities, who can expect greater harmony with the rest of the society and freedom to act according to their own beliefs;

- Pakistan as a whole, from progressing in all fields of endeavor and becoming a respected nation around the world; and
- the Muslim *ummah* for having a country dedicated to the welfare of its own people and willing and able to support the genuine causes of all Muslims.

Who Would Lose by Reform?

There would be some who would lose from the proposed agenda. The possible losers would include:
- landed aristocrats, who hold property beyond the limits set by law, would lose their excessive holdings and power;
- bureaucratic rulers, who would lose their discretionary powers and their bribes and would be forced to become civil servants;
- all who have made money illegally, bureaucrats, politicians, business-men, military officers, who can expect accountability; and
- divisive religious leaders, who will see a reduction in their power.

Minimizing the Opposition

Opposition by sincere individuals sharing the vision of a prosperous Pakistan but who do not agree with the means should be welcomed. They should be convinced by results. It is necessary to show that the general welfare of the society will eventually help even those who may lose in the short run. It is important to sharpen and test ideas to ensure their practicality and their contribution to the general welfare. Debate is healthy to promote positive ideas.

From a moral perspective, it is essential to affirm fear of Allah and to be reminded of the temporary nature of this life. The party should always remain aware of the religious nature of Pakistanis and encourage and support the faithful.

Gaining Acceptance of the Ideas

Gaining acceptance of all like-minded individuals under the same platform is the key. They must be encouraged to work together to achieve the common goals. In order to inform the people, discuss ideas with them, and eventually convince them, the proponents and *supporters would need* to
- visit and communicate with the poor (in slums and villages), the unemployed (at unemployment offices, vocational schools, universities),

women (at women's NGOs and other organizations), supporters of decentralization, active groups in small provinces and district towns, intellectuals, families of military personnel, religious reformers, etc.;

- relate to the people, dress in popular local clothes for the occasion, speak their language if possible, let the local people speak up for the party;
- take positions to support the causes which appear to be right;
- cultivate the press and the opinion-makers;
- seek opportunities to establish contact with people, and demonstrate what can be achieved;
- establish a core of promoters consisting of a paid staff and volunteers; and
- demonstrate the qualities that the people like: honesty, physical stamina, risk taking for the general welfare.

The difficulties of uniting Pakistanis, the power of the national leadership, and the influence of international interests should not be underestimated. There are good and valid reasons why they all behave as they do. Those who desire change have to understand the motivations of all the key players and offer incentives for support of the reforms.

CHAPTER 20

CONCLUSIONS AND RECOMMENDATIONS

Leadership

286. *Public Opinion.* Governing Pakistan is a very complex task. That is partly why, with the exception of the founder of the nation, none of the leaders is widely remembered with affection and kindness. None of them is credited with meeting the true aspirations of the people.

Some of the leaders including General Ayub Khan and Zulfiqar Ali Bhutto were initially committed to the general welfare of Pakistanis. They listened and implemented the right advice. However, something changed them after their initial period in office. Some have argued that the desire to show their personal greatness or eagerness to perpetuate their own rule led them astray. Others have argued that pressures relating to Kashmir or internal security considerations led them away from the right track.

Governing is a function of at least two basic criteria—right policies and sincere implementation. People believe that right policies have always been recognized by the rulers. Pakistan has never had a shortage of brilliant adminintrators, economists, entrepreneurs, or political analysts. It has been really up to the leaders themselves to pick the right experts and to listen or discard their advice. However, they have generally picked experts on the basis of personal loyalty rather than expertise.

Many Pakistanis view their leaders as selfish, corrupt, unaccountable, cruel, and isolated from common citizens. The government must be made transparent and the people must be consulted regarding key decisions. The leaders must be prepared to make policy changes over a period of time on the basis of available information. The interest of the people rather than the ego of the leaders must be paramount.

It is difficult to stop those who are ready to sacrifice everything that they have, including their lives. The job of stopping them becomes doubly difficult if they happen to be competent and know what they want. Whether one agrees with them or not, the determination of Jinnah, Zulfiqar and Benazir Bhutto, and General Zia are examples.

The government should take citizens into its confidence, telling them the facts and why the government is taking certain decisions, e.g., those managing the public utilities should explain why the price of rail or airline tickets, electricity, telephones, water supply, etc., needs to be increased at a given time.

287. *Power Politics*. Political parties have often been formed to advance causes of a particular individual or a few individuals. Such parties have died with the achievement of the objectives, abandonment of the objectives or simply death of the individual. Most parties have been handicapped by limited appeal due to regional, ethnic or sectarian foundations. PPP and PML are the only two significant national political parties.

The power structure can be changed with: (a) the ability of the majority of the population to stand up for their rights; (b) a reduction of excessive power held by feudal lords and bureaucrats; (c) the reduced cost and/or public financing of elections enabling qualified candidates to contest; (d) elections on the basis of program and total party vote rather than individual constituencies; (e) greater education and tolerance on the part of religious leaders; (f) positive direction from outside forces, e.g., the West or the Islamic block.

As the declassified documents and memoirs of those previously in power confirm, successive governments in Pakistan have followed the policies of dividing the people, politicians in particular, in order to gain and maintain power. The policy has facilitated rule in the initial phases; however, it has brought instability to the country and caused long-term damage. Often the divisions so created become permanent and lead to much bigger problems.

Pakistani rulers have often misjudged their friends and foes in the domestic field. Overwhelming reliance has been placed on "unquestioned loyalty." In a representative form of government, removing the causes of discontent among people rather than continuing one's own power must be the number one priority.

Political change must take place in conjunction with social change. Leaders must have an understanding of economic issues in order to cope with the current needs and expectations. Leadership must be encouraged from the top down as well as from the bottom up. Steps must be taken to ensure that the leaders feel obligated to the populace. The votes must be given and received voluntarily. Leadership positions must be filled on the basis of a transparent process with full accountability for leaders at all levels.

Leadership must be decentralized to provincial and local government. Leaders most knowledgeable about the concerned issues should be given the authority to resolve them. The civil bureaucracy must be reviewed with the objective of minimizing its size. Its quality must be improved by the introduction of full accountability, by giving greater power to locally elected representatives, and by increased decentralization.

Can Pakistan ever find a perfect ruler who is immune to personal, domestic or external constraints? Probably not! The best hope is to find a way to strengthen the hands of the citizens and the democratic process with built-in checks and balances which will keep the leaders on track. Only consistent, effective and timely pressure by people can ensure implementation of the right policies.

Senior appointments, including those of cabinet members, secretary-level officials and senior judges should be made following their confirmation by the National Assembly. Their past experience and performance should be the basis for their confirmation and appointment.

The middle class, educated citizens have largely stayed out of politics in view of heavy expense and risky carrer opportunities. Politics has been primarily left to very wealthy agriculturists and industrial families. The middle class can contribute to the policy making process through their positions in the civil service, outspokenness in the media, and public addresses and seminars. However, in order to have the needed role in policy making, they must find ways to become part of the direct electoral process.

288. *Full time National Assembly.* There are existing detailed studies prepared by local and international experts on most of the problems and issues facing Pakistan. The majority of the studies are gathering dust because of inadequate arrangements for (a) review of the studies by concerned public officials and private citizens and (b) implementing the results after the review. A full time national assembly (along the lines of the American Congress) is needed to digest the available recommendations and to enact necessary legislation.

Poverty and Unemployment

289. *Education.* The latest available data show that more than 70% of Pakistan's people are illiterate, i.e., unable to read, write or count. The launching of a sustained massive literacy program is a must. An educated populace leads to political accountability and stability, economic progress, use of technology, improved household management, and sensible population planninig.

Educational standards must be raised. Graduates of a few good private high schools are able to compete successfully at home and obtain admission and scholarships to prestigious universities abroad. However, the majority of students cannot. The success stories must be replicated in every school in Pakistan.

290. *Poverty*. Pakistan must devote its resources to finding better and faster ways to decrease hunger, reduce poverty, develop human resources, improve the standard of living, and reduce underemployment and unemployment. Without success in these areas, Pakistan is doomed to remain an unhappy place for its citizens.

291. *Policy Recommendations*. There is an urgent need for a greater and more dedicated effort for: (a) high economic growth policies; (b) low population growth; (c) accelerating rural development in order to bring development to the majority of citizens and to discourage large-scale movement of labor to already congested urban areas; (d) well-designed and directed public works projects; (e) support for schemes which maximize labor utilization; (f) reasonable minimum wages; (g) incentives for self-employment; (h) incentives for large-scale employment generation in the private sector through reforms in trade policies, the financial sector, investment regulations, taxation and public enterprises; (i) well-directed educational policies matching skills with job opportunities; and (j) removal of discrimination against ethnic, racial, tribal, and gender groups.

Medical facilities in the public sector have become a joke in terms of quality and timely availability. The facilities must be made functional on the basis of increased accountability.

Creation of Higher Living Standards

292. *Economic Overview*. Pakistan's fiscal deficit as well as the external gap are too large. The nation is living off old investments; new investments in the infrastructure are relatively few. Population growth is high. The benefits of the country's limited economic growth are going to the upper and middle classes alone. The incomes of the poorest lower and middle income groups are further declining.

293. *Economic Reforms*. There is an urgent need for fiscal, monetary, and banking reforms. The financial regulatory system needs critical review and upgrading. The municipal governments are unable to provide services from their limited resources and federal allocations. There is an urgent need for establishment of a viable municipal system throughout the country.

There is a need for an effective educational system; female education as well as the quality of education need special attention. The rich and middle classes are able to pay for quality education in private or a few prestigious public schools. The poor who are totally reliant on the local public facilities are being left further behind.

Pakistan must learn from successful development efforts in other countries. Continued control of national resources by a few, based on services rendered to past rulers and on corruption, should not be allowed to decide Pakistan's future. By contrast, the fruits of honest entrepreneurship should not be denied. Serious thought must be given to fairer distribution of economic benefits. There must be honest land reform. Past failures in reform should not be obstacles to revitalize efforts.

294. *Agriculture.* The agricultural land-holding system should be reviewed and modified with the objectives of increasing agricultural productivity (e.g., through full use of the unutilized land owned by large landholders) and providing an honorable way of making a living for the rural population. Suitable ways must be found to continue increasing agricultural incomes and collecting an equitable share in income taxes.

295. *Population.* There is an urgent need to reconcile social, economic, and spiritual aspects of population planning to achieve a growth rate that is consistent with the best interest of the nation. There is an urgent need for people to learn to live within their resources and practice the Islamic principle of *Qinaat.*

296. *Taxes.* The existing tax laws must be enforced and established taxes must be collected. Powerful individuals and interest groups should not be allowed to escape paying their taxes as specified by law. An honest, independent, efficient, and impartial taxation department is needed. The tax administration must be made more efficient and corrupt tax officials must be punished.

The reform of the income tax to make it more equitable should be a high priority. Specific steps should be taken for expanding the tax base; treating income from agriculture on a par with that from other sectors; eliminating loopholes which permit industrialists to escape income tax; introducing a capital gains tax; introducing severe penalties for tax dodgers and thieves; and introducing measures to ensure adequate reporting of financial transactions to tax authorities.

297. *Deficit Reduction.* The national deficit must be reduced through increasing national revenue and controlling costs.

298. *Debt.* In terms of *borrowing*, the average cost of foreign loans is about 3% per year. However, domestic borrowing is being done at about 17% per year. While efforts must be made to reduce all debt, it is more important to reduce the domestic debt. Proceeds from the privatization process must be used to pay off the domestic debt.

299. *Financial Institutions.* While the government pays its debts, it is neglecting to *collect debts* from its favorite citizens. The banking system has a huge bad debt portfolio. Banks are often unable to recover loans, resulting in their financial ruin. Outstanding loans must be collected. Reform of financial institutions is urgently needed.

300. *Public Service.* How to motivate Pakistanis to become active in public service is a great challenge. Many highly educated young people are desperate because they are unable to find productive employment. They must be encouraged to take appropriate examinations, find scholarships or jobs abroad, or start a small business at home. These people have the core skills and can become net contributors to the society with just a push. They must be helped. Motivating people to return to public service is a challenge. Good examples will obviously help. Punishment for those who cheat the public in the name of charitable organizations will help restore confidence, too.

Simplifying bureaucratic rules is a critical factor in removing the obstacles to Pakistanis' becoming prosperous. Issuing required permits for starting and running local businesses, and issuing visas for foreign workers in a timely manner by simplified procedures can go a long way.

301. *Foreign Aid.* Foreign assistance deemed to be in Pakistan's interest must be continued. Nevertheless, self-reliance must be increased. Lessons in self-reliance may be learned from the experiences of (a) China from the 1940s through the 1970s; (b) Iraq since the end of the Gulf War; and (c) Iran since the Revolution. It may mean hardship and lowering an already low living standard. However, eventually, Pakistan will emerge stronger, and will be able to deal with the rest of the world on equal terms.

302. *Private Investment.* Domestic private investment funds seem to be again moving into real estate or abroad. The government needs to provide a new push to accelerate investment from both domestic and foreign sources in the

country. Without substantial new private investment, the country will not be able to grow and meet many of its needs.

Some Pakistanis see privatization as the handing over of large chunks of publicly-owned assets to the favorites of the ruling government. The favorites may be local political allies who are branching out into business, or they may be businesses from Western countries which the local government is eager to attract. Pakistanis need to be assured by their government that privatization is a worthwhile exercise in the national interest.

Proceeds from sales of public assets must be used to achieve agreed upon and visible objectives, e.g., repayment of loans relating to the particular asset and reduction of other loans. A long-term action program is needed to eliminate undue benefits to feudal lords and other advantaged groups.

Religious Tolerance

303. *Islamic Principles.* The solutions to Pakistan's problems as discussed in this book cannot ignore Islam. While the solutions must work in a modern context, they must not be "repugnant" to Islam, otherwise, the people will just not accept them. On the other hand, solutions which are consistent with the needs of current times and which have full support in Islamic principles have a much greater chance for success.

304. *Solution.* The solution to religious intolerance lies in education and understanding. There is a need to (a) return to the basic tenets of Islam, namely, unity of Allah, the prophethood of Muhammad (PBUH), prayer, Haj, Zakat, belief in the day of judgement, and moral and just living; (b) withdraw official patronage to all sectarian organizations; (c) state clearly to Iran and Saudi Arabia that their patronage of different sects is not welcome and will not be tolerated; (d) strictly punish those convicted of crimes regardless of the sect involved; (e) ensure that sensitive religious beliefs are protected.

The staff, budget, powers, and influence of the Ministry of Religious Affairs must be used to ensure that:

- there is no compulsion in religion and that citizens are free to choose the religion or sect of their choice;
- current religious controversies are resolved in an orderly manner;
- facilities are provided for the sound education and training of *imams* and religious scholars; facilities must also be provided for conflict resolution;
- Arabic instruction must be incorporated in the educational curriculum in order to facilitate a better understanding of Qur'an and Sunnah among the masses; and

- adequate protection and necessary facilities are provided for religious minorities.

305. *Religious Leaders.* Leaders of the religious parties must increase cooperation in the context of the Milli Yakjehti Council or other comparable frameworks. If the spirit of cooperation is maintained and leaders of the various religious sects agree on fundamental points of day-to-day concerns to all Muslims, the Pakistani population will be faced with less intolerance and will probably reward the religious parties with more electoral success.

306. *Religious Parties.* People of Pakistan wish to have an "Islamic" form of government, but they have repeatedly rejected the existing religious parties in elections. They have voted primarily against those who propose to follow Islam in letter but not in spirit. With the recognition and practice of *Ijma* (collective thinking and consensus) and *Ijtihad* (individual effort), the teachings of Islam and the demands of modern times can be reconciled. The 1973 Constitution has already made a promising statement. Sincere implementation coupled with some refinements can meet our goals. The result can be achievement of an ideal government for Pakistan and renaissance for Muslims everywhere.

Empowering the People

307. *Basic Needs.* In order to restore power to citizens, there is a need to
- allow democracy to take root,
- minimize concentration of power and maximize decentralization,
- amend the constitution and relevant laws to give meaningful options to the people during elections and to make it possible to elect people responsive to needs of the citizens (e.g., introducing public financing of elections and proportional representation),
- reduce excessive immunity for public officials,
- make it difficult to reelect representatives who fail to keep their promises to the electorate, and
- make it rewarding for opposition to play their lawful role.

308. *Question of Democracy.* Many Pakistanis feel that if democracy is given a chance to take root through several elections, people will learn how to make a distinction between good leaders and bad, and the current "democratic" system will improve. Others argue that the democratic process has been hijacked by the privileged class for their own benefit and democracy

will not provide progressive leaders. They argue that the violence and loss of property which has continued for years will only increase and be more expensive than a one-time loss caused by a revolution. They wish to cut losses and make the change now.

If people hear a party making genuine promises on critical issues, they will support that party. Zulfiqar Bhutto's electoral victory in 1970, and MQM's victories in Karachi are testimony to that fact. People will be happy with even limited progress as long as there is movement in the right direction. Anyone who can deal with and solve even some of the key problems facing Pakistan as outlined in this book can have a great success in politics in Pakistan. Above all, people value implementation of promised action.

Democracy and free market policies must work hand in hand—the free market provides incentives and creative energy while sustained democracy provides periodic approval by the general population and limits power.

309. *Opposition Parties*. Opposition parties have failed to play a constructive role. Following an electoral defeat, they should provide constructive challenges to keep the government on the right path, revitalize their party, and offer options to the people for the next round of elections.

310. *The Press*. Based on their past performance, with the exception of a few shining stars, the bulk of the local press cannot be considered as responsible voices for the people. They are largely owned by greedy vested interests. They survive by supporting the powerful. They have failed to speak for the people during times of excesses by the army against citizens in East and West Pakistan and the abrogation of the 1956 Constitution. Efforts must be continued to develop a free but constructive press.

311. *Islamic Government*. The feasibility of an Islamic government in Pakistan is questioned by many because of the failure of its proponents to satisfy others on several issues, including dealings with other sects of Islam and minorities, adequate resource mobilization in the absence of interest (*riba'*), social justice, and the role of women. The Constitution already requires that laws repugnant to the basic principles of Islam not be enforced. Citizens must choose their leaders on the basis of democracy which is mandated by Islam (as discussed above).

312. *Sacrifice*. A few dedicated and selfless people can start change in Pakistan, provided they are willing to sacrifice themselves for the cause. If they touch the hearts of the people, they will receive all the support that is needed.

The democratic process should not be stopped by armed forces or powerful minorities for any excuse; systematic and periodic elections will give confidence and experience to the people who will eventually learn to choose the right leaders.

313. *Electoral Reform.* On the whole, as discussed in different parts of this book, the country can be improved and made to work by sincere people. In order for it to be a viable option, at least the following changes need to be made in the current system:

- Public financing of elections must be introduced and private financing must be banned in order to provide opportunities to otherwise qualified candidates.
- At least 50 percent of the seats must be allocated on the basis of party program and votes rather than on individual constituencies controlled by feudal lords.
- Elections must be held on fixed schedules, regularly and freely under international supervision.
- Equal media access must be provided to all candidates and parties.

Law and Order

Robberies, kidnapping, extortions, destruction of public property, and killings have become common in many parts of Pakistan, particularly in Karachi and other parts of Sindh. It has started spreading North into Punjab and the NWFP. Peace must be restored and maintained in Karachi and throughout the country by sincere dialogue and open channels of communications. Deliberate violation of the law of the land must be stopped at all costs. There are many reasons for the breakdown of order. The nation must address all of them and work on several fronts simultaneously, including:

- reform of the police and judiciary;
- finding political solutions for political conflicts;
- control over terrorist organizations, including involved and identified feudal lords;
- control over weapons;
- reduction of greed and corruption; and
- empowerment of common citizens through basic military training.

Many speculate that India is encouraging the breakdown of law and order in Pakistan. Peace with India is essential to stopping sabotage activities within Pakistan.

The police should be so structured that avenues for corruption and political interference will be closed. It will be fully accountable to the interior and the home ministers for administrative purposes and to the judiciary for legal purposes.

Peace within Afghanistan is essential for stopping the flow of arms and immigration into Pakistan. This poorly regulated immigration is one of the causes of the law-and-order problem.

There must be increased understanding and cooperation between the people and the government of Pakistan. Arbitrary arrest and torture in jail must be stopped. Human rights, as guaranteed by the constitution, must be respected.

Sectarian and ethnic issues which provide excuses for some of the law-and-order controversies must be addressed.

Small Provinces/Backward Areas

314. *Secessionists.* Through their votes in numerous elections, Sindhis have already rejected secessionist groups, repeatedly handing them defeat in elections. It is time to close that part of the debate. Like most of their Sindhi brethren, the remaining few secessionists should work within the framework of Pakistan to achieve their genuine goals for economic development of their people.

The central government and Pakistanis from all provinces must realize that an overwhelming portion of the population wishes to remain a part of Pakistan. The decisionmakers must therefore remove the cloud of suspicion about national loyalty floating over almost every Sindhi and Baloachi.

315. *Legitimate Grievances.* The various governments have in the past underestimated and downplayed the legitimate grievances of the people. The concerns and justified demands of the people of Sindh (urban and poor) and Baloachistan need to be fully understood and acted upon.

The small provinces suffer from all of the problems that the country as a whole suffers. In addition, they suffer from issues peculiar to them. The government must pay special attention to development of the less-developed and backward areas. Special incentives must be provided to invite new industries, particularly those providing employment and future growth, e.g., electronics. Interprovincial projects, e.g., allocation of water and financial resources, must consider special developmental needs of backward areas.

Sindh as a whole is experiencing a very high growth of population. In rural areas this is due to natural fertility; in urban areas it is due to immigration from within Pakistan and overseas, particularly India, Bangladesh, Iran, Afghanistan, Burma etc. Effective measures must be taken to reduce immigration into Sindh.

Education and hygiene for women which tend to slow natural fertility must be promoted. Integration of the existing population must also be promoted. The richer parts of Sindh (e.g., some people of Karachi) wish to separate from the rest of Sindh and take most of the resources with them. The separation movement must be resisted and resources must be spent equitably.

Sindh and Baloachistan suffer from feudal practices. Feudalism must be eradicated and a middle class must be developed. Alternative organizations which can assume the benefactor roles of the feudal lords must be developed.

Sindhi and Baloachi people are particularly concerned about the lack of government efforts to preserve their languages and cultural heritages. Special encouragement and resources must be provided. Sindhi and Baloachi intellectuals must reassess their own culture. They must discard the ideas of decay. The issues of refusing to leave the villages for education and a better life, dowries at the time of marriages, "marriage to the Qur'an" in case of the non-availability of suitable matches, killings at the slightest suspicion of sexual misconduct, etc., must be constructively addressed.

Sindhi journalists have articulated the cause of their language, culture, people, and the province. They have already played a significant role in providing political education to the masses. They can be a great source of motivation for further awakening the masses and a vehicle for bringing about much needed reform in the political, economic, and cultural arenas.

316. *Constitutional Changes.* A constitutional provision is needed to protect the rights of all ethnic minorities. It should, *inter alia,* include provisions for protection and enhancement of their language, culture, economic development, and human rights. The need for provincial and local government autonomy is particularly strong in Sindh and Baloachistan where a large number of civil servants are not willing to transfer and work in the backward areas.

317. *Compromise.* Mohajirs and Sindhis are all citizens of Pakistan. Their genuine demands have to be met. However, it must not be at the expense of anyone else. Genuine compromise must be fair to all and must include:

- greater effort by public and private means to integrate the native and new Sindhis in the province;
- holding local government elections throughout the country, including Karachi and Hyderabad, as demanded by Mohajirs and other communities;

- decentralization of the government and giving as many powers to the local governments as possible—local governments of Karachi and Hyderabad should receive the same powers and responsibilities as others on the basis of their population size and other relevant criteria;
- focused and phased quotas for the really deserving, limited to residents of areas lacking adequate college and higher learning facilities. Within a short period, say five years after the requisite facilities are producing graduates, the quotas should be phased out;
- joint efforts by Mohajirs and natives for full rights; an increased share for Sindh of the overall allocations of national, educational, employment, investment and other resources provided by the government; and
- mutual recognition of Urdu and Sindhi languages and culture and their protection through educational institutions, public administration, and official media, as done for others in the countries. The mutual learning and speaking of both languages in high school should be encouraged.

318. *Social Contract.* There is a need for a social contract among all citizens of smaller provinces such as Sindh; they must stop hurting each other and begin providing mutual assistance that will enable them to make progress.

Quotas for educational facilities and jobs which are meant to develop the backward people are used by the feudal lords and sardars to advance their own families and a few loyal associates. The quotas are needed by backward com-munities but measures must be established to ensure that the facilities are well-targeted and used by the most deserving within each community. The quotas for people of Baloachistan and rural Sindhis must be used by the most deserving among them rather than by nominees of the powerful.

319. *Political Merger.* An effective merger of MQM and the Jiai Sindh parties could work well for the interests of Sindh as a whole. However, the ideal combination would be that of a reformed PPP and a reformed MQM which could work for welfare and development of all Sindhis, with particular attention to: maximizing resources for development of Sindh; meeting the economic needs of all "have nots"; political representation on the basis of merit and competence rather than feudal power and loyalty to party leader.

This type of merger will be opposed by the people who have benefitted from the current strife. However, it will be supported by the middle and poor classes among both Sindhis and Mohajirs. It appears idealistic at the moment. The realities of the problem may eventually convince both sides.

Corruption

There are many aspects of bribery, such as payment to police, which are impossible to quantify. Nevertheless, the total estimated loss to the economy from leakage of federal government spending alone is much higher than the foreign assistance received each year from all sources. If the economy could conserve the leakage of money through bribery, there would be no need for foreign assistance at the current level of investments.

The solutions include:

- establishing an *ethical environment*;
- setting *good examples at the top*; high officials in government must set a proper example, must be held to a higher standard, and should be subject to higher punishments for corruption;
- in the context of procurement of goods and services, review the government's cost structure to determine what the cost of different items ought to be; establish *disincentives for padding costs*;
- set and enforce *exemplary punishment* on a systematic and consistent basis. Civil servants are ready, willing, and able to do everything to protect their jobs. If they get a firm signal that bribery will lead to termination of employment or confiscation of property or jail, they will stop doing it;
- *adjust salary levels* of public officials to assure them that they can live comfortably without being corrupt. Accordingly, salaries of all public officials must be reviewed and suitably revised;
- permit lower level civil servants *to accept second jobs* in their spare time to help meet needs. However, all must be expected to work diligently during office hours;
- more *education* of citizens, *transparency* of government, and *accountability* on an individual basis to reduce corruption;
- *reform of police, judiciary and anti-corruption apparatus* is urgently needed;
- *fear of Allah* and *punishment* right here in this world is essential;
- *less emphasis on consumerism* by the society; and
- financial insecurity is one of the main causes of corruption. Introduce an economic *safety net* for the "have nots" to discourage corruption.

Human Rights Violations

Essential human rights are already guaranteed under the constitution and the laws of Pakistan. Implementation is, however, lacking. Every strong person who decides to violate these existing laws, whether a feudal lord, a terrorist organization, a local police inspector, a chief minister, or a general, claims to have a "higher purpose" in mind. If Pakistan citizens decide to accord high priority to human rights for all, then such rights will be implemented.

320. *Action.* Additional action must focus on:
- legislation covering areas not addressed by the constitution or existing laws, and closing loopholes for more effective implementation;
- accelerating process for dispensation of justice;
- repealing laws or parts thereof which offend fundamental human rights (e.g., Maintenance of Public Order (MPO); Frontier Crime Regulations); Stopping use of state machinery to suppress political dissent;
- vigilant action by citizen groups;
- creation/strengthening of human rights monitoring agencies at the local, provincial, and national level; and
- coordination with and support of human rights organizations at the international level.

The new ministry in charge of protection of human rights must be strengthened.

Settlement of the Kashmir Issue

The government should continue to make an effort for the right of self-determination for Kashmiris through an international conference on Kashmir. Life will be easier for all if such a conference takes place soon and the issue is resolved satisfactorily. In any event, the government eventually will have to initiate an open debate of all aspects of its Kashmir policy.

Following two to three months of free debate, there should be a well-supervised secret referendum to decide Pakistan's future actions in this regard. All realistic options including going to another war, continuation of the current bleeding, acceptance of the results of the international conference, if any, and formal acceptance of the status quo should be presented. All politicians should agree to accept and abide by the verdict of the people. If the military, politicians in power, and the politicians in opposition (who have been in power earlier) are courageous enough to tell people what they know, the people will probably accept the "less than desired results." The population must recognize that Pakistan may be forced to accept the unacceptable. In any case, the minimum package must include:

- maximum autonomy for occupied Kashmir;
- protection for all Muslims in India; and
- renunciation of disruptive activities in each other's territories by India and Pakistan.

321. *Treaty with the United States.* The United States should be fully involved in the final negotiations concerning Kashmir in order to ensure that other issues will not reignite threats of war. In exchange, Pakistan can offer to pursue policies which converge with the West, including assurances that the nuclear technology will not be shared with others, and religious tolerance will be officially endorsed and implemented.

322. *Support from Muslim countries.* The endorsement of the defense strategy should be solicited from the Organization of Islamic Conference (OIC). In addition, the military should develop strategies to strengthen their solidarity with other Muslim countries in case of future threats.

323. *The West.* The strength and influence of the United States cannot be denied. The historical relationships with Pakistan and the services it provides must however be respected. The strategy of dealing with the West must include the following elements:
- learning to coexist with the West, particularly the United States;
- avoiding undue expectations, emotionalism, and confrontation;
- working within areas on which views converge—these happen to be of particular importance to Pakistanis in any case; and
- promote sympathetic understanding of issues critical to Pakistan and Muslims through representations by the national leaders and by Pakistanis and Muslims living in the West.

324. *Foreign Involvement.* Foreign countries will continue to absorb labor from Pakistan and continue to play prominent roles in policy formulation, providing moral, financial, and other types of assistance to their favorite groups. They are eager to expand their influence. Some wish to have bases. Other seek to spread their religious views. However, they do not appear interested in taking over the country to assume responsibility for its affairs.

National Defense

The government has repeatedly failed to recognize the limitations of relying on military power to conduct domestic affairs. The military may have the destructive power to enforce order, but it cannot stop motivated public sentiments on a long-term basis. The government must minimize use of the army to control domestic political disputes and must find suitable political solutions.

There is some evidence suggesting that parts of the government, including military officers, planted personnel in Kashmir which led to the 1965 war.[237] The military establishment has in the past concocted terrifying scenarios of a nation at risk in order to keep justifying additional resources for defense. Thank God, most of these scenarios never materialize. This happens in practically all countries. Nevertheless, there should be some realistic limits to allocation of resources for non-productive purposes.

325. *Past Errors.* In defense-related matters, the government of Pakistan has misjudged many situations, including:

- India's military capacity, its willingness to fight for Kashmir, and its sabotaging East Pakistan;
- Kashmiri willingness to sacrifice freedom from India in recent years but failure to do so at the time of the Indo–Pakistan wars in 1948, 1965, and 1970;
- East Pakistani alienation due to linguistic, economic, and political reasons and ultimately due to oppression by the military; and
- continual warfare in Afghanistan after the fall of communism.

These and other miscalculations have resulted in unpleasant surprises. The government needs to be more discriminating.

Defense Strategy

The government should introduce universal military training. Other elements of the national defense strategy should, among other things,

- minimize provocation of India and other countries which may encourage them to retaliate against Pakistan. Pakistani citizens must press the government to resolve outstanding issues with India and other adversaries;
- review the internal administration of armed forces. Take corrective actions to reduce internal corruption and make it more efficient;
- use the technical capabilities and disciplined manpower of the armed forces for implementation of economic development schemes for the nation;

---

[237] Gauhar, "Pakistan's Adventure in Kashmir," Chapter 8.

- stop official bribery of the armed forces through lavish housing schemes, allocation of urban and rural land for personal use of military personnel, and special gifts to the higher echelons (e.g., BMW cars to generals during the Nawaz Sharif regime); and
- Pakistanis living abroad must stop pampering military officials, and treating them as conquering heros. They must encourage adoption of a suitable defense package through personal influence on their adopted homelands.

326. *Weapons.* The military should detonate a nuclear device, if India chooses to carry out additional tests. There should be tactical confirmation that Pakistan possesses a nuclear arsenal, including equipment for delivery of nuclear devices. There should be further development of the defense industry.

327. *Cost savings.* There should be a reduction in the purchase of high technology equipment. The standing army should be reduced. A start can be made by scrutinizing the practice of providing "soldier servants or batmen" to commissioned and noncommissioned officers. There should be a gradual reduction of the national budget's allocation for defense.

328. *Intelligence Agencies.* If democracy is to have meaning, the unregulated power of the intelligence agencies has to be limited to its national security functions. Their role has to be governed by legislation or statutory authority, as is the practice in much of the world. Only then will they be able adequately to perform their vital national security task.

Overall

The people of Pakistan appear to want a major change in society, particularly in government. Without realizing their common purpose, practically everyone would like to achieve the demands outlined in this book. However, most of them have found a way to operate within the existing system. At the time of this writing in 1996, they do not appear to be ready to make major sacrifices for the change. They are hopelessly divided on ethnic, linguistic, and religious grounds.

There is no leader in sight who is knowledgeable enough to spot and correct the flaws in the existing system. Pakistan needs a leader bold enough to confront the defenders of the status quo, regardless of the cost to his or her person and family, charismatic enough to motivate the people to unite for the major changes that they all desire, and respected enough to prevent foreign sabotage and gain the essential support of foreign powers.

The key centers of power—the military, politicians, religious leaders, bureaucrats, and the business community—are comfortable within the system. They feel that they can survive and prosper under the status quo. All they want is more power in their hands. A major shock of some kind, at home or abroad (e.g., God forbid, a military defeat, national catastrophe, economic collapse) can change the behavior of the people and the powerful interest groups. The scene can change quite suddenly.

Pakistanis must learn from good examples abroad and incorporate them into day-to-day life. However, a bloody revolution is not likely to solve all the problems. The long-term objective of the government and the people must be to strengthen the democratic form of government in Pakistan. While there are compelling reasons to change the current controlled and manipulated form of democracy, the best option appears to be to nourish the current democratic process through patient and gradual development rather than through another authoritarian experiment.

At first glance, the Pakistani constitution includes most of the required provisions for establishing and maintaining a good government of the people, by the people, and for the people. It guarantees essential rights and protections for the people. Yet it is amazingly impotent in meeting the essential demands of the people, as outlined in this book. It must be carefully reviewed by representatives of the people, and suitably amended to ensure that the loopholes are closed and that citizens are able to achieve their reasonable demands within the constitutional framework. Special attention must be paid to meeting the demands of the people, particularly:
- reducing poverty and unemployment,
- providing basic infrastructure and services,
- making Pakistan richer,
- bringing back religious tolerance,
- restoring power to people ,
- restoring law and order,
- stopping human rights violations,
- meeting basic concerns of the people in the smaller provinces and relatively backward areas,
- stopping corruption,
- ensuring peace at the borders at an affordable price, and
- coexisting with the West.

Prayer

I pray for Pakistan to be a country of prosperous and content citizens, at peace and secure with themselves; a country where citizens acknowledge, glorify, and benefit from their diversity in terms of ethnicity, culture or belief, and yet unite on broader interests of the nation. I pray for it to be a part of the Islamic Nation and at peace with its neighbors, with each Muslim government, and with the West, particularly the United States. I pray for Pakistan to continually develop, grow, and blossom, participating as an equal under the new world order.

PERSONAL NOTE

I believe in universal brotherhood. I believe that we all are children of Adam and Eve (Hawwa') and are related to each other as members of the same family. We ought jointly to manage the affairs of this planet for the welfare of all of us. My fascination with international affairs started from early childhood. Almost thirty years of service with the World Bank (which is a specialized agency of the United Nations) provide testimony to that fact.

While I have been fortunate enough to work in about thirty countries, I have felt that I have not done enough for my "own branch of the family." I feel that within the universal brotherhood, I happen to be a part of Muslims, Pakistanis, Sindhis, as well as my own immediate Memon families. I feel that for the universal family to be strong, all branches of the family have to be strong. If Muslims, Pakistanis, Sindhis, or Memons are weak, they will not be able to play their role in advancing the universal brotherhood and strengthening it. Accordingly, while continuing to work for the universal brotherhood, I wish to attach special priority in my remaining life to family, Sindh, Pakistan, and the Islamic Nation around the world. I have worried about all four since my childhood. I want to make life better for all four.

It must be understood that I cannot advance my branch of the universal human family tree by cutting other branches of the same tree. I shall never advocate harming any other part of my universal family in order to advance mine. My work will focus on strengthening my branch so that it can be a live branch of the universal tree and coexist and grow as an equal member of the family.

Whenever I am with members of my extended family (father, uncle, cousin, or own child), I am thinking and often talking about how to improve the family's lot. When I am with Sindhis or even other Pakistani friends, I am discussing the hardships faced by ordinary Sindhis. Among Pakistanis and other friends of different nationalities, I keep focusing on short and long term issues faced by Pakistan. Every time I open a newspaper in any part of the world, I am struck by tragedy which has befallen one or other Muslim country. I wonder why! I keep thinking about what can be done to bring peace and prosperity and make Muslims equal partners on God's earth.

The results of my belief in universal family have been reflected in my output at the World Bank. Several projects and reports relating to Syria,

Singapore, Malawi, Liberia, Ghana, Nigeria, Saudi Arabia, Indonesia, etc., have been implemented with my input and are well-documented.

The results of my thinking about Muslims have been presented in my earlier book *The Islamic Nation: Status and Future of Muslims Under the New World Order*. The present book aims at Pakistan, particularly Sindh.

Pakistan has been the main focus of my attention since the time of my childhood. As a school boy, I often spoke during the school debates and wrote in the Sindhi press about the problems. Most of it is unrecorded. However, I still have a copy of the Government High School Larkana Magazine of 1956 which contains an article titled "Azadi" or independence in which I commented about the unfulfilled promise of Pakistan. I concluded that we the ordinary people were to be blamed because the leadership was from among us. I wrote that article when I was around thirteen years old.

Since then, I have had the good fortune of traveling around the world, and living in several countries. Most of the time I have been in United States. Nevertheless, I have never stopped thinking about Pakistan.

I have noted unhappiness among people and have wanted to make it better for them. I have taken note of their broken dreams and wanted to sound a wake-up call. What to do and how to do it remain largely unanswered. The problems are many. Nevertheless, I have tried to look at the most basic and urgent of the current problems, draw some conclusions, and make some recommendations. The research material available is large, and it is easy to get lost in detail. I have tried to stick to the basic or fundamental points and relied on what I have learnt from teachings of my religion and experience.

I hope that Pakistanis and others who are interested in the welfare of people of Pakistan will (a) read this book, (b) discuss the conclusions and recommendations, (c) debate the issues, (d) provide their comments and reactions to those who can help in resolving the issues with the objective of making it all more practical and "do-able," and (e) finally take some practical steps in making Pakistan a better place in which to live.

Reconciliation of My Life Objectives

Within the universal brotherhood, my immediate objectives relate to self, family, Sindhis, Pakistanis, and Muslims. I wish to see all of them prosper. It is my goal to work for the happiness and welfare of all of the above. I derive pleasure from it. However, what shall I do when the interests of one of my dear ones conflicts with those of others. In fact, I occasionally find myself in conflict with members of my own family. I find Sindhis in conflict with other Muslims of Pakistan. I cannot and should not avoid taking sides in a constructive manner. One has to stand for what is right and just. However, it is easy to get emotionally involved on the basis of emotional considerations. I should stick to my objectives through: (a) working for reconciliation of all conflicts among all loved ones; (b) avoiding any work which is against any of the loved ones; and (c) working for removal of causes for the conflict.

The reconciliation must be on "any cost," but on basis of merits and justice. The struggle for reconciliation must be very hard and must take precedence over every other thing. I should actively work for the removal of causes of conflict among the loved ones, and I intend to. Most of the causes and possible solutions have been discussed in my earlier book, *The Islamic Nation,* and this one.

I gratefully acknowledge all those whose thoughts and material are reflected in this book. May Allah bless and compensate all those who have contributed directly or indirectly. I am particularly thankful to M. Abdul-Salaam Ahmad, Phyllis Muhammad, and M. Afzal Khan for their help in reviewing and editing this book. To the best of my knowledge, the book does not contain any confidential information from my employer. This is my personal statement of the agenda for Pakistan's reform.

List of Discussants

The author has drawn on broad discussions with the individuals listed below concerning issues facing Pakistan. Each discussion has added to the understanding of the issues and the solutions. However, none of the discussions covered all aspects of the book and few of them were held in context of this book. None of the discussants can be held responsible for any particular view, conclusion or recommendation unless otherwise stated.

Field Marshal Ayub Khan, former president of Pakistan
Zulfiqar Ali Bhutto, former president and prime minister of Pakistan
Benazir Bhutto, prime minister of Pakistan
Mohammed Shoaib, former finance minister of Pakistan
General Mirza Aslam Beg
Sultan Khan, former foreign secretary of Pakistan and ambassador to China, the United States, etc.

Syed Salar Kirmani, former director of the World Bank
Tariq Husain, World Bank
Abdul Fatah Memon, former ambassador of Pakistan to Saudi Arabia
Nizamuddin Memon, advocate, Larkana
Syed Sathar, World Bank
Dr. Hammid Naz
Senator Hamid Raza Gilani
Senator Iqbal Haider
Senator Husain Shah Rashdi
Senator Abdul Hai Baloach
Ali Raza Memon, hotel management specialist
Azizullah Memon, advocate, Quetta
Kazi Abid, former minister of Pakistan
Hakim Mohamad Ahsan, former ambassador of Pakistan
Dr. Mohammad Yaqub, governor, State Bank of Pakistan
Fakhre Imam, former speaker of the National Assembly of Pakistan
Sardar Qayum, prime minister of Azad Jammu and Kashmir
Sardar Atiq, chief organizer of Azad Jammu and Kashmir Muslim
    Conference
Nawab Nasrullah, MNA
Hafiz Mohammad Taqi, MNA
Salek, minister of minority affairs
Abdul Razaq Soomro, ambassador
Several graduate students of Pakistani origin studying in the United States
Manzoor Memon, businessman, Houston, Texas.
Dr. Maleeha Lodhi, ambassador of Pakistan to the United States
Reshma Memon Yaqub, reporter, *St. Louis Post-Dispatch*
Lt. Col. (Ret) Altaf Elahi Malik, president, Malik Maula Bakhsh Memorial
    Trust, Islamabad
Professor M. Qasim Jan, University of Peshawar
Anwar Memon, president, Soil Probe Ltd., Scarborough, Ontario, Canada
Humayun Mirza, World Bank (Retired)
Inder Malhotra, political commentator and Nehru Fellow, New Delhi
Hafiz Muhammad Taqi, member, National Assembly, Pakistan
Nawabzada Nasrullah Khan, MNA, chairman, Special Committee on
    Kashmir
Muhammad Haneef Ramay, speaker, Provincial Assembly of Pakistan
Mohammad Kalim, president, ESCON Ltd., Karachi
Najam Sethi, chief editor, *The Friday Times*, Lahore
G.M. Qureshy, advocate, Karachi

Nauman Quraishi, Bureau of Buildings, City of Portland, USA

Sikandar Memon, businessman, Cairo, Egypt

Shahab M. Qarni, executive director, Asian American Union, Baltimore

Prof. Jamshed Uppal, The Catholic University of America, Washington, D.C.

Shakil H. Siddiqui, former deputy commissioner of Hyderabad, Sindh

Zafar Mirza, Asian American Republican Club

Shahid Siddiqi, Asian American Republican Club (Retired from Pakistan Air Force)

Makhdoom Syed Hamid Raza Gilani, chairman, Senate Standing Committee, Cabinet Establishment & Management Services, Islamabad

Professor Mir M. Ali, University of District of Columbia

Dr. Abdul Hayee Balouch, senator, Islamabad

Pir Mazhar-ul-Haq, minister, Law and Parliamentary Affairs, Sindh

Dr. Jamal H. Qadri, chief engineer, Weksler Instruments Corp.

Dr. M. A. Halepota, World Sindhi Congress, U.K.

M. Afzal Khan, APP representative in Washington

Mushahid Hussain, information secretary, Pakistan Muslim League, Islamabad

Mohammad Sarwar, Montgomery Watson, Indonesia

Agha Murtaza Pooya, chairman, Institute of Strategic Studies, Islamabad

The author has benefited from reading the views of many persons discussing related to Pakistan on the Internet.

Oh Allah, show us the right path and keep us away from the path you forbid. You have already taught us and we already know what is good for us in the long run, and how You want us to act, but our own immediate interests stop us from acting that way. We know that You forbid falsehood, but in our day to day life, we fear for our existence without it and call it diplomacy. We know that You forbid arrogance, but we cannot intimidate and control the weaker than us without it. We know that we are brothers and sisters in Islam, but we feel insecure without cutting each other's throat. We know that You are the only God, but we obey everyone we fear. We know that You forbid bribery and ill-gotten wealth, but we fear the rainy day without a large bank account. We know that we should support the good and oppose the evil, but we do just the opposite because the power of evil in our daily life is stronger and we fear it. We try to follow the prescribed rituals but relegate the duties to the poor, weak and helpless because the rituals are easier to follow and bring us a good name. We know that our religious teachers are often in the pocket of our rulers, but we follow them because we are too lazy and scared to learn in depth and act on our own. Oh Allah, bring us back to Your true path and give us wisdom and courage to follow it!

SELECTED BIBLIOGRAPHY

Abdulla, Ahmed. *The Historical Background of Pakistan and Its People.* Karachi: Tanseem Publisher,1973.

Arshad, Mohammad. *An Advanced History of Muslim Rule in Indo-Pakistan.* Dacca: Ideal Publications, 1967.

Aziz, A. *Discovery of Pakistan.* Lahore: Sh. Ghulam Ali & Sons, 1957.

Bhutto, Benazir. *Daughter of Destiny.* New York: Simon and Schuster, 1989.

Bhutto, Zulfiqar Ali. *The Myth of Independence.* Oxford University Press, 1969.

Blood, Peter R., ed. *Pakistan, A Country Study.* Washington, D.C.: Library of Congress, 1995.

Crescent & Green, A Miscellany of Writings on Pakistan. London: Cassell & Company, 1955.

Duncan, Emma. *Breaking the Curfew.* Arrow Books, 1990.

Gordon, Irving L. *Reviewing World History.* New York: Amsco School Publications, 1964.

Jalal, Ayesha. *The State of Martial Rule.* Lahore: Vanguard Books, 1991.

-----. *The Sole Spokesman.* Cambridge University Press, 1985.

Lamb, Christina. *Waiting for Allah.* London: Hamish Hamilton, 1991.

Landau, Jacob. *The Politics of Pan-Islam.* Oxford: Clarendon Press, 1994.

Mahmood, Safdar. *Pakistan Political Roots and Development.* Lahore: A-H Publishers, 1994.

Memon, Ali Nawaz. *The Islamic Nation,* Beltsville: Writers' Inc., 1995.

Nixon, Richard. *Beyond Peace.* New York: Random House, 1994.

Noon, Firoz Khan. *From Memory.* Pakistan, 1969.

Saulat, Sarwat. *Maulana Maududi.* Karachi: International Islamic Publishers, 1979.

Syed, G.M. *Sindhu Desh.* Karachi: G.M. Syed Academy.

U.S. State Department Profile. U.S. Government Printing Office, 1995.

Vasil, Raj K. *Governing Singapore.* Selangor: Eastern Universities Press, 1984.

Wallbank, T. W. "World History." *The World Book Encyclopedia,* 1994.

Wheeler, J. T., ed. *Early Records of British in India.* Delhi: Ankit Book Centre, 1991.

Wolport, Stanley. *Zulfi Bhutto of Pakistan.* Oxford University Press, 1993.

INDEX

Q
Qur'an, 48, 51, 57, 155, 157

R
reform, 73, 83-87, 92, 105, 106, 116, 119, 125, 126, 138-140, 152, 171, 172, 194, 195, 226, 275, 276, 282, 283, 296, 300, 302-304, 313, 319, 321-323, 329, 330, 334, 336, 338, 348
reforms, 66, 68, 86, 106, 123, 127, 140, 151, 152, 162, 275, 304, 324, 328
religion, 7, 8, 15, 19-21, 39, 43, 48, 54, 58, 60, 78, 86, 89, 92, 93, 109, 148, 155, 157, 160, 161, 164, 178, 181, 191, 228, 230, 231, 241, 251, 277, 283, 288, 290, 294-296, 304, 310, 320, 331, 347
religious leaders, 39, 57, 67, 74, 92, 96, 130, 156, 158, 161, 165-167, 241, 284, 295, 297, 298, 301, 321-323, 326, 332, 343
religious tolerance, 14, 47, 159, 267, 289, 301, 315, 317, 331, 340, 343
representatives, 51, 63, 64, 74, 81, 118, 159, 163, 173, 175, 176, 193, 206, 213, 237, 312, 327, 332, 343
resources, x, 42, 43, 46, 47, 49, 62, 69, 77, 86, 90, 94, 98, 117-119, 121, 126-128, 131, 134, 136, 147, 150, 151, 153, 170, 171, 185, 186, 190, 193, 196, 201-203, 206, 209, 211, 212, 238, 249, 252, 255, 259, 262, 264, 273, 278, 284, 289, 290, 301, 302, 309, 313, 314, 316, 328, 329, 336, 337, 341
revolution, xi, 29, 101, 139, 150, 151, 163, 164, 195, 226, 259, 279, 281-284, 291, 301, 302, 310, 330, 333, 343
rituals, 39, 94, 158, 159, 276, 350
robberies, 55, 133, 178, 185, 334
Russia, 4, 101, 180, 223, 242, 252, 263, 318

S
sacrifice, 156, 250, 258, 287, 289, 302, 304, 320, 322, 325, 333, 341
Saudi Arabia, 53, 94, 150, 164, 167, 232, 243, 268, 269, 279, 290, 291, 331, 347, 349
science, 12, 43, 97, 98, 130, 143, 243, 252, 289, 309, 319
sects, 15, 48, 143, 155, 161, 164, 165, 167, 178, 297, 315, 331-333
Shari'ah, 34, 166, 289, 290
Sindhis, 44, 46, 58, 68, 103, 108, 179, 186, 189-198, 200-208, 316, 335-337, 346-348
Singapore, 96, 121, 130, 149, 150, 153, 223, 263, 284-287, 353
solutions, 9, xi, 53, 75, 83, 123, 139, 149, 156, 167, 170, 184, 185, 225, 226, 236, 249, 250, 266, 275, 278, 280, 311, 331, 334, 338, 341, 348
standard of living, 122, 128, 131, 179, 206, 224, 277, 286, 328
strategy, 98, 119, 122, 169, 233, 266, 303, 316, 340, 341